To

a friend e

colleague

Nani

feb 2007

An Alternative Path

An Alternative Path

The Making and Remaking of Hahnemann Medical College and Hospital of Philadelphia

NAOMI ROGERS

RUTGERS UNIVERSITY PRESS
New Brunswick, New Jersey, and London

*Allegheny University of the Health Sciences gratefully acknowledges
the generous contribution of The Barra Foundation, Inc.,
to publish additional photographs in this book.*

Library of Congress Cataloging-in-Publication Data

Rogers, Naomi, 1958–
    An alternative path : the making and remaking of Hahnemann Medical
College and Hospital of Philadelphia / Naomi Rogers.
        p.   cm.
    Includes bibliographical references and index.
    ISBN 0-8135-2535-7 (cloth : alk. paper). — ISBN 0-8135-2536-5
(pbk. : alk. paper)
    1. Hahnemann Medical College and Hospital of Philadelphia—
History.   2. Medical colleges—Pennsylvania—Philadelphia—History.
3. Homeopathy—Study and teaching—Pennsylvania—Philadelphia—
History. I. Title.
R747.H23R64   1998
615.5'32'071174811—dc21   97–43595
                                                                          CIP

British Cataloging-in-Publication data for this book is available from the British Library.

Manufactured in the United States of America

Contents

Illustrations

Preface and Acknowledgments

In 1988 the Allegheny Health, Education, and Research Foundation (AHERF) merged with the Medical College of Pennsylvania (MCP, formerly the Woman's Medical College), and in 1993 with Hahnemann University (formerly the Hahnemann Medical College and Hospital of Philadelphia). The last classes of the separate schools entered in 1994, and in 1996 the new institution was renamed Allegheny University of the Health Sciences. A health care company's merger with two prominent medical schools was unprecedented in American medical history. Allegheny's administrators recognized the power and precariousness of history: in 1998 Hahnemann's alumni would have celebrated their sesquicentennial, and in 2000 the alumni of MCP would have celebrated theirs. The administrators at Allegheny decided not only to go forward with these celebrations but also to welcome the past into the present and future of this new institution with commissioned histories of each school.

This history of Philadelphia's Hahnemann Medical College and Hospital, commissioned by AHERF in September 1995 and completed in September 1997, has been a challenging assignment. I was asked to write not a coffee table book but a serious historical work with proper documentation, a work that would place Hahnemann's history into a larger social and political context. I decided to write a history of Hahnemann warts and all, deliberately rejecting as a model medical school histories that are structured around the reigns of presidents and deans and offer unblemished stories of progress and success. Hahnemann achieved a tremendous amount, coming as it did from its position as an outsider: in the nineteenth century teaching homeopathy, an alternative medical system, and in the twentieth century lacking the endowments and the university base that would have given it a firm financial foundation. Hahnemann's trustees, faculty, and supporters were forced to construct an alternative kind of institution to enable the college to survive. How it achieved this and how, in the 1950s, it was able to remake itself into a mainstream academic health center are the major focuses of this book.

Most academic history books are researched and written over longer periods of time than this history was, and it, therefore, leaves out a lot. For example, I examine Hahnemann Hospital only as it becomes part of the history of the college; a full history of the hospital remains to be written and would make a fascinating tale. This is also not a study of Hahnemann's other important training programs: its nursing school, its schools of radiologic and medical technology, its physicians' assistants program, and other programs that made up its school of allied health professions in the 1960s and beyond. This is primarily a history of Hahnemann's medical school: its faculty, administrators, trustees, and students, as well as its supporters and detractors in the local community.

Sources for this study are drawn heavily from one archive: the Hahnemann Collection of the Archives and Special Collections of Allegheny University of the Health Sciences. I could not have completed this book without the assistance of Hahnemann archivist Barbara Williams, who shared her rich knowledge of Hahnemann's past with me, and whose commitment to the history of Hahnemann saved hundreds of documents that would otherwise have been thrown out and helped raise an awareness of the importance of the past among numerous administrators, heads of departments, librarians, and alumni. This is not the book that Barbara might have wanted, or that individual Hahnemann alumni might have wanted, but without her there would have been no book at all.

Librarians and archivists at the Historical Library of the Yale University School of Medicine, the Free Library of Philadelphia, the Historical Society of Pennsylvania in Philadelphia, the State Historical Society of Wisconsin in Madison, the Bentley Historical Library in Ann Arbor, Michigan, the Association of American Medical Colleges Archives in Washington, D.C., and especially the College of Physicians of Philadelphia and the Urban Archives of Temple University have generously helped me and my research assistants, Devorah Lissek and Craig Repasz. Devorah and Craig have given me careful, consistent, and creative work, and their interests in social history and in homeopathy, respectively, have made this a more interesting book.

This history was written under the auspices of the Sesquicentennial Book Committee, headed by Carol Hansen Montgomery, and I thank Carol and the members of the committee for their encouragement and criticisms. The project was overseen by Allegheny's Office of Development, and I am grateful to Vice President Michael O'Mahoney and his assistants, especially Murielle Telemaque and Jackie Adamczyk, for their help in organizing my many trips from New Haven to Philadelphia.

I wrote this book with two audiences in mind: Hahnemann alumni and others who have worked or taught or been cared for at Hahnemann, and historians. A number of Hahnemann alumni, faculty, and supporters have given up their time to be interviewed: my thanks to Horst Agerty, Wyrth and Katherine Baker, Phyllis and Stephen Baer, Marilyn Blum, SallyAnn Bowman, Charles Cameron, Walter Cohen, Peter Eisenberg, Ronald Feigin, Seth Fisher, Lonnie Fuller, George Gardiner, Margaret Giannini, Alterman (Chip) Jackson, Karl Koiwai, Burton Landau, Warren Landau, Ernest Leiss, Patricia Lyons, Robert McMichael, Catherine Mather, John Moyer, Ana Nuñez, Wilbur Oaks, Charles Paxson, John Storer, Beatrice Troyan, Suzanne and Vincent Zarro, Sidney Zubrow, and especially Joseph DiPalma, who generously shared his love and knowledge of Hahnemann as well as his autobiographical manuscript. To the extent that I have managed to address issues of importance in social and medical history, I would like to thank the following readers who took time from their own work and lives to accommodate my schedule: Jim Connor, June Factor, Sue Lederer, Janet Tighe, and John Harley Warner. Doreen Valentine, my editor at Rutgers, read chapters quickly and with insight; and Carlotta Shearson, my copyeditor, helped smooth and sharpen my prose.

I worked at my home and at the homes of my mother and my in-laws, and therefore efforts to create a peaceful environment were crucial for the creation and completion of this book. For their work in helping to counter the household confusion created by two children—one born three months before this project began, and the other during the writing of chapter seven—I thank my baby-sitters: Sheryl Anderson, Shelley Choy, Renee Faulkner, Elizabeth and Peggy Flanagan, Gretchen and Alison Krueger, Amy Nuernberg, Sue and Steve Pierce, Jenny Raybin, Kumiko Sullivan, Megan Tripp, and Megan Wega. My mother, June Factor, and my parents-in-law, John and Dorothy Warner, not only cared for their grandchildren but also kept me fed and relatively calm. Finally, I thank my husband, John, for his forbearance, assistance, and love, and my children, Nathaniel and Dorothy, for forcing me out of my study.

All illustrations in this book are courtesy of the Archives and Special Collections, Hahnemann Collection, Allegheny University of the Health Sciences, except as noted.

An Alternative Path

Medical Alternatives
before 1848

IN THE EARLY nineteenth century, physicians were not a crucial part of most American patients' experience, and most hospitals were for the destitute. Sick people relied on the advice and help of neighbors, midwives, and other wise women, and on domestic health guides, some of which were best-sellers and as valued as the family Bible. When patients did seek out a medical practitioner they faced a plethora of options, perhaps the widest choice in American history.

In the decades before the founding of Hahnemann Medical College and Hospital there was no single medical profession in the United States. There were no national boards, specialty boards, government or private research institutes, or accreditation committees. American medicine was diverse and competitive, perhaps the most open medical marketplace of any Western nation.[1] Medical practice in the United States has never been completely unified—doctors often disagree, not only about therapy but also about diagnosis—but in the early nineteenth century, in the absence of national examining or regulatory agencies, the way doctors practiced was even more idiosyncratic than it is today and depended on the teaching of their preceptors, their own experience and that of their colleagues, and what they might be reading in current medical journals and texts. Practice also had to be responsive to the context in which it occurred: doctors frequently complained (in vain) that as they entered a patient's home, it was not the doctor but the patient and family who made the final choice of treatment.

Until the 1850s most medical education did not take place in medical schools; an American practitioner did not need to have a medical degree or any formal certification from the state to be regarded as a legitimate physician. Medical training was by apprenticeship. Young African-American men and women, enslaved and free, learned medical skills and the knowledge of plants from older skilled healers in their communities; midwives were trained by other midwives, often their mothers; young white men with an interest in drugs and healing sought out a recognized medical practitioner as a preceptor. A small group of elite white men supplemented their apprenticeship by attending lectures at a medical school (only four existed in the United States in 1800) or by studying medicine in Europe. It was this last group that would later be a nucleus around which the ideology of medical orthodoxy would coalesce.

The medicine that nineteenth-century healers practiced varied. For some it had roots in African or West Indian medicine; for others it was framed in a Western European tradition. But American medical practices in this period did have some things in common. A healer's diagnostic tools were primarily his or her senses: the body and its products were seen, touched, smelled, tasted, and heard. Therapies too were surprisingly similar. Historian Charles Rosenberg has argued that American physicians and their patients shared the belief that the sick body was in a constant state of imbalance.[2] The practitioner's job was to monitor this imbalance, primarily by manipulating the secretions of the body to elucidate its inner workings, and by dramatic action designed to return the patient to health. Herbal and mineral drugs could induce vomiting, sweating, and the production of urine; a lancet could be used to let blood, as could a heated glass cup placed on scarified skin. Such practices, known as "heroic" therapies, came to symbolize the practice of educated physicians, who began to see themselves as America's regular or orthodox profession. While not all healers used bloodletting and blistering, all practitioners did share a holistic conception of the sick body, and they advised their patients about "regimen," or the role of diet, exercise, and lifestyle in maintaining health and preventing disease.

Formal medical education became a politically charged issue in the 1820s and 1830s when some groups of American healers began to argue that good medicine was domestic medicine, that the state should not privilege any kind of practitioner or medical system through licensing laws.[3] The most important group was known as the Thomsonians, after its founder Samuel Thomson. Thomson (1769–1843), a New Hampshire farmer, developed a system based on indigenous botanic medicine, a system that gained a tremendous following from the 1820s to the 1840s. His popular health book *New Guide to Health* (1822) and his movement's slogan, "Every Man His Own Physician," resonated with Jacksonian populism. Thomsonians believed that an open medical marketplace would ensure the best health care and assailed regular physicians for their elite position in society, for hiding medical knowledge from their patients, and for harming their patients by using European drugs rather than American plants and herbs. By the end of the 1840s Thomsonians had gained enough political clout to convince all but two state legislatures to repeal the already weak state licensing laws; these laws were not reintroduced until the 1870s and 1880s.[4]

Thomsonians castigated formal medical training as both harmful and elit-ist. The medical school, as they saw it, harmed patients not only by producing a privileged group of physicians who practiced dangerous, debilitative medicine but also by depriving ordinary men and women of the knowledge to care for their bodies. Medical schools, claimed Thomson and his followers, taught men tricks like the use of Latin terms that obscured medical knowledge instead of making it available and accessible to all.[5] (In fact, Thomsonian rhetoric assigned American orthodox medicine influence, unity, and strength that it would not actually have until the mid–twentieth century.)

These attacks resonated powerfully with other political and cultural forces that were already shaping the American medical world, and became part of a popular health movement that was developing during the 1840s, a movement whose proponents shared Thomson's distrust of medical authority and heroic therapies. Hydropathy or water therapy, for example, reached the United States from Germany in the 1840s and gained widespread public support. Hydropaths rejected chemical and herbal drugs and attacked regular doctors for ignoring pre-ventive medicine and for not teaching patients about their own bodies and how to keep themselves well.[6]

Although populist medical rhetoric did not disappear, by the late 1840s Thomson's suspicion of formal medical education was no longer so widely per-suasive. The number of American medical schools doubled and then tripled as medical students began to seek out medical lectures and an M.D. degree: in 1820 there were thirteen schools; by 1850 there were forty-two. These were private institutions, established by a few physicians who bought or rented a building and offered lectures for fees. Patients still turned to popular health books, and students continued to rely on preceptors for practical training; but medical schools began to play a newly important role in medical education. Not only orthodox physicians but also anti-orthodox groups established medical schools and embraced other trappings of a new professionalism. For example, the botanic practitioners known as Eclectics or Reformers, who considered themselves suc-cessors to Thomson, began publishing the *Reformed Medical Journal* in 1832. Eclectics organized a chartered school in Worthington, Ohio, in 1830, and in 1845 established the Eclectic Medical Institute in Cincinnati, which lasted un-til 1939. In 1850 Eclectics gained a charter from the Pennsylvania legislature and in 1851 opened an Eclectic school in Philadelphia that granted Eclectic doctor of medicine degrees.[7] In 1853 Russell Thatcher Trall (1812–1877) opened one of the earliest hydropathic schools in New York City, which in 1857 was chartered by the state to award M.D. degrees.[8]

Homeopaths entered the American landscape amid this cacophony of voices. Homeopathy was first introduced to the United States in the 1820s and 1830s by German-speaking immigrants, the United States' largest ethnic group

in the nineteenth century, and it spread through the efforts of individual practitioners and patients.[9] One of the earliest homeopathic physicians was Hans
Burch Gram (1788–1840), who had encountered homeopathy while studying
at the Royal Medical and Surgical Institute in Copenhagen. Gram, the son of
Danish immigrants, set up a homeopathic practice in New York City in 1825
and began to win converts among both patients and fellow physicians; in 1835
he published the United States' first English-language homeopathic journal, the
American Journal of Homoeopathia.[10] Homeopathy was introduced separately into
Pennsylvania by German immigrant physicians, including William Wesselhoeft
(1794–1858), Henry Detwiller (1795–1887), and Constantine Hering (1800–
1880). The efforts of these men and their supporters in numerous German immigrant communities made Pennsylvania a key state in the development of
American homeopathy. In the 1830s they founded, with the support of local
clergymen and businessmen, America's first homeopathic school, the North
American Academy of the Homeopathic Healing Art, in Allentown, Pennsylvania (known as the Allentown Academy), which received a state charter in
1836 to award M.D. degrees.[11] They also founded the Hahnemannian Society,
America's first homeopathic society, which had as members both physicians and
laymen, and the Homeopathic Medical Society of Philadelphia, one of the
United States' earliest homeopathic medical societies. Between 1835 and 1836
they published the United States' first homeopathic journal, *Correspondenzblatt
der Homöopathischen Aertze*. The writings and teaching of these practitioners, as
well as the popular and professional health texts they published, helped to bring
homeopathy to the attention of both physicians and patients.[12] In 1860 homeopathic physicians made up around 3 or 4 percent of the fifty-five thousand physicians in the United States, and the states with the greatest number of
homeopathic physicians, in rank order, were New York, Pennsylvania, Massachusetts, Ohio, and Illinois.[13]

Homeopathy had been developed by the German physician Samuel
Hahnemann (1755–1843). Trained in the learned medical tradition, Hahnemann
graduated in 1779 with a medical degree from Erlangen and taught briefly at
the University of Leipzig before turning to private practice. He became dissatisfied with the medicine of his day, especially with the impurity of drugs and the
imprecise way they were combined, and with bloodletting and other therapies
that he felt were useless if not harmful and were prescribed without any coher-
ent theoretical justification. By studying eighteenth-century medical writings and
by experimenting on himself, Hahnemann developed a new system of therapeutics he called "homeopathy" (from the Greek *homoios pathos*, or "like-suffering"),
which was most fully spelled out in his major work, *Organon der rationellen
Heilkunde* (1810). There were two major components: the law of similars (*similia
similibus curantur*, "likes are cured by likes") and the law of infinitesimals, both

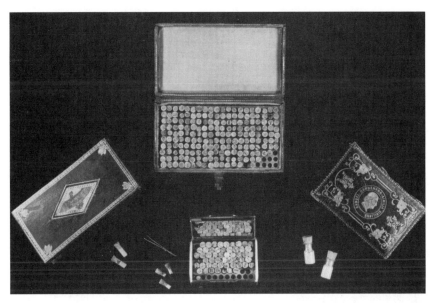

Figure 1. Homeopathic medical cases and vials owned by Constantine Hering (top); Henry N. Guernsey (bottom); an unknown homeopath (the case at right inscribed with Samuel Hahnemann's bust); and Henry Detwiller (at left), possibly the vials from which he prescribed the first homeopathic dose in Pennsylvania in 1828.

based on Hahnemann's own experience with the effects of drugs. In 1790 Hahnemann performed an experiment on himself: he took cinchona bark, a source of quinine, and discovered that the drug produced the symptoms of malaria, the disease it was known to cure. From this and similar tests he called "provings" (from the German *Prüfung,* or "testing") Hahnemann concluded that a sick person could be cured of a disease by a drug that in a healthy person produced symptoms similar to those of the disease. Hahnemann also concluded from his experiments that very small doses appeared to work better than the typically large doses used by most physicians. He proposed that drugs gained potency through dilution, and he developed a system of drug preparation in which powders or tinctures were mixed with water or alcohol, shaken in special ways, and then placed in small vials in liquid, powder, or globule form.[14]

Hahnemann's homeopathy was both part of learned medical culture and critical of it. Hahnemann disliked the tendency of physicians to explain and classify diseases, and he argued that these disease classifications were erroneously constructed and that all a doctor could truly know, unless he engaged in foolish speculation, was individual symptoms. Given this focus on symptoms, homeopathic therapy required a close collaboration between doctor and patient, and a detailed initial history that could take up to two or three hours. In other ways, Hahnemann's system reflected the mainstream medicine of his day. He believed that disease was the result of the disturbance of the body's "vital force," a term he used to refer sometimes to a physiological principle, sometimes to a spiritual one. Homeopaths' mild therapies, he argued, allowed the body's vital force time to heal.[15] Before 1800, scientific medicine, based on the best teaching in Leyden and Edinburgh, meant an elitist, highly theoretical, rationalistic system of medicine. Hahnemann proudly termed his a "rationalistic" system, and his discoveries "laws." By the 1830s rationalism, however, had become a term of abuse among America's most prominent medical reformers. The new scientific medicine, now drawn from Paris, depended on empirical observations made at the bedside and during autopsy rather than on system building.[16] Hahnemann's emphasis on external symptoms was an implicit attack on the new materialist interest in pathology, but his stress on active research and self-experimentation by physicians drew on a empiricist tradition. As these elements of homeopathy—both original and derivative—were carried into the nineteenth century they came to be characterized as "homeopathic" and "unorthodox." Many of Hahnemann's American followers continued the designation of homeopathy as "law" but stressed as well that Hahnemann's experimentation and his close observation of symptoms fit well into the new empirical way of thinking. Many of Hahnemann's own ideas changed as he taught and practiced homeopathy over his thirty-year career, especially during the last eight years of his life, when he lived and practiced in Paris. Thus, when American homeopaths studied in Paris, they could both pay homage to Hahnemann by visiting his widow, Melanie, herself a homeopathic practitioner, and learn Parisian medicine from clinicians at the Hôtel Dieu and other great Paris hospitals.

It is important to recognize the differences between the context in which Samuel Hahnemann developed his ideas and the context in which they flourished in the United States. Homeopathy was developed in reaction to German learned medicine by someone thoroughly trained within that tradition. In the United States the social and medical context differed profoundly. There was no equivalent state-sanctioned "learned" medicine: anyone could set up a medical school, gain a charter, and issue medical degrees. In Germany, by comparison, no medical school has ever had a homeopathic professor, and no homeopathic medical degrees have ever been awarded. Further, by the time homeopathy crossed the Atlantic, orthodox American medicine was in the midst of significant philosophical change: from a faith in rationalistic systems (like Benjamin Rush's "one disease" theory) to a commitment to empiricism based on bedside and pathological observation. Thus, it is not historically accurate to designate, as homeopath-historian Harris Coulter has done, regular medicine as rationalist and homeopathy as empirical. Both were always more complicated and more responsive to each other and to the social and intellectual climate in which they developed than a simple dichotomy would suggest. In the United States homeopaths responded to the challenges of orthodox medical science by more fervently emphasizing homeopathy's experimental and empirical basis. They agreed it was a system, but one that provided more reasoned answers to the problem of explaining illness and the effect of therapies than did orthodox medicine, one that was open, based not on one man's theory but on laws of nature discovered by Samuel Hahnemann that did not alter simply because additional pathological facts were unearthed. The emphasis on continually "proving" drugs in order to develop an extensive and lengthening list of symptoms for which to prescribe made homeopathy appear progressive, and numerous historians have remarked that nineteenth-century homeopaths were more "scientific" than regular physicians.[17]

In assessing the impact of homeopathy on American medicine in the nineteenth century, it is difficult to separate out the influence of homeopathy from that of other anti-orthodox critics of American medicine.[18] Regular physicians did begin to alter their practice, blaming the excessive use of heroic therapies for the popularity of these anti-orthodox medical groups, which they called "sects." Recognizing the political and social force of medical populism, many regular physicians protested little about the repeal of state laws and agreed that a physician should be judged by practice and character rather than by some state-ratified privileged position. At the same time, American regulars also became more conscious of their own identity and developed what one historian has termed an "ideology of orthodoxy."[19]

One of American homeopathy's most lasting critiques of orthodox medicine came from the term "allopathy" (from *alloison pathos*, or "unlike-suffering"), which was drawn from Samuel Hahnemann's description of learned medicine that he characterized as based on the Galenic theory of *contraria contrarii*, the opposite of "like cures like." Homeopaths argued that this theory was not only wrong but also unacknowledged by its practitioners.[20] Orthodox practitioners scorned the term allopathy as a description of the basis of their practice.[21] Their efforts were in vain though; the term was widely adopted by all anti-orthodox groups and is still sometimes used today as an epithet by those critical of biomedicine. "Although the antiquarian friends are somewhat an[n]oyed at the title [Allopathist], and just at this time are calling up each other not to answer when so addressed," Pitman Dinsmore, a homeopathic student from Providence, Rhode Island, prophesied in 1852, "yet in spite of all their efforts it will adhere to them."[22] In this book I avoid the term, as it is both inaccurate (nineteenth-century orthodox medicine was not based on a law of contraries) and derisive; I use instead "orthodox" or "regular." Similarly, I avoid the term "sectarian," which has generally—both then and now—been used as an epithet with connotations of religious fundamentalism; I use instead the terms "alternative" and "unorthodox."

American homeopathy, thus, trod a middle ground. Although rooted firmly in a learned European tradition, it was consistently responsive to popular cri-

tiques of medicine. Yet at heart American homeopathy was not a populist movement but an alternative medical profession. In 1844, three years before the founding of the American Medical Association (AMA), homeopaths established their
own national medical organization, the American Institute of Homeopathy, and
by 1870 the United States had become the leading center of formal homeopathic
training in the world. Although homeopaths on occasion joined Thomsonians
and other anti-orthodox groups in attacking regular medicine and published domestic medical guides and kits, they were not populist healers in the Thomsonian
tradition.[23] Indeed, homeopaths practiced among prosperous farmers, clergymen,
and merchants and established large urban practices among the emerging middle
class and especially among intellectuals.

In this period when a physician's character was considered a central part of
his professional identity, many homeopaths chose to adopt a liberal social and
political stance.[24] A few of these physicians had ties to German liberalism and
had fled their homelands to escape political and medical persecution. William
Wesselhoeft, for example, who was born in Jena and took his medical degree in
1820 at the university there, was arrested and sent to prison as a result of his
radical activities in the Burschenschaften. He escaped from prison and joined
the growing number of German communities in eastern Pennsylvania before
moving to Vermont. In the United States a number of leading homeopaths became part of a community of liberal urban intellectuals and were caught up in
their social and political movements, such as temperance, abolition, and tran-
scendentalism. Prominent supporters of homeopathy included Harriet Beecher
Stowe, Daniel Webster, Susan B. Anthony, and Henry Wadsworth Longfellow.
These associations were a source of both strength and vulnerability for homeopathy. In 1858, for example, when a New York City commission rejected a request by homeopaths to control some of the wards at Bellevue Hospital, the
commission argued that homeopathy was based on a "wild transcendental
theory."[25]

Most homeopaths consciously sought to create a medical tradition that was
in keeping with the spirit of learned medicine. Their assumption, for example,
that dissection was a necessary part of homeopathic education clearly distinguished them from hydropaths, with their notions of medicine as preventive hygiene, and from Thomson, with his drugs drawn from the garden and field.
Samuel Hahnemann's concept of the "vital force" attracted intellectuals already
intrigued by other philosophies that sought connections between the material
and the spiritual.[26] When an editor of a homeopathic journal praised the faculty of Philadelphia's Homeopathic Medical College as "all sound in the faith,
and imbued with the spirit of the *Doctrines of Homeopathy*, as taught by
Hahnemann," he used the religious metaphors common to homeopathic debate
during the early and mid–nineteenth century.[27] This language, used by homeo-

paths especially in the 1840s and 1850s, reminded supporters that in this period becoming a homeopath *was* part of a conversion into a new world. Indeed,
a number of physicians converted both to homeopathy and to Swedenborgianism
(the latter also known as the New Church or New Jerusalem Church), and
American homeopathy claimed the title the New School and derided orthodoxy as the Old School. Emanuel Swedenborg, a scientist and mystic whose work
offered a way to connect the physical and the spiritual, attracted homeopaths
such as Gram and Hering.[28]

American homeopaths constantly faced the charge that their drugs were so
mild that they were in fact inactive, that nature, rather than homeopathy, was
the healer. This argument was part of an attack by orthodox reformers who were
themselves critical of heroic therapies. In 1835, for example, Harvard professor
Jacob Bigelow published his ideas on "self-limited diseases," reinvigorating the
discussion on the healing power of nature; and in the 1840s Oliver Wendell
Holmes and Worthington Hooker, both of whom published attacks on heroic
practice, explained the so-called efficacy of homeopathy as the result of the pla-
cebo effect.[29] Clearly, homeopathic therapies were milder than orthodox medicine; indeed their mildness was part of the reason homeopathy had become the
preferred medicine for many women and children.[30] By midcentury a number
of families began to select different systems of medicine for different family members and different kinds of disease. But at the same time American homeopaths
prided themselves on their ability to treat serious epidemic diseases and publicly compared their successes to orthodox failures during and after epidemics.
Homeopaths' success during the cholera epidemic of 1849 and the yellow fever
epidemic of 1853 helped to give the new system prominence and demonstrated
its contribution to the civic good.[31] William H. Holcombe (1825–1893), for example, a graduate of the University of Pennsylvania, read about the successes of
homeopaths in Cincinnati treating cholera victims in 1849, and went there to
study homeopathy before establishing his own homeopathic practice in Natchez,
Mississippi. Holcombe became a major figure during the series of yellow fever
epidemics in the South, wrote a guide to homeopathic treatment of yellow fever in the 1860s, and headed the Homeopathic Yellow Fever Commission of
1878.

Thus, by 1848, homeopathy in the United States had started to spread beyond German-speaking communities and was beginning to attract urban middle-
class families, especially intellectuals. Homeopathy was developing as an
alternative profession to orthodox medicine but was still treading the middle
ground between medical populism and elite learned medicine. Unlike heroic
medicine, homeopathic therapies were mild and pleasant; that they also cured
disease was an additional appeal for the American public already dissatisfied with
orthodox therapies and practitioners.

The First Fifty Years, 1848–1898

Part I

Creating a School and a Distinctive Identity

Chapter 1   Proudly Homeopathic

The Homeopathic Medical College of Pennsylvania, 1848–1869

I<small>N THE WINTER OF</small> 1848, Constantine Hering, Jacob Jeanes, and Walter Williamson met to establish a homeopathic medical school in Philadelphia. On April 8, 1848, the state legislature in Harrisburg granted the Homeopathic Medical College of Pennsylvania an act of incorporation, and over the summer the organizers found a building on Arch Street which had been used previously as a schoolroom and also as a Swedenborgian church and now housed a homeopathic pharmacy in its front rooms. The first lectures began in October 1848 and were attended by fifteen students, six of whom received a doctor of homeopathic medicine degree the following March. The college was financed and managed by a group made up of faculty, other eminent homeopaths, and some business and philanthropic supporters. This group, whose powers were formalized in 1849, was initially known as the board of managers, but the name was later changed to the board of trustees.

Why Found a Medical School?

That the founders of the Homeopathic Medical College of Pennsylvania decided to found a medical school rather than to continue American homeopaths' practice of teaching by preceptor demonstrates that they were aware of the changing social and medical currents. They chose to establish the school in Philadelphia (a mecca for medical study). This new school was intended to offer an educational alternative not a supplement. It would provide students with a full course of lectures, all in English. The founders were not sure which aspects of the new theory and culture of homeopathy would fit best in American soil, but they felt confident that the way to introduce and institutionalize homeopathy in the United States was through a medical school. It was not difficult to obtain a legal charter, a building and some equipment, and a small group of physicians who agreed to split the profits from student fees. Despite the technical ease, founding a medical school remained a politically charged issue.

The Thomsonian critique of formal medical training hung over homeopaths' heads as they considered establishing a school. For example, although the editor of the *Homeopathic Pioneer* in Philadelphia in 1845 asserted that founding a homeopathic school could counter those who look at homeopathy "as a sheer humbug, unworthy of the attention of any but enthusiasts or ignorant and unsuccessful practitioners," he nevertheless suggested that "in the present state of the public mind" getting a charter from the state legislature and "making it a corporate body invested with certain powers and privileges" would meet "with too powerful opposition." Instead, he suggested, the school should begin independent of state privilege and then gain some "standing in the public opinion" that would "induce the Legislature to grant those privileges now denied to all except the self-styled scientific schools of Allopathic doubts and uncertainties."[1]

Since no American homeopathic institution was state supported until the 1870s, homeopathic physicians were dependent from the beginning on the lay public, who raised funds for the building of medical schools, hospitals, and dispensaries. The Homeopathic Society of Cincinnati was founded in the wake of that city's 1849 cholera epidemic, with about one thousand members, in order to promote homeopathy and to encourage the founding of a homeopathic medical school. Homeopathic journals and public lectures in these early years were directed to both physicians and the lay public. In the 1830s the Hahnemannian Society of Pennsylvania and the New York Homeopathic Society were made up of, in one historian's words, "physicians and believers."[2] The opening lecture at the Homeopathic Medical College, on October 16, 1848, was given not only to its fifteen students but also to "ladies and gentlemen interested in homeopathy."[3] And, most importantly, homeopathy was practiced not only by those with medical training but also by laypeople, only some of whom later chose to take a medical degree. Christopher Columbus Slocomb (1824–?), for example, practiced homeopathy as a layman for four years in Rutland, Massachusetts, before coming to Philadelphia in 1865 to attend medical school. And John J. Garvin (1819–1893), the captain of a steamer that traveled between Philadelphia and Savannah, always used homeopathic medicines at sea, and only when his vessel was laid up in 1857 did he attend medical lectures in Philadelphia, where, some years later, he received a degree.

Before the founding of the Allentown Academy and the Homeopathic Medical College in Philadelphia, all homeopathic physicians in the United States had been trained as orthodox physicians. That is, all were converts to homeopathy. Many continued to consult with orthodox colleagues, count them as friends, and go to medical society meetings. In the 1840s, for example, all the members of the Massachusetts Homeopathic Fraternity were members of the Massachusetts Medical Society.[4] For many of these early homeopathic physicians, the practice of homeopathy was a kind of intellectual experiment. Homeopathy in the 1830s and 1840s is best understood as a form of complementary medicine; only gradually did its practitioners come to see themselves as fully antagonistic to orthodox medicine, as offering a medical alternative rather than an addition, as committed to overthrowing orthodoxy rather than simply improving it. Indeed, for some practitioners, it was not so much being homeopathic as being anti-orthodox that distinguished them. A few homeopaths, for example, were also hydropaths:[5] in the 1840s, William Wesselhoeft, a German immigrant and one of the first practitioners of homeopathy in Pennsylvania, moved to Brattleboro, Vermont, where he and his brother Robert established a hydropathy spa that became the leading water-cure institution in the nineteenth-century United States. A number of early homeopaths wrote popular health texts to attract patients, as Samuel Thomson had done. Nevertheless, although historians today lump all these groups under the category "alternative," they in fact were rarely colleagues and considered their practices distinctive and usually in competition.

As homeopathy spread across the East and Midwest, relations between homeopaths and orthodox physicians began to worsen. Medical societies began to expel or ostracize outspoken homeopaths, and orthodox teachers ridiculed medical students who openly professed a commitment to homeopathy. Homeopaths claimed that a student needed to "humiliate" himself by "persistent concealment of his professional creed before graduating, and afterwards, foregoing the common professional courtesies due from his classmates." Some orthodox faculties even ordered "their janitors to exclude from their lecture rooms *their own alumni.*"[6] Orthodox leaders used attacks on homeopathy to unite regular physicians. They accused homeopaths of quackery and lumped them together with Thomsonians and hydropaths. Leading reformers such as Oliver Wendell Holmes and Worthington Hooker made their national reputation, in part, on antihomeopathic tirades.[7]

A New School in Philadelphia

For Constantine Hering, Jacob Jeanes, and Walter Williamson, founding a homeopathic school was an expression of their commitment to the cause to which they devoted much of their lives. Their own conversion to homeopathy had not taken place through formal schooling. All were trained in regular medicine and had graduated from medical schools in an era when apprenticeship was regarded as a fully adequate training for a physician. For some years they had been actively

IN DUBIIS LIBERTAS   **IN CERTIS UNITAS**   **IN OMNIBUS CHARITAS**

HERING

JEANES   WILLIAMSON

..☙ THE FOUNDERS. ❧..
1848

Figure 2. The three founders of the Homeopathic Medical College of Pennsylvania (Constantine Hering, Jacob Jeanes, and Walter Williamson) and the college's motto chosen by Hering in 1867: In Certis Unitas, In Dubiis Libertas, In Omnibus Charitas (In Things Certain Unity, In Things Uncertain Freedom, In All Things Charity). Thomas Lindsley Bradford, *History of The Homeopathic Medical College of Pennsylvania: The Hahnemann Medical College and Hospital of Philadelphia* (Philadelphia: Boericke and Tafel, 1898), frontispiece.

involved in teaching and practicing homeopathy. All three had been prominent in founding the American Institute of Homeopathy (AIH), and Hering was its first president. Hering, perhaps the United States' most erudite and influential homeopath, had organized the Allentown Academy, published homeopathic texts in German and English, and helped to found the American Provers' Union, a group modeled on Samuel Hahnemann's German Provers' Union, which had been organized for the cooperative investigation of the effects of drugs by "provings." All three clearly saw institutionalized teaching as part of their larger vision of homeopathy as a medical profession.

Both Jacob Jeanes (1800–1877) and Walter Williamson (1811–1870) were graduates of the University of Pennsylvania, Philadelphia's oldest and most respected medical school, and both were Quakers from eastern Pennsylvania (religious unorthodoxy was typical of many early American homeopaths). Of the three founders, Jeanes could claim the highest prestige in Philadelphia medical circles. After graduating from Pennsylvania in 1823, he had practiced as an orthodox physician for twelve years, holding prestigious positions such as physician to the Philadelphia Almshouse. Jeanes heard about homeopathy from his fellow Friends, taught himself German, read Hahnemann's works, did his own investigating, and began practicing as a homeopath. In 1845 he was elected the second president of the AIH.

Williamson was a successful homeopathic practitioner but also a scientist, in a time and place when scientific studies were little rewarded and had only a marginal part in a professional medical career. Williamson had graduated from Pennsylvania in 1833 and set up a large and successful practice in Newtown, his hometown. Williamson heard the controversy raging over homeopathy in Philadelphia at the Delaware County Institute of Science, of which he was a member. He went to a bookshop in Philadelphia and bought every English-language book on the subject, carried out his own experiments, and then began to practice homeopathy. He attended the first AIH meeting in New York in 1844 and helped organize local and state homeopathic medical societies. In the 1840s he moved to Philadelphia and became successful by specializing in obstetrics, an area homeopaths had up to then largely overlooked. (Male Philadelphia homeopaths came to appreciate more and more strongly the powerful influence of women as patients and homeopathic supporters.)

Constantine Hering (1800–1880), born in Oschatz, Saxony, was studying surgery in the early 1820s when he was asked to research and write a book for a Leipzig publishing house to demolish Hahnemann's theories. His reading led him to investigate homeopathy for himself, and he was finally convinced of its efficacy when a serious dissection wound in his arm, which threatened to necessitate amputation, was healed by homeopathically prepared doses of arsenic. Hering graduated with a medical degree from the University of Würzburg in 1826; his thesis, entitled "De Medicina Futura," included the proposition "Materia Medica is to Hahnemann what Pathology was to Hippocrates."[8] He found that as an avowed homeopath his colleagues ostracized him, so he left for South America to undertake a zoological expedition sponsored by the king of Saxony. Because of his connections at the Academy of Natural Sciences, and an invitation to establish a homeopathic cholera hospital, Hering went to Philadelphia in 1833 and found the German-speaking communities of eastern Pennsylvania more accepting of homeopathy.

Although Hering published the United States' first homeopathic domestic health guide, *The Domestic Physician*, which was accompanied by a medical kit of forty homeopathic medicines in globule form,[9] he made it clear that he believed homeopathy could best be promulgated through formal medical training. In his introduction, reprinted in the book's numerous editions, Hering warned the American public of "the glaring absurdities of the old system of physic," offering them "a more judicious and rational system of domestic practice." But most importantly he argued that "No one can be a successful disciple of Hahnemann who is not well versed in the learning of the medical schools, and it would be just as impossible for him to act judiciously without a knowledge of anatomy, surgery and materia medica, together with mineralogy, chemistry and botany, as for a man ignorant of navigation and seamanship to carry a vessel with safety into port without a compass or chart."[10]

The failure of the Allentown Academy in 1842 helped to convince Hering that the continuing success of homeopathy on American soil meant fully institutionalizing homeopathic education and reaching out to English-speaking supporters. Hering's involvement with the Allentown Academy had begun in 1835, when a group of German immigrant physicians, including Henry Detwiller and Wesselhoeft, asked him to organize and direct a homeopathic school. He had agreed to do so as long as he received a salary "equal to that of a first-class Allentown clergyman," thus becoming, in effect, the school's first salaried clinician.[11] The academy folded after seven years because of financial problems, a fate not unusual for an American medical school in this period. Its education directives resembled the early bylaws of the AIH, which stated that an applicant for membership not only had to be assessed by three current members to be "properly qualified in the theory and practice of Homeopathy" but also had to "have pursued a regular course of medicine studies, according to the requirements of the existing medical Institutions of our country."[12] The Allentown Academy was not conceived as proselytizing outside its original ethnic community: all the lectures were in German; it was, one later commentator remarked, "in no sense American."[13]

It was no simple matter for the founders of the Philadelphia college to decide what kind of homeopathy to promote. Samuel Hahnemann had died in 1843, but long before his death, homeopaths in Germany and America had begun fighting over his tenets, especially over what it meant to be a pure homeopath and how to fit Hahnemann's more controversial theories—including his later theory of "psora" or skin eruption as a central cause of disease—into mainstream scientific ways of thinking. American homeopaths from the beginning had interpreted homeopathy in multiple ways. Hans Burch Gram, America's first homeopath, had consulted with orthodox doctors and used orthodox medical works; by contrast Walter Channing (1800–1855), an early New York homeopath, had defined homeopathy as exclusive and antagonistic to regular medicine. The men who founded and taught at Philadelphia's Homeopathic Medical

College and their supporters recognized that the faculty would be seen as representatives of the present and future of American homeopathy and would be publicly established as a legitimate alternative profession.

In the early years supporters of the college argued that its teachers were "pure homeopaths." In 1852, for example, a local medical editor praised the faculty for having "not a mongrel or an Eclectic among them."[14] Such assessments were as freighted as any assessment a church congregation might make of its minister. Theirs was not an arrogant purity, the school's organizers explained, trying to assuage the fears of other homeopathic physicians and patients that a school would institutionalize privilege and give one group of homeopaths special power over the training of future generations of homeopathic practitioners. Their school, the founders assured their friends, would counter the dangers of orthodoxy: the threatened professional isolation of homeopathic colleagues and the orthodox efforts to co-opt the homeopathic system into mainstream medicine.[15] This fear of orthodoxy was the reason that positive reviews of homeopathic ideas and books in orthodox medical journals were sometimes more disturbing to the homeopathic community than orthodox attacks.

The timing of the founding of this school was no coincidence. Hering, like other early homeopaths, believed that homeopathic teaching could take place between preceptor and student, and even after the founding of the college he offered weekly lectures on materia medica at his home.[16] But in 1846, just a few years after the founding of the AIH, a small group of orthodox physicians had met in New York to discuss forming a national medical organization. In 1847 the group met in Philadelphia to draw up the constitution and a code of ethics for the American Medical Association (AMA). These efforts were part of a new sense of professionalism and were a way of trying to separate in the public mind orthodox physicians from the myriad other practitioners in the nineteenth-century American medical world.

A clear sign of growing antagonism between homeopathy and orthodoxy was the creation of the AMA's code of ethics. The code required that the group's members refuse to consult with what were termed "irregular" practitioners, those whose practice was "based upon an exclusive dogma, to the rejection of the accumulated experience of the profession." Only orthodox doctors were defined as "regulars," and in opposition to the regulars the code placed vagabond healers, Thomsonians, hydropaths, eclectics, and homeopaths. Self-proclaimed homeopathic converts were to be cut off from social and intellectual communication with other physicians. At the same time the AMA warned its members against accepting into a medical school any student who had studied with a preceptor who was "avowedly and notoriously an irregular practitioner."[17] This action threatened the professional worth of homeopathic physicians, who were now denied the opportunity to teach new ideas to young students without turning them into professional pariahs. Although the 1847 code was simply pre-scriptive—and throughout the nineteenth century some orthodox doctors con-tinued to consult and work with homeopaths—it did contribute to the sharpening of boundaries between orthodox doctors and others. And by 1855, when the AMA required all members to adopt the 1847 code, the code spelled out on paper what many orthodox physicians had begun to feel professionally.

Organizing the School

The founders of the college felt that obtaining legal recognition for the school was crucial. Any building could be fitted out for medical teaching, any organi-zation could send an advertisement to a newspaper, but to attract the kind of student who would want to attend and graduate from a school as distinctive as this one, Philadelphia homeopaths, like the leaders of eclecticism and hydropa-thy, believed they must be able to legally offer M.D. degrees.

The charter granted in 1848 by the state legislature indicated to the public and other physicians that even this small group of homeopaths had enough po-litical clout to influence the legislature. The charter was the result of pressure from Congressman Charles Brown, who was Jacob Jeanes's brother-in-law and a former state legislator, and from petitions by homeopathic supporters with "hun-dreds of signatures," according to Walter Williamson. "The great revolution," Williamson later proclaimed at an AIH banquet in 1870, "commenced with the people, was carried out by the people, and we, as homeopathic physicians, are put forward and sustained now by the people, by the friends of Homeopathy, by the friends of progress, by the friends of advancement."[18]

In keeping with the guidelines of the AIH and with Hering's philosophy of medical education, the Homeopathic Medical College was structured on the typi-cal model of orthodox medical schools of the 1840s. Some of the college fac-ulty, the school's third catalog admitted, had considered organizing the school "on an entirely new basis, in accordance with the spirit of the great law." Un-der this radical scheme, a student could, "on the principle of perfect liberty," have acquired his medical education "wherever he pleased." He would not have needed to attend college lectures, and when he felt ready he would have been examined by an independent board of examiners elected by the college.[19] But even in proposing this unusual system, the professors had felt it necessary to ex-plain why college faculty members would have been better examiners than doc-tors wholly engaged in the "daily routine of practice." In words that showed as early as 1849 that the founding of a school could exacerbate tensions between faculty and physicians outside the college, the college compared "physicians en-gaged in the daily routine of practice" to faculty members who were engaged in "cultivating a particular branch of medicine," although, in fact, many of the college professors, like orthodox faculty, moved from chair to chair as needed. Equally important, while outside physicians might not be disinterested in their assessment of students, college teachers would be even less "likely to have their favorites."[20]

That this argument was played out in the school's own catalog suggests both the fluidity of the definition of a good homeopathic education and the tenuousness of support for the school and its faculty among the wider homeopathic community. The faculty reminded their fellow physicians of the youth of most students, reminded them that the students' young minds were "so easily moulded." The homeopathic law of cure, they argued, "does not merely govern us in the practice of medicine or the materia medica but is also capable of revolutionizing the practice of surgery and midwifery"; they argued that students needed to be taught by teachers imbued with "the true spirit of homeopathy."[21] A few years later the college also felt it necessary to defend the length of its school year, which was a standard four months. The course length, the school argued, demanded so much attention and study from the students that they barely had time for rest or exercise in order to keep healthy (perhaps an indirect reference to the constant threat of tuberculosis for those in medical work). They did not lengthen the school year because, they reasoned, if the course were longer, the minds of the pupils would become "perplexed," their teachers "careless," and the students therefore "indolent and more prone to succumb to the temptations of the city."[22] These doubts were briefly played out in these early catalogs, but from the mid-1850s on, the college consistently and proudly modeled itself on standard orthodox institutions.

The first lectures of the Homeopathic Medical College of Pennsylvania were held in October 1848 in a building on Arch Street. There were fifteen students at the first session, and the following March six graduates received a doctor of homeopathic medicine degree. During the following years the number of students increased, and by the mid-1850s the school averaged around ninety students, with about one-third of the class graduating seniors.

Initially most of the students were not local; of the first six graduates, only one was from Pennsylvania. Some students, in this era before extensive rail travel, traveled extraordinary distances. In 1851, thirty-two of the sixty-nine students were from Pennsylvania, and nineteen from six neighboring states; but eighteen came from places like Texas, Maine, Alabama, Canada, and England in order to attend one of the few degree-granting homeopathic schools in the world.[23] Indeed, those from far away were more likely to be older physicians who had decided that the cost of travel, lodging in an unfamiliar city, and study was justified. Of fifty-five students in 1849, eight of whom already had medical degrees, one each came from Massachusetts, Rhode Island, and Wisconsin. Thirteen of the seventy students in 1850 had M.D.s, from schools that included the

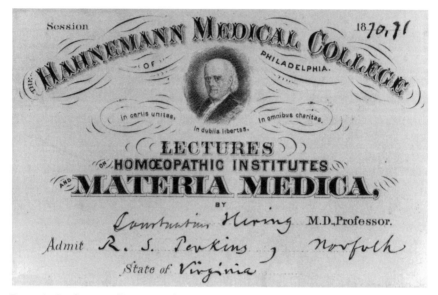

Figure 3. Students at all nineteenth-century American medical schools had to buy tickets to their professors' lectures. This ticket admits Robert S. Perkins to Constantine
Hering's 1870–1871 materia medica lectures at Hahnemann, a crucial course in a homeopathic college.

Universities of Missouri, Virginia, and Edinburgh. The 1867–1868 school catalog boasted of its graduates that "not a few of these physicians are known to
have left important fields of labor, at a very considerable present pecuniary sacrifice to themselves."[24]

Typical of medical schools throughout the United States in this period, standards for admission to and graduation from the college were low and were structured around the faculty's confidence in being able to assess a student's ability
and character. No entrance exam or high school diploma was required for admission, but a student did need a recommendation from a respectable physician,
presumably his preceptor, stating that he was of good moral character and had
studied medicine in apprenticeship for three years. Students at the college were
required to continue as "the private pupil" of a "respectable practitioner of medicine" during the two years of their college course; lectures at this school, like
most other American schools, were considered a supplement to practical medical training. As a sign of the importance of continuing apprenticeship, for the
first two decades college catalogs publicly listed students' preceptors, often faculty members or other leading local homeopaths. To graduate, students were expected to attend two four-month courses of lectures at the college (only one
course was required if they had already attended lectures at another medical
school). They were required to write a thesis, prove that they had attended the

requisite lectures, and pass final examinations, given orally at the professor's home. They also had to pay a matriculation fee of five dollars, a ten-dollar fee for a course of practical dissection, one hundred dollars for each term of lectures, and a graduation fee of thirty dollars. The length of study, the admission and graduation requirements, and the costs of tuition were all typical of American medical schools in the 1850s.[25]

One-third of the college's matriculants in the 1850s and 1860s did not graduate, a figure that was not unusual for this period. Before the Civil War a number of physicians used medical schools as a form of continuing education, and experienced physicians with a medical degree would sometimes take time off to attend lectures at a leading school just to catch up. With the repeal of most licensing laws by the 1840s, very few states required practitioners to have an M.D. to practice legally. Still, a degree was helpful in the competitive marketplace for any ambitious practitioner who wanted to gain respect from his colleagues and patients.

The decision to attend a homeopathic school had special meaning, especially for this early generation of homeopaths. Attending the college gave students the opportunity to establish a network of physicians who shared their special view of medicine. But most significant, the founding of the college enabled some physicians to formalize for the first time a system of practice that had up to then been simply an individual choice. It enabled them to claim an alma mater that could publicly reinforce their new sense of identity as alternative practitioners; in fact, it was like joining a new church as an adult.

The example of the Gardiner family demonstrates how the college helped to integrate a family's medical choice into a formal educational system. In 1849, at the age of fifty-six, Richard Gardiner (1793–1877), the father of William Gardiner, the college's professor of anatomy, became a student at the school, graduating a year later with a thesis on the use of forceps. Richard Gardiner, born in Darby, Pennsylvania, had studied medicine with his father and had attended lectures at the University of Pennsylvania. In 1835, he had moved to Philadelphia, built a large practice, and become a homeopath. Gardiner, like many early medical converts, raised his family as part of the city's homeopathic community, and he and his son William were among the original corporators of the college.[26] Richard's second son, Daniel (1828–1889), also a homeopathic physician, became a student at the college the same year as his father and was one of its first six graduates. During the 1849–1850 school year, Richard Gardiner attended classes not only with his son Daniel but also with his own pupils and those of his son William. In the next year William, Richard, and Daniel all sent pupils to the school.

Richard Gardiner and his sons exemplified the culture of the college, a culture mixed in age but close-knit in facing medical adversity. The faculty recognized the potential of older students, like Joseph Griswold Loomis (1811–1853), who was thirty-nine when he graduated with Richard Gardiner. Loomis had an 1834 medical degree from the New York College of Physicians and Surgeons of Fairfield and had been practicing for around ten years when he became interested in homeopathy after reading Samuel Hahnemann's death notices in 1843. He became professor of obstetrics at the college in 1852, two years after his graduation.

While the course content of the Homeopathic Medical College was distinctive, the organization of medical knowledge was not. This organizational similarity between the college and regular medical schools became a source of professional pride; for example, one year the college catalog boasted that "during the first twenty years of the College's existence, its course of study and its requirements for graduation were almost precisely like those of the best class of American allopathic schools."[27] In 1848 the college organized itself into nine standard departments: principles and practice of medicine, midwifery and diseases of women and children, botany, surgery, materia medica, chemistry, anatomy, pathology, and physiology. In its first session all of these professorships were held by men trained at orthodox schools, six of them at the University of Pennsylvania.

Of the three founders, only Walter Williamson became a central figure at the school, teaching obstetrics and materia medica for a decade. Jacob Jeanes did little formal lecturing; in 1848 he taught principles and practice of medicine, but his resignation in March 1849 attests to the difficulty of combining active involvement in a medical school with a successful private practice. Hering, similarly, was not much visible as a formal faculty member. After the first session he resigned his chair of materia medica (he was replaced by Caleb Matthews [1801–1851], an 1822 graduate of the University of Pennsylvania). But throughout the 1850s Hering taught private courses to supplement the college lectures, and he remained the intellectual backbone of the school, with his growing national and international reputation adding to its luster. He also, according to one of his students, "retained an old German custom to have a couple of students from the College reside in his family to keep in touch with the work and progress of the College."[28]

During the 1840s and 1850s, a core of approximately twelve men made up the rest of the faculty, most of whom taught at the college for between five and ten years. Many were graduates of the University of Pennsylvania and had become intrigued with homeopathy as a practical and intellectual alternative to orthodox medicine. Matthew Semple (1813–1867), an 1838 Pennsylvania graduate, became a pupil of Jeanes after reading about homeopathic successes in French hospitals and then saving one of his own patients, a child dying of scarlet fever, with a homeopathic remedy. From 1848 to 1862, Semple taught chemistry both

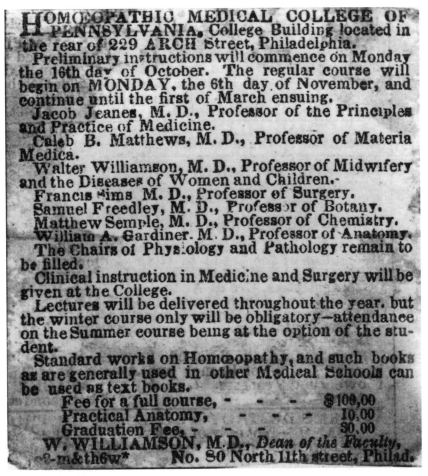

HOMŒOPATHIC MEDICAL COLLEGE OF PENNSYLVANIA, College Building located in the rear of 229 ARCH Street, Philadelphia.

Preliminary instructions will commence on Monday the 16th day of October. The regular course will begin on MONDAY, the 6th day of November, and continue until the first of March ensuing.

Jacob Jeanes, M. D., Professor of the Principles and Practice of Medicine.

Caleb B. Matthews, M. D., Professor of Materia Medica.

Walter Williamson, M. D., Professor of Midwifery and the Diseases of Women and Children.

Francis Sims M. D., Professor of Surgery.

Samuel Freedley, M. D., Professor of Botany.

Matthew Semple, M. D., Professor of Chemistry.

William A. Gardiner. M. D., Professor of Anatomy.

The Chairs of Physiology and Pathology remain to be filled.

Clinical instruction in Medicine and Surgery will be given at the College.

Lectures will be delivered throughout the year, but the winter course only will be obligatory—attendance on the Summer course being at the option of the student.

Standard works on Homœopathy, and such books as are generally used in other Medical Schools can be used as text books.

    Fee for a full course, -   -   - $100,00
    Practical Anatomy,   -   -   10,00
    Graduation Fee, -   -   -   30,00

W. WILLIAMSON, M. D., *Dean of the Faculty,*
  o2-m&th6w*   No. 80 North 11th street, Philad.

Figure 4. The opening of the Homeopathic Medical College was announced in local newspapers; of its seven original faculty members, six were graduates of the University of Pennsylvania; one was a graduate of Jefferson Medical College. *Philadelphia Public Ledger,* October 2, 1848.

at the college and at Philadelphia's Woman's Medical College. The professor of physiology, Alvan Edmund Small (1811–1886), an 1841 graduate of the Pennsylvania Medical College (one of Philadelphia's many short-lived medical schools), had become a homeopathic convert after reading Swedenborgian works.

A number of the prominent college teachers had come to homeopathy through a combination of personal experience with illness and the influence of a homeopathic mentor. William Sheaff Helmuth (1801–1880) was an 1823 Pennsylvania graduate whose chronic neuralgia had been cured by his classmate James Kitchen (1800–1894). Kitchen had returned from Paris in 1824, where

he had become a homeopathic enthusiast, and his notes on the lectures of Rene
Laennec and his new stethoscope are some of the earliest extant in the United
States. Kitchen sent a number of his pupils to the college, and one, William
Ashton Reed (1827–1895), an 1852 graduate, first became a demonstrator in
anatomy and then, in 1855, replaced Small as the chair of physiology. Charles
Neidhard (1809–1895), whose health had suffered during his medical study at
the University of Pennsylvania and the Pennsylvania Hospital, was healed by
William Wesselhoeft, one of Pennsylvania's earliest homeopaths. Afterward,
Neidhard, who had been born in Bremen, Germany, traveled to Leipzig and Jena
to study medicine and, after his return to Pennsylvania, graduated from the
Allentown Academy in 1837. From 1846 to 1852 he held the chair of clinical
medicine at the college.

    As homeopaths in other cities began to establish their own schools, the col-
lege was drawn into a wider social and medical world. For some Philadelphia
homeopaths these other institutions offered more promising prospects for medical advancement than did the college. Faculty turnover was typical at medical
schools; homeopathic conversion, it became clear, did not always mean collegi-
ality. Alvan Small, for example, left Philadelphia in 1856 for private practice
in Chicago and later became dean of the Hahnemann Medical College of Chicago. At the end of the 1850s, a small group of college faculty left to take up
positions at the recently established New York Homeopathic Medical College,
which remained homeopathic until the 1930s, the second longest-lasting homeopathic school in the United States after Hahnemann Medical College. Isaac
Moreau Ward (1806–1895) taught obstetrics at the college from 1853 to 1860
and then left to teach at the New York Homeopathic Medical College. In 1863,
Ward and Clemence Sophia Lozier (1813–1888)—an 1853 graduate of the Central Medical College, an Eclectic school—helped found the New York Medical
College and Hospital for Women, and Ward became its dean and professor of
obstetrics. This homeopathic school later became a rival of the orthodox school
for women in New York founded by Elizabeth Blackwell in 1868 (the Woman's
Medical College of the New York Infirmary).[29] Ward had been trained as an
orthodox physician at Rutgers Medical College and had turned to homeopathy
after comparing its success with orthodox failures in treating cholera during the
1832 New York epidemic. He introduced homeopathy to his patients secretly,
telling them only after they noticed its efficacy. Jacob Beakley (1812–1872), an
1834 graduate of the New York College of Physicians and Surgeons of Fairfield,
had become a homeopath in the 1840s while practicing in New York City. He
came to Philadelphia and taught surgery at the college from 1853 to 1860.
Beakley returned to New York after a public pamphlet battle and threatened
lawsuit from three students he refused to pass: the students called him "shame-
fully ignorant of Anatomy" and "not even a second rate operator" and claimed

that his lectures were "a disgrace to the Homeopathic Medical College."[30] He helped to organize the homeopathic college in New York and was dean and professor of surgery there for ten years. By the early 1860s, as a result of this turnover, the Homeopathic Medical College no longer had a stable core of faculty, and of the early faculty only Matthew Semple and William Gardiner remained.

What Was Taught

The college kept copies of students' theses, and almost all of them survived and today serve as an impressive source for historians trying to assess what the faculty taught and what students considered important. The college theses, like the theses required at orthodox schools, were handwritten and ranged in length from twelve to thirty pages. The choice of topics suggests that students and their teachers were interested in current medical issues of the day—such as smallpox vaccination and the use of chloroform—and in professional relations between physicians and patients and between orthodox and homeopathic physicians. But the most striking fact revealed by a brief analysis of the forty theses written by the 1857 seniors is that the college expected students to master standard medical topics. The teaching at this homeopathic school was distinctive but, unlike that of hydropathic and eclectic schools, clearly part of a medical mainstream.

Fifteen of the forty theses (around 40 percent) dealt with medical conditions, especially diseases that physicians faced in ordinary practice: pneumonia, bronchitis, dysentery, typhoid fever. Two students from Southern states wrote on yellow fever, a regional concern. That these works centered around various diseases attests to the flexibility of the homeopathic teaching at the college: "pure" homeopaths taught by symptoms rather than by disease categories. Nine of these seniors wrote on physiology, most on the workings of major organs and systems such as the heart, the blood, or the reproductive system, but two theses dealt with pathology, including one entitled "The Pathology of Tubercles." Pathology, a topic of major interest in contemporary medical science, was seen by some homeopaths as the antithesis of the Hahnemannian emphasis on external symptoms.[31]

Three of the theses dealt explicitly not only with homeopathy but also with one of the more contested realms of medicine: medical history. History, for American homeopaths, was part of their special identity, and to some extent the mission of the early homeopaths was to create and reinforce a new medical history. The founders of the college cared about history, and at one of their first meetings, the faculty set up a committee to draft a history of the school.[32] To a large extent the college's calendar was based on important events in the history of homeopathy: the first meeting of the college trustees in 1848, for example, was held on Hahnemann's birthday, April 10. As one student wrote in his 1853 thesis entitled "Medicine as a Science," "thanks to this age of liberal thinking, the practice of medicine is not always to remain beclouded by Egyptian darkness. . . . The ancient, though illfounded Structure of Medicine is being rebuilt, and erected upon a foundation of principles truly scientific."[33] In this kind of homeopathic history medicine began with Samuel Hahnemann.

But homeopaths began increasingly to recognize the power of medical history in situating their system in the respected Western medical tradition. Homeopaths at the college sought to characterize their system as a natural development of the orthodox medical tradition, as based on a body of writings that referred to long-standing learned medical texts. Hahnemann himself had pointed to medical luminaries such as Hippocrates and Paracelsus to find precedents for his ideas, and homeopathic educators similarly instructed their students. In an 1857 thesis entitled "Pre-Hahnemannic Homeopathy," David Hindman explained that the principle of "like cures like" had been around since the days of Hippocrates, both in the writings of the best medical authorities and also in the popular and domestic practices of almost every age and country. "In the writings of Hippocrates we find many valuable foreshadowings of the law of homeopathy and also admissions and vindications for that law as a law of nature." Hindman pointed out that even Galen, claimed by orthodox physicians as a father, had called for similars in medical practice. Hindman called on "allopaths" to stop "their great hue and cry against modern homeopathy" and "examine the evidence of their Father in medicine," as well as the work of Paracelsus, John Hunter, and others "of the most scientific and enlightened authorities of ancient medicine," among whom "the homeopathic law was not only recognized but . . . taught and practiced."[34]

It is difficult to judge how successful the college was in its first few decades, or why medical students and practitioners came to study there. It proudly noted its growing enrollment and its place as "the oldest of its kind in either hemisphere, striving against prejudice amidst those other time-honored Institutions backed by habit and influence."[35] Occasionally a student would leave some evidence to allow us to glimpse some of the reasons behind his choice of school, although these reasons may have been phrased so as to please his teachers and satisfy himself. Take the 1857 thesis of Georgia physician William Nephew King simply entitled "Homeopathy." King had practiced "allopathy" for ten years after graduating from the New York University Medical College, where he had attended lectures by eminent orthodox physicians such as Valentine Mott, Granville Sharp Pattison, and John William Draper. With his diploma in hand he had gone forth "armed with a panacea for every disease," but by the end of his first year of practice he found his "beautiful fancied theories of the nature of disease and the action of medicines empty nothingness." During his third year of practice, he found himself "lost, lost in the infinite labyrinth of Contraria

Conrais [sic]," and he wrote: "too proud to look to any other sources of light, I groped in the dark." After his discovery of Hahnemann's work, especially the law of similars (a law "founded upon pure induction, not *invented* but *discovered*"), King regained his professional equilibrium but was then confronted by his orthodox former colleagues. He was frequently asked by his "allopathic brethren" why he had "descend[ed] to the palpable absurdities of infinitesimal doses, and the use of the contemptible 'little pills'—what can you accomplish with them?" "You learn all in the *hands* of *nature*," King replied. "She perfects her cure and you get the praise." A homeopath, King argued, does not need anatomical knowledge or some imagined concept of disease, for "to obtain the object we are to *listen—write*—interrogate—and lastly arrange."[36]

These theses also show that the college continually aspired, like its urban supporters, to a comfortable middle-class status; it was never a poor-boy's school. College teachers sought a standing in the community as gentlemen and offered their students appropriate models of professional behavior, which many were quick to adopt. "The good physician," student George William Dennett wrote in "The Physician and His Duties," recognized "the many sacrifices of comfort & social enjoyment to which he is likely to be subjected to." He visits "not only the wealthy and those comfortabl[y] situated, but the distressed and miserably poor." Dennett admitted that he knew a homeopath who "refused to attend a great many poor people, because the wealthy would not employ him if they knew he answered such calls." "I think it is a disgrace to Homeopathy," Dennett commented, "that it has among its advocates those who entertain no higher views of the objects of the 'healing art.'" A true homeopath "should be a gentleman in the fullest sense of the word," a man of culture and elegance who disdained "coarse brutish language" as well as alcohol and tobacco, was self-disciplined and cheerful, kept the private matters of his patients secret, and was never in "habit of gossiping."[37] Despite their somewhat diverse backgrounds and internal divisions, the faculty also clearly saw themselves in a different world from the school's janitor, say, and especially from their dispensary patients and dissection subjects. In 1859, for example, the faculty decided to go to the janitor's funeral and attend "in carriages," a gesture to indicate their concern to the wider community while maintaining their class distance.[38] One catalog referred to the "multitude of poor" who asked for aid, and assured students that some of these patients could be used as obstetrics cases for the graduating class, something that would never have been considered for the faculty's private women patients.[39]

Surgery and Homeopathy

Before the Civil War surgery at the college was poorly taught and poorly regarded. In a damning 1865 student thesis entitled "Homeopathic Surgery,"

Samuel Gibbs Tucker (1851–1897) argued that "homeopathists are notoriously unskilled in surgery," and he placed the blame both on homeopathic teaching in his own school and on the popular image of homeopathy as a weak, anti-interventionist medical system, an image that was, he admitted, part of its attraction for some converts. Tucker deplored the "farce" of surgical teaching, claiming that "our professors of other chairs lose no opportunity to sneer at the use of the knife [and cry] . . . Surgery your shame and the knife a disgrace to him who uses it." Consequently, he wrote, "the students of our college to a great degree imbibe a disgust for surgery and many of them enter practice with the determination to have as little as possible to do with it."[40]

Yet Tucker warned that without surgical skills a homeopath would lose not only patients but also his public reputation. Although Tucker indicated that homeopaths "would not deviate from the path of duty, for the sake of popularity," he nonetheless argued that the public faced with surgical ignorance would "contemptuously turn to the 'scientific men of the old school,' leaving us, as they facetiously remark 'to doctor the babies & the ladies who *play* sick.'" The management of childbirth especially required surgical skills for both homeopaths and regulars. Tucker cited the example of Henry Guernsey, "our own professor of obstetrics," whose pregnant patient from "an intelligent family" had previously employed "an allopath." She had asked Guernsey what he would do if she needed a catheter, supposing he would not be acquainted with it "*simply because he was a homeopath.*" Surgical skill, Tucker concluded, was therefore far more important for a homeopath than for an orthodox physician, for unlike the latter, who could "choose whether to make one or other branch of the profession a specialisation," the homeopath "stands alone in the community where he practices" and "must master every skill" or lose certain cases and the public's respect.[41]

The Civil War impressed the public with the importance of skilled surgical care.[42] The public's perception was especially challenging for homeopathic educators, for one of their earliest identifying claims was that they offered an alternative to drastic surgical intervention. Indeed, before the war homeopaths had prided themselves on offering patients medical solutions to what orthodox physicians defined as surgical problems. The school's 1849–1850 catalog claimed, for example, that homeopaths were able to cure "by far the greater proportion of what are usually denominated surgical diseases . . . without any dexterous handling of the gorget or scalpel."[43] Under homeopathy, the college also boasted, one-half of all surgical operations "may be dispensed with," and "the surgeon is enabled to relieve without resort to painful operations many diseases which were formally surrendered to the knife."[44] This argument was especially convincing to prospective general practitioners who recognized the public's well-justified fear of surgical intervention in an era when many surgical patients died from shock and wound infection. Homeopaths also claimed that when they did operate, their results after surgery were better than those of regulars. "While surgical operations are similar in all schools," the 1863–1864 catalog commented, "*our* after treatment demonstrates most clearly the advantage to the patient of Homeopathic treatment over any other."[45] With a homeopathic treatment of women in labor the "act of parturition would become more and more natural" and would require less mechanical intervention, another catalog assured the public, although, it added, all these techniques were taught nonetheless to the student.[46]

The Civil War forced the college faculty to reassess their attitude to surgery. As it did at other Philadelphia schools, the war hurt the college's enrollment: the number of graduates dropped from thirty-one in 1861 to fifteen in 1862.[47] The faculty became even more aware of the demands of students and the expectations of the public and, in its 1867–1868 catalog, stated that surgery's "vast importance, as illustrated during the late war, and the claims of humanity upon us in their direction, give special force to the universal demand for surgical knowledge."[48] Students began to select surgical topics for their final theses, sometimes graphically drawing on their experience during the war. In 1865, in a study based on his own military experiences, Robert Wilkie Martin (1841–1907) discussed gunshot wounds, including his own.

In response to the demand for surgical knowledge, the college began to hire young men whose less prestigious medical backgrounds were compensated for by strong military surgical experiences, men such as John Coleman Morgan (1830–1903). Morgan, who had been a drug clerk and surgeon's steward in the navy, graduated in 1852 from the Pennsylvania Medical College and taught materia medica at the unorthodox Penn Medical University, the only medical school in the city that had chairs in "homeopathy" and "allopathy."[49] Morgan then moved to St. Louis, where he helped to organize a homeopathic school. After being refused many times because of his homeopathic identity he finally gained a surgical commission in the Union Army and became surgeon of the Twenty-ninth Missouri Volunteers. He taught at the college from 1865 to 1876 and then left to teach theory and practice at the new homeopathic department of the University of Michigan. Malcolm MacFarlan (1841–1921), who became professor of surgery and surgical pathology, had been an army hospital steward and an assistant surgeon. During the war, while posted at Fort Morgan, he worked as a quarantine officer, where he read Hahnemann's *Organon*, and after experimenting with drug proving, he began practicing homeopathy.[50] With the addition of these new faculty members, the teaching of surgery at the college improved somewhat, but as historian Gert Brieger has pointed out, most nineteenth-century schools still taught surgery through lectures and the observation of operations in amphitheaters. Ambitious American surgeons had to go to Europe to gain practical experience.[51]

During the 1860s, in addition to seeking surgeons with military experience, the college for the first time appointed a few teachers who were not physicians. In 1860 H. Ryland Warriner, a lawyer and later a college trustee, taught medical jurisprudence, and in 1863 chemistry was offered by Lemuel Stephens (1817–1892), a physical scientist with European training.[52] Stephens, an 1835 chemistry graduate from Harvard College, had studied in the early 1840s at the Universities of Göttingen and Berlin and then taught chemistry, mathematics, and natural philosophy at the University of Pittsburgh and Girard College. Stephens held the chair of chemistry and toxicology at the college from 1863 to 1886, but not until 1894 was it again held by a non-M.D.[53]

Physical Structure and Moral Mission

From its first years the school suffered financial instability. By as early as June 1849 the school had already run up a debt of $750, $240 of which was due to unpaid student fees.[54] Money became a constant theme in structuring relations among faculty members and between the faculty and the school's trustees. In spite of its financial difficulties, the school continued to exist, and perhaps the most significant factor in ensuring its existence was physical stability. In September 1849 the school moved from Arch Street to a building on the north side of Filbert Street between Eleventh and Twelfth Streets; the Arch Street building was subsequently taken over by the newly established Female Medical College (later renamed the Woman's Medical College).[55] The Filbert Street building, originally built for the Philadelphia Institute for the Instruction of Young Men, had been redesigned as a medical school by the private Medical Department of Pennsylvania College.[56] The Homeopathic Medical College rented the building and bought Pennsylvania College's equipment, including glass cases, gas fixtures, benches, and curtains; six years later it bought the main building and two adjoining buildings.[57] Filbert Street housed the college from 1849 until it built a more modern building on Broad Street in 1886.

The college's physical space, and the way the school occupied it, tell us much about the mission of mid-nineteenth-century American medical schools. The Filbert Street building became a crucial part in the making of the identity of the college and its alumni. In his 1898 history of the college, for example, Hahnemann historian and 1869 graduate Thomas Lindsley Bradford (1847–1918) devoted a whole chapter to walking his readers through the Filbert Street building, based mainly on his memories as a student some thirty years earlier.[58] Bradford had a private practice in Philadelphia but began collecting documents pertaining to the college's history. In 1890, he was appointed librarian of the college and later lecturer in the history of medicine.[59]

Historian William Rothstein has aptly characterized midcentury American medical schools as consisting of "one main building with two lecture halls," one

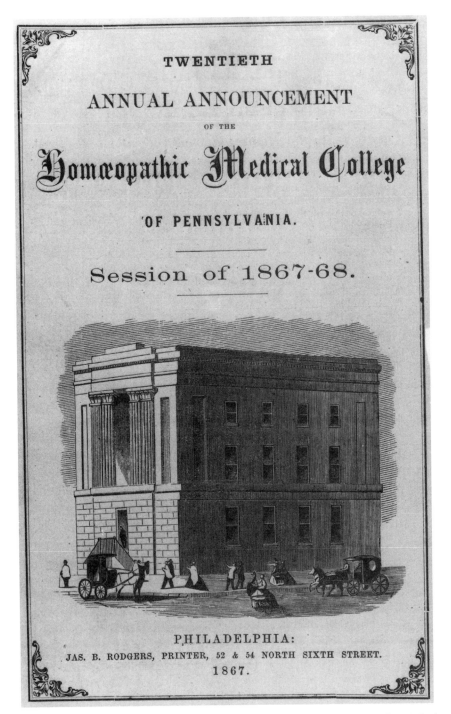

TWENTIETH

ANNUAL ANNOUNCEMENT

OF THE

Homœopathic Medical College

OF PENNSYLVANIA.

Session of 1867-68.

PHILADELPHIA:
JAS. B. RODGERS, PRINTER, 52 & 54 NORTH SIXTH STREET.
1867.

Figure 5. Front cover of the *Twentieth Annual Announcement of the Homeopathic Medical College of Pennsylvania: Session of 1867–1868.* In 1849 the college moved to this building on Filbert Street, where it stayed until 1886.

used for "chemistry, materia medica, and theory and practice of medicine" and another, "which had a skylight . . . used for anatomy, physiology and surgery."[60] These schools were not designed to provide students with clinical training; the college, for example, required that students study with a preceptor during the years they were attending lectures. The school year was short, around four months, and students were expected to spend the rest of the year gaining clinical experience by working with their medical preceptor or, although this was less openly acknowledged, by practicing medicine themselves.[61] The college's main lecture room was also available for the use of outside medical groups, such as the Homeopathic Medical Society of the County of Philadelphia (founded in 1866); sharing space was an effective way to indicate to the larger medical community that this building was not to be a place of privilege separate from other physicians.[62]

Medical teaching in the nineteenth century, thus, was largely didactic. Lectures were given in large classrooms by teachers who read notes that then formed the basis of a student's library. Until the 1870s most schools, homeopathic and orthodox, needed only a few lecture rooms, for all students attended the same set of lectures. Filbert Street's main lecture room extended the entire width of the building and could seat six hundred. At the front of the room was a low platform with a long desk and a stand where the lecturer could place his notes. As the school year lengthened and formal apprenticeships became less common, medical schools felt under greater pressure to provide clinical teaching. The college began to hold "clinics," but they were mostly lectures with a patient present, offering students limited opportunity to see and none to touch. Surgical techniques, for example, were demonstrated with anatomical models and, "when opportunities offer," by patients shown before the class.[63]

The quality of these lectures depended on the teacher's ability to command the attention of his audience and to speak clearly and slowly. In an 1856 thesis entitled "Scientific Lecturing," Harrison O. Apthorp, without naming names, complained that few of his teachers sought "the most simple, natural, and intelligible mode of presenting his science," a mode that would "favor the taking of notes . . . and facilitate the transcribing of them, so as to present a methodical and well-arranged view of the subject." Instead, many spoke in "a low, muttering indistinctness," used technical terms ungrammatically, and "couple[d] the singular & plural of different languages."

Apthorp's thesis demonstrates more than frustration with poor lecturing techniques. It shows that the college faculty were trying to develop a style of teaching that would distinguish the medical school professor from the university professor or the master of a grammar school. To their students, the college faculty made unfavorable comparisons between the academic humanist or "literary pedant" and the scientific physician who chose, as Apthorp phrased it, a "manly adherence to plain facts & the naked statements of principles" and understood the "general distaste in the scientific world to all that is ornamental in style, or figurative in diction." The faculty told students to set aside "the dandyism of letters" and to "beware of rhetoric, despise the polish of diction, and confine themselves to fact." These rhetoric flourishes suggest the development of a self-conscious academic medical style that defined science in masculine terms and implicitly drew on the teachings of the Paris Clinical School in valuing empiricism over speculation. Apthorp hoped, wistfully but without much conviction, that his teachers would add "a grace to knowledge" by "investing the treasures of science in the garb of refinement & taste."[64] Perhaps the stridency of this teaching style that Apthorp so disliked was intensified by his teachers' fear that the public and other physicians did not believe homeopaths were proper professionals able to treat serious disease.

Lecturing style was important because, as we have seen, lecturing largely defined American medical education until the late nineteenth century. But the founders of the Homeopathic Medical College recognized that a medical school had to have broader function, that it also had to provide facilities for medical care for the poor and opportunities for students and their teachers to gain clinical experience in an institutional setting. Until the 1870s there were no homeopathic hospitals in Philadelphia separate from the college. Thus for two decades the college remained the central force in organizing institutional homeopathic care in Philadelphia. In many cities homeopathic physicians and students were barred from orthodox hospitals. In the late 1850s, for example, attending orthodox physicians at both Chicago City Hospital and New York City's Bellevue Hospital threatened to boycott the hospitals rather than turn any wards over to homeopaths.[65] But in Philadelphia, by the 1860s, homeopaths were allowed to walk the wards at the Philadelphia Almshouse, the Pennsylvania Hospital, and Wills Eye Hospital.[66] Visiting the wards was so central a part of the college curriculum that the school's teaching schedule was organized so as not to interfere with clinics at the Philadelphia and Pennsylvania hospitals.

When the college opened, its founders immediately established a dispensary, providing free outpatient care for the sick poor, in part to win the public's loyalty by displaying a philanthropic spirit and in part to attract students seeking clinical instruction. The dispensary's 1849 published regulations listed both of these goals: "To afford to all indigent sick persons, medicine and advice gratuitously" and "To afford students the opportunity to study disease and witness the practical application of homeopathic medicine."[67]

The college used the dispensary in its advertising to students; in the 1849–1850 catalog the college boasted that its dispensary would enable students to learn medicine "in a more effectual manner than can be learned from books" and, in a later catalog, that "from the numerous patients applying to the

Dispensary for medical aid an extensive range of disease presents for study."[68] Under the eye of an attending physician, students and recent graduates could prescribe for patients (they could also visit those who were too sick to come to the dispensary). Students were obliged to keep accurate records, which would be copied and sent to the board of managers.[69] But the faculty saw dispensary work more as demonstrative teaching than as a replacement for experience gained from a preceptor, telling students "opportunity will be afforded for witnessing the practice of a large number of the homeopathic physicians."[70] Overall, the college dispensary functioned more as a health facility and a community showpiece than as a place for clinical instruction. In the 1880s Israel Tisdale Talbot, an 1853 graduate who had become dean of the homeopathic medical school of Boston University, reminded his fellow alumni that the dispensary was "the solid foundation of our system," for "here the poor, who will not always be poor, learn the advantages of Homeopathy." When homeopathic dispensaries are established and managed, Talbot added, with "public effort on the part of the laity," potential middle-class patients will then identify the dispensaries "with our system and [this] interests them and acquaints them more thoroughly with Homeopathy."[71]

Despite these grand claims, the dispensary was open only from noon to one every day except Sunday; although by 1852 the college claimed it aided thirty patients a day, and in the 1860s it refigured this as five to six thousand patients a year.[72] Until 1877 the college dispensary was housed in the basement of Filbert Street with its entrance immediately under the college's front steps (it remained a physical part of the college until 1890, when it was moved into a new building, known as Clinical Hall, that also housed the amphitheater).[73] At the rear of the dispensary were a small surgical clinic and also rooms for the preparation and storage for what Thomas Lindsley Bradford tactfully called "anatomical material."[74]

In this period when even the best orthodox schools in the city did not control their own hospitals, dispensaries were a small but symbolically important part of the American medical school.[75] Providing medical students the opportunity to see and touch patients was a highly problematic issue in this era when most hospitals were run by charitable lay men and women who saw themselves as the patients' protectors and doctors as possible experimenters and students as disrespectful.

The dispensary of the college suffered constant administrative problems. The dispensary's board of managers found it difficult to attract and keep a medical director and was unable to decide whether to pay the attending physician (in hospitals such work was provided free by philanthropic physicians). Within a few years, the board began selecting young men from the college, providing professional rewards in exchange for service. In 1852 they chose Randolph Titsworth

(1821–1890), who graduated the following year, to serve as the attending dispensary physician from March to October (the off-school months) in exchange for one year's tuition, and later the board hired recent graduates. In 1857 the board permitted one faculty member to attend each day to oversee the dispensary and select patients for college clinics, but in general the board successfully kept the college faculty at arm's length, treating the institution more like a hospital than an educational training facility.[76] In 1862, for example, the faculty asked the board in vain for the power to select the dispensary's visiting physicians. The board, indeed, seems to have seen the dispensary as providing training and experience to the city's entire homeopathic community, not just to college physicians. Not until 1879 was a recent graduate, Charles Mohr (1844–1907), a newly appointed lecturer in pharmacy, made the dispensary's chief of staff, a position he retained until 1885. He became the first in a series of faculty officials who helped to integrate college teaching into the dispensary.

In the nineteenth century most medical care took place in the patient's home. Hospitals, which were usually the size of a large house and had between twenty and sixty beds, were used only by the poor and by strangers far from their family and private doctor. Hospitals were known, justly, as places of dirt and disease, and the poor generally preferred dispensary to hospital care. Hospital training provided students with kinds of patients different from those whom private physicians hoped to attract. Physicians engaged in two types of patient care; one to make a living, the other to show their civil responsibility and gain clinical experience.

The college faculty always felt that the growth of homeopathic education in Philadelphia demanded a hospital. In 1851 the college announced that "to render the course of instruction of the College complete, nothing more was wanting than the establishment of a hospital."[77] In 1852 the Philadelphia homeopathic community established a small hospital with around forty beds in a four-story building on Twenty-fourth and Chestnut Streets. Although it was some streets away from the college, the school's 1852–1853 catalog referred to it together with the college dispensary as the means for students "to witness Clinical practice,"[78] and the last page of the catalog showed a woodcut of the Homeopathic Hospital of Pennsylvania.[79] College faculty and alumni ran it: Richard Gardiner was the president of its board; Caleb Matthews and William S. Helmuth were vice presidents, William Gardiner was secretary, and Walter Williamson was treasurer. But the hospital collapsed after two years, owing to a lack of money and interest on the part of homeopathic physicians.[80]

In 1862, a group of women, including a number of faculty wives, met at the college to raise money for a new hospital, which was to be called the Homeopathic Hospital of Philadelphia for Sick and Wounded Soldiers. This hospital was designed to raise public awareness of soldiers' need to have access to homeopathic treatment, and to demonstrate the patriotic and philanthropic spirit of Philadelphia's homeopathic community. The women raised enough money to buy two buildings at the rear of the college on Cuthbert Street and convert them into a hospital. The buildings were close enough for one upper story to be connected to the college amphitheater by a covered walkway. The hospital was unable to gain government support for its homeopathic treatment of Civil War soldiers, but during the war it did treat some fifty soldiers who had been discharged "uncured" from the army.[81] By the end of the war the hospital collapsed and became a boarding house for college students; the collapse left the faculty struggling to find ways to link homeopathic education with a homeopathic hospital.[82]

In trying to distinguish itself from the numerous small medical schools in the city that offered only lectures, and with an eye to the model of the University of Pennsylvania and Jefferson Medical College, the faculty also proudly promoted their dissecting rooms. From the first session students were required to pay a separate fee of ten dollars for "practical anatomy," a fee that continued until the 1880s. In 1850 a demonstrator in anatomy, the first nonprofessorial faculty member, was hired. Early catalogs boasted about its "ample supply of *material*" and its "large well ventilated room for anatomical purposes," which was open during the colder weather from October to March, and assured students that it used gaslight for illumination, critical for dissection that took place in dark winter months. Later, the college also boasted that students were "invited to practice operations upon the cadaver under the direction of the Professor."[83]

Nonetheless, medical educators knew that dissection and the procurement of bodies were aspects of medical training disliked by the lay public. Only in 1867 did Pennsylvania legalize medical dissection in a law the school's catalog immediately praised as "in accordance with the enlightened spirit of the age."[84] At Filbert Street the winding college stairs led from the basement (which housed the dispensary and anatomical storage rooms) to a trap hole in the fourth floor. Through the hole hung a rope on a windlass that was used to draw bodies up to the top floor for dissecting.[85] Perhaps placing the school's dissecting rooms at the top of this winding staircase kept them somewhat hidden.

The way the rest of the building was organized also showed that the college was trying to model itself on good orthodox schools. A central and continuing point of college pride was its museum, which took up most of the second floor and was housed in the largest room in the building.[86] That medical museums were a critical aspect of medical training in the eighteenth and nineteenth centuries reflected a movement in natural science that valued cataloged order and the presentation of selected materials to teach science through physical demonstration. Filbert Street's museum, like many other medical school museums, contained wax models, life-size anatomical plates, mineral and plant samples, and specimens and preparations. And interspersed throughout this "means of scientific demonstration," the college noted in its 1852–1853 catalog, were "many specimens of natural curiosities, and anomalies of the human species."[87] This reference to freaks and monstrosities, which fascinated the lay public, suggests that the museum was a showpiece for visitors and for prospective students.[88] When the college split in 1867, the first thing the faculty of the new school did was to ask the Philadelphia homeopathic community for donations of pathological specimens and apparatus, perhaps those that were a "source of inconvenience" for the busy practitioner with limited space. Within a year the new college boasted that it had fifteen hundred "objects" and invited the profession to view the museum as part of an examination of the whole school.[89] By 1871 the merged college claimed that the museum contained five thousand specimens, and it was particularly proud of the sixty-eight-piece set of "celebrated Auzaux clastic anatomical models from Paris," which were "marvels of beauty of finish and accuracy of detail."[90] Even Abraham Flexner, visiting the college in 1909 with an extremely critical eye as part of his inspection of American medical schools, praised the school's "large and very well kept museum," although by this time such comments also suggested that the college spent too much time on an old-fashioned source of medical instruction. Nonetheless, the lasting power of this kind of teaching can be seen in Thomas Lindsley Bradford's memory of his experience as a student with a mannequin in which "all the muscles could be taken off separately; the internal organs also removed." Bradford wrote that he well remembered "the delight of taking apart an arm and then trying to get the muscles back again."[91]

The college was also proud of its amphitheater. A medical school's amphitheater was designed to be both instructional and demonstrative. It offered students the opportunity to see the practice of medicine and surgery and especially to admire the skill and performance of the surgeon. One distinctive note at the Filbert Street amphitheater was a long table at its center, on either side of which hung a skeleton. The skeletons, Bradford remembered, frequently became the butt of jokes while students waited for the medical performance to begin, and the skeletons are prominent features in the only extant sketch of the interior of this college. Students in the front rows, he wrote, would "take grotesque liberties with these relics of departed humanity."[92] These skeletons reminded the spectators of the special world they were now in, and their accessibility reinforced the message that doctors were permitted a privileged and perhaps less reverential attitude to the human body. This irreverence, part of a wider medical culture in which medical students frequently chose to be photographed with skeletons or skulls, was reflected in a poem written by William Tod Helmuth (1833–1902), whose preceptor-uncle had taught at the college. Helmuth, an 1853 graduate, had become a prominent New York surgeon and medical poet

Figure 6. Sketch from the student notebook of Theodore S. Geiger (18?–1863, class of 1854) showing the amphitheater of the college on Filbert Street, including two skeletons hung on either side of the lectern. Theodore S. Geiger Collection, Hahnemann Collection.

and was American homeopathy's equivalent to Oliver Wendell Holmes. Speaking at an AIH banquet in 1871, Helmuth read a poem that could have been written by any orthodox graduate; he drew on his student days at the college twenty years earlier:

> What visions of that careless, motley crew
> Who studied medicine, and mischief too . . .
> I sought thy classic precincts, mother dear,
> I wore thy benches smooth year after year . . .
> Laughed o'er the dead in "parlors of the sky"
> Carved bone and muscle, nerve and artery,
> "Crammed" for each quiz, applauded with my feet,
> And cut my name upon a chosen seat.[93]

Academic Conflict in the Early Years

Within the first weeks of the school's opening, members of the larger homeopathic community began to protest about the way the school was organized, particularly about the power delegated to the faculty. A lay committee made up of five of the school's original corporators rewrote the school's constitution, and the new constitution, adopted in March 1849, placed power not in the hands of officers elected from the corporators but in a twelve-person board of managers, none of whom, the rules now specified, "shall be medical men." This board of managers was to have the ultimate control of all aspects of the school, including faculty appointments and salaries, student admissions, tuition, and the conferring of degrees. The new board also altered the school's charter so that graduates received not only a doctor of homeopathic medicine degree but also a doctor of medicine degree.[94]

This brief upheaval was not just about homeopathy. It pitted doctors against lay gentlemen and suggested that the status of physicians was still unsettled in this era. Doctors were not necessarily seen as men who could be trusted with the moral management of the various groups making up a medical school: the housekeeping staff, the students, the patients, and even the faculty themselves.[95] Trustees, by comparison, were financially secure men who could manage an institution morally and responsibly. The changes in the 1849 constitution also implied that the judgment of the college's homeopathic founders, many of them enthusiastic converts, might need to be tempered by wiser lay heads concerned with both the internal workings of the college and also its trappings. The addition of a traditional medical degree to the school's homeopathic degree suggests that lay homeopathic supporters were not convinced that the wider public would value a newly minted physician with only an odd title on his diploma. By 1861 the college itself boasted that its diplomas conferred on graduates "*all* the professional rights to privileges granted by Allopathic Colleges, as Doctor of Medicine."[96]

The power of lay men and women in shaping medical education has frequently been underestimated by historians of medicine. Certainly, their power was a significant force in the history of American homeopathy. It is impossible to understand the early history of the college without recognizing the power of lay networks, and, as later chapters will show, the local community continued to shape education at the college in the twentieth century as well. By the mid-1860s the school's constitution no longer specifically required that trustees not be medical men, and in 1867 a prominent and respected homeopathic physician, Augustus Koch, became a full trustee of the college. For some years the faculty called themselves professional trustees, but the title designated no additional control of the institution.

Lay management did not ensure stability. In the 1850s and 1860s the college was rocked by a series of internal conflicts that hurt its reputation and eventually, in 1867, split the college in two. The conflicts began in October 1854, when the faculty asked Frederick Humphreys (1816–1900), the recently hired chair of institutes, pathology, and practice of medicine, to defend himself against the charge that he had been involved "in the Manufacture & Sale of 'New Era Medicines'" and had promoted "certain advertisements of Secret Medicines."[97]

Humphreys was an alumnus; he had attended the college's first session of lectures in 1848, graduated in 1850, and in the early 1850s gained professional recognition and a position on an AIH research committee after publishing his provings of the poison of the honey bee. Like a number of early graduates, he had had a varied career before coming to the college; he had been a merchant, a farmer, and a minister in the Methodist Episcopal Church. He had studied medicine with his father, Erastus Humphreys, a respected homeopath in Utica, New York, and had published a number of homeopathic pamphlets. Humphreys assured the school's investigatory committee that he had received no profit from the drugs in question and had never authorized the use of his name. He did, however, defend a set of pills he had developed in Utica known as "Blessings for the Multitude." The sale of these globules, which resembled homeopathic medicines, to the public as homeopathic therapies for infant dysentery and other more serious infant diseases was not, he claimed, a departure from legitimate homeopathic practice.[98]

The college faculty members were not convinced. Perhaps because they were conscious of the precarious position of so many medical schools in the country, their response to Humphreys showed their fear that a college could rise and fall on its public reputation. They warned Humphreys that his association with patent medicines created "distrust and discontent in the minds of the students and a deep feeling of regret on the part of those interested in the college." While they had "no wish to abridge his rights as a man or a physician," they believed that Humphreys's association with these drugs could "give rise to evil reports capable of indefinite exaggeration."[99] That his pills combined two "specifics" was also a serious transgression against standard homeopathic prescribing. Humphreys resigned a few weeks later and was subsequently expelled from the Philadelphia and New York homeopathic societies. His career as a popular writer and homeopathic drug manufacturer, however, burgeoned. He became one of the college's best known early alumni, amassing a fortune with his Humphreys Specific Homeopathic Medicines Company, a fortune that enabled him to maintain houses in New York City and in his home town of Monmouth Bay, New Jersey, as well as a winter house in Thomasville, Georgia. He always claimed that homeopathic patent medicines did not undermine the standing of homeopathy, and in the 1890s, after hearing about the history of the college Thomas Lindsley Bradford was preparing, Humphreys encouraged an employee to write to Bradford explaining that his company "brought [homeopathy] to the attention of thousands to whom it was entirely unknown, and to whom it would remain unknown if confined simply to the lines of purely professional practice."[100]

The college faculty was anxious to squash any association between homeopathy and patent medicines because the line between professional activity and the selling of pills by quacks was somewhat fuzzy, especially among American homeopaths. It was difficult to separate the work of a homeopathic professional from that of a patent medicine promoter because homeopaths were so dependent on lay support that much of their work—including journal writing, college teaching, and especially therapeutic practice—involved gaining popular attention through a high public profile. The notion of a "professional" practitioner was also problematic because until after the Civil War many homeopaths were lay practitioners (although most homeopathic historians have overlooked this fact). Some laypeople had studied serious medical works like Samuel Hahnemann's *Organon*, but many others based their practice on homeopathic popular health books and used homeopathic medical kits. Indeed, some eminent homeopaths made their professional reputation by publishing such books. Hering's *Domestic Physician* remained in print for some decades, and it inspired other college faculty: Walter Williamson wrote a popular health book entitled *The Homeopathic Treatment of Women and Children*, and Alvan Small, like Hering, wrote a book on domestic practice. Similar guides were written by anti-orthodox practitioners, like Thomsonians and hydropaths, but many others were by orthodox physicians, some of whom provided testimonials for patent medicine manufacturers as well.[101]

As a question of medical ethics the issue of patent medicines was largely ignored by medical societies and schools, although the 1847 AMA code and the 1869 AIH code did prohibit secret remedies. Homeopaths boasted that their system was open for all to see. As Hering argued in 1853, homeopathy "recognises no nostrum, deals in no secrecy, but displays its treasures and courts inquiry."[102] For the faculty in Philadelphia, there was additional pressure for the college to keep itself professionally pure. Students interested in studying non-orthodox medicine had a wide choice of medical schools, including the Penn Medical University and the Eclectic Medical College of Philadelphia. And not all local homeopaths were satisfied with the college teaching. During the same year that Humphreys was investigated, Philadelphia's leading homeopaths, Constantine Hering and Adolph Lippe, who were not then formally connected to the school, tried unsuccessfully to organize an opposing homeopathic school, to be known as the Independent Medical School, and then offered private lectures in their homes, perhaps as an alternative to college teaching.[103] After a series of conflicts in the early 1860s resulting in significant faculty turnover, Hering and Lippe headed a new slate of college faculty.

Selecting new faces did not solve the college's internal troubles.[104] The most serious conflict within the college in this period occurred in 1867 and concerned both homeopathic theory and money. The central figure was Adolph Lippe (1812–1888), one of the school's early organizers. Lippe, the Prussian-born son of aristocrats, had come to the United States in 1839. He studied homeopathy with Hering and graduated from the Allentown Academy in 1841. He held the chair of materia medica at the college from 1864 to 1869, traditionally in homeopathic schools the most ideological and conservative of positions. In 1865, to try to deal with its perennial financial problems, the college trustees reorganized themselves into a joint stock company, worth sixty thousand dollars, offering stockholders three thousand shares at twenty dollars each. Trustees were now elected by the stockholders, and the faculty was chosen for one year at a time. In 1867 Lippe managed to get control of a majority of college stock, and at the end of the 1866–1867 session he announced that the existence of a chair in special pathology and diagnostics (which had been introduced in 1864 as "thereby supplying a *desideratum* demanded by modern researchers")[105] was contrary to true homeopathy. This announcement led Hering to resign his professorship, partly to protest Lippe's concept of homeopathy and partly because his friend, Charles Godlove Raue (1820–1896), had held the chair in question.[106] Hering and a group of physicians (including college faculty Raue, John Morgan, and Lemuel Stephens) then set up an opposing homeopathic school. They bought the 1853 charter of the Washington Medical College, a defunct Philadelphia medical school, changed its name through the city courts, calling it the Hahnemann Medical College, and installed Hering as dean. They first rented the second and third floors of a building at 1307 Chestnut Street and then moved to 18 North Tenth Street near Market Street.

For two years the new college (led by Hering) and the old college (led by Lippe and staffed mainly by a group of new faces, including Robert John McClatchey [1838–1883], a major figure in the local homeopathic society) divided Philadelphia's homeopathic students and college supporters. The split was ended in January 1869 by a clandestine agreement between the faculty at both colleges: Lippe's colleague Henry Guernsey, having convinced Lippe to use him as a broker to sell his shares, sold Lippe's shares to Hering. When Lippe discovered this, he resigned, and within months the two colleges merged under Hering's new name, the Hahnemann Medical College.

In part the split was a story of homeopaths struggling to defend their concept of homeopathy. The teaching of pathology and experimental physiology became pivotal issues in American homeopaths' efforts to define themselves in relation to orthodox scientific changes.[107] College catalogs in the 1850s had claimed that homeopathy was in fact more scientific than orthodox medicine, for its "only known law of cure" provided "the only scientific basis of practical medicine," and assured students that they would be introduced to "microscopical anatomy and physiology" so they could trace the "deeper law of Homeopathy."[108] But clearly some teachers disagreed and taught their students differently. In 1865 one student wrote confidently in his thesis that the true homeopath does not diagnose the case and that "according to the teaching of Hahnemann, he has nothing to do with pathology."[109]

The 1867 split was also about money and public relations. The college faculty were dependent on the support of physicians outside the school. Until the 1940s no senior member of the faculty received a full-time salary from the college, and all college teachers therefore had private practices. Teaching and administration, however, took time and energy away from practice, and the faculty clearly cared about the income they did receive from the college.[110] Throughout this period, however, the college remained in debt, and the faculty underpaid, mostly because its board accepted partial payment of student fees, which were the financial fuel of the school. As a result the college was frighteningly responsive to social and economic upheavals: for example, it was, as we have seen, significantly disrupted by the Civil War, although, unlike a number of other private medical schools in Philadelphia, it was able to recover. In 1864 the faculty wrote a letter appealing to the alumni and the public for funds but then rewrote it as the first letter's tone was "too despondent."[111]

The ease with which Hering and his friends set up the new school suggests how uncomplicated it was to set up a medical school in the United States of the mid–nineteenth century. But it also became clear, as the new college's constitution recognized, that a medical school was more than a charter: a school had to establish a convincing identity and solidify relations with other homeopaths not only as colleagues but also as preceptors who would recommend the school to their students.[112]

The organization chosen by the founders of the new Hahnemann Medical College demonstrated that the Homeopathic Medical College had not had a good relationship with the wider medical community. Hering's new college publicly presented itself as more responsive to community concerns about standards of medical training than the old school and as more liberal in its interpretation of homeopathic theory. As well as a board of trustees and a core of faculty, which, interestingly were now tenured for life, the new college's constitution created a medical advisory board. Although these advisors could not vote in ordinary college affairs, they could be called on, when a graduating candidate "demanded the action," to take the place of the designated faculty in examining candidates in any subject. The members of the new board, the college argued, "have no interest in the institution, inconsistent with *the advancement of medical education, and the welfare of the medical profession*."[113] This new board, in other words, was a check on faculty power and perhaps a response to the legal and pamphlet fight some years earlier, when three students had claimed faculty prejudice in denying them the right to graduate. This accusation became more convincing when the students' families and communities realized that final examinations were private oral exams held in the home or office of the individual faculty member. The new board, boasted the first catalog (1867–1868) of the new college, was established "for the double purpose of assuring the public and the profession of the fitness of graduates to practice medicine."[114] The symbolic power of this new board was such that it was retained when the colleges merged and lasted until 1886.

Hering's college also tried to present good homeopathic teaching as liberal as well as homeopathically pure. Its 1867–1868 catalog attacked homeopathic eclecticism and, to demonstrate the proper homeopathic identity of its faculty, pointed out that every one of its faculty was a member in good standing of the Homeopathic Medical Society of the County of Philadelphia. The same catalog proudly announced the appointment of Francis E. Boericke, the well-known homeopathic pharmacist who in 1869 formed with Adolph Tafel what became the nation's best known homeopathic pharmacy and publishing house. But, typical of Hering's homeopathic philosophy, the new college allowed freedom on disputed homeopathic issues such as the question of the dose: "while strict adherence to pure Homeopathy is inculcated, and the principle of the *minimum* dose is both taught and practised in the clinic, the student must judge for himself what that dose should be in each individual case."[115] Thus, Hering assured both high- and low-dose physicians that they could confidently send their students to his school. The motto Hering chose for his school expressed this powerfully: In Things Certain Unity, In Things Uncertain Freedom, In All Things Charity.

Although the structure of the two colleges was almost identical, there were some minor changes. Hering's college listed a few new books, although it retained all the old ones. Students were now advised to read Cazeaux's *Midwifery* and Davis on parturition, Da Costa on diagnosis, Hughes on auscultation and percussion, and Simon's *General Pathology*. In Hering's college one chair was now physiology, general pathology, and microscopic anatomy (its equivalent at Lippe's school was physiology and general pathology). The critical chair that had initiated the split was retained as practice, special pathology, and diagnosis in Hering's college but renamed homeopathic institutes, pathology, and practice of medicine in Lippe's.

Hering's faculty took Lippe's attack on pathology seriously. The new college claimed to be distinctive (and better) because it offered students proper scientific training. Its first announcement proclaimed, "Homeopathy, however pure, if not based upon general medical science, must, in common with all other modes of practice, end only in quackery."[116] Hering's concept of a modern, scientific homeopathy included experimental laboratory physiology, using animal experiments. Richard Koch (183[8?]–18?) was appointed to teach physiology with "*vivisection* and other experimental illustrations." Koch, the 1868–1869 catalog boasted, had "given more numerous *vivi-sections* than have ever before been given in any medical institution in this city" and would teach "on the European plan," using "microscopes of high power."[117] The effort to cast the new college in the same mold as the best orthodox schools was one way to try to convince local physicians to send their students to the college for their entire education, rather than, as had been more common, to send them to good orthodox schools for lectures in medical science and surgery and then to a homeopathic school for training in homeopathy and a homeopathic degree. In orthodox schools such students, the new college's catalog warned, would be poorly taught, for they would have to face the ridicule of orthodox teachers who would sow "sources of doubt and error in the after-life of the physician."[118] But, in fact, the split openly politicized changes in medical teaching already in process in the college during the 1860s, for as early as 1861, physiology teachers used vivisections, which were described as "a *desideratum* in this important branch of medical science."[119]

The debate between the colleges allows us to explore some of the underground history of the school in that it shows conflicts that were not visible in college minutes or catalogs. During a pamphlet war Hering's college accused the old school of being "subject to the caballing of a ring" and of having sold diplomas, or at least of having graduated unsatisfactory candidates. The new school noted the number of applicants who "applied for the purchase of our diploma" and alluded to two cases in which their own candidates had attended only one course of lectures and "desired our diploma for the *money*." The old college refuted this accusation by arguing that Hering's college was based on a shaky charter bought from William Paine, an Eclectic physician and editor of the *Eclectic Medical Journal of Philadelphia,* and that the new school's teaching reflected this Eclectic origin. Hering's college responded that its graduation requirements were "very liberal [but] . . . fair and adhered to in every instance."[120]

Lippe's college similarly claimed to be liberal and modern but sought its authority not in membership in a local society or in teaching methods used in local orthodox schools but in the broader international scientific world.[121] In particular, and perhaps surprisingly, Lippe's school claimed to be aiming at educational standards equivalent to the best in Europe. One faculty member had visited Paris and London, and on returning, the college catalog boasted, he had proposed curriculum changes—especially the use of anatomic figures and mannequins he had ordered from the 1867 Paris Exposition, as well as microscopes and tissue preparations from "Messrs Vaisseau of Paris."[122]

Liberalism, which both colleges were defining as indicating philosophic flexibility and receptivity to modern medical science, was hardly new. Since 1850, the Homeopathic Medical College had proudly described itself as open and undogmatic. It claimed to offer students a better education than they could obtain by studying with a single homeopathic preceptor, for it "will give the student an opportunity to view the Homeopathic practice in a more diversified aspect. The peculiar and often diverging views of the individual Professor will be thus more brought to light, to the manifest advantage of the student."[123] Teachers at the college also recognized the concern among Philadelphia homeopaths that students would be taught only one way. In 1853 one student, in a thesis entitled "Medicine as a Science," argued that, while in some cases "a large size [dose] is required," all cases required that "reference be had to the reactive state of nature, and sensibility of the patient, and not to whether they will come under the head of Infinitesimals in In[su]bstantials."[124] Thus, the changes that Hering and Lippe proudly proclaimed were significant only in heralding the already transformed nature of Philadelphia's homeopathic training, in showing its clear responsiveness to changes in broader medical science and education.

Philadelphia Homeopaths in the City and the Nation

Even in these early evangelical years of the college's history, its founders and teachers largely defined themselves in the shadow of orthodox medicine. The models they adopted in organizing a school; local, state, and national professional societies; and later a hospital were based firmly on already established orthodox structures. Homeopathy, nonetheless, retained a distinctive appeal to the lay public and, especially after the Civil War, in its relations to the state.

The issue of distinctiveness remained crucial in the early years, when homeopathy was seen partly as an intellectual experiment that could be adopted by orthodox and other practitioners, when practice, in other words, did not indicate an immutable identity. Within the homeopathic world, Philadelphia homeopaths were under constant pressure from patients and local physicians to remain flexible. The college faculty feared that students who attended orthodox schools would view homeopathy this way rather than imbibe the true spirit. In 1857 one student commented on the problem of what he termed "so-called homeopaths" who consult "the preferences of the patient, in a choice, between the 'Homeopathic' treatment and the Allopathic," and he referred to "a well known homeopath in New York" who mixed drugs. A doctor, he concluded, has no right "to trifle with the sick" or to "deceive the public," and "if he adopts a certain name & subscribes to a certain law of cure he must do so in good faith, and adhere to it in practice."[125]

For the first generation of homeopaths, the college was a key part of defining the place of homeopathy in the city and defining homeopaths as gentlemen, as educators, and as private physicians. But the history of the Homeopathic Medical College suggests that by the 1860s, if not publicly then at least in private, American homeopaths were developing a new identity, distinct from that of the first generation of converts. In 1864 the college demonstrated its awareness of its distance from the "first generation" by inviting the "pioneers of Homeopathy" to attend the school's commencement: men who could be honored but not seen as part of the school.[126] The practitioners of the 1830s and 1840s were now considered too inflexible, too evangelistic, and perhaps too close to that early blurred distinction between lay and professional homeopaths. The new generation of the 1860s, of physicians formally trained at homeopathic schools, wanted to be considered reasoned gentlemen of science; they sought an identity that went beyond the searing power of the conversion experience but yet was more serious than seeing homeopathy as an intellectual puzzle.

Defining homeopathy in a new way was an inextricable part of a conversation between homeopathic practitioners and their patients and supporters. Sometimes, as we have seen, this conversation was made explicit in the school's published literature; more often, I think, the college faculty and students responded to the feelings and fears of lay networks that throughout the school's history both supported and criticized the institution. Indeed, without exploring these networks we have only a partial history of the school. The Alumni Association of the Hahnemann Medical College and Hospital of Philadelphia (established in 1884) was one public forum for this debate, but other organized supporters were critically important as well in shaping the school's social and cultural persona. Although women were not admitted as students until the 1940s, they nonetheless played a crucial although less visible role in supporting and criticizing the institution. Women homeopathic supporters, especially the families of faculty members, organized themselves into private fund-raising groups, and their work enabled the school to establish a hospital and a scholarship fund for poor students. By the 1870s, as we will see, some began to pressure the college to admit women for formal training. While the faculty were flexible in their homeopathic philosophies, their social and pedagogic ideals were more rigidly orthodox.

At heart, the college was and remained a white, middle-class, male-oriented institution. It drew its support from religious and religious-fraternal groups such as Quakers, Swedenborgians, German Lutherans, and Masons in the 1840s and 1850s and, later in the century, from Presbyterians and the Republican Party. The college survived at first with the support of lay and professional enthusiasts, but its survival created another crucial network: its own homeopathic graduates. They became leaders in national homeopathic education and were on the faculties of most other homeopathic schools in the country. Other graduates, the majority, became private practitioners in Pennsylvania or surrounding regions; they decided whether to send a student or son to the school, to buy the school's medical journal, or to attend its commencement and other ceremonies. They defended the image of homeopathy as presented by their former teachers, supported the school financially, consulted with its professors, and allowed their patients to appear at its clinics and later to enter its hospital. When the school began to change in the last decades of the nineteenth century, many of the alumni clung more closely to their memories and traditions and watched with some sadness and with some pride as the college embraced first the new scientific medicine and finally orthodoxy.

Chapter 2

Becoming a Homeopathic Leader, 1869–1898

Hahnemann Medical College and Hospital of Philadelphia

Wᴵᴛʜ ᴛʜᴇ ᴍᴇʀɢᴇʀ of the two colleges in 1869 and the decision to rename the school, Hahnemann Medical College had to confront the anger of the Homeopathic Medical College's alumni at losing a heritage and a name. Pemberton Dudley, an 1861 graduate, recalled the effort "to give the least possible cause of offense and dissatisfaction to alumni and other friends of the Colleges," especially the many who "could not help feeling grieved that the name of the pioneer College had been changed." To older alumni "it was almost as if their Alma Mater had ceased to exist." Dudley admitted, "I confess to having been myself among the number who, for a time, felt that the mother college was dead, and that her children were orphaned."[1] Similarly, in 1871, William Tod Helmuth, an 1853 graduate who had become professor of surgery at the New York homeopathic school, complained that he was now "a step-son of Hahnemann, and a son of the Homeopathic Medical College of Pennsylvania," for his alma mater for reasons that he "could never distinctly understand . . . saw fit *to change her name* (many young ladies, yea, and old ones too, appear to delight in similar transformations)."[2]

The school's alumni, as the trustees and faculty recognized, were concerned that a new name presaged a new identity. When the first catalog of the merged college appeared, it offered the history of the Philadelphia school from 1848 to the present, seeking to merge the two schools together in the past as well as present. The retelling of the school's history, the catalog promised, was done "in order that the profession may have a clear conception of the whole matter, and especially that the Alumni of the Homeopathic Medical College of Pa., may not think that we have injured them in the person of their Alma Mater."[3] But in the same catalog the college also took the opportunity to criticize the name the original founders had chosen. It was "scarcely a name at all" and only "partially true," the college argued, for the school was intended "to educate men for *physicians* and not merely as homeopathic doctors."[4]

The college's new name did portend a new kind of homeopathic education, one based on the model of leading orthodox schools. In 1869 the college introduced an optional three-year graded course, in addition to its standard two ungraded years, in an effort to break away from any association with other private medical schools, which frequently had low standards. With this gesture Hahnemann began to position itself among the leading late-nineteenth-century medical schools in the United States, rather than as a school comfortable to be alternative and less rigorous in its educational standards.

By the late 1860s orthodox reformers had begun to focus on the medical school as a way of raising the standards of the medical profession, recognizing that schools had begun to play a defining role in medical education. As early as 1867 the AMA had urged schools to introduce a compulsory three-year graded curriculum, but most schools had been too wary of the expected concomitant decline in student enrollment to attempt such a radical move. Finally, in 1871 Harvard University's president, Charles Eliot, forced his medical faculty to adopt a three-year, nine-month course, and other orthodox schools began to follow. The Woman's Medical College of the New York Infirmary, Elizabeth Blackwell's school, offered a three-year graded course in 1876, and in 1877 so did the homeopathic medical department of Boston University and the medical faculty of the University of Pennsylvania. The homeopathic New York Medical College and Hospital for Women followed in 1879.[5]

The college's responsiveness to these changes was the result of a growing awareness of its place in the American homeopathic profession. After the founding of the Homeopathic Medical College in 1848, five other homeopathic schools were established before the Civil War; eight more were established in the 1870s, and six more in the 1880s. Numerous Eclectic and hydropathic schools also appeared, and a common charge by regulars was that these unorthodox schools provided an "easy" diploma. Still, while the college began to adopt some of the changes befitting a modern medical school, it remained hesitant to make three years compulsory. Instead the college chose a middle road. Like a number of schools in the 1870s and 1880s, Hahnemann introduced an optional summer course, providing extra subjects to round out the education of two-year students. Not until 1890 did Hahnemann introduce a four-year option. Homeopathic Boston University had introduced this option in 1878 and made it compulsory in 1891, as did Harvard in 1892, Pennsylvania in 1893, and Hahnemann in 1896.

Introducing graded lectures signified a profound transformation in the role of the medical school in training physicians. No longer were medical schools simply providing classroom lectures to supplement the training of a student by a preceptor. In 1869, when the college began to defend its three-year graded course to the wider community, it assured the prospective student that he would "gain what would otherwise require years to attain . . . and admit of his beginning his professional life upon an elevated plane which would at once command the respect and confidence of the intelligent laity." This argument recognized that the American public was becoming more supportive of expert training for professionals. Such a course, the college continued, would even help men "not designed to follow the calling of medicine" because "the age demands scientific farmers, mechanics, merchants, teachers, lawyers and clergymen, and above all, scientific physicians."[6]

In 1886 the college used its move to a new building on Broad Street as the occasion to make its three-year course compulsory. By this time it was lagging behind its rivals in the city: Jefferson had made three years compulsory in 1884 and in 1885 had abolished its thesis requirement, as Hahnemann did the next year. Perhaps an indication of the wisdom of delay, Hahnemann did not lose a significant number of students. Indeed during the 1880s and 1890s enrollment increased, reaching a peak of 77 graduates in 1893 and 281 matriculants in 1894. As a result of the greater income, financial pressure eased, and the faculty began to increase the number of senior and junior teaching positions and expand the number of departments. The college began to modernize its teaching of pathology and physiology by introducing courses on practical microscopy and histology. In 1891 the specific course on microscopy was dropped for one in normal histology, which assumed a familiarity with the microscope: thus the students in the normal histology course would engage in laboratory work, rather than in drills on the use of the instrument and on the preparation and mounting of specimens as they had in the microscopy course. In the late 1890s the college also reorganized its internal space, transforming a second-floor room that had been used for the preservation of botanic and zoological specimens into a histological laboratory (the specimens were moved to the pamphlet room and to cases in corridors). The faculty also removed the janitor and his family from the second floor, where they had been living since 1886, and turned that space into histology, pathology, and bacteriology laboratories.[7] By the time of the school's Golden Jubilee celebrations in 1898, the college was one of the leading homeopathic schools in the nation. As an advertisement for the school boasted in the late 1890s, "our alumni are in every state and on the faculty of every Homeopathic Medical College in the country."[8]

During the 1870s and 1880s homeopathy became firmly established in the American medical landscape. Membership in the AIH rose from 575 in 1865 to 830 in 1880 to 2,100 in 1903. By the late 1890s there were nine national homeopathic societies, thirty-three state and eighty-five local societies, one hundred forty hospitals, fifty-seven dispensaries, twenty medical colleges, and thirty-one medical journals. In 1881, 17 percent of Philadelphia's 1,480 physicians were homeopaths; in 1900 observers estimated that around 8 percent of physicians in the United States were homeopaths.[9] New homeopathic leaders appeared, representing a generation of physicians who were trained at homeopathic schools, were members of homeopathic medical societies, and were consultants at homeopathic hospitals and dispensaries.

For the college this was an era of commemoration and memorialization, as the early founders of and teachers at the school died, including Constantine Hering, Jacob Jeanes, Walter Williamson, Robert McClatchey, Alvan Small, Henry Guernsey, Adolph Lippe, and Richard Gardiner. With the passing of these men, the mission of homeopathic education began to change, although its aims remained the same: producing private practitioners. There were new opportunities for homeopaths to express their civic duty, by serving on city and state boards of health and as visiting physicians to city hospitals and state asylums. In 1878 a homeopathic physician was chosen as a member of the national Yellow Fever Commission investigating the New Orleans epidemic of 1878, and a group of homeopaths, including Jabez Philander Dake (1827–1894), an 1851 graduate who taught materia medica at the college in late 1850s, set up their own separate commission as well.[10] In the mid-1880s the college introduced a new course on sanitary science, reflecting these new possibilities for civic service and the growing popular interest in public hygiene since the Civil War.

The 1869 Fair

With Philadelphia homeopaths joined in a newly merged college, supporters of the school began to seek ways to impress this sense of solidarity upon the public and to enlarge and modernize the institution. A major celebratory event in the merged college's early history was the hospital fair held in the Horticultural Hall for two weeks in November 1869. Efforts to raise money for a new hospital had been made in 1866 and 1868, but the college split made it impossible for homeopaths to gain united medical and public support.[11] The fair was organized by women associated with the college and was staged to raise money for a homeopathic hospital for the sick poor and for improving homeopathic medical education; one fund-raising letter urged potential donors, "in the name of humanity and science do what you can for this cause."[12]

Hahnemann's fair, modeled on a successful one held a few months earlier for Boston University's school, provided an opportunity for Philadelphia homeopathic supporters and physicians to come together, celebrate, and remind one another of the special system of medicine that distinguished them from the rest of the medical world. It was an event that did not raise divisive issues in medical theory or educational curriculum but, rather, pointed to aspects of a shared Philadelphia homeopathic identity.

First, it reinforced the idea that homeopathy was a family and community affair. The fair was organized by a group that called itself the Ladies Homeopathic Hospital Fair Association, which was made up of women from the families of college faculty, college trustees, and philanthropic leaders of the city. One organizer, Caira Skelton Starkey was the wife of George Rogers Starkey, an 1855 graduate and registrar of the college from 1860 to 1864.[13]

Second, the fair publicly displayed the crucial role local women played in supporting and shaping homeopathy, a role not evident from college catalogs and medical journals. These women, commentators later agreed, had "taken over" the fund-raising that had received only lukewarm support from most of the college faculty.[14] The way these women structured the event also gave it a distinctly middle-class feminine touch. Before the fair, for example, some money was raised by "Soirées Dramatiques" held at local halls, and the women also organized a strawberry festival. The fair itself was on two temporal levels. By day, twenty-two tables offering various goods for sale, many decorated in brilliant colors, attracted buyers, mainly women, decorated in equally colorful and impressive hats. By night, the fair continued by gaslight while Carl Sentz's orchestra played light opera tunes by Offenbach.

Third, the fair was a public relations success, demonstrating the widespread and deep support of homeopathy among the public, particularly among respectable members of Philadelphia society. Homeopaths had always prided themselves on their appeal to the American middle and upper classes, and during and after the fair commentators emphasized how many of the city's wealthy citizens appeared publicly to show their support. It was "the centre of attraction for the intelligence, wealth, and beauty of our city," wrote one observer; there were "immense throngs of our best citizens," agreed another.[15] The organization of the fair allowed participants to revel in the breadth of homeopathic support. Tables, for example, were sponsored by women's groups from communities including Pittsburgh, Harrisburg, Pottsville, Reading, Easton, Chester, Chestnut Hill, Germantown, Woodbury, Norristown, and Camden, and from Wilmington, Boston and Baltimore.[16] This sense of the college's place in the region and nation was reinforced even more strongly by the major role later played by faculty members in organizing and hosting the 1876 World's Homeopathic Convention, part of Philadelphia's celebrations of the American Centennial. During the Centennial, college faculty members were organizers, speakers, and historians, the latter a crucial professional role.

The 1869 fair was designed to link the college to homeopathy's past and future. On entering the hall, visitors were confronted with two large gilded columns joined by an arch on which "letters of fire" spelled the word "Hahnemann," a reference both to homeopathy's founder and to the college.[17] Homeopathic veterans—and long-time college supporters—such as Constantine Hering, Walter Williamson, and Henry Guernsey were invited, as was William Wesselhoeft, now of Boston, who came with a check from Boston supporters. There were also corporate sponsors such as the A. J. Tafel Homeopathic Pharmacy and the Atlantic Mutual Life Insurance Company, which offered special rates for homeopathic patients on the assumption that they would remain healthier and live longer than patients under orthodox care.

The fair raised over seventeen thousand dollars, enough to buy the college property on Filbert Street and an adjacent property at the rear on Cuthbert Street; to raze the two buildings that had been used as a hospital during the Civil War; and to construct a five-story brick building with thirty beds making up two large public wards and four private wards.[18] The new Homeopathic Hospital opened in January 1871. Circulars were sent to local industries, reminding employers that the institution had been designed "to devote especial attention to those suffering from accidents requiring surgical aid,"[19] and it remained the only homeopathic hospital in Philadelphia until the founding of the Children's Homeopathic Hospital of Philadelphia and the Pennsylvania Homeopathic Hospital for Children, both in 1877. The success of the fair could "serve as a wholesome lesson to those who are so foolish as to assert that 'homeopathy is going down,'" asserted one commentator.[20] As one sign of the fair's public relations success, the Pennsylvania legislature gave the hospital five thousand dollars shortly after it opened, beginning the continuing state support of homeopathic health care institutions.

The Woman Question

After the Civil War the college faculty came under significant pressure to explain why the school refused to admit women as students. In Philadelphia and in neighboring communities and states, as the 1869 hospital fair made clear, there were hundreds of homeopathic supporters. Increasing numbers of school catalogs and journals demonstrated that new homeopathic schools were claiming a place in the sun. One distinguishing characteristic of these schools was their organizers' acceptance of coeducation. During the 1870s women were admitted both to state-supported homeopathic schools like Boston University and the University of Michigan and to private colleges like the Detroit Homeopathic Medical College and the Hahnemann Medical College of Chicago. There were also women's homeopathic schools in Cleveland and New York. Indeed, by 1880, of eleven existing homeopathic schools, only Philadelphia's Hahnemann Medical College and the New York Homeopathic Medical College did not admit women. The latter argued that local female students could attend Clemence

Lozier's homeopathic New York Medical College and Hospital for Women.[21] In Philadelphia women medical students could attend the Woman's Medical College, but it did not teach homeopathy.

During the 1850s and 1860s Hahnemann Medical College made a few exceptions to its men-only policy. In 1859 at the old college, Sarah Brooks Pettingill (1810–1877) was permitted to attend lectures as long as she sat behind a partition shielding her from the view of the male students. Pettingill was not allowed to apply for a diploma, however, and in 1860 she graduated from the Penn Medical University, a private medical school in the city that taught a mix of eclectic, orthodox, and homeopathic medicine. In 1871 she became one of the first women to be admitted as a member of the AIH.[22]

The pressure to admit women to the college increased in the 1870s as women were admitted as full members to first the Philadelphia homeopathic society in 1870 and a year later to the state society and the AIH. Mercy B. Jackson (1802–1877), a Pittsburgh homeopath, published "A Plea: For the Admission of Women to the Medical College and Institute of America" in the *Hahnemannian Monthly*, in which she pointed out that Samuel Hahnemann had encouraged his wife to practice with him.[23] Unbeknownst to Jackson, Samuel Hahnemann had requested a diploma for his wife, Melanie, from the Allentown Academy in 1841, telling one Allentown teacher "she is better acquainted with Homeopathy, theoretically and practically, than any of my followers." In 1848, at her trial for practicing medicine and pharmacy without proper qualifications, Melanie Hahnemann had pointed to the Allentown medical degree as part of her defense. She lost the case and was fined 100 francs but continued to practice.[24]

In 1871 a group of women, recognizing some support among the trustees and the faculty, decided it was time for the college to follow the lead of the homeopathic societies. After all, a number of the faculty had taught women before coming to the college: Dean Amos Thomas had lectured on artistic anatomy at the Philadelphia School of Design for Women and had taught anatomy at the coeducational Penn Medical University from 1854 to 1862. Hahnemann botany professor Samuel Freedley (1799–1885) and Thomas's anatomical demonstrator, Rufus Weaver, had also taught there. The college faculty discussed the issue of admitting women as students at a July 1871 faculty meeting and decided against admission, but at a later meeting the faculty did propose a summer course exclusively for women, a course that never took place. In 1870, according to Thomas Lindsley Bradford, the dean received a request from a woman physician from Ohio who had been in practice for some years, and the faculty refused to admit her.[25] Later a positive editorial in the college's journal, the *American Journal of Homeopathic Materia Medica*, entitled "The Medical Education of Women," referred to the "numerous applications by women" the college regularly received, and the article proposed a full course for women, to be offered in the spring and summer for the "milder weather." This course never took place either.[26] A new charter in 1885 made women doctors eligible as residents or visiting physicians or surgeons to the college hospital, but no woman was appointed until the 1940s.

In 1886 the homeopathic Women's Medical Club of Philadelphia wrote to the college formally asking that the school admit women.[27] The letter's first signature was that of one of the club's founders, Harriet Judd Sartain, a local homeopathic physician. Sartain (1830–1923) was the daughter-in-law of John Sartain, the engraver and inventor of mezzotint and one of the college's original trustees. Harriet Judd had spent 1851 at Mary Grove Nichols' American Hydropathic Institute in New York and in 1854 had graduated from the Eclectic Medical Institute in Cincinnati. After her marriage to Samuel Sartain, she moved to Philadelphia, where she raised children and practiced as a physician. She had been the first woman elected to membership in Philadelphia's homeopathic medical society in 1870 and in 1871 was the first woman admitted to the state society and the AIH.[28] The organization of the Women's Medical Club in 1883, probably in response to the founding of the all-male Hahnemann Club, was a public sign of the growing number of women homeopaths practicing in Philadelphia. The members included Mary Branson and Amelia Landis Hess, both graduates of Philadelphia's orthodox Woman's Medical College; Mary Ann Cooke, an 1888 graduate of the University of Michigan's homeopathic medical department; Mary Brewer, an 1894 graduate of the homeopathic New York Medical College and Hospital for Women; and Elizabeth Baer, an 1898 graduate of the Hahnemann Medical College of Chicago.

Dean Thomas responded to the 1886 request of the Women's Medical Club in a long letter that was sympathetic but firm. He acknowledged that "the question of co-education has received much attention from the Faculty during the past decade" and assured the club that the college was "not opposed to the admission of women," pointing as proof to "the architecture of our new building [that] has provided for them" (small stairs were built leading from the main floor to the third story, so that women, if admitted, would be able to attend the lectures in the amphitheater without entering in front of the class). However, Thomas explained, while "the trend of public sentiment" favored coeducation (and, he added, "especially is this manifested by those who do not intend to become students of medicine"), nonetheless there was still "old time conservatism." He explained that the faculty had asked its medical advisory board for advice on admitting women, and the board had not deemed it "advisable" for two reasons. First, faculty members had pledged one thousand dollars a year toward supporting a hospital "for the use of the college." "It therefore behooves us to avoid any experiment that may jeopardize our ability to accomplish this." Second, the faculty had agreed to support a compulsory three-year graded course "in compliance with the demand for a higher education and our mature convictions of the requirements of our profession," and they were concerned that the change might initially decrease the number of students. Thomas wrote, "we do not feel prepared to hazard the changes you ask us to make until we see what will result from the adoption of the lengthened course and enlarged curriculum." He concluded by saying, "we wish you to believe what seems to us, after mature deliberation, to be for the best interests of the Institution we serve and the Hospital the profession is trying to establish" and by signing the letter "fraternally yours."[29] Clearly, women were considered too disruptive to be admitted at a time when the college was in transition and seeking public support. And yet, just five years earlier, without any public discussion or debate, the college had begun admitting African-American students for the first time, and continued to have at least one black student admitted every eight or nine years until the last graduated in 1912. Women would have to wait until 1941.

The New Faculty

The period from the 1869 merger to the college's Golden Jubilee celebration in 1898 saw the establishment and institutionalization of school traditions, epitomized by the founding of the Alumni Association in 1884. A new stability of leadership was achieved in 1874, when, with the death of Dean Henry Guernsey, Amos Russell Thomas, who had been teaching anatomy at the college since 1867, was chosen as dean, a position he would hold until his death in 1895. The length of his tenure also established another school tradition: an ensconced dean who, despite the school's bylaws, was not subject to annual election.

During the 1880s and 1890s, students developed their own distinctive culture, and so, in a different way, did the college faculty. A new group of faculty became united in opposition to what they considered old-fashioned notions of medical education, notions held especially by their own trustees. They also were forced to conduct their campaign to restructure the college curriculum within the limitations and expectations of the city's homeopathic supporters and opponents, and by the 1890s they had found an uneasy peace with the wider community. The faculty distanced itself from American homeopathy's past, especially its association with the populist, anti-orthodox values of the early nineteenth century. The Philadelphia faculty embraced a modern conception of homeopathy, an odd and sometimes uneasy combination of redefined tradition from homeopathy's heritage and the new conceptions of medical education and professionalism developed by leading orthodox medical schools. Indeed this period saw the high point in American homeopathy in adopting both the trappings and the heart of a new kind of medical professionalism. These changes stemmed from external influences such as the AIH and the AMA, other medical schools both orthodox and homeopathic, as well as from local and internal pressure on the college to distinguish itself in the Philadelphia medical world and in the homeopathic community.

Moving from Filbert Street to Broad Street was a major step. In 1884 the ground for a new building was broken, and, as the founders of the Allentown Academy had done, the Hahnemann faculty collected symbolic materials to make up a cornerstone, including copies of the *Hahnemannian Monthly*, the transactions of the 1876 World's Homeopathic Convention, and the 1881 fifth edition of Samuel Hahnemann's *Organon*. The cornerstone ceremony was conducted with Masonic rites, befitting the growing number of graduates who were Masons (the affiliation between Hahnemann and the Masons continued into the 1920s and 1930s).

The college faculty expanded significantly during this period, from seven professors and a demonstrator of anatomy in the 1850s to sixteen professors, fourteen lecturers, and ten demonstrators by 1898. While they were not listed as formal faculty, there were additional college teaching staff: quiz-masters were hired by the college in 1873 to replace the private system of quiz-masters (senior students and recent graduates) that students had established as part of their efforts to cram for exams. These junior positions were part of the college's faculty "track," and indeed some of the major figures of the college faculty in the 1880s and 1890s were graduates who had first been brought to prominence by being chosen as quiz-masters: Benjamin Franklin Betts (1845–1909), an 1868 graduate who was quiz-master in practical and clinical medicine in 1872 and became professor of physiology and microscopic anatomy in 1873; William Howard Bigler (1840–1904), an 1871 graduate, who was quiz-master in physiology, general pathology, and microscopic anatomy in 1872 and in 1891 became professor of physiology and pediatrics. Dean Amos Thomas's son Charles Monroe Thomas (1849–1916), an 1877 graduate, was a quiz-master in 1876 and a demonstrator and lecturer in surgery, and in 1878 he became professor in operative surgery and ophthalmology, a position that enabled him to push for clinical specialty teaching at the college. In the 1870s this group of younger men founded a homeopathic specialty society, the Philadelphia Clinical Society, which in turn founded the Pennsylvania Homeopathic Hospital for Children in West Philadelphia that merged with the college's Hahnemann Hospital in 1886.

The faculty in this period also achieved a stable core, a welcome change from the upheaval of the 1860s. By the mid-1890s Betts, Charles Thomas, and six other professors had been teaching at the college for over twenty years: Amos Russell Thomas (1826–1895), dean and chair of anatomy; John Edwin James (1844–1910), surgery and then gynecology; Charles Mohr (1844–1907), clinical medicine; William Colby Goodno (1850–1932), histology and pathology;

Erving Melville Howard (1840–1904), pharmacy and materia medica; and John Nicholas Mitchell (1847–1923), obstetrics. Another important presence at the college since 1870 was anatomy demonstrator and museum curator Rufus B. Weaver (1841–1936), who became a professor of applied anatomy in 1897 and retired in 1925. In 1888 Weaver completed a dissection of the cerebro-spinal nervous system, and in 1893 he presented the dissection at the Columbian Exposition, where it received an exhibition medal and ribbon. The dissection, named Harriet after its subject, became one of the college's prized research pieces.[30]

Almost all of these men, who helped to define the school's character up to the turn of the century, were Hahnemann alumni, most having graduated in the late 1860s and early 1870s. The faculty members were also linked by family connections. William Bigler married the daughter of Augustus Koch, the first physician member of Hahnemann's trustees and a prominent homeopath. Charles Thomas was the son of Amos Russell Thomas. And John Mitchell, a former student of the older Thomas, married his mentor's only daughter, Florence, in 1877. While this shared background contributed to an impressive academic esprit de corps, it also created a sense of parochialism that lingered through the school for many years. Of this group only Amos Thomas (an 1854 graduate of Syracuse Medical College), John James (an 1866 medical graduate of the University of Pennsylvania), and Rufus Weaver (an 1865 graduate of Pennsylvania Medical College) had not attended Hahnemann.

Defining Experiences: Paris, the Civil War, and Germany

Another distinctive element drawing together this generation of Philadelphia homeopaths was a commitment to a new kind of medical education, a commitment inspired by their experiences studying medicine in Paris, by their experiences as soldiers and surgeons in the Civil War, and, during the 1870s and beyond, by medical study in Germany. These experiences encouraged many of them to place a high value on clinical instruction and laboratory work and led some to construct a new conception of modern scientific homeopathy that by the 1890s would become a crucial part of the college's identity.

Before the Civil War most medical schools had simply provided lectures and some dissecting opportunities to accompany the bedside training a student gained from his or her preceptor. For ambitious physicians seeking greater clinical experience, the state-controlled hospitals of Paris offered extensive access to living and dead bodies. In the United States, few hospitals allowed medical students to walk their wards, apart from large public hospitals like New York's Bellevue, New Orleans's Charity, and Philadelphia's Blockley. After the Civil War medical school educators, especially those at state-supported schools, gradually began

Figure 7. In 1888, despite warnings from his colleagues that he would exhaust himself, Hahnemann anatomist Rufus Benjamin Weaver (1841–1936) worked for five months to prepare a dissection of a complete human nervous system, known as "Harriet," after its subject. In 1893 the dissection won an exhibition medal and ribbon at the Chicago World's Fair Exposition, and it became a centerpiece in Hahnemann's museum. Photograph dated 1898, reprinted in "Scrapbook of the Class of '99."

to build their own hospitals so that they could control access to patients for their students' clinical instruction.[31] It was even more difficult for homeopathic educators to make up for the lack of clinical facilities for their students because homeopaths initially controlled so few hospital beds.

The effort to rethink the role of the medical school, and especially to make clinical instruction more central, was shaped initially by physicians' experiences with Parisian medicine. As historian John Harley Warner has shown, even those who did not journey to Paris themselves were caught up in its new expression of medical science: a faith in experience gained in the clinic and dissection room, a belief in the importance of correlating bedside observations with lesions found at autopsy, a distrust of theorizing and heroic therapies given without strict clinical assessment, and a belief in the numerical method.[32] Homeopaths embraced only some of these ideas. Although they based their system on a theory, they denied that they were therefore "sectarians," a hated term that suggested an unthinking believer in a dogmatic faith. Instead they claimed that they were continually testing and retesting Samuel Hahnemann's laws in practice and by conducting drug provings. Homeopathic teaching also emphasized therapeutic theory and clinical skills over pathological analysis. Homeopaths did embrace the Parisian critique of heroic therapy but denied the orthodox claim that homeopathy succeeded only because many diseases were "self-limited" and would often improve with no drugs at all. Homeopaths did not accept the assertion by regular physicians that their diluted medicines were ineffective, but they did agree that their treatments aided nature's healing processes.[33]

Influences that were even more important in shaping homeopathic medical education before the Civil War were a feeling of difference, a sense of martyrdom, and a reaction to orthodox professional and theoretical challenges. Compared to the faculty at other leading medical schools in the antebellum period, relatively few physicians from the college, not surprisingly, went to Paris or made a visit a central part of their professional identity. On occasion, however, a physician associated with the college did go, and at times the college tried to tap into the prestige that Parisian travel could bring. In 1868 Lippe's college, for example, boasted that at least one faculty member (probably Henry Guernsey) had traveled to Paris and returned with pathological and other specimens that would bring obstetrical teaching "up to the standing of the same Chair in Paris."[34]

Medical historians have long pointed to the impact of the Civil War on American orthodox medicine: after the war, orthodox physicians paid greater attention to preventive medicine and sanitation, to surgery, to hospitals, and to an appreciation of the value of professional nursing. The war had similar effects on homeopathic practice and education. During the war faculty members and many students gained practical experience on the battlefields. Amos Thomas was a surgeon at the Battle of Bull Run. William Gardiner resigned his college chair in 1863 and became a surgeon to the Eighty-first Pennsylvania Reserves, and he was later made a brigadier surgeon. William Ashton Reed (an 1852 graduate and a teacher from 1852 to 1860) and Bushrod Washington James (an 1857 graduate and member of the college's medical advisory board) visited the battlefields as members of the Christian Commission. James (1838–1903) was a surgical assistant for the commission at the Antietam and Gettysburg battlefields and later wrote about his experiences in a collection of poetry and prose entitled *Echoes of Battle* (1895). For him, as for physicians of all schools, it was a shattering experience. He recalled that at Gettysburg,

> the hospital tents were run in rows along avenues on the level area to the north. Every surgeon in the hospital was kept busy nearly a week amputating limbs, probing for and removing bullets, or sewing, bandaging and dressing the wounds of those who were too badly mangled and shattered to be aided in any more hopeful manner. . . . The compulsory use of the knife was sadly trying, but, oh, it was far worse to see the wounded who were awaiting their turn, burning with fever or wasting with gangrene, which came quickly in the hot, sultry days of that weary season. . . . Even now, how vividly that row upon row of tents full of suffering humanity comes before my mind, and how powerless I felt to do even a modicum of good among so many![35]

A month later, James recalled, "I became so completely overtaxed that I was compelled to return home to recuperate."[36]

Although the war disrupted the medical education of many students, it also provided them with an extraordinary breadth of clinical experience. Robert Wilkie Martin, for example, attended lectures at the college from 1857 to 1859, joined the army, and then returned to attend the 1864–1865 session and graduate, basing his thesis on his Civil War experiences. Harry Eldridge Williams (1840–1917) practiced in the 1850s as a dentist in Philadelphia and attended medical lectures at the Penn Medical University. During the war, he was a hospital steward, a druggist in Philadelphia, and an assistant surgeon in the army, and after the war he graduated with a homeopathic degree from the college in 1866. Oliver Parker Barden (1839–1892) spent from 1861 to 1864 in the Pennsylvania Cavalry and graduated from the college in 1868.

Military experience may have brought a sharper sense of separate identity for many homeopaths, for the United States Army refused to recognize or commission homeopaths, and some homeopaths had to hide their affiliation.[37] A number of college men nonetheless managed to serve as surgeons. Rufus Sargent (1824–1886), an 1852 graduate, worked as an army surgeon from 1862 to 1865. Lewis Henry Willard (1838–1906), who attended college lectures from 1861 to

1862 and then became a hospital cadet, served at Satterlee Hospital in West Philadelphia, Georgetown Hospital in Washington, and as an assistant surgeon of the United States Navy. After the war Willard returned to the college as a student, and while there he also lectured on surgery from 1865 to 1866, graduating at the end of the term. He later became a member of the State Board of Medical Examiners. Benjamin Barr (1829–1913), an 1855 graduate, was the surgeon-in-chief of an army corps at Lee's surrender.

The war also inspired some young men to turn to homeopathy. Henry Noah Martin (1829–1889), a journalist who before the war had briefly studied law and medicine, served as a lieutenant and then judge advocate. He was healed by homeopathic medicines after the war, and he studied as an apprentice in Buffalo with Rollin Robinson Gregg (1826–1886), an 1853 college graduate. Gregg sent Martin to Philadelphia, where he graduated from the college in 1865 and then briefly taught obstetrics and clinical medicine there.

The war disrupted medical travel to Europe, and when peace came ambitious American physicians increasingly tended to head not to France but to German-speaking centers, a part of Europe that had always had special meaning for homeopaths. The state-run general hospitals at Vienna and Berlin provided impressive opportunities for medical study, especially for clinical specialties. In fact by the 1860s and 1870s a trip to Europe had become a commonplace way to finish medical training, and the college, like many other schools, began to choose faculty who had demonstrated their ambition and commitment in this way.

Even those with war experience felt the need to continue their medical study in Europe.[38] Charles Herman Haeseler (1830–1903), for example, the son of a German homeopath, had graduated from New York's orthodox College of Physicians and Surgeons in 1853 and worked as a surgeon during the Civil War, later establishing a successful homeopathic practice in Pottsville, Pennsylvania. In 1867 Haeseler went to Europe and then published a study of his European trip (*Across the Atlantic*), something many medical travelers did. In the early 1870s he briefly held the chair of practice, special pathology, and diagnostics at the college, after which he returned to private practice.

In his book Haeseler recounted a trip typical for an American medical student: he visited physicians and hospitals in London, Paris, and Vienna, and he rarely mentioned homeopathy or homeopaths. But he did comment on his time in Leipzig, where he visited the monument to Samuel Hahnemann, which, he remarked, "is truly a noble piece of art, and exhibits the learned Doctor in a sitting posture, an open book in his left hand, a pen in the right, and on his naturally fine and open countenance is depicted a well-drawn expression of thoughtful meditation." While in Paris, Haeseler became ill and stayed at a maison de santé, a kind of hotel-hospital. He complained that the "food doses" were "exceedingly Homeopathic," and he was especially unhappy when the "medical allopath" offered him first salts, castor oil, ipecac, and then quinine. Haeseler refused this standard orthodox therapy, telling the physician, as he later recalled: "Oblige me by keeping it in your bottle; it will look so much nicer than in my stomach. . . . Let us trust to the 'Vis Medicatrix naturae,' and you will see how well-founded will be our faith."[39]

The desire for foreign clinical experience abated a little as homeopathic hospitals and asylums were established during the 1870s and 1880s, and college students could become hospital interns and residents. The college began to expand its dispensary, and it became one avenue for postgraduate clinical training. Herbert Eugene Aldrich (1856–1917), for example, who had been a school teacher, graduated from the college in 1883 and for the next four years worked at the college dispensary before establishing a successful private practice. But for most ambitious homeopaths, German-speaking centers beckoned with their promise of opportunities for gaining experience in a particular specialty that would have professional currency back at home.

Homeopaths who decided to study in Germany in the 1870s and 1880s could have sought out well-known European homeopaths. Most, however, chose the less "homeopathic" route and instead sought specialist clinical training alongside orthodox physicians. In keeping with their effort to make the college modern and scientific, Hahnemann faculty members had not hesitated to adopt the latest improvements in clinical technology and were aware of orthodox European examples. As early as 1868, for example, one of the rooms of the college dispensary was fitted for the use of the ophthalmoscope and laryngoscope. In 1876, the college offered its first course in practical obstetrics based, it was claimed, on the Vienna model, and during the 1870s and 1880s, before incorporating them into the main curriculum, the college offered courses in specialist topics in its regular summer course.[40] Clinical specialty training was considered a continuation of the homeopathic emphasis on detailed attention to symptoms and was also a way to attract ambitious physicians seeking a distinguishing clinical skill. Homeopaths' interest in clinical specialties was also reflected in the growth of specialties sections in the AIH and of homeopathic journals such as, in the 1880s, the *Journal of Obstetrics and Diseases of Women* and the *Journal of Ophthalmology, Otology, and Laryngology*. By the early twentieth century all of the college clinical teachers called themselves specialists and advertised their particular skill on the back pages of the student yearbooks.

The success of some of the faculty who did travel to Germany was impressive. William Bird Van Lennep (1853–1919), a missionary's son who became one of the college's most famous surgeons, had an 1876 college degree from Princeton, and he graduated from the college in 1880 with its highest gold medal. He spent six months as resident physician at the homeopathic Ward's Island Hospital in New York and then took over the private practices of vacationing

Spring Course.	HAHNEMANN MEDICAL COLLEGE,				April 7 to May 31, 1890.	
HOURS	MONDAY	TUESDAY	WEDNESDAY	THURSDAY	FRIDAY	SATURDAY
10 A.M.	Dermatology. Dr. Gramm.	Diseases of the Lungs. Dr. Snader.	Hospital.	Minor Surgery. Dr. Giles.	Obstetrics for the beginner. Dr. Mercer.	Hospital.
11 A.M.	Refraction. Dr. Messerve.	Diseases of the Heart. Dr. Van Baun.	Hospital.	Electro-Thera- peutics. Dr. Bartlett.	Urinary Analysis. Dr. Oatley.	Hospital.
12 M.	Bacteriology. Dr. Vischer.	Chemistry of Foods. Dr. Hamer.	12.30 P.M. General Medical Clinic.	Materia Medica Characteristics. Dr. Knerr.	Nose, Throat and Ear. Dr. Ivins.	12.30 P.M. General Surgical Clinic.
1 P.M.	Sub-Clinics.	Sub-Clinics.	Dr. Haines.	Sub-Clinics.	Sub-Clinics.	Dr. Van Lennep.

Medical Sub-Clinics by Dr. O. S. Haines.   Gynæcological Sub-Clinics by Dr. I. G. Smedley.
Surgical   "   "   " Dr. W. B. Van Lennep.   Ophthalmological Sub-Clinics by Dr. H. I. Jessup.

Figure 8. Schedule for Hahnemann Medical College's 1890 spring course. Hahnemann, like many other schools, offered an optional spring course with "extras" including instruction in clinical specialties and on subjects considered less crucial to the main course, like bacteriology, dermatology, and electrotherapeutics.

friends in Philadelphia. He then spent two years studying surgery and pathology in the hospitals of London, Paris, and Vienna. Van Lennep was put in charge of the surgical department of the college dispensary in 1886, lectured on general pathology and morbid anatomy from 1886 to 1890 and later on surgery, and gained the chair of surgery in 1895. He also became consulting surgeon at the Children's Homeopathic Hospital in Philadelphia and at homeopathic hospitals in Camden, Trenton, and Wilmington.

For other graduates it took some time for their college position to match their German specialty training. William Bigler spent two years in the clinics of Berlin and Erlangen and returned to work in the college dispensary and as a lecturer on ophthalmology. In 1879 he headed the ophthalmology and otology section of the dispensary and in the early 1880s taught courses on the ear and eye for the college optional spring course. In 1890 he became associate professor of physiology and in 1891, as we have seen, professor of physiology and pediatrics. In private practice, however, he remained an eye and ear specialist. Edward W. Mercer (1859–1941), an 1884 college graduate, worked first as resident in the college hospital and then spent 1886 in the hospitals of Vienna. He returned to specialize in obstetrics and gynecology, teaching first as a demonstrator of obstetrics and finally in 1897 gaining the chair of obstetrics. Charles Thomas, an 1871 graduate and the dean's son, spent 1872–1874 in Vienna, Heidelberg, and Edinburgh and returned interested in specializing in surgery and diseases of the ear and the eye. Initially the college employed him only as a quiz-master, museum curator, and librarian. But he later became a demonstrator and then lecturer of surgery, and in 1878 he gained the chair of operative surgery and ophthalmology. In 1879 he and Bigler offered a course on diseases on the eye and ear for the college's summer course, and from 1881 to 1884 Thomas was the appointed ear and eye specialist for the college hospital. In 1892 Thomas transformed his position into a new chair of ophthalmology and otology, and from 1903 to 1906 he was dean of the college. William Weed Van Baun (1858–1930) took the college's optional three-year course and graduated in 1880, whereupon he became a resident at the college hospital. He later spent 1888 and 1891 in Vienna. In 1899 he was appointed an instructor in pediatrics, and he became professor in 1905, in private practice specializing in the heart, throat, and lungs. Benjamin Franklin Betts spent 1868–1870 in Berlin, Vienna, Paris, and London and returned to work first as a quiz-master and later as professor of physiology and microscopical anatomy (a position a number of recent European travelers were given); he finally gained the chair in his chosen specialty of gynecology in 1876. His appointment as lecturer in physiology and microscopical anatomy in 1873 and his return from Vienna were mentioned in that year's college catalog.[41]

Aspiring homeopathic specialists were frustrated, however, by the refusal of orthodox professionals to allow them practical access to this new knowledge and way of thinking in their own country. During the 1880s and early 1890s homeopaths in Philadelphia, Cleveland, and Chicago founded specialty clinics for postgraduate training.[42] Hahnemann graduates were rejected by the Philadelphia Polyclinic and College for Graduates in Medicine, which had been established in 1883 and merged with the University of Pennsylvania in 1918. The Philadelphia Post-Graduate School for Homeopathics was founded in 1891 and lasted for seven years, directed in part by James Tyler Kent (1849–1916), whose writings on homeopathic philosophy and materia medica later won him significant renown. Unlike the college, it accepted women students as well as men.

Before 1900 very few college faculty members went to German laboratories to study bacteriology, as was true of most orthodox graduates. Despite the defeat of Lippe's argument in the 1860s that pathology was not "true homeopathy," the notion remained that homeopathy trained a young man for general practice and clinical work. The study of drugs and symptoms was clearly part of the homeopathic lineage; but the study of germs was not so clear. Of the generation that taught students into the early twentieth century, only Philip Sharples Hall (1866–1919) went to Heidelberg from 1894 to 1895 to study the techniques of the new science of bacteriology. Hall, the son of a prosperous coal dealer, graduated from the college in 1891, spent 1891 as a resident at Hahnemann Hospital and a demonstrator in histology, and in 1892 married Gertrude Ervin, daughter of a city banker. Together they spent 1894–1895 in Europe, and Hall returned to Philadelphia to practice as a private pathologist and bacteriologist. On his return he lectured on pathology and bacteriology and became the college hospital's pathologist. In 1897, at the age of thirty-one, he was appointed professor of pathology and director of the college's histology laboratories. Clearly, Hall's choice of German specialty had helped his career, in part because in the Philadelphia homeopathic community there was so little competition in that field. However, at the hospital he faced constant shortages of space and nursing support, and he complained of medical staffs who did not properly prepare specimens, signs that hospital administrators recognized the importance of a pathologist but did not necessarily know how to reorganize the institution to take advantage of his skills.[43]

Whose Hospital?

These experiences on the battlefields of the Civil War and in the medical clinics of Europe urged the Hahnemann Medical College faculty to rethink the mission of their school, particularly the place of clinical instruction. During the school term, students' access to patients had come mainly, as we have seen, from the college dispensary, which also played a role in attracting patients and linking the college to the local community. But the college faculty members were not satisfied with the dispensary as the major facility for student instruction; they wanted a hospital that could be a central part of teaching. And in their campaign to get one they began to criticize passive, didactic methods of instruction. The school catalog of 1885–1886, for example, argued that "the methods of imparting instruction have undergone a complete revolution, and instead of a dependence on the old routine of didactic lectures only, the use of recitations, illustrations, laboratory work and manipulative drills . . . can more thoroughly equip the young physician for the practice of his Art."[44]

For many reasons the major tensions in the 1870s and 1880s centered around the college hospital. The Homeopathic Hospital, which had opened in 1871, was located on college grounds, but it was an independent body; and its lay trustees were fiercely protective of its patients and unwilling to allow faculty to bring students into the wards. Although proud of the hospital, the school's catalogs had to admit that students could obtain clinical instruction only by attending Blockley (Philadelphia's general hospital), Pennsylvania Hospital, or Wills Eye Hospital. The wards of the Homeopathic Hospital were closed to the college faculty and students, except for occasional surgical procedures, for which patients were sent from the hospital to the college amphitheater.

Hospitals had become increasingly important in forming medical careers. A hospital, controlled by faculty, could be both instructive and philanthropic and could provide carefully monitored opportunities for improving relations with

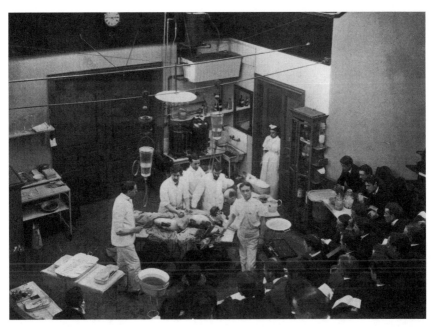

Figure 9. Most of the photographs of lectures and surgical operations published in Hahnemann's catalogs and yearbooks were staged, but the messy realism of this one from the 1899 yearbook, showing college surgeon Herbert L. Northrop at work, suggests otherwise. "Scrapbook of the Class of '99."

local physicians as well. As historian Charles Rosenberg has shown, ambitious young researchers, fresh from experience in Europe, demanded from hospital trustees regular opportunities to teach their students through clinical instruction. When their pleas fell on deaf ears, medical educators began to build their own hospitals.[45] Hahnemann Medical College became aware of the achievements of leading orthodox schools in the city: the University of Pennsylvania had opened its own hospital in 1874 and Jefferson had in 1877; in 1881 the Medico-Chirurgical College of Philadelphia, a new medical school, opened with its own hospital and dispensary and remained an important medical force in the city until it merged with the University of Pennsylvania in 1916. There were also some new homeopathic hospitals in the city: two children's hospitals opened in 1877, and the Hospital and Dispensary of the Women's Homeopathic Association of Pennsylvania opened in 1884. But, while providing some opportunities for graduates as residents, even these homeopathic hospitals were not available for college teaching.

The 1869 hospital fair had created an uneasy relationship between the college faculty and the hospital trustees. The new college and hospital properties had been bought with the fair money, and the trustees allowed the faculty to

rent the college at sixteen hundred dollars a year: six hundred dollars for payment on the mortgage, and one thousand as a contribution to the hospital fund.[46]
The faculty resented their subordination to the trustees and were unhappy with
the hospital that had been built with the fair's proceeds. Even its name, the Homeopathic Hospital rather than Hahnemann Hospital, suggested a stronger link
to the community than to the college. Yet, outside the college, the hospital was
seen as a college building, inaccessible to other homeopathic physicians.

Legally the hospital was incorporated under the college's charter, which suggested that it was bound by college rules. But the trustees made it increasingly
clear that they were in control. Within a month of its opening, they kicked out
the college janitor, who had taken up rooms in the new hospital, as he had done
in the old hospital. He had been paying the faculty three hundred dollars a year
in rent, which they now lost, but the trustees refused to alter the yearly faculty
rent payment.

As early as 1872 the trustees had proposed getting a separate charter for
the hospital so that it would be fully independent of the college and able to
hold title to real estate. Both supporters and opponents of the separation began
to acknowledge that the reason that the hospital had never been able to receive
much support either from the lay public or the wider homeopathic community
was that, whatever the reality, the hospital was seen as too closely connected
with the college. A later dean called it "a small ill-contrived Hospital" and noted
that "a sentiment was created which for some years rendered it exceedingly
difficult to raise further sums for hospital purposes." The college faculty were
accused of improperly taking the money raised by the 1869 fair and using it for
college purposes; but more insidious, I believe, were the implications that college faculty had too much control in running the hospital and that patients were
threatened with public examinations by students and, even worse, faculty experimentation. These threats were implied in a series of articles in a local city
paper that attacked the hospital and charged the faculty with incompetence. In
1873 Dean Henry Guernsey admitted that the hospital had never received "that
general support from the profession and community at large which it would otherwise receive." Guernsey said that when applying for financial assistance from
the public, he and his colleagues had to constantly explain that "the Hospital
was a separate institution" from the college.

Relations between the faculty and trustees worsened when in October 1873
the two groups could not agree on how to appoint a single committee to approach the legislature for state funds. As the trustees began to apply for a new
charter, John Morgan, a member of the faculty and of the hospital's board of
managers, filed a suit in court to stop the new charter, claiming that it had been
composed behind the faculty's back. Perhaps the real issue, however, was the
one raised by faculty member Lemuel Stephens at a stormy meeting of faculty

and trustees in September 1873: why had the proposed new charter left out the promise to allow the college "the advantages of hospital practice"?

The college journal, the *Hahnemannian Monthly*, published an unsigned article that blamed Philadelphia's hospital problem on the "jealousies of individual practitioners, and the extreme bitterness of opposing parties, together with a general indifference to the common advancement of Homeopathy, and a lack of proper *esprit du corps* [sic]." Homeopathic hospitals, the article argued, were usually in an "accustomed and chronic condition of mediocrity," for most were "either too limited in their means and objects and too much under the control of other organizations to promise much assistance to the cause they represent." Organizing a hospital, the writer made clear, was a critical way to advance homeopathy. Doctors must "become manly enough to rise above all personal prejudices, and . . . sacrifice the present interests of the individual, the party, the clique, to the permanent well-being of the whole profession, the honor and glory of homeopathy, and the benefit of the human race." This conception of what a hospital could accomplish was based on European models and relied on a faith in the efficacy of the numerical method of Pierre Louis. "A large general hospital and special hospitals under homeopathic control, in every city in the land, sending out annual volumes of statistics showing the results of homeopathic treatment, would be conclusive arguments in favor of Homeopathy, not only with the public, but with the allopathic branch of the medical profession also," he wrote, explaining his aspirations for the advancement of homeopathy. "Let us, then," it concluded, "have HOSPITALS."

By 1874 it was clear that the small hospital on Cuthbert Street had not served the purposes that homeopathic supporters, physicians, and college faculty had intended. Philadelphia homeopaths unconnected with the college began their own campaign to remake the hospital. The Homeopathic Medical Society of the County of Philadelphia proposed a different charter, for a "Homeopathic Hospital of Pennsylvania at Philadelphia." The society conceived of a kind of homeopathic Philadelphia General Hospital, a charitable institution for the sick poor, with facilities for medical, surgical, obstetrical, and insane patients. In this proposal, the trustees would be elected by the corporators, and private patients could admit their doctor if he was "in good standing." A similar argument was made in a local homeopathic journal, which blamed the problems with the current hospital on the "selfishness of a few men" and proposed that new trustees of a new public hospital be elected by the whole profession of Philadelphia. Financial stability would be assured by help from two hundred homeopathic doctors in and around Philadelphia "whose friends represent great wealth."

By the late 1870s the college faculty began to attack the Cuthbert Street hospital. They demanded either increased clinical access to hospital patients or a legal separation from the Homeopathic Hospital and its trustees so that they could build their own hospital, and they conducted a publicity war to convince the homeopathic community of Philadelphia of the validity of their grievances, sending out a series of printed circulars, including printed postcards asking homeopathic physicians to respond whether the college should build a clinical amphitheater and be allowed hospital ward visits, or build a new hospital.

The college faculty were able to draw on powerful new arguments to make their case, especially the increased value accorded to clinical training drawn from experience in France and Germany. With the growth of other homeopathic schools around the country, the Philadelphia faculty could also argue that the college needed to remain competitive, and the faculty called on college alumni who depended on the reputation of their alma mater to maintain the value of their training and the reputation of their medical diploma. "Mere reputation and prestige will not save us from certain decline in popularity," the faculty argued; the college "must be able to compete, or else fail to come up to the requirements of the times; requirements on the part of both the profession and the public." In particular, the faculty pointed to the necessity of "making the hospital in reality a part of the educational system of the school, a clinical hospital in fact, and by placing its medical control entirely in the hands of the professors of the college."

In a powerful move the faculty began to try to undermine the nostalgia with which many alumni viewed the Filbert Street college building and to re-present this physical space in ways that highlighted its deficiencies. In the early 1880s the faculty further politicized the physical space by complaining that the urban environment was destructively forcing itself into the daily sounds and smells of college life. In a letter to the trustees the faculty used the college building as a symbol for their own low status and argued that the college no longer offered a proper gentlemen's educational environment. The college building, the faculty pointed out, was situated next to the largest market in the city, right opposite the fish market. Its lecture rooms were too small and poorly heated, lighted, and ventilated. The clinics were overcrowded; the library had no reading room; the dissecting room and the chemical laboratory were too small; practical surgery had to be done in the cellar, where there was no daylight and little fresh air; and practical obstetrics was taught in the very same room. Microscopy was taught not in a laboratory but in a lecture room; and there were no large rooms for faculty or trustee meetings and no private rooms for any professor. There were also, the faculty revealed, no washrooms or water closets, and the cellar smells were made worse by outside urinals and the storage of chemicals and bodies waiting for dissection. These latter problems were endangering the health of not only the college occupants but also patients, for the college staff engaged in the "bad practice of having surgical operations performed in a college building contaminated by subjects for dissection." The faculty also argued that a dispensary was "out of place" anywhere inside a college building and that, in any case, as there were forty narrow winding steps required to enter it, its structure already prevented some patients, such as serious cases, from attending. Echoing what had become a central motif, the faculty argued that the most significant problem was the college's lack of a proper teaching hospital. "A clinical hospital must be provided," the faculty explained, to make the *"practical and clinical instruction of students . . . an essential part* of the College work."

In 1883 the college and hospital severed ties. The college retained control of its library and museum, continued to rent the building, and engaged in further fund-raising. In 1886 the college opened a new college building on 1.8 acres it had bought on Broad Street between Race and Vine. The college opened a new hospital, called Hahnemann Hospital, in 1890 and established a school of nursing at the hospital. The women supporters also split: in 1886 a group calling itself the Women's Hospital Association of Hahnemann Medical College separated itself from the Women's Homeopathic Association of Pennsylvania founded in 1882. The Women's Hospital Association raised money for Hahnemann Hospital; the Women's Homeopathic Association raised money for a smaller hospital that would be opened in 1890. The hospital trustees sold the old building on Filbert Street to the Hilton Hotel company.

The college faculty had won the battle for linking the professionalization of homeopathy with institutionalized care directed by medical educators rather than outside physicians. But the new hospital's trustees proved almost as skeptical of the notion of a teaching hospital as the earlier group, although with a significant difference. These businessmen recognized that students needed to learn and practice their skills with patients and allowed ward patients to be used in clinical teaching. Private patients, however, a group that many hospital administrators were seeking to attract, remained off limits to students until the 1950s.

Student Life

A self-conscious student culture with a clear sense of its own identity began to develop only gradually at Hahnemann, for, in the college's early decades, classes were small and mixed by age, experience, and geographic background. By the 1870s the students were younger; fewer had practiced as physicians or worked with a preceptor; and many had only a limited education, for the college's high school admissions requirement was frequently ignored. Students' geographic diversity also began to disappear, and, as American students in the North, South, and Midwest could attend local homeopathic schools, the college began to take its place in the mid-Atlantic regional medical market.

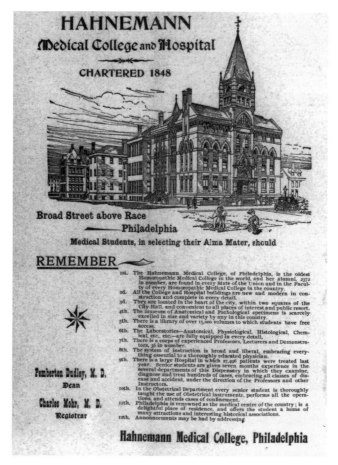

Figure 10. In 1886 Hahnemann built a new college building and, in 1890, a new hospital building on the site they still occupy today. These impressive edifices were featured in an 1890s advertisement for the school in the *Hahnemannian Institute,* 1899.

Although students at Hahnemann in the last decades of the nineteenth century were proud of their distinctive badge, they were conscious that with their medical degree they would be welcome only in homeopathic medical societies and hospitals and that orthodox physicians might refuse to consult or even socialize with them. Nevertheless Hahnemann students were also part of a wider American medical culture, in which medical students were allowed kinds of behavior before and during classes more typical in later decades of high school students.

Joseph Guernsey (class of 1872) recalled in the 1890s that in the late 1860s "a favorite song of the students was John Brown's body, not then as hackneyed as now." When the popular professor Charles Raue would appear, climbing "those

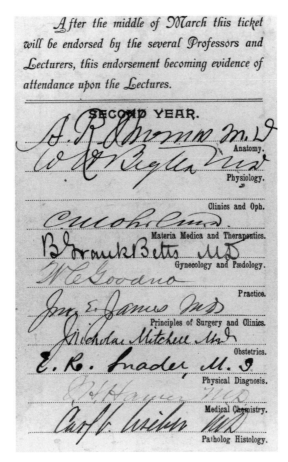

Figure 11. The back of the second-year matriculation ticket of H[enry] B. Justice, 1892–1893. Teachers at Hahnemann Medical College took roll, and their students—many of them young men who had not completed high school—had to get their teachers' signatures showing they had attended lectures in order to graduate.

old stone steps just as we students did" (most of Raue's colleagues entered by the back way so that they "suddenly appeared upon the platform before the students"), the students would change "the chorus to 'Raue is marching along,' and then came the stormy applause."[47] William Rufus King (1859–1926), who became a professor of ophthalmology and otology at the Southern Homeopathic College in Baltimore, offered some examples from the safe distance of twenty years. Remembering his years at the Filbert Street college in the late 1870s, he asked fellow alumni:

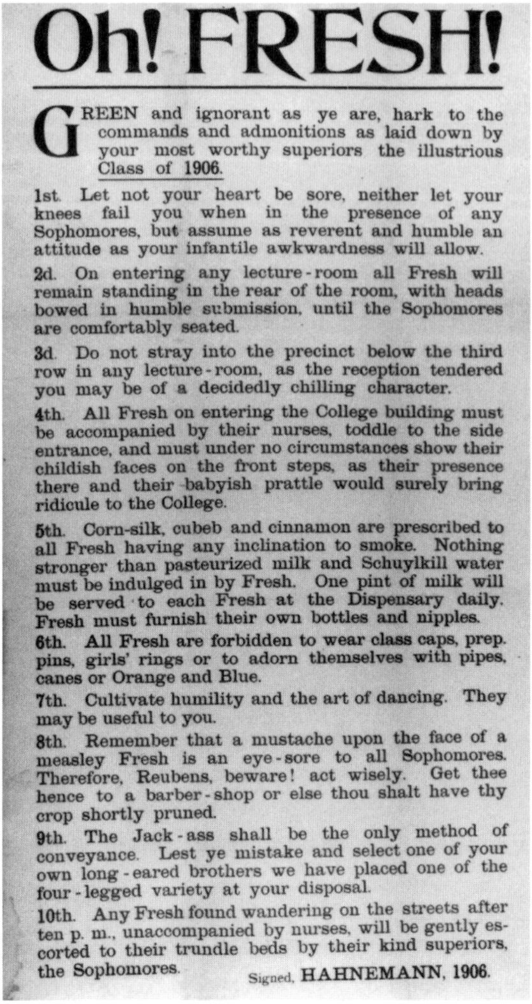

Oh! FRESH!

GREEN and ignorant as ye are, hark to the commands and admonitions as laid down by your most worthy superiors the illustrious Class of 1906.

1st. Let not your heart be sore, neither let your knees fail you when in the presence of any Sophomores, but assume as reverent and humble an attitude as your infantile awkwardness will allow.

2d. On entering any lecture-room all Fresh will remain standing in the rear of the room, with heads bowed in humble submission, until the Sophomores are comfortably seated.

3d. Do not stray into the precinct below the third row in any lecture-room, as the reception tendered you may be of a decidedly chilling character.

4th. All Fresh on entering the College building must be accompanied by their nurses, toddle to the side entrance, and must under no circumstances show their childish faces on the front steps, as their presence there and their babyish prattle would surely bring ridicule to the College.

5th. Corn-silk, cubeb and cinnamon are prescribed to all Fresh having any inclination to smoke. Nothing stronger than pasteurized milk and Schuylkill water must be indulged in by Fresh. One pint of milk will be served to each Fresh at the Dispensary daily. Fresh must furnish their own bottles and nipples.

6th. All Fresh are forbidden to wear class caps, prep. pins, girls' rings or to adorn themselves with pipes, canes or Orange and Blue.

7th. Cultivate humility and the art of dancing. They may be useful to you.

8th. Remember that a mustache upon the face of a measley Fresh is an eye-sore to all Sophomores. Therefore, Reubens, beware! act wisely. Get thee hence to a barber-shop or else thou shalt have thy crop shortly pruned.

9th. The Jack-ass shall be the only method of conveyance. Lest ye mistake and select one of your own long-eared brothers we have placed one of the four-legged variety at your disposal.

10th. Any Fresh found wandering on the streets after ten p. m., unaccompanied by nurses, will be gently escorted to their trundle beds by their kind superiors, the Sophomores.   Signed, HAHNEMANN, 1906.

Figure 12. A 1903 poster written by Hahnemann sophomores of the class of 1906. Hahnemann's student classes,
like those at many other schools, practiced a friendly ri-
valry that sometimes extended into scuffles and fights.

Don't forget the many pranks that were played during those happy days, for a medical student is apt to be a boy again occasionally. These were mainly of the harmless, laughable and enjoyable kind. Did you ever see one of the boys "passed down"? Was the sulphuretted hydrogen bottle ever left uncorked in the chemistry room during lecture hour? Did the gas [light] ever go out in class-room suddenly by reason of a mischievous student being actively engaged in blowing in a pipe down stairs? Did you

ever find the lecture-room doors securely fastened by rope and wire at
the end of the hour? Did you ever slide down those old steps to the
lower hall by reason of the packing of snow along the stair-way? Did you
ever leave a "stiff" hanging part way up the shaft in the spiral stairway to
frighten some timid and belated dispensary patient?[48]

Hahnemann students had first established a student society in 1849, which
became known as the Hahnemannian Medical Institute, and the institute played
a crucial role in providing tutoring support and even issued its own diplomas. It
was later renamed the Medical Student Institute, and during the 1920s became
the organized student government body, expressing student grievances to the
dean and organizing the annual Blue and Gold Ball. From the 1880s into the
1910s, however, it also tried to formalize social and professional interactions between students and professors, and at its regular meetings both college faculty
members and senior students presented papers that were discussed after dinner.
In 1886 the institute began to publish a journal by the same name, which included some of the faculty's lectures—especially the introductory philosophical
ones—as well as personal and professional news. The journal was oriented toward both students and alumni, and it offered news of graduates in private practice, especially those in unusual or prestigious work. By 1886, for example, John
B. Wurtz (class of 1876) was physician to a carpet manufacturer; Pemberton
Dudley (class of 1861), a member of the Pennsylvania State Board of Health;
John K. Lee (class of 1851), a member of the Pennsylvania State Board of Public Charities; Israel Tisdale Talbot (class of 1853), dean of the Boston University medical school; and Tullio Suzzara Verdi (class of 1856), a member of the
National Board of Health, a short-lived federal public health department.[49]

One of the most striking changes in Hahnemann's student culture during
the 1880s was, as we have seen, the introduction for the first time of African-
American students. Hahnemann's first black student, Thomas Creigh Imes
(1852–1923), was admitted in 1881 without public fanfare, a year before the
graduation of Nathan Mosell, the University of Pennsylvania's first black student. Imes graduated in 1884, with a thesis entitled "The Physiognomy of Disease." It was a conservative piece, arguing against the idea that homeopaths must
understand the cause and etiology of disease through pathology and experimental physiology. Hering, "one of the most noted Physicians of his day," Imes argued, had explained that "all diseases are known and distinguished by their
symptoms," so that "the causes may be in the darkness, but the symptoms are in
the light." A good physician, Imes believed, watched rather than touched. "This
thumping and jerking of the patient as I have seen done by some of the so-called
'eminent' diagnosticians of the present day, is as harmful to the patient as the
disease," he wrote. "In numerous instances, death has evidently been the result

Figure 13. Thomas Creigh Imes (1852–1923, class of 1884), shown
in this undated photograph, was Hahnemann's first African-American
graduate. Thomas Creigh Imes Collection, Hahnemann Collection.
Courtesy of the family of Thomas Creigh Imes.

of exhaustion from repeated and prolonged examination, and with persistent
rough handling." Instruments such as the clinical thermometer, the stethoscope,
and aspirator were, he believed "very good in their place," and "it would be impossible to get along without them," but most of them "should be a last resort."
For Imes the strength of homeopathy was its emphasis on expectancy and observation: "Think of the devastation of human lives from the blind prescribing
of druggists and physicians of the dominant-school of medicine. They think they
must give something, they do give something, but what is it, and what effect
does it have upon the patient: frequently the 'Undertaker' is called in to finish
the case."[50]

Hahnemann's black graduates seem to have been fully integrated into
Philadelphia's black medical world; perhaps the limited number of black physicians in Philadelphia forced a sense of community that overcame sectarian differences.[51] Imes became a member of the board of directors of Mercy Hospital,

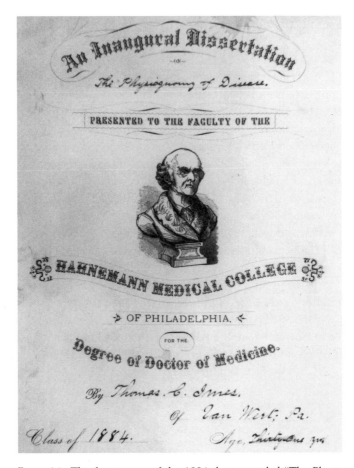

Figure 14. The front cover of the 1884 thesis entitled "The Physiognomy of Disease" by Thomas Creigh Imes, Hahnemann's first black graduate.

an institution founded in 1907 by black orthodox physicians. Isaac Walter Sutton (1877–ca. 1938), a 1903 graduate, was chief of the department of obstetrics at Mercy Hospital; and Henry Lytle Gowens Jr. (1884–1953), a 1908 graduate, was chief of the eye department there.

Like most women physicians in this period, African-American physicians were restricted from careers in most medical schools and from government work. William Edwin Morgan (1879–1938, class of 1900) was the only one of the group who did not make his living primarily as a private practitioner. Morgan worked at Hahnemann's dispensary after his graduation and then for a year at the Reading Homeopathic Hospital. For the rest of his career, however, he worked as a medical bureaucrat: first as a medical examiner for the Pension's Bureau in

Washington, D.C., and then as a bacteriologist for Philadelphia's city water department.[52]

By the 1890s Hahnemann students and faculty had found an established and prominent place in Philadelphia medicine and in the homeopathic profession nationally. The college offered graduates a distinctive but not inferior status, and the medical education it provided was of a standing equal to that of most orthodox medical schools and superior to that of many homeopathic colleges. Students at Hahnemann Medical College founded branches of homeopathic medical fraternities that brought them into a national network of homeopathic students, and they engaged in social activities that demonstrated their pride in their alma mater. For example, when in 1893, students at Pennsylvania and Jefferson refused to march at the annual medical parade (held on a Saturday at the end of October) if Hahnemann students were to lead it, Hahnemann's students marched down Broad Street accompanied only by students from the dental college. Students from Jefferson and Pennsylvania watched the parade from the sidelines and taunted them with: "Sugar pill, sugar pill, Never cured and never will." Led by a squad of mounted police and a brass band, 250 college students carried canes decorated in blue and gold, the school colors, and when they passed their college they called out the school cheer: "Rah, rah, rah, Hahnemann, Hahnemann, sis boom ah." [53] It was a glorious moment.

Part II

The Second
Fifty Years

An Alternative Path
from Medical Orthodoxy

THE MIDDLE THIRD of Hahnemann's history was a wrenching and difficult period during which the college was forced to remake its identity: at the start of the period the college aspired to national leadership, but by the end it was comfortably second-ranked and locally oriented. Not until after World War II did the school again aspire to become a major academic medical center. By the 1920s it had carved out a place as an institution whose structure and mission were tolerated but not encouraged by national medical leaders: it had become a school with pragmatic goals, limited efforts in medical research, and a focus on producing practitioners.

At the same time, however, Hahnemann also become aware of a new and special responsibility: by the 1920s, it was one of only two homeopathic schools left in the United States.[1] In an era when the number of American medical schools was declining rapidly, Hahnemann's homeopathic heritage enabled its faculty to argue that the survival of the institution was crucial because it supplied communities with homeopathic physicians. Although by the 1930s most graduates left intending to combine orthodox and homeopathic practices, just as they had been taught, they nevertheless left with an alternative identity, a feeling that they were distinct from but not outside the medical mainstream. This sense of distinctiveness was reinforced by the school's increasingly diverse student body. As Hahnemann's homeopathic reputation made it more difficult for the school to attract mainstream medical students, the college began to offer places to students whose religious and ethnic affiliations had barred them from other medical schools.

By the mid-1930s, though, external and internal changes pressured the school to begin to shake off its unorthodox past and to deviate from the alternative path it had carved out in American medical education. Faculty turn-over and dissension, changing student demands, state educational requirements, and a society that increasingly valued scientists and specialists over routine general practitioners contributed to this shift. Physicians who identified themselves as homeopaths became increasingly alienated from the medical world, and Hahnemann's faculty either retreated into a familiar role as teachers and local practitioners or reached out to join orthodox associations. The professional probation imposed on the college in the 1940s was the final pressure to push the school into the orthodox mainstream.

Chapter 3

The Turbulent Years
1898–1928

İN THE DECADE after its Golden Jubilee the college went through a series of upheavals, elements of which were already visible to revelers at the 1898 celebrations. Hahnemann's faculty and trustees were conscious of the growing desire
among medical professionals and the public to improve and standardize medical training. In 1896, spurred by new state requirements and the rising expectations of the AIH and AMA, Hahnemann made its four-year course compulsory,
and, in the wake of this change, in contrast to the introduction of a compulsory three-year course a decade earlier, the relative stability in student enrollments provided a measure of the success of this change.[1]

Not only the structure but also the content of Hahnemann's medical training began to alter. Like many other schools in this period, Hahnemann began
to introduce new courses and ways of teaching reflecting the growing esteem
for the hallmarks of German medicine: laboratory science and clinical specialization. Hahnemann increased its laboratory teaching and introduced new
courses in bacteriology, experimental physiology, and clinical specialties such as
ophthalmology. While some homeopaths worried that this rapid adoption of
"German science" was potentially unhomeopathic, Hahnemann educators recognized that, in the competitive medical world of the new century, laboratory
and specialty training was expected by students and patients. During the 1870s
and 1880s Listerism and the bacteriology of Pasteur and Koch had been quickly
integrated into American homeopathic practice. Homeopaths linked the use of
antisepsis to Samuel Hahnemann's call for physicians to prevent disease and, as
they had with smallpox vaccination, saw the new serum and vaccine therapies
developed in German laboratories as expressions of homeopathic law.[2] Philadelphia homeopaths were also conscious of the lay public's interest in the new

scientific medicine. College gynecology professor Benjamin Franklin Betts acknowledged the importance of the lay public's support of germ-killing policies
when he admitted in 1887 that Hahnemann and other homeopathic hospitals
recognized "the necessity for disinfection" and that "in all things," other than
the reliance on homeopathic law to treat disease, "our hospitals are conducted
as other hospitals," for such institutions need "liberal aid from the charitably
disposed citizens of this city; and *they* should know that in the matter of care
and sanitation they compare favorably with the best."[3]

Homeopathy and the State

During the 1880s and 1890s state legislators began to pass laws that actively
sought to define standards of medical practice and medical education. These laws
reflected the fact that the medical populism and egalitarianism of a bygone era
had been supplanted by the American public's new faith in special expertise and
in the knowledge of elite professionals. Homeopathic supporters in the 1890s
were wary of these efforts to regulate medical practice but were pleased to see
that their political influence had helped create boards that institutionalized state
recognition of homeopathy.[4] Indeed, as one historian has pointed out, although
in the 1830s and 1840s alternative practitioners felt that unregulated practice
best protected their freedom against an orthodox medical monopoly, by the 1880s
and 1890s they saw state licensing itself as a protection.[5]

For the first time since the 1840s, states began to define what a physician
would have to demonstrate to practice legally: typically, a medical diploma from
an "acceptable" school. Because homeopaths and eclectics continued to carry
social and political weight in this period, defining "acceptable" became so politically charged that a number of states initially retreated to establishing standards for good practice. They did this by assuming a role that medical societies
had played in the early nineteenth century and then largely ceded to individual
medical schools: examining candidates for licensure. Selecting examiners became
another political fight, and in the 1890s states with a relatively strong unorthodox presence established what were known as mixed boards, in which orthodox,
homeopathic, and eclectic professionals wrote their own questions and examined their own candidates. It was a sign of the political and popular decline of
these unorthodox groups when states replaced these boards with a single board.
Pennsylvania had established three medical boards in 1894, but in 1912 the state
replaced the three with one carefully balanced mixed board of seven members.
Only the exams in therapeutics and materia medica were kept separate. Pennsylvania also began to define what constituted an acceptable medical school, at
least in terms of admission and graduation requirements.[6] The blueprint for the
acceptable school was drawn partly from professional models developed by or-

ganized medical groups such as the AMA and AIH. The structure of the new state licensing laws suggests that by this period Philadelphia homeopathic leaders had accepted a modern notion of homeopathy and that the basic content of medicine was shared across systems; that is, homeopaths no longer accepted the idea of a distinctive homeopathic obstetrics or physiology. This acceptance reflected a wider consensus that homeopathy's new role in American medicine might be as a therapeutic specialty, as a complementary rather than alternative medicine. Thus, in 1899, the AIH formally redefined homeopathy's law of similars as "let like be cured by like," making it less a law than a guide to therapy.

During this period the problem of homeopathy's relation with the state increasingly polarized Pennsylvania's homeopaths. Urban practitioners who taught at medical schools worked comfortably with regular physicians to support the new boards, for both groups were unhappy with the rise of new unorthodox practitioners, such as osteopaths, chiropractors, and Christian Science healers. Philadelphia homeopaths were also pleased when the state established the State Homeopathic Hospital for the Insane in Allentown (week-long trips to this hospital became an annual event for college seniors and gave them a sense of homeopathic treatments for mental illness). But other homeopaths, especially those outside the big cities, remained skeptical of any collusion with either regular physicians or the state. These homeopaths, especially in rural eastern Pennsylvania, promoted a proudly separatist practice, and in the *Homeopathic Recorder*, their journal published in Lancaster, they attacked the faculty at Hahnemann as representatives of a misguidedly modern and antihomeopathic way of thinking. In an editorial attacking the proposal for a mixed board, entitled "You Cannot Bridge the Gulf," the editors argued: "there is only one way in which the two can unite in peace and for the public welfare, and that way is for the allopath to fully and completely acknowledge the validity of the law known as Homeopathy and teach it as the central truth of therapeutics."[7]

Much of this resistance must be understood not only as a continuation of urban-rural tensions among the state's homeopaths but also as part of the traditionalists' older view of their homeopathic identity. As one historian has noted for other unorthodox groups in this period, traditionalists "wanted to be recognized for possessing Truth, not simply for having an expert skill."[8] The change in the AMA's code of ethics in 1903, allowing homeopaths to become members, and the 1910 Owen Bill, proposing a federal public health department, only exacerbated tensions between urban homeopaths, such as the Philadelphia faculty, and rural practitioners, which included many college alumni. The AIH was sympathetic to the Owen Bill; but a number of homeopathic antagonists joined the National League for Medical Freedom, which included osteopaths, antivivisectionists, and patent medicine manufacturers, in order to defeat what was seen as a federally mandated takeover by the orthodox profession of

American medicine. "Mr. Legislator should keep [his] hands off," wrote the editor of the *Homeopathic Recorder* in 1912, "unless he is fully satisfied" that the "particular clique (though it calls itself the whole show, as does the A.M.A.) has arrived at medical truth."[9]

Although historian Kenneth Ludmerer has recently argued that until 1910 state licensing laws were "an insignificant factor in the development of American medical education,"[10] it is clear that not only for Hahnemann but also for other Philadelphia medical schools the new state demands defining a medical school and the qualifications for legal practice significantly altered the city's medical marketplace such that, in various ways, the medical schools began to change their curricula and structures.[11] When the state legislated a two-year college-equivalent requirement for all medical schools to begin in 1918, for example, Hahnemann as well as other medical schools introduced premedical years and then began to promote them as the best kind of preparation for medical school. Some of these changes may seem less obvious in retrospect because many of these state laws came about not as the result of elite orthodox medical leaders' single vision of the proper medical school but as part of a political process that tried to ensure only that practitioners were properly trained, not that they all practiced the same kind of medicine or even shared the same view of medical science.

Hahnemann Medical College did especially well in the reorganization of Pennsylvania's medical licensing laws in the 1890s because the new laws reinforced its place as a leading homeopathic school in the nation and as a prestigious rival within the local medical arena. Hahnemann graduates and faculty were appointed as members of the state homeopathic examining board, and during the period of the three boards (1894–1911), Hahnemann graduates consistently outperformed other homeopathic graduates in the homeopathic board exams. Robert Jones Abele (1875–1929), one of Hahnemann's few African-American students, scored the board's highest general average in 1895; and of the top ten homeopathic candidates in this period, seven were Hahnemann graduates, all from classes in the late 1890s, a decade whose graduates were to make up the majority of the college's departmental chairs by the 1920s.[12]

Not surprisingly, the rates of failures of graduates from the state's various medical schools became a powerful weapon. The schools used their ranking to compete for students and popular support, but these rankings could also be turned against schools by outside regulatory bodies such as the AMA and the AIH. Hahnemann performed well in the mixed board exams, with individual students sometimes ranking second or third in the state, but, in the 1930s and 1940s, its failure rate doubled (from 9 percent in 1933 to 18.3 percent in 1942).[13] This public sign of inadequate preparation and poor educational standards fueled major internal changes that led to a curriculum and faculty upheaval and, ultimately, to a complete transformation of the Hahnemann Medical College after 1946.

The 1910 Flexner Report

More than anything else, historians have pointed to the 1910 *Report on Medical Education in the United States and Canada* prepared by Abraham Flexner as a major turning point in twentieth-century American medical education. Flexner, not a physician but a professional educator, was hired by the Carnegie Foundation to improve the standards of medical schools by exposing their faults to the public. The tone and ideology of Flexner's report became (and have remained) a central part of the debate over the direction of medical education. Historians of medicine have long argued that many of the changes Flexner promoted were already in process: the closing of weak medical colleges, the raising of admission and graduation standards, and the introduction of intensive laboratory and clinical teaching. Nonetheless, his widely read report, backed by foundation funding, contributed to the professional and public notion of the ideal or model American medical school. While some aspects of this model have been consistently lauded—small classes, less didactic and more hands-on teaching, a faculty who devoted their attention to teaching and research, the creation of academic medicine as a career—other elements of the report have been castigated as leading to the homogenization of medical students and of the content of medical knowledge.[14]

The disappearance of alternative medical schools has been a crucial part of this story of homogenization. Historians have tended to assume that, after the public and prospective students read Flexner's scathing comments on what he called "medical sectarians," alternative schools quickly collapsed, and their followers, embarrassed by their unscientific ethos, also retreated to the orthodox fold. Central to Flexner's argument was the idea that truly scientific medicine no longer needed a "democratic" responsiveness to public interest in medical alternatives. Reformers like Flexner and his supporters from Johns Hopkins medical school believed that the new science provided a universalized explanation of the natural world and that dissent implied ignorance or blind faith in a dogmatic system, be it allopathy or homeopathy. "Modern medicine has . . . as little sympathy for allopathy as for homeopathy," Flexner argued in his report. "It wants not dogma, but facts." In particular Flexner saw an allegiance to the new German sciences as antithetical to medical creeds, especially to self-identified unorthodox medical systems such as homeopathy and osteopathy. "One cannot simultaneously assert science and dogma; one cannot travel down the road under the former banner, in the hope of taking up the latter, too, at the middle of the march. Science, once embraced, will conquer the whole."[15]

As a good Progressive reformer, Flexner saw himself as unprejudiced and objective, and in his report he recognized the strengths of a few of the fifteen homeopathic schools he examined. The Philadelphia, Boston, and New York schools, he admitted, "possess the equipment necessary for the effective routine teaching of the fundamental branches. None of them can employ full-time teachers to any considerable extent. But they possess fairly well-equipped laboratories in anatomy, pathology, bacteriology, and physiology, a museum showing care and intelligence, and a decent library."[16] He noted that the Boston University's homeopathic medical school had "a model dispensary" and that the dispensaries attached to the New York, Chicago, and Philadelphia schools enabled them to "command material enough."[17] Flexner also recognized that homeopaths and other unorthodox groups had accepted significant parts of the new sciences and integrated them into their teaching. "They have practically accepted the curriculum as it has been worked out on the scientific basis," he wrote. "They teach pathology, bacteriology, clinical microscopy."[18] But he nonetheless concluded that "the logical position of medical sectarians to-day is self-contradictory," for the "scientific method cannot be limited to the first half of medical education." The sectarian, Flexner asserted, "at the beginning of the third year produces a novel principle and requires that thenceforth the student effect a compromise between science and revelation."[19] And he vehemently rejected any role for such schools in a modern American society committed to true science and Progressive ideals.

Flexner examined thirty-two unorthodox schools: fifteen homeopathic, eight osteopathic, eight eclectic, and one physio-medical.[20] He dismissed chiropractors as "unconscionable quacks" who were not "entitled to serious notice in an educational discussion," and he did not visit any of their schools. Flexner took homeopathy most seriously of all the alternative groups he examined. He acknowledged that "historically it undoubtedly played an important part in dismissing empirical allopathy."[21] This admission drew on the arguments of nineteenth-century reformers like Oliver Wendell Holmes, but Flexner also used the language of nineteenth-century homeopaths who had tried to discredit orthodox medicine of their day by seeing it as empirical rather than rationalistic. Flexner's use of the homeopathic epithet "allopathy" was especially pointed. However, his argument undermined any homeopathic claims to scientific importance. Homeopathy, Flexner explained could not withstand the explanatory power of the new sciences that had allowed medicine to become "scientific." In the modern medicine of 1910, he believed, "everything of proved value in homeopathy belongs of right to scientific medicine and is at this moment incorporated in it; nothing else has any footing at all, whether it be of allopathic or homeopathic lineage." Thus, the ideology of the new science denied the validity of the past, refusing to grant former systems the right to claim any signifi-

Figure 15. Hahnemann, like many American medical schools, offered more anatomy lectures than dissection classes and relied heavily on didactic teaching. Here anatomists Amos Russell Thomas and Rufus Benjamin Weaver lecture in the college. *Forty-sixth Annual Announcement of the Hahnemann Medical College and Hospital: Columbian Edition, 1893–1894: With Illustrations.*

cant contribution to medical progress, and made their adherents ridiculous and pathetic. Turning to the language of the Progressive United States, in a metaphor that made medical creeds as irrelevant to progress as ethnic immigrant allegiances, Flexner continued: "Homeopathy has two options: one to withdraw into the isolation in which alone any peculiar tenet can maintain itself; the other to put that tenet into the melting-pot."[22]

Flexner's report played a significant role in shaping American alternative medicine in general—and American homeopathy in particular—not just because it influenced public opinion and had the backing of powerful foundations but also because leading unorthodox educators, such as those at Hahnemann, wanted to be judged by the same standards as orthodox medicine and shared with orthodox medicine many of the same assumptions about the proper direction of medical education and the place of the new science in a modern curriculum. Hahnemann, as we have seen, had already begun to alter its teaching in accordance with these values. Nonetheless, a close examination of Hahnemann's response to the Flexner report demonstrates that medical alternatives did not simply disappear or collapse in its wake. For all Flexner's attacks, osteopaths and chiropractors not only continued to attract students and patients but have endured through the late twentieth century as prominent features of the American medical landscape.[23]

Homeopathy, the oldest of the medical systems investigated by Flexner, did not fare as well as osteopathy and chiropractic, although it began the race with better resources and a more established public reputation. My examination of Hahnemann's history here can offer only tantalizing hints as to why that occurred. Homeopathy, unlike other, newer unorthodox systems, was no longer seen as alternative enough. Many of its leaders spoke the language of the new science, and increasingly homeopathy's claim to medical distinctiveness had become narrowed to therapy alone, a specialty that could be and was practiced alongside all other aspects of orthodox medicine. Still, the case of Hahnemann suggests that Flexner's report did not provide an automatic death blow to alternative medicine. Historians have assumed that, in the wake of the report, American medicine experienced an increase in medical orthodoxy and homogeneity that continued uninterrupted for the following sixty years. But despite Hahnemann's integration of many aspects of the new science and educational ideals, the college's survival shows that this notion of American medical history is too simplistic. Thus, Hahnemann continued to offer an "alternative" model of medical education between the 1910s and the 1940s.

Certainly, the decline of American homeopathic schools was quickened by Flexner's report, although the worst and most vulnerable schools had already begun to disappear in the preceding two decades. After the report, the New York Homeopathic Medical College began to phase out its homeopathic training, although it did not drop its homeopathic title until 1936; the New York women's homeopathic school collapsed in 1918. Flexner had urged medical faculties to merge with universities, but merging was a disaster for the homeopathic schools that chose that option. In 1914 Cincinnati's forty-two-year-old medical college was merged into Ohio State University; the university's homeopathic division closed in 1922. In 1915 San Francisco's Hahnemann School of the Pacific merged with the medical school at the University of California at San Francisco, which subsequently, despite a significant endowment, maintained only a few homeopathic electives. In 1918 Boston University's medical school, which had been fully homeopathic since its opening in 1873, became an orthodox school; and in 1919 Iowa State University's homeopathic department closed.[24] By comparison, only the two private medical colleges, both founded before the Civil War, Hahnemann in Philadelphia and the New York Medical College, managed to survive as homeopathic institutions into the 1920s and 1930s.

Hahnemann after Flexner

The immediate impact of Flexner's report at Hahnemann was the rewriting of its school catalog and the reorganization of its curriculum to more closely mirror elements of Flexner's ideal school.[25] Hahnemann increased its hours of laboratory teaching and intensified its clinical training for third- and fourth-year students. As Dean William Pearson informed the alumni, "the modern physician must be able to apply modern science to the treatment and elimination of disease. Samuel Hahnemann, Constantine Hering and many other prominent Homeopathic physicians have realized the necessity of a solid scientific foundation."[26] Hahnemann's faculty and trustees also tried to alter some of the most egregious faults in organization that Flexner had pointed to, some that had long been concerns to the faculty. Responding to Flexner's specific attack that Hahnemann students had inadequate clinical experience because the college faculty was allowed to use only a handful of beds at the adjacent Hahnemann Hospital for student teaching, the college instituted a closer relationship between the college faculty and hospital staff and also institutionalized student access to other local homeopathic hospitals: Children's, St. Luke's, and West Philadelphia.[27]

The college catalogs published in the years after the report made much of these changes. They included a "Block Plan" of Hahnemann's Broad Street site, demonstrating, as the text pointed out, that the buildings on the block were "practically all in direct communication." The catalogs also stressed that "the Faculty of the Medical School and the Staff of the Hospital are one" and proudly listed the advantages of the three-hundred-bed hospital "under complete control of the medical school," a claim that was not and has never been true.[28]

These changes caused the faculty, as one member later recalled, to be divided "into several camps." When the college enrollments began dropping, to a low of fourteen graduates in 1914, Dean William Van Lennep was forced to leave, in an episode that William Pearson, the man who succeeded him, later described as a "vitriolic schism" of the faculty. "No artist can paint the meeting where he was crucified, but he still loved Hahnemann Medical College," Pearson concluded.[29] Faculty minutes from this period have not survived, so we can only guess at the kinds of issues that raised such a level of emotion.

Hahnemann's 1911 catalog commented on the changes taking place in American medical education, in an effort to transform the fervor stirred by Flexner's report into an open dialogue in which homeopaths could take part as equal professional reformers. "Students of medicine in this country," the catalog's introduction read, "cannot fail to observe the gratifying degree of uniformity in medical teaching which is rapidly being attained coincident with the general improvement in our medical schools." The catalog described the "official and unofficial criticisms and arraignments of medical college defects," adding "to

these advances, Hahnemann Medical College, as in the past, most heartily subscribes." Responding to Flexner's characterization of unorthodox education as
outdated, directionless, and incoherent, the catalog commented: "It is the prime
object of this medical school to give a broad and thorough medical education,
and, to this end, it has availed itself of the benefits derived from the most recent advances in medical teaching and equipment, while not departing from
that conservatism which gives stability, not standardizing its courses to the ex-
tinction of initiative." The college proudly pointed to "the obvious advantages
accruing from new laboratories . . . and small classes which enhance the amount
of individual instruction" and described in detail its plans to reduce the number
of its lecture rooms to three in favor of laboratory space, to build new physiology and pharmacy laboratories, to improve its pathology and bacteriology laboratories, to reorganize its museum, and to establish a homeopathic research
laboratory. This catalog also began to lay out what became Hahnemann's defining philosophy, which was reiterated throughout the 1920s and 1930s: that the
college was seeking to be not unusual or pathbreaking but part of a general trend:
"There is nothing novel in this general plan of instruction; it is common to many
medical schools. And this college claims no startling innovations in its teaching."[30]

Flexner's model required funding, a factor he recognized in his report. While
unsuccessful in gaining the kinds of endowment support Flexner envisioned for
the best schools, in 1910 Hahnemann did receive a significant gift from Walter
Hering, Constantine Hering's businessman son (who founded the Globe Ticket
Printing Company), in order to fund the Constantine Hering Professorship of
Homeopathic Materia Medica and Therapeutics and the Hering Research Laboratory. "The endowment of Mr. Hering," Dean Van Lennep commented in 1911,
"has opened the door for the *sine qua non* of success, or even of continued existence, in an up-to-date medical school." "This magnificent gift," Van Lennep continued, "guarantees the teaching of Homeopathic Materia Medica and
Therapeutics in our College for all time" and "protects" the college's doctor of
homeopathic medicine degree. In addition to the research laboratory, Hering
also funded a clinical laboratory in the hospital, where, the dean reported proudly
to the alumni, "each senior student has his desk, with locker for microscope and
reagents, his 'Pathological Home,' while in the same room are complete outfits
for the examination of urine, blood, sputum, bacteria, etc."[31] Between 1910 and
1912 the school raised two hundred thousand dollars in endowments.[32] During
this transition period, part of the dean's job was to reassure skeptical alumni that
modernizing the college did not mean rejecting its homeopathic heritage and
traditions. Thus, in 1915 the dean assured the alumni: "your prestige, the prestige of the college and of Homeopathy itself, demanded that these suggestions
be carried out. The result is: your status has not suffered, a model college, and
the advancement of Homeopathy."[33]

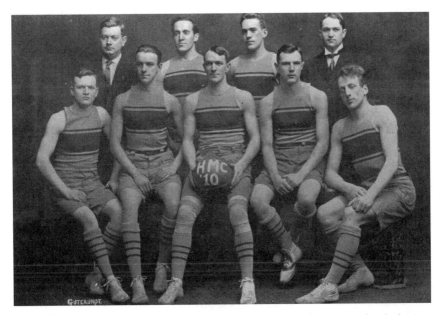

Figure 16. By the 1910s Hahnemann students had developed a strong school identity. College sports teams, like the 1910 championship basketball team pictured in this photograph from *Similia* (the student yearbook), played against other Philadelphia medical schools.

In 1910 Hahnemann was Philadelphia's fourth largest school, after the University of Pennsylvania, Jefferson, and Medico-Chirurgical. Despite Flexner's effort to segregate and denigrate unorthodox schools, a comparison of Philadelphia medical schools suggests that the structure of the college after the report came out was not especially distinctive. In 1911 Hahnemann students paid $150 yearly in tuition fees, compared to $140 at the Woman's Medical College, $150 at Medico-Chirurgical, $180 at Jefferson, and $200 at Pennsylvania.[34] Hahnemann students were required to have a high school diploma or its equivalent, which was a standard admission requirement in Philadelphia schools until 1913, when the state raised it to a year of college-equivalent courses. Typical of graduates of all other Philadelphia schools, graduates at Hahnemann had to be at least twenty-one; they had to have achieved a general average of 75 percent, to have attended four full thirty-two-week terms of medical lectures, the last of them at Hahnemann itself, and to have attended at least two childbirths at the homes of dispensary patients.[35] The moral behavior of students remained a concern of the faculty and trustees: students were expected "to observe such rules of decorum and order in the lecture rooms, laboratories and halls of the college as are becoming gentlemen."[36] Graduates were encouraged to complete a year's hospital internship, something Pennsylvania required for licensing, and Hahnemann's list of its graduates' placements began to include hospitals beyond immediately local institutions, reminding readers of the broader role of homeopathy in American health care and the influence of a Hahnemann medical degree in the region. In the early 1910s the list included National Homeopathic Hospital in Washington, D.C., the McKinley Memorial Hospital in Trenton, the Crozer Hospital in Chester, the West Jersey Homeopathic Hospital, the Wilmington Homeopathic Hospital, Metropolitan Hospital in New York City, the Cumberland Street Hospital in Brooklyn, the Buffalo Homeopathic Hospital, the Rochester Homeopathic Hospital, the Reading Homeopathic Hospital, and the Pittsburgh Homeopathic Hospital.[37]

To understand many of the choices that Hahnemann's leaders made in the early and mid–twentieth century it is crucial to emphasize the school's persistent financial troubles. Both the college and the hospital continually operated under deficits; in 1915 the deficit was 10 percent of the institution's $31,088 annual budget.[38] The difficulties in transforming the school to resemble Flexner's model were in part due to the lack of money.[39] Small classes taught in properly equipped laboratories and clinics meant high teacher-student ratios, and fewer students meant either less income from fees or fees that were not competitive. The new facilities were costly, but so were schools' efforts to hire and put on salary even a limited number of full-time staff, never mind Flexner's vision of a completely full-time faculty.[40]

In 1920 Hahnemann's dean, William Pearson, and Charles Barney, chair of the board of trustees, traveled to New York to meet with Abraham Flexner in order to apply for a grant from the Rockefeller Foundation. In 1913 Flexner had been appointed as assistant secretary of the Rockefeller Foundation's General Education Board, which provided major grants to medical schools considered "deserving" of support. Pearson and Barney asked for a continuing grant of five thousand dollars a year and were assured by Flexner that their school's homeopathic identity would have no "detrimental influence" on its application. With their request they included a letter pointing out that the founder of the foundation, John D. Rockefeller Sr., had a homeopath as his personal physician.[41] As Flexner had already publicly expressed his abhorrence for medical sectarianism and his feeling that such schools had no place in a modern scientific education, and as Rockefeller's advisors were fervently trying to convince him of the uselessness of homeopathy, it is not surprising that the foundation did not offer Hahnemann a grant.[42]

While this part of the story of American homeopathy and medical education fits nicely into the accepted picture of the history of American medical education, the acceptance in 1913 of Hahnemann by the Association of American Medical Colleges (AAMC) does not. The AAMC, which was made up of medical school deans and had been active since the 1890s, was distinct from the AMA and had somewhat more pragmatic goals for directing medical education and improving the status of American physicians. Its annual meetings and its regular unpublicized inspections of schools helped to reinforce its growing power in determining the ranking of American medical schools. At least in the first few decades of its membership Hahnemann seems to have been fully accepted, in spite of its unorthodox medical philosophy, and, according to one report, when the AAMC urged Hahnemann to become a member it "definitely assured [Hahnemann] that never would the question of Homeopathy reflect against the College."[43]

Homeopathy after Flexner

Although it becomes increasingly difficult in the decades after 1910 to discern the kind of homeopathy practiced and promoted at Hahnemann, it is clear nonetheless that in the first few decades of the twentieth century a separatist identity remained a crucial aspect of the school. The AMA had begun to open its doors to homeopaths who did not prominently identify themselves as unorthodox, but many American homeopaths continued to meet in separate societies, treat patients in separate hospitals, and support separate medical journals. In 1918 Hahnemann historian Thomas Lindsley Bradford listed around fifty homeopathic journals then published in the United States.[44] Hahnemann's students, Dean Van Lennep remarked in 1911, "are beginning to realize that they must go out with a united front as members of the minority school."[45]

In his 1910 report Flexner had lumped homeopaths together with "medical sectarians," but Hahnemann's faculty, students, and supporters did not necessarily see themselves as colleagues or peers with other alternative groups. In the 1910s and 1920s, despite Flexner's attacks, unorthodox "drugless healers," such as osteopaths, chiropractors, and Christian Scientists, remained popular, and antivivisectionists continued to gain a public hearing in their attacks on modern scientific research.[46] Yet Hahnemann's faculty were not welcoming to these newcomers. In the 1910s pathologist Samuel Sappington was the college representative to the Pennsylvania Society for the Protection of Scientific Research, a lobbying group set up to counter the activities of antivivisectionists in the state.[47] While the faculty agreed to allow students of "drugless healing" to attend lectures in 1913, a year later they refused to let the American Osteopathic Association use Hahnemann's Clinical Hall for its Philadelphia meeting.[48] In 1915 the faculty also refused to allow osteopathic students to transfer courses from osteopathic schools with credit.[49] During World War I the *Hahnemannian Monthly*, which had become the organ of the state homeopathic society but continued to be supported by college faculty, praised the decision by Surgeon General William Gorgas not to appoint "osteopaths and other sects" to the Army

Figure 17. Student Army Training Corps, Colonel John A. Lockwood, Commanding Officer, November 20, 1918. Students and faculty from Hahnemann, like homeopaths around the country, played a major role in World War I.

Medical Department.[50] And in a 1918 editorial G. Harlan Wells pointed in horror to the twenty or thirty schools of "drugless healers" that had appeared in Pennsylvania in the previous several years. Wells believed the inappropriately high demands of medical training imposed by the state had created too many "difficulties placed in the way of a man obtaining a medical degree" and had "led to a uniform increase in the number of poorly trained practitioners commonly known as 'drugless healers' . . . [who] have no education that is worthy of any consideration from a scientific standpoint."[51]

Hahnemann's continuing commitment to homeopathy was reinforced by homeopathy's national prominence and respectability during the first two decades of the twentieth century, respectability that is often overlooked in accounts of the decline of alternative medicine in the United States.[52] On June 21, 1900, for example, a monument dedicated to Samuel Hahnemann was formally installed in Washington, D.C., with the dignitaries at the opening ceremony including President William McKinley. And unlike their fathers and uncles, who had been rejected during the Civil War, homeopathic graduates in this period were welcomed as commissioned physicians during the Spanish-American War and World War I.[53] Hahnemann faculty and students were well represented in the latter conflict: some three hundred alumni and one-third of the faculty served, and at least nine Hahnemann graduates died in service. In 1917 the AIH pressured the Council of National Defense to include two homeopathic physicians as members, and one was a former Hahnemann dean, William Van Lennep.[54] The Hahnemann Hospital Unit organized by the college was not recognized by the Red Cross, but the unit organized by New York's homeopathic Metropolitan Hospital was; and other homeopathic hospitals played a prominent role in medical care in France.[55] Homeopaths also proudly pointed to their patients' low mortality during the 1918 influenza epidemic.[56] During the last months of World War I, Hahnemann students who were part of the Student Army Training Corps at Hahnemann were each given a bottle of "Gelsemium [homeopathically prepared yellow jasmine diluted to the power of] 3X" and told to take one tablet frequently, and, unlike other young soldiers, they did not develop influenza or pneumonia.[57]

Although by the 1910s and 1920s homeopathy was no longer supported by prominent intellectuals, it nonetheless retained a national political presence. The most famous public homeopath during this period was Senator Royal Copeland (1868–1938), a homeopathic graduate of the University of Michigan, and formerly dean of the New York Homeopathic Medical College and New York City health commissioner. Copeland's support of the 1938 Food, Drug, and Cosmetic Act helped ensure legislative recognition of the homeopathic pharmacopeia at the federal level.[58] While Hahnemann Medical College could not claim Copeland as a graduate, Dean Pearson claimed him as a crucial personal supporter. When Pearson had first become dean in 1914, with the faculty divided over the fall in the number of the school's graduates and over how to respond to the Flexner report, Pearson recollected, in a reflective history of the school written in 1948, that Copeland deserved "much credit for formulating the policy of The Hahnemann Medical College during this tense period."[59] Hahnemann could proudly point to 1913 graduate Joel T. Boone (1889–1974), a much decorated military physician, who became a vice admiral and was White House physician to Harding, Coolidge, and Hoover.[60] Dean Pearson must have mentioned Boone often: the student yearbooks used as one of the dean's typical quotes "my friend Admiral Boone." And in 1919, a few months before he was elected president, Ohio senator Warren Harding, the son of a homeopathic physician who had served in the Civil War, gave the school's commencement address.[61]

During this period, the catalogs did not significantly downplay the college's homeopathic heritage and reputation. Although the 1911–1912 catalog no longer contained the boast, as had the 1909–1910 catalog, that "the college is aggressive in the teaching of homeopathy,"[62] the former nonetheless pointed out that the college was the "oldest homeopathic medical college in existence" and called readers' "special attention" to the "Department of Materia Medica and Therapeutics," where "the materia medica of Hahnemann, Hering, Dunham and other noted investigators is thoroughly elucidated throughout the course, and a number of enthusiastic and experienced clinical teachers demonstrate the principles and efficiency of homeopathic practical work."[63] Philadelphia and Pennsylvania remained a central locus for homeopathic activity. In 1917 Pennsylvania had fourteen homeopathic hospitals, six of them in Philadelphia.[64] As late as 1933 Dean Pearson told his "hand-picked" freshmen that they had chosen the "best medical college in the world" and "were a very select and chosen few who had been awarded the privilege of studying medicine, and more especially the . . . privilege of studying the Homeopathic Practice of Medicine."[65] And some of the Hahnemann professors played public roles as homeopathic professionals: in the 1920s Herbert Northrop and Morris Golden were presidents of the state homeopathic society, as were, in the 1930s, Joseph Clay, Harlan Wells, and Garth Boericke. Boericke was also president of the AIH in 1932.

Nonetheless, being a homeopathic educator after Flexner meant constantly being on the defensive. Although faculty members publicly warned that only a properly supported homeopathic school could provide the large numbers of homeopathic physicians demanded by the public, within their ranks they admitted that homeopathy was less popular with patients, students, and the public. The faculty began to play down its homeopathic identity. As early as 1918 the faculty urged every colleague to become a member of the orthodox Philadelphia County Medical Society, in order to "justify his position in the Homeopathic School by attending all meetings of the Phila. County Society and to take an active interest in all proceedings tending to advance interest in scientific medicine."[66] That not all agreed with this position was demonstrated when the debate resurfaced in the 1920s over whether any member of the faculty or hospital staff should be permitted to be a member of "Old School" county, state, or national societies (this did not include the AAMC).[67] But by the late 1930s it was clear that the issue had tacitly been resolved, as a number of the faculty began listing their membership in societies such as the Philadelphia County Medical Society and the AMA. In the 1930s, the Alumni Association, which was more conservative than the faculty, began to push for Hahnemann faculty members to publicly identify themselves as homeopaths. In 1938 William Hunsicker, an officer of the Alumni Association, a clinical professor of urology, and a representative of the local homeopathic society, wrote in vain to the trustees asking them to require that all faculty be members of their local, state, and national homeopathic societies.[68]

This sense of defensiveness and professional inferiority permeated student ranks. In a satirical examination of the school's admissions and promotions policies, seniors outlined the following requirements for admission to advanced standing:

(a) Have been refused admission at some previous time,
(b) Have substituted the first two years at some dominant school,
(c) Swear by homeopathy and sneer at the rest of the world.[69]

In the 1928 yearbook, Higinio Mendoza, a twenty-six-year-old Filipino senior, argued in a piece entitled "A Misconception" that "a number of people have the erroneous impression that the Hahnemann Medical College teaches nothing but homeopathic therapeutics, and that its graduates are not cognizant of Old School methods." But, in fact, Mendoza explained, "this institution gives full and thorough instruction in Allopathic therapeutics as well as the specialty of Homeopathic therapeutics. In this additional method of therapy lies the only difference between a homeopathic medical college and others."[70]

In the 1920s it remained true that most of Hahnemann's students were attracted to the school because they had some interest in homeopathy or some family connections to the school. Boericke's department had a student proving squad, and students at the School of Science, Hahnemann's premedical school, were taught the "principles of homeopathy" by college dermatology professor Ralph Bernstein with the goal of making them "true and practical followers of Samuel Hahnemann."[71] Students at the college sought out indications that Philadelphia was not the only urban center active in homeopathic education. In Chicago, the 1929 yearbook remarked, there was a drive for a new homeopathic college and hospital to be known as the "Mid-West Homeopathic Institute," and in Cleveland there were plans for a new college. Boston had a postgraduate institution run by the American Foundation for Homeopathy, which offered summer courses that were "growing rapidly." These "many events," one student commented, "are occurring to indicate that the ostracism and ill-will of the last century are nearly over."[72]

Hahnemann students also noted proudly that homeopathy was not losing its place in the international arena. The 1929 yearbook pointed to the four homeopathic schools in the Americas: in New York, in Philadelphia, and in Rio de Janeiro and Mexico's Faculty of Medicine and Surgery of the Hahnemann Institute, with some two hundred students. In a disturbing way, homeopathy seemed to be becoming an alternative medical system especially well suited to groups aspiring to cultural or ethnic superiority. Observers could point to the homeopathic personal physicians to Britain's Prince of Wales and the kings of Italy and Spain, as well as Joel Boone's appointment as physician to Presidents Harding, Coolidge, and Hoover. In Germany over the preceding five years homeopathy had "progressed with great strides," students noted with pride. The University of Stuttgart had a homeopathic postgraduate college, "which does not have room to care for all who are clamoring for entrance," and the University of Berlin, a chair of homeopathy.[73] Homeopathy continued to gain support in Germany during the 1930s, attracting the interest of a number of Nazi leaders.

These yearbook remarks were deliberately polemical. Within the walls of the college and the hospital, students faced a confusing dichotomy between homeopathic tradition and medical science. The Student Health Service, for example, founded in 1937, was run by a physician who practiced regular medicine, but he had a homeopathic assistant. At the hospital pharmacy, as seniors in 1934 described it, "one pharmacist dispenses the homeopathic remedies while another is employed for the standard physiological preparations."[74] Wyrth Baker recalled his senior clerkship at the hospital in 1929: "When you were working under a homeopathic professor you used homeopathic medicines, under a non-homeopathic [teacher] you used non-homeopathics."[75] A telling sign that homeopathy was no longer the assumed professional identity of all Hahnemann students came in 1933, when a group formed the Hahnemann Research Society, with Garth Boericke as its faculty sponsor, for the purpose of "cultivating Homeopathic knowledge and thought." Members met with Philadelphia homeopaths in their homes, and "in this way intimate, informal contacts are had with practitioners who use successfully Homeopathy in their therapeutics."[76]

College homeopathic students began to boast of their prowess as diagnosticians and clinicians; as one yearbook editor explained it in 1930, "acceptance of Homeopathy has always been by the intelligent minority; for despite the simplicity of the law, there is nothing easy about its practice."[77] Praising homeopathy for its therapeutic efficacy was a well-worn argument among homeopathic supporters; suggesting that its strength lay in its complexity did not seem convincing. Nonetheless, the argument that homeopathic training produced skilled clinicians was well suited to Hahnemann's role as a practical school. In 1918, one 1893 graduate described homeopathy as "the broad, general practice of medicine [that] embraces any agent or means by which sick people can be made well or suffering ones relieved" and, as a way of clarifying the meaning of Hahnemann's double degree, reminded his peers that they graduated "as doctors of medicine first, and, in addition to that, doctors of homeopathic medicine."[78]

In practice, however, many of the physicians at the college and hospital did not use homeopathy; as one student commented in 1931: "Prescriptions, so far as possible, should be solely for recognized homeopathic medicines."[79] By the 1930s the formal teaching of homeopathy at the college had become somewhat routine and was easy for students to mock. Every year Garth Boericke read his notes on "principles of homeopathy" to the first-year class. His lectures on practice to seniors had moved from showing how to understand and individuate symptoms to describing a set list of homeopathic drugs and the generalized physical and psychological profiles or types they were best suited to, a kind of cookbook homeopathy. As one satirical yearbook put it, Boericke's lectures "emphasize that all drugs were probably first proven by Hahnemann and are pocket case remedies without which one could not risk a trip to the corner cigar store. Clinical tips abound as to the value of the sixth decimal trituration of the auro of the blue moose for curing oboe players who find it difficult to urinate in the teeth of a strong wind."[80]

In 1935 senior Charles Cameron, who became Hahnemann's dean and president in the 1950s and 1960s, was called into Dean Pearson's office. Pearson asked him to organize "something entertaining" for the one hundredth anniversary of the founding of the Allentown Academy to be performed at the college following a ceremony at the original school in Allentown. Cameron wrote a play he entitled "A New School for the New School," set in Constantine Hering's parlor in 1834. Based, he later recollected, not on research but on his own imagination, the play centered on a debate about whether to found a homeopathic school. After an "impassioned" discussion the group of homeopaths voted "aye" or "ja" in favor, and there was a "boisterous tumult of rejoicing" which Hering quieted "with his gavel." "The curtain falls on a scene of jubilation and gemutlichkeit," Cameron recalled at a historical symposium fifty years later. The play was performed only once, and according to Cameron: "For this production my roommate, Charles Dotterer in the role of [William] Wesselhoeft, got carried away in the spirit of the thing and rented a false beard. At that point he indulged in some unrehearsed by-play and, to my complete astonishment, pulled out a cigar and lit it. In his nervousness he also lit his beard, which was quickly snatched off by the doctor from Hellertown."[81]

Although the popular press in Philadelphia continued to report on the homeopathic state society's annual meetings throughout the 1920s and 1930s, homeopaths as a distinctive group were getting less public attention and respect. For those Hahnemann graduates and faculty members who were not visible in the public homeopathic profession, the practice of homeopathy became more a therapeutic choice than a medical identity. The college had prided itself as an educator in therapy when other medical schools ignored the subject; but now Boericke's Department of Therapeutics, formerly a pivotal place for homeopathic teaching, contained an eclectic group of therapy experts, including radiologists and physical therapists. Hahnemann graduates found that even though homeopathy was no longer a central feature of their education, the professional stigma remained. Internships and residencies at orthodox hospitals were closed to them, as well as many professional associations. Not until the late 1940s did the Philadelphia County Medical Society and the prestigious College of Physicians of Philadelphia admit Hahnemann graduates.

Resisting Women at Hahnemann

Chiropractic and osteopathic schools had opened their doors to women from the beginning, and the Philadelphia College of Osteopathic Medicine established in 1899 had women professors on its faculty. Homeopaths in other cities had embraced the idea of homeopathy as offering an alternative kind of medical profession, but Philadelphia's Hahnemann Medical College had resisted. Even as

Figure 18. Inside cover, untitled 1907 student yearbook. During the 1890s and 1900s Hahnemann students began intermittently to put out a yearbook, offering a lighthearted but revealing look at their culture and educational experiences. The typical Hahnemann student was, as seen here, a white, Protestant, middle-class man.

the college became conscious that it was becoming one of the few and then the only homeopathic medical school in the country, its faculty consistently refused to admit women students. While the school's stated goals were to encourage the spread of homeopathy and homeopathic practitioners, and while many nineteenth-century male homeopaths had prided themselves on the high proportion of homeopathic physicians who were women (which one historian has estimated was around 12 percent compared to 5 or 6 percent of regular practitioners),[82] Hahnemann faculty continued the school's conservative exclusionary tradition.

During the 1910s the school was under persistent pressure to admit women, especially as women homeopaths settled in Philadelphia, became established members of the local and state homeopathic societies, and ran their own Philadelphia hospital, the Women's Southern Homeopathic Hospital. Female homeopathic groups also consistently supported the school financially; both the Woman's Homeopathic League of Pennsylvania and the Women's National Homeopathic League, for example, raised money for student scholarships.[83] But one group of faculty—all alumni—remained adamantly opposed to the admission of women and continued to view their exclusion as part of the school's proud nineteenth-century heritage. Indeed much of the faculty and student culture was a comfortably segregated one of clubs, sports teams, and smoking rooms, a world of male exclusiveness where women had accepted but tangential roles, like housekeeper and secretary.[84]

With the threatening decline in student enrollment that resulted from the state's 1918 requirement for two years of college, the issue returned, and it became clear that the faculty was divided, the trustees were open, and the Alumni Association was adamantly opposed. In 1918 Harlan Wells, a member of the Department of Medicine, published an article in the *Hahnemannian Monthly* praising the recent "growing sentiment in favor of co-education at Hahnemann." Wells commented on the active part women were playing in social service, public health, and laboratory work during the war.[85] Spurred perhaps by the passing of the Twentieth Amendment granting the vote to women, in 1919 the Hahnemann faculty formed a committee to investigate coeducation, but the vote the following year was ten for, nineteen against.[86] At a special meeting of the faculty called to discuss the issue again in 1928, Edward Steinhilber (1886–1980), head of the Department of Neurology, quoted testimonials from former (male) class presidents of the coeducational Johns Hopkins Medical School as evidence against the idea; the vote was eleven in favor, twenty-six against.[87] Women were admitted finally in 1941, but as late as 1938 the faculty executive decided not to accept women who applied for intern positions at Hahnemann Hospital.[88] This consistent resistance to coeducation can be explained partly as an effort to hold on to the "Old Hahnemann" tradition, which was threatened by German sciences, educational reform, and new therapies; many alumni saw these threats as implicit attacks on their training and identity as Hahnemann men.

Without public debate, in this same era, Hahnemann stopped admitting African-American students, perhaps as a response to the wider racism in American culture, which had led to a reemergence of the Ku Klux Klan and President Woodrow Wilson's resegregation of the federal bureaucracy in Washington. When the widow of Lemuel Taylor Sewall (1887–1973), one of Hahnemann's last black graduates, was asked about her husband's experience at Hahnemann from 1907 to 1911 she replied that he had had "four friends."[89] A more likely explanation for the decision to resegregate Hahnemann was the school's growing responsiveness to the local and national medical culture; in Philadelphia and across the United States medical schools were not accepting even the token black students that they had in the previous decade.[90] Flexner had made it clear in his report that he felt that black physicians needed to be trained as "sanitarians" for the black community. With the survival of Howard and Meharry, other schools chose to try to homogenize their student body. However, financial pressures would prevent Hahnemann from following this path, and by the end of the 1940s it had become an educator of a diverse range of students too often denied entrance to other Philadelphia schools.

Chapter 4	Survival through Diversity

The 1920s and 1930s

In 1910 ABRAHAM FLEXNER examined fifteen homeopathic medical schools; by 1922 only Hahnemann and the New York Homeopathic Medical College remained.[1] How did Hahnemann survive and how did it continue to remain homeopathic? These are the crucial questions that we must ask in exploring the history of Hahnemann in the interwar period.

To answer these questions, we must recognize that, contrary to the expectations of regular physicians in the 1890s, unorthodox medicine did not disappear with the impressive achievements of German medical science. The American public had become fascinated with the heroes and culture of scientific medicine, and their fascination was epitomized by the use of men in white coats to sell products ranging from deodorants to cigarettes and by the popularity of Hollywood films such as *Arrowsmith* (1931) and *The Story of Louis Pasteur* (1936). But the lay public also continued to support healers whose views conflicted with and were sometimes antagonistic to mainstream modern medicine. Osteopathy and chiropractic, both founded at the outset of the bacteriology revolution, were expanding and were legally protected by state licensing boards. In 1923, for example, forty-six states legally recognized osteopaths; by 1930 twenty-five states licensed chiropractors; and by 1938 all but seven states had laws recognizing such practitioners. In 1932 one study estimated that almost one-quarter of American healers were unorthodox practitioners.[2] Christian Scientists continued to speak out against modern medical technology; antivivisectionists continued their campaigns to gain state regulation of medical research; and birth control advocates such as Margaret Sanger were publicly critical of organized medicine's refusal to discuss contraceptive technology or teach it systematically in medical school.[3]

Hahnemann Medical College was able to withstand the continuing regular attacks on homeopathy, spearheaded by Morris Fishbein, the editor of the *Journal of the American Medical Association*, by expanding its physical space with a new hospital in 1928 that allowed the college to move into the old hospital building that had been built in 1890. Hahnemann also formed a premedical institution called the School of Science, which operated from 1916 to 1929 and was used as a "feeder" to the college. The School of Science, which offered a bachelor of science after two years of study, attracted students who otherwise might not have come to Hahnemann, and it also attracted students anxious to study medicine but prevented from doing so by their class, race, ethnicity, or religion. After Hahnemann closed the school it continued this policy of admissions diversity, and while it, like other American medical schools, retained a quota for Jews and Catholics, Hahnemann's percentage remained somewhat higher than at other city schools, a situation that continued into the 1960s.

Although the strategies pursued by Hahnemann's trustees and faculty tended to be reactive rather than visionary, they can be summed up as stability, integration, and expansion. The school's stability came primarily from its senior faculty, almost all Hahnemann alumni, who both created new traditions and continued the traditions of what came to be known as "Old Hahnemann." Although faculty members were mostly barred from orthodox medical associations and students found it difficult to gain internships in any hospitals other than those founded by homeopaths and still part of a homeopathic network, Hahnemann's teachers and especially its students nonetheless felt themselves an integrated part of the American medical culture. Orthodox groups may have considered Hahnemann men outsiders, but in their politics, student life, and professional aspirations they differed little from medical students and physicians across the country.

Hahnemann Faculty after Flexner

Hahnemann's great success through these turbulent years was not only surviving but also maintaining a presence in Philadelphia medical education while retaining its homeopathic identity. Even after surviving the derisive criticisms in Abraham Flexner's 1910 report, Hahnemann had to confront a reinvigorated attack on unorthodox medicine. The 1920s and 1930s saw the rise of a new sense of orthodoxy among the leaders of the AMA. Those "outside" organized medicine were now commonly designated not as "sects" but as "cults," a term suggesting that these groups sought not to convert patients to a sincerely held belief in an alternative medical view but to dangerously and deliberately brainwash the American public. The terms "cults" and "cultist" also linked together, in ways Flexner had not done, so-called drugless healers like Christian Scientists, who distrusted medical intervention, with unorthodox practitioners like osteopaths, naturopaths, and homeopaths, who did use drugs and other medical technologies.

This vision of unorthodox medicine as cultist was promulgated most fervently by Morris Fishbein, the man who became clearly identified in the public mind as the "voice" of orthodox American medicine. In 1924 Fishbein was appointed as editor of the *Journal of the American Medical Association* and the AMA's popular health magazine *Hygeia,* and he held those positions until 1949. In the mid-1920s he began writing articles that vehemently attacked what he called the "Healing Cults," and he collected these articles in a study entitled *The Medical Follies,* in which he placed homeopaths together with osteopaths, chiropractors, antivivisectionists, birth control advocates, and supporters of government health insurance.

Samuel Hahnemann, Fishbein claimed, had been neither a creative nor a careful scientist, had borrowed his ideas from Paracelsus, and had allowed "all kinds of more or less qualified individuals" to test his medicine.[4] Fishbein did acknowledge that two of "the world's greatest medical historians" had argued that the influence of homeopathy had been "on the whole, certainly for the good," at least in individualizing the patient and showing the value of testing drugs by trial. But, "the fact is," he concluded, "homeopathy died from within," for—and here he used Flexner's argument about alternative groups—"scientific medicine absorbs from them that which is good, if there is any good, and then they die."[5]

Homeopaths were frustrated with Fishbein's efforts to place homeopathy in the same category as the Christian Science movement and other movements that explicitly rejected the teachings of modern science. In their own analyses of American medicine, they tried to separate themselves from such groups by designating them as "non-medical cults."[6] Critics of Fishbein and medical orthodoxy pointed out that homeopaths were part of the medical profession and hardly drugless healers; modern homeopaths, Annie Riley Hale wrote in her rejoinder to Fishbein's *Medical Follies,* subscribe "loyally to all the fallacies and barbarities of modern Medicine, even borrowing some of its bigotry."[7] An awareness both of the bad press homeopathy was receiving and of the lessening interest in homeopathy among the lay public and prospective students was reflected in the founding in 1921 of the American Foundation for Homeopathy, a lay group dedicated to educating the public.[8]

In struggling to integrate homeopathic tradition with the new scientific medicine, Hahnemann reconstituted itself as a pragmatic facility and achieved a stable place in Philadelphia medical training and health care. Until World War II it mostly hired its own graduates, men whose homeopathic training made it almost impossible for them to obtain academic positions elsewhere but whose influence in Philadelphia and the surrounding region ensured a critical referral network for students seeking hospital positions and private patients. The school consolidated its new identity with an extraordinarily low faculty turnover: between 1910 and 1945, of twenty-eight heads of departments, twenty-two held their positions for over ten years, and, of those, six headed their departments for more than twenty years.

The school's administration, after a decade of upheavals at the beginning of the century, was consolidated impressively under the leadership of a dean who retained that position for thirty years. In 1895, after twenty-one years as college dean, Amos Thomas died. During the next two decades the college had a series of short-term deans, all Hahnemann graduates: obstetrician John Edwin James, 1895–1896; Pemberton Dudley, 1896–1903; ophthalmologist Charles Monroe Thomas, 1903–1906; surgeon and anatomist Herbert L. Northrop, 1906–1910; and surgeon William Van Lennep, 1910–1914. After Van Lennep was toppled in the wake of the Flexner report, the trustees chose chemistry professor William Alexander Pearson (1879–1957) as dean, and he remained dean from 1914 to 1943. Although Pearson over time lost much of his administrative power to a small group of clinical faculty who had the ears of the trustees, his long tenure provided stability and predictability to Hahnemann. Only in the mid-1940s was the administration again transformed, as an opposing group of faculty—both clinicians and basic scientists, dissatisfied with the school's declining reputation and standards—began to push for organizational change and was able to pressure resistant trustees by turning to outside professional bodies. Breaching Hahnemann's entrenched stability and altering its faculty, structure, and institutional mission were achieved only with great friction and upheaval, as we will see later.

Unusual in Hahnemann's history, Pearson was neither a Philadelphian, nor a Hahnemann graduate, nor a physician. Born in Ohio, Pearson had studied chemistry at the University of Michigan (Ph.D. 1902) and, after a brief career as a commercial research chemist, had begun teaching as professor of chemistry in the college in 1909.[9] Throughout his deanship Pearson headed the Department of Chemistry, which played a prominent role in socializing students, in part because chemistry was the first lecture every day for all freshmen. Numerous yearbooks report the caution, "Nine o'clock, point zero, zero, zero," with which Pearson concluded each one of his annual introductory lectures, reminding new students to be punctual for their first class of the day.[10]

Pearson also played an important role in selecting students. Students remembered him as "the first man to greet us when we applied for a medical education,"[11] and he seems to have told every new group of freshmen that they were his "hand-picked class."[12] An article on him in a Philadelphia newspaper in 1932 described him as a "rare judge of men" who

Figure 19. Seated at his office desk in the college is William Alexander Pearson, dean of Hahnemann Medical College from 1914 to 1943 and for many years Hahnemann's "admissions committee." *Medic* 1930.

> for 20 years has been interviewing applicants to the medical school and watching their reactions [when he says] "If I were you, I'd go back home and forget it. The study of medicine is a long, heartbreaking thing. Maybe you think you're the exception, that you'll get along where others have failed. If you have any illusion on that score let me tell you that 20 per cent of the medical students in the United States fail to finish the course. . . . If I were you I'd study something else."[13]

In their yearbook the graduates of 1933, for example, remembered being described as "the one hundred and seventy select" and imagined Pearson sitting at his mahogany desk looking at the stack of applications:

> [There] sat Dr. Pearson, moulding from that stack of papers his creation, the Class of '33. He worked rapidly yet deliberately because ours was to be a "hand-picked" class. Here was a letter from an applicant in Iowa; another from a doctor's son in Indiana; here an alumnus has recommended this man, and still another from South Philadelphia. Each must be weighed in its turn to determine, if possible, the fitness of the men to administer to the ills of the people. Gradually, carefully he

created. . . . After days of tireless effort a secretary was called and this list was given to him. "There are the hand-picked men," he said.[14]

Pearson's admission decisions were ratified by the board of trustees, whose political friends, such as state senators, also felt they had a singular opportunity to recommend and enforce the admission of individual students. The school's financial and status problems in this period left it particularly vulnerable to political pressure. In the Pennsylvania legislature the college could count on the support of Senator Ernest Tustin (1862–1921), who was a member of its board of trustees.[15] But Tustin died in 1921, and although Hahnemann continued to benefit from state appropriation—receiving twenty-five thousand dollars in 1928, for example—the school had to rely on other, hidden ways of ensuring state support. For example, during the 1920s, and probably beyond that period, the college admitted students "recommended" by state senators and provided them with a "scholarship" (that is, waived their tuition fees).[16]

In addition to the long tenure of Dean Pearson, the tight and parochial relations between the college's senior faculty members, who were tied together by their shared experience as former Hahnemann students, further consolidated the stability of the college. By 1920 most of the college's senior teachers of the 1880s and 1890s had died: Dean Amos Thomas died in 1895, his son Charles in 1916, Benjamin Franklin Betts in 1909, William Bigler in 1904, Bushrod Washington James in 1903, his brother John Edwin James in 1910, Charles Mohr in 1907, Erving Howard in 1904, and William Van Lennep in 1919.

The few professors who had been teaching at the college since before the 1890s all retired in 1925 when the board of trustees mandated that professors retire at age sixty-five. Rufus Weaver (1841–1936), for example, had been teaching anatomy at Hahnemann since the 1870s. He became a professor of applied anatomy in 1911 and retired in 1925 at the age of eighty-four. Oliver Sloan Haines (1860–1936) who had taught obstetrics at Hahnemann in the 1880s, became the Hering Professor of Materia Medica and Therapeutics in 1909 and headed the Department of Therapeutics until he retired in 1925 at sixty-five. Clarence Bartlett (1858–1936), an 1879 graduate, had taught neurology at the college since the late 1880s. He became professor of medicine in 1909 and headed the Department of Medicine until his retirement in 1925 at the age of sixty-seven.

The new group of men who became the established face of Hahnemann in the interwar period were classmates from the 1890s and students of the group that retired in 1925. That this new group headed the major college departments from the 1920s into the 1940s reflects the static nature of both the structure of and the teaching at the institution. Family connections continued to play a role in the selection of senior positions, as they had in the 1870s and 1880s. In 1908, for example, John E. James Jr., a 1902 graduate and the son of obstetrician and gynecologist John E. James (class of 1886), became head of the Department of Obstetrics, a position he held for thirty years. In 1910, when James senior retired as head of gynecology, David Bushrod James (class of 1896), the son of Bushrod Washington James and nephew of John E. James, took his uncle's place and held the position until his own death in 1932. In 1919, after the death of surgeon William Van Lennep (class of 1880), Herbert Northrop, an 1889 graduate who had been teaching at the college since the 1890s, became the new head of surgery, and when Northrop retired in 1935 he was replaced by Gustave Van Lennep (class of 1894), William's nephew.

Like professors at all American medical schools in the first half of the twentieth century, Hahnemann's professors were private practitioners, many of them specialists. The faculty's relations with their patients helped to anchor the college to the community and also brought the physicians significant academic influence. In both the college and the hospital, the senior clinical men were the most powerful, not only because they were well respected and often wealthy but also because their patients frequently became trustees and major donors. In fact, Hahnemann depended on these clinicians as a means of ameliorating the institution's consistent financial problems, which were exacerbated by the Great Depression. In 1935, for example, the college's new provost, Frederic von Rapp, praised the ten men on the hospital staff who "send to the institution, yearly, between twenty and thirty thousand dollars of work." He found, however,

> numerous instances where men of our faculty and homeopathic persuasion have permitted families with considerable financial resources to go unapproached as to making contributions to the Hospital. While I realize that this, to some, may seem like taking an undue advantage of their position of trust, one must remember that if they neglect to put in a good word for their own institution, in the end someone else will do it and attract their interest and charitable inclination toward some other institution. May I suggest—if you have a rich patient, that from time to time you drop the suggestion that Hahnemann is in need of money and that they should either make a contribution now or write such in their wills.[17]

Or, as Dean Pearson asked, a few years later, with a building plan in mind: "Have you a wealthy patient who would be willing to pay for the equipment of one or more of these new laboratories?"[18]

Hahnemann did not adopt Flexner's full-time model and did not put senior clinical faculty on salary until the 1950s. From the 1910s on, however, the college did pay some basic science teachers a salary. In this practice the college resembled most other American schools with limited endowments: they could not afford to match the income that successful specialists could command but were able to pay men who made their careers more as academic teachers than as private practitioners. In 1913 Hahnemann had seven men on salary: William Pearson as dean and head of chemistry; Rufus Weaver as professor of applied anatomy; Samuel Sappington as head of pathology; a lecturer on pharmacy; and three demonstrators, one in anatomy, one in pathology and bacteriology, and one in histology.[19] By the mid-1920s, a time when the income of a specialist was around ten thousand dollars, Pearson, Sappington, and Widman were paid three thousand dollars each; and Thomas Phillips, an associate professor of anatomy identified as "full time" in the college budget, was paid five thousand dollars. The only anomaly that made Hahnemann distinctive among medical schools was the salaried position of Garth Boericke, professor of materia medica and head of the Department of Therapeutics, who was hired in 1926 at a salary of five thousand dollars.[20] Boericke was a clinician, a basic scientist, and the teacher of the college's required homeopathic theory courses. The existence of a separate department of therapeutics—which was not abolished until the 1950s, when Boericke retired—shows the continuing legacy of Hahnemann's homeopathic past.

The faculty members who held their positions from the 1910s and 1920s into the 1940s helped to give the college a distinctive character. As teachers they cultivated personas and kept alive Hahnemann's old traditions and continually created new ones. They were closely connected with student life and culture: they invited students to annual parties, sponsored student study and social groups, and gave speeches at student, faculty, and community gatherings. In many of these ways, the school's golden years continued with the large group of alumni who had become teachers. A particularly large number of the faculty during this period had graduated in the 1890s, including Sappington and Van Lennep; John Jay Tuller (1861–1931), who became professor of neurology in 1905 and headed the Department of Neurology until he retired in 1925; Frank H. Widman (1871–1939), who was professor of physiology until his death; Charles Sigmund Raue (1873–1965), who was professor of pediatrics until 1945; and laryngologist Harry Sands Weaver (1868–1938), who headed the Department of Oto-Laryngology and Rhinology from 1924 until his death in 1938. Graduates from the 1900s who gained senior positions included the James cousins; George Harlan Wells (1880–1970), head of the Department of Medicine from 1931 to 1948; and Frank Orthmer Nagle (1884–1957), head of a new Department of Ophthalmology created in 1935.

Many of these men remained vivid in the memories of their students. Sappington, for example, was remembered as an austere man with a dry wit, always hurrying off to his laboratory after lectures; this laboratory, at the back of the main hall, had a red line drawn on the floor in front of it so that students learned never to enter.[21] "He was so austere," one yearbook claimed, "that when the lab wanted a frozen tissue section they merely had him look at that tissue."[22] Hahnemann alumnus Horst Agerty, a 1934 graduate, remembers that Sappington "looked down" on homeopathy as "a sort of quackery" without saying so "in so many words," and his oral exams were tough and feared.[23] The lecture hall's seats were numbered, and Sappington was one of the professors who carefully counted heads.[24] His white coat and horn-rimmed spectacles were so distinctive that they were easily parodied in post–final exam celebrations like one by the 1928 seniors.[25] Dean Pearson not only interviewed almost every college applicant but was famous for ending his exams by telling his students to "put a caboose on it."[26] Thomas Phillips (1887–1975), teacher of anatomy, always began his first lecture with the words "Men, the clavicle."[27] The jokes, lines, and stories about these teachers became part of Hahnemann life and legend.

The way of speaking and the personal habits of these teachers defined both a student's four-year training and his memories and conceptions of the college. Obstetrics professor John E. James Jr. was, one yearbook claimed, "a human being who could speak at the rate of two hundred words a minute and enunciate each and every syllable very clearly and completely without as much as swallowing." Students tried to take notes but then decided that they "might better supplement [their] notes with the mimeographed sheets put out by the student-company of Ridall and Maxwell."[28] James conducted his exams on the fifth floor of the hospital's women's building, and in the 1928 yearbook, students described suddenly hearing their names being called and being told, "have a chair doctor—go ahead and smoke if you care to—well, let's see what you know about Obstetrics."[29] Joseph Hepburn, or "Heppy," a 1913 Ph.D. from Columbia University, was both the associate chemistry professor and also a teacher and archivist at his alma mater, Central High School, and he provided a connection for the many Hahnemann students and faculty who were Central High alumni as well. One graduate remembered him as a bald-headed "typical absent-minded professor" who wore long baggy suits.[30]

A few professors were not Hahnemann graduates, including Garth Boericke; although he was respected as a diagnostician and clinician, his compulsory homeopathy courses became easy targets of student mockery. Born in 1893, Boericke had received his homeopathic M.D. from the University of Michigan in 1908, but he claimed association with Hahnemann through his family connection with Philadelphia's prominent homeopathic pharmaceutical firm, Boericke and Tafel. Boericke "kept us awake" even in the dry subjects of materia medica, Wyrth Post Baker (class of 1930) recalled.[31] The other non-Hahnemann men who gained senior positions during the 1930s were basic scientists who were hired to placate external complaints that the college was too parochial and not scientifically rigorous enough. In 1936 Reinhold Beutner, who had an M.D. and a Ph.D. from the University of Berlin, was appointed head of a new Department of Pharmacology created by the college to demonstrate a commitment to scientific research in pharmacology separate from the analysis of homeopathic drugs. Beutner, whose thick German accent gained him the nickname "Desert Fox," was attracted to Hahnemann through his interest in homeopathy, which he pursued in postgraduate work at the college.[32] Stanley Reimann, a 1913 University of Pennsylvania graduate, was appointed head of a new Department of Oncology created in 1939, probably in recognition of the public's increasing interest in cancer research, which was reflected, for example, by the establishment two years earlier of the National Cancer Institute.[33] Physiologist John Scott (1900–1978), who had a 1929 Ph.D. from the University of Pennsylvania, had worked under Frank Widman in the 1920s and 1930s, and after Widman's death in 1939 Scott became head of the Department of Physiology and remained there until 1968. Scott, committed to teaching students research skills through active laboratory instruction, was considered by later accreditation committees as one of the few praiseworthy preclinical faculty.

Connections among most of the faculty and students, many of whom were members of the same college fraternities, reinforced the school's sense of ethnic and cultural coherency. While throughout the interwar years the college did accept Jewish and Italian students, the faculty did not reflect this diversity. Morris Golden (1876–1931), an 1899 graduate, was one of Hahnemann's few Jewish senior faculty members and the only Jewish department head in this period. A respected homeopathic clinician and in 1922 president of the state homeopathic society, Golden headed the Department of Medicine from 1925 until his death in 1931. Bacteriologist Grant Orante Favorite (1903–1948) was the only Italian senior faculty member before the 1950s. Favorite, born in Italy in 1903, had come to Hahnemann to do premedical work, and he graduated with his M.D in 1927. After studying bacteriology at Harvard with the eminent bacteriologist Hans Zinsser and then working in Sappington's pathology department, he was appointed head of the new Department of Bacteriology in 1941.

Neither the personnel nor the curriculum of the college altered much in the interwar period. There was some expansion, with the number of departments growing from ten in 1920 to eighteen by 1943, the year Pearson resigned. Some of these changes were in keeping with national trends—the department of pediatrics established in 1925, for example—but others reflected the college's individualist response to physicians who brought money or influential patients and patrons. In 1925, for example, the trustees offered gastroenterologist Harry Martin Eberhard (1866–1962) his own department of gastroenterology. Eberhard, an 1898 graduate born in Philadelphia, had interned at Hahnemann Hospital and then studied in Berlin and London. He was appointed a lecturer in gastroenterology in 1915 and a clinical professor in 1916, and he remained head of the Department of Gastroenterology from 1925 until 1958. Students admired him for his professional success and his teaching style. In 1935 the seniors dedicated their yearbook to him:

> for his keen interest in our welfare as students
> for his admirable knowledge of gastroenterology
> for his scientific approach to medical problems.

But the following class satirized him as "his Excellency of the belly-ache."[34] Wyrth Baker, who was his assistant in the early 1930s, recalled him as a "good businessman with a high class practice" who had a "wonderful bedside manner" and "would tell people what they wanted to hear."[35]

Although a homeopath by training and inclination, Eberhard, like many of his colleagues, nonetheless showed himself professionally adaptable in his affiliations, and by the early 1940s he was a member of the AMA and the regular Philadelphia County Medical Society. Although he was prominent and extraordinarily powerful within the college, he did not play a role as a public homeopath. That is, unlike other prominent Hahnemann professors in this period, he never became president of the state or local homeopathic society. Eberhard was a successful physician, and he gained his wealth by practicing a form of gastric irrigation that attracted many rich patients, including some of the college trustees. By the 1940s he had, a graduate later recalled, "all the Board members in his back pocket."[36] Sidney Zubrow (1913–), a 1938 graduate, remembered Eberhard as "the head of the Board," and Zubrow remains grateful to Eberhard for helping him to get a leave of absence that was normally against school policy.[37]

Both Eberhard and urologist Leon T. Ashcraft (1866–1945), an 1890 graduate who was appointed head of the new Department of Urology in 1925, quickly became members of the College Committee of the Board of Trustees, which decided the major administrative and academic issues in the college.[38] By the mid-1940s, as AMA and AAMC representatives were later shocked to discover, Eberhard was the only member of the faculty on the board and also a member of every major college committee. Although Eberhard's influence was increasingly resented by other college teachers, his fellow board members protected him and refused to hear anything against him. When, in 1930, he was accused of sending a series of anonymous letters to other members of the faculty and a typewriter expert argued the letters were written on Eberhard's typewriter, the trustees claimed this was not conclusive evidence and refused to proceed further.[39] Through incidents such as this one, members of the faculty quickly recognized that power at Hahnemann came not through teaching or research prowess or through loyalty to the school or to the alumni but through personal connections to trustees and to patients who could become patrons of Hahnemann. Trustees reinforced this feeling by permitting the faculty less and less control over administrative and academic affairs.[40] In 1935 they created the new position of provost, appointing Frederic von Rapp, a board member, to oversee both the hospital and the college, and in 1940 the board appointed Eberhard to a new position as vice president of medical affairs with jurisdiction over the dean, the admission of all new students, and "all things medical connected with the College and Hospital."[41]

A Hahnemann Novel

In 1929, William Trites, son of 1896 Hahnemann graduate Charles Sutton Trites and grandson of 1869 Hahnemann graduate William Budd Trites, published *Paterfamilias*, a fictional study of William R. Stanton, a small-town homeopathic physician living in Wawa, Pennsylvania, around 1910. Trites drew on the experiences of his father and grandfather, and his town of Wawa closely resembles Manyunk, Trites's hometown. Stanton is a graduate of Hahnemann who becomes a professor at the college, and his son Jack is a student there. William Stanton is a good man and a good, old-fashioned doctor living in a modern cynical world that resembles the 1920s more than the 1910s. His patients value him for his medical skills, but his sense of medical ethics and reforming spirit impress no one. As a homeopath he is flexible, willing to consult with regular physicians, and he believes in bacteriology. The novel provides an unusual source for exploring the generational shifts between Hahnemann teachers and students.

Jack attends Hahnemann Medical College and represents the selfish generation of the new century. Jack resents his dependence on his family, telling a friend "How would you like it . . . if you had six more years of schooling ahead of you? How would you like it, when you wanted a smoke, to have to ask your people for a dime to buy a box of cigarettes with? 'Gimme a dime, papa, to get my beard trimmed.'" Jack would like to leave Hahnemann and go to work, but he has no desire for any other career. He acknowledges that "work only appealed to him because it meant money, freedom from study, and evenings devoted wholly to the pursuit of *fun*."[42] Jack identifies homeopathy as socially and culturally inferior to mainstream medicine. He complains that his family is Methodist ("Why the hell wasn't I born an Episcopalian? That's the correct, fashionable religion") and that his father's medical ideas are also "all wrong": "Why'n hell's name did he want to study homeopathy? Homeopathy! It's damn near's bad as osteopathy." Jack is also conscious that his father's medical practice has not provided his family the kind of secure middle-class life they long for. Stanton has enough paying patients but is interested more in trying to reform his community than in billing his patients. Thus, the family spends its summer vacation at Ocean Grove rather than at Asbury Park (105–106). Jack secretly frequents clubs and pursues show girls, and, in order to sustain this profligate life, he steals money from his father. When his theft is discovered by his father, Jack is transformed into a repentant and serious medical student, winning college honors in order to use the prize money to help pay back his father.

Stanton, a man in his fifties, is almost a caricature of an older generation of physician and homeopath. As his son describes him, both with scorn and admiration: "how noble, how indomitable and how pathetic his father looked in his shabby frock coats! An unselfish man in a selfish world, a good man in a bad world, an honest player in a crooked game" (191). Trites makes clear that Stanton is "a good doctor and a good man" who treated "all the poor in Wawa for nothing" and has a book "on nervous diseases" that was "an authority" (16). Stanton refuses to rush to see the wife of a rich family, losing the family to the town's other homeopath after he tells the husband "there's nothing serious[ly] the matter with your wife. It's imagination mostly" (155). Stanton has cordial relations with the town's orthodox physician, but they are strained when a child breaks her leg and Stanton asks "old Doc Dalrymple, the allopath" to assist by giving the anesthetic to "save this child from torture." Dalrymple says, "No, sir. I can't consult with you. We regulars don't recognize homeopathy. You know that." Stanton reflects that "he would have to set the leg without an anesthetic, after all. Too bad, too bad" (174–175). Stanton's sense of ethics is established when he turns down the offer of a position as the head of the medical department of a private insurance company with the impressive salary of twelve thousand dollars after his businessman-sponsor announces that the doctor must drop his public protests against the pollution of the town's water caused by the local iron works (176–182).

As a homeopath Stanton is forward-thinking and has integrated his notion of homeopathy into the new medical sciences such as bacteriology. He distinguishes himself from an "old line homeopath," who "believed in homeopathy as Jimmy Bonner believed in the Bible, as if there had been no progress, no discoveries, no Pasteur" (341). The old-liner had been professor of materia medica at Hahnemann Medical College but had been kicked out and now "talked in a continual stream" against the "ultra-modern faculty" who, he claimed, "had abandoned Samuel Hahnemann's precepts" (342). Stanton, by contrast, astounds a neighbor by claiming that there is no difference between homeopathy and allopathy because "the germ theory has revolutionized medicine. It has made medicine as exact a science as surgery. No more blind beating about the bush. If you've got malaria it's because your blood is full of malaria germs, and there's only one way to cure you—that is, get rid of those germs. . . . The fact is, Pasteur showed us all up. We're all Pasteurians now" (327–328).[43] It is interesting to see Flexner's language of modern science as a universalizing force in medicine permeating even this novel, with its portrayal of the doctor as resolutely antimodern in most other things, for example, as compared to his children, who drink and smoke and drive a car instead of a horse and buggy as their father does.

Jack Stanton, representing the new generation in medicine as well as morals, tells a friend that he wants to "go in for medical research. Medical research is a splendid thing. . . . To discover the germ that causes a disease, and then to find out how to kill the germ and abolish the disease forever—that's worth devoting your life to, isn't it?" (289). His father also believes that "Medical research is the noblest calling in the world" (326). When Jack finally admits to his father that he wants to study "regular medicine," Stanton agrees reluctantly to let him leave Hahnemann for another school, saying "if you were a homeopath, you'd be barred from the big research laboratories, but now they'll be open to you, and you'll have a chance at all the scholarships and fellowships besides" (330). But Stanton still takes Jack's rejection as a personal betrayal and a betrayal of the family's medical tradition, and he says he himself will continue to practice homeopathy "out of sentiment" (331).

Stanton is appointed to the chair of clinical medicine at Hahnemann, a part-time position. He see his appointment primarily as a form of professional improvement: "This is a great chance for me. Woodruff leaves me all his lectures. What a chance to study and improve myself!" (205). Nevertheless, he is conscious of his limitations: "Three lectures a week. I could never get them up without Woodruff's notes to help me" (206). He receives no salary but explains to his family: "it's a great honor. Besides, there's a kind of salary in the long run. Your students, you see, because they learn from you year after year, come naturally to have faith in you; so when they graduate and begin to practice for themselves they call you in as a consultant" (206). His family members are excited with his position as a college professor not for its professional glory but for the social standing they expect it to bring. When Stanton considers raising his rich patients' rates from a dollar to a dollar and a half a visit, his confinement cases from ten to fifteen dollars, and his office prescriptions from fifty cents to seventy-five cents, his wife replies, "Why shouldn't you, Will? You're a professor now" (279). His family imagines him being promoted from professor to college dean, saying "you'll be taking us to live in one of those big brownstone houses in Walnut Street near Rittenhouse Square, and we'll have a butler and footman in livery" (268).

At Hahnemann, Stanton meets some of the real faculty, including William Van Lennep, Hahnemann's professor of surgery, who, Stanton reflects, is "a surgeon of renown, . . . a tall, robust chap, rich, fastidious, elegant, a club man, a society man, his opposite in external things, but a good deal his counterpart within" (268). Stanton worries about the difficulties of holding his position—which involves an hour-long train ride to Philadelphia three times a week and must be fitted in between his general practice in Wawa. "He thought of his lectures, to which he did not give enough time. Worst of all at the end of each lecture were the students' questions—those questions brought home his ignorance to him so painfully" (211). But during his lecture on pneumonia, faculty members listen attentively at the back of the room, and such is their respect for him that when Stanton is sick, "every night in turn a member of the faculty of Hahnemann, a pillar of the profession, watched by his . . . bed" (421). The students remind him of his son Jack: "They applauded heartily as he hurried in. A little out of breath, he stood in the cockpit and smiled up at those tiers of young faces smiling down. They had, those friendly, smiling faces, a patronizing air, due to the firm belief that their generation was better and wiser than his own" (267).

It is as a practitioner not as a professor or city reformer that Stanton is shown as the most successful: in visiting patients, Trites comments, "he gave of his own courage and strength and happiness as he gave of his drugs, and the former gift was infinitely more precious than the latter. William R. Stanton, indeed, was the doctor, the healer, personified" (209). In Trites's conclusion—the least believable part of the novel—Stanton, although initially defeated when he runs for a local political office, becomes governor of Pennsylvania, which, we are left to assume, will end his family's financial woes forever. It is an ending that points to the commercial values of the 1920s and suggests a new kind of medical culture.

Hahnemann and a Wider Medical Culture

While most of Hahnemann's faculty members and students continued to identify themselves as homeopaths, their distinct identity did not mean they were distant from the broader medical culture of the United States in the 1920s and 1930s. Hahnemann Medical College, like most medical schools in this period, was a politically conservative institution, with most faculty and students supporting the Republican Party. Garth Boericke commented sadly on a debate about the New Deal by members of the Hahnemann Club, an exclusive faculty club of which he was secretary: at one meeting the host read a "personal indictment of the New Deal, Franklin D. Roosevelt, and all his works"; and although it was "extremely painful" to Boericke, it was "obviously relished by all the Republicans present," and "discussion, accusations, fantasies and prognostications flew thick and freely."[44] In surveys of seniors conducted by yearbook editors in the 1920s, almost all the students called themselves Republicans.[45]

Hahnemann students largely embraced American popular and medical culture of the interwar period. For example, in student surveys the 1925 novel Arrowsmith, on which the popular 1931 film was based, was rated among the most popular works of fiction, and its author, Sinclair Lewis, among the most popular fiction writers.[46] Further, students were clearly offered a vision of a medical career that closely resembled the AMA's view. They anticipated being businessmen and wanted practices in large urban centers which would bring them quick returns and the excitement of an active medical community. In 1918 Clarence Bartlett, the professor of medicine, commented sadly that "too few enter practice in rural communities where fees are small and do not warrant the outlay for adequate medical equipment. Referring to an opportunity to practice in one of these rural towns a young man remarked to us: 'I would rather be a lamp post in Philadelphia than a prosperous physician in————.'"[47] Similarly, in 1928 one of the college's instructors told his class:

> Now that you men are about to enter the profession of the practice of medicine, it is important for you to heed well the advice I am about to give you. A physician never starves—there are tricks in every trade. I advise you to borrow about fifteen thousand dollars and buy yourself a good automobile (not a Ford); get a chauffeur, establish a big office, put up a big front, and it won't be long before you'll pay this money back![48]

And in 1936 seniors, giving as an example Harry Eberhard's description of traveling to Florida in the winter with a patient, recalled that "the amenities of practicing among the wealthy are well described to us."[49]

Hahnemann, like many medical schools before the 1950s, accepted more students than it could handle. It collected the tuition from freshmen and then gave them harsh midterm and final exams, winnowing the classes down, sometimes by as much as one-third. The students who entered recognized this policy and kept other career options open. In 1924, of the freshmen who left before the end of the first year, one accepted a position as a veterinarian with a large dairy company, and another went into dentistry.[50] Carl Fischer, who became the head of Hahnemann's pediatrics department in 1945, recalled that Dean Pearson frequently told freshmen that he could predict the future. Pearson told Fischer's seventy-five-member freshman class of 1924 that 10–15 percent would not graduate (23 percent did not), several would commit suicide (three did), two or three would become drug addicts (several did), and some would become abortionists (one was suspected of doing so).[51]

The students attending Hahnemann throughout the 1920s and 1930s were young men, often only one or two years out of high school. It is not surprising to find the boisterous parts of their medical training recollected with great glee in their yearbooks. Faculty recognized this immaturity by taking attendance and acting in a paternal fashion that only during the 1960s would begin to seem out of place as medical students demanded to be treated more like graduate students than college or high school students.

Hahnemann student traditions that had developed in the 1880s and 1890s solidified. Students continued to compete class against class, with sometimes vigorous fighting. The School of Science provided another group of even younger students to battle with. One yearbook recalled a fight with first-year science students to make them cut their hair and wear the caps known as dinks.[52] If a professor was late to class (1928 seniors were willing to wait ten minutes) the students began war cries, counted the time down, and then left.[53] Freshmen in 1924 later recalled greeting one of their chemistry teachers with "a deafening din of applause, shouts, shrill whistles, cheers, howls, kicking on the back of seats, mixed in with a shower of torn bits of paper, airships, and erasers."[54] Students also played up when left alone. As one class recalled, when "the dissecting room became too deserted, and the group in the smoking room too large and noisy, we generally heard the cry, 'Beat it, here comes Doctor Widman,' from one of the look-outs. Within a few minutes the place would be deserted, and seventy-one men were industriously at work over a cadaver."[55] Seniors in 1928 recalled how much they had enjoyed the "dog hunt" (they received two dollars for each dog) that had begun when Pearson announced that the college needed more animals for experiments. Protests by pet owners and the Society for the Prevention of Cruelty to Animals halted that effort.[56] As late as the mid-1940s when a chemistry professor did not check attendance he found that "'cutting' has increased greatly and loitering and 'bumming' throughout assigned periods."[57]

The level of training at Hahnemann seems to have compared fairly well with that of other schools. Hahnemann alumnus Warren Landau recalled that "everyone felt they were almost flunking out"; he "saw very little of Philadelphia" and "never even went to the Academy of Music."[58] Charles Cameron felt he held his own with residents from Duke and Yale at the Philadelphia General Hospital in the late 1930s.[59] And Horst Agerty remembers topping the state boards but finding it very difficult in 1934, as a Hahnemann graduate, to get an internship at a "good hospital."[60]

Expansion through Diversity

Hahnemann, like other private medical colleges in this period, wanted to tighten standards and yet not lose its attraction to student applicants. The transition to a four-year school had been achieved smoothly, in part because the change had been mandated throughout the state and thus had had the same effect on all schools. Despite the boasts in its catalogs, Hahnemann did not alter its curriculum significantly or increase its faculty, and, as had occurred in the school's earliest years, second-year students in the 1910s and 1920s sat through some of the same classes as freshmen.[61]

Raising admission qualifications proved more difficult. Flexner had deplored the low admission standards typical of medical schools around the country, and he had found Philadelphia, despite its proud medical heritage, no exception. Of the seven medical schools in Philadelphia only Jefferson Medical College, for example, consistently rejected applicants who did not have a high school diploma. Hahnemann also compared poorly with other homeopathic schools and was not listed by Flexner as one of the five out of fifteen homeopathic schools around the country that in practice required a high school diploma.[62] Flexner, a college graduate and educator, believed that medical students needed a college degree to prepare them properly to enter medical school. But most American medical educators, while agreeing that students did need better preparation, especially in science, were not convinced that a full four-year degree was necessary. In 1900, Hahnemann's dean Pemberton Dudley had remarked that the group suggesting a college degree requirement "does not include a very large percentage of practical and experienced medical teachers."[63] Still Hahnemann educators recognized the problems incurred by admitting students with weak educational backgrounds, and during the 1890s and 1900s the school was forced to offer freshmen "preparatory instruction in general science."[64]

Hahnemann changed its admission standards only under pressure from the state government. In 1913 the Commonwealth of Pennsylvania required all medical schools to accept only students with a high school diploma and one year of college-equivalent science subjects. Hahnemann's 1913–1914 catalog quickly pointed out the advantages for those students needing "condensed premedical courses" in choosing "independent medical institutions" over "lay colleges."[65] In fact, Hahnemann's faculty had been debating the idea of offering a premedical year since it had been raised in a memo sent to the school by the AMA's Council on Medical Education and Hospitals in 1912, but the faculty did nothing until the state law was passed.[66] Then, like two other Philadelphia schools, Jefferson and Medico-Chirurgical, Hahnemann introduced a premedical year in the summer of 1913, and in 1916, when the state instituted a two-year requirement that was to start in 1918, Hahnemann's School of Science was established. The new school was, Dean Pearson explained, "designed to give the high school graduate the instruction necessary for admission into any first class medical college and to furnish a comprehensive scientific foundation upon which to build a modern medical education."[67]

The School of Science enabled the college to offer a premedical education and the promise of further study to students who might not otherwise have been able to afford college. The school also pushed Hahnemann further onto an alternative path, in this case in terms of the ethnic and class diversity of students. Flexner had implied that the ideal medical student was a young white man with a college degree and a middle- or upper-class upbringing. Certainly Hahnemann, like other medical schools throughout this period, continued to seek out such students. But its admission policies increasingly undermined Flexner's claim that medical training was or should be a privilege and that schools favoring working-class students with limited funds and educational backgrounds—through low fees, low admission standards, and flexible or part-time schedules—were inappropriate and should not exist. Hahnemann educators, for example, boasted of its student scholarships, as Dean Pearson explained in 1916: "Modern medical education would be entirely confined to the rich were it not possible to furnish financial assistance for young men in moderate circumstances."[68] Indeed, the choices made by Hahnemann in the 1920s and 1930s, and by some other small medical schools around the country, suggest that, although not as a deliberate policy, these schools, desperate for survival and professional respect, managed to develop a different structure for medical education by providing a place for some "alternative" students who found the elite medical world otherwise increasingly discriminatory and financially out of reach.

The School of Science offered the college an opportunity for both expansion and financial stability. Although it never solved the problem of Hahnemann's continuing debts, the school's fees brought in around 9 percent of Hahnemann Medical College's income.[69] More importantly it became a crucial feeder institution for the college, which had begun having serious problems in attracting students. In 1913, faculty minutes show that one student was offered a 20 percent discount on his yearly college tuition in return for acting as a "procurer."[70] Dean Pearson admitted in 1915, with an entering freshman class of only ten, the smallest in decades, that "there has been considerable censure on account of our small freshman class."[71] He engaged in an active program of recruitment: in 1915–1916 he visited nine local and regional colleges and traveled to more than fifteen cities, where he presented a promotional lecture accompanied by a series of lantern slides of the college and hospital, and he also organized an exhibit at the annual meeting of the AIH.[72] By the following year Hahnemann's freshman class had increased to thirty-three.

Because Hahnemann accepted almost all of the School of Science graduates, the school provided young men who were not able to attend college, usually for financial reasons, with an opportunity to go to medical school, thus ensuring that working-class and lower-middle-class boys, despite the tightening of medical school admissions requirements and the decreasing numbers accepted across the country, were still able to find a way to become physicians. Italian immigrant Grant Favorite, for example, earned his bachelor in science from the school in 1925, before attending Hahnemann as a medical student, and he graduated with his M.D. in 1927. While Hahnemann's steady increase in fees for both science and medical students ensured that the class range would remain relatively narrow, the school did enable Hahnemann to resist the forces of homogenization for some decades and led to a student body with surprisingly diverse ethnic and religious backgrounds. Horst Agerty remembers the school as "a convenient back door" and that admission to the medical school was "almost automatic." It offered a "good education," especially as it "was not easy to get into a good university."[73]

Hahnemann Medical College
First Year And Graduates, 1900-1970

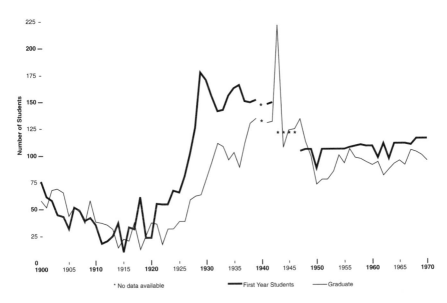

Figure 20. Graph of the number of Hahnemann freshmen and graduates, 1900–1970, showing increasing enrollment in the 1920s and 1930s.

While it is difficult to get a definite sense of what impact the School of Science made and how much Hahnemann Medical College's admissions policies began to change, there is some evidence available. By analyzing the graduates in selected years from 1906 to 1935, we can see the student body become increasingly locally based. Of the fifty-two Hahnemann graduates in 1906, 64 percent were Pennsylvania residents (27 percent from Philadelphia), 8 percent from New Jersey, and 4 percent each from nearby New York, Washington, D.C., and Ohio, with the other 12 percent coming from other states. As other homeopathic educational options began to disappear, small groups of students came from distant states such as Maine (8 percent of graduates in 1910) and Iowa (5.4 percent of graduates in 1911).[74] In 1935, the proportion of graduates from Pennsylvania remained around the same as it had been in 1906, but the school increasingly drew large numbers of students from nearby states rather than from across the country. For example 15.7 percent of the 1935 graduates were from New Jersey, and 47 percent of the Pennsylvania students were from Philadelphia. This high proportion from the city suggests that atypical students—especially Italians and Jews—were finding a path, initially through the School of Science, to Hahnemann's medical school.

Before the founding of the School of Science the percentage of students with college or other degrees had also begun to drop, falling from 19 percent of graduates in 1906 to 8 percent in 1911, as students who had been the typical Hahnemann graduate began to choose other, perhaps nonhomeopathic, schools. However, by 1927, with the School of Science as a feeder institution, some 40 percent of the graduates (whose total number was only slightly larger than in 1906) had college or other degrees. By 1935 with double the number of graduates, 53 percent had college or other degrees, mostly bachelor of science degrees.[75] That a bachelor of science degree was recognized as inferior to a full-length college degree, especially from a prestigious school, can be judged by the experiences of college student Carl Castle Fischer, who arrived in 1924 with a bachelor of arts from Princeton. Both his skills and his degree helped give Fischer status at Hahnemann: he was made vice president of his sophomore class and president of his junior class, he was voted "most representative Hahnemannian," and his nickname was "Princeton."[76]

That Hahnemann did begin to accept unusually high numbers of Italian, South American, and Jewish students reflects its lowered status in the medical marketplace. Other major medical schools deemed these students, even those who were highly qualified, unacceptable or restricted them by quota systems.

Hahnemann also had informal quotas, but its need for students forced greater flexibility in its admission policies. During the 1930s and 1940s in particular it developed a surprisingly diverse student body. Horst Agerty, class of 1934, who had gone to high school at the prestigious Friends Central, remembers as a freshman being shocked by having Italians as fellow students: the only Italians he had ever met before had been street peddlers.[77]

These new kinds of students began to form their own ethnic associations, including clubs and fraternities, such as the Jewish fraternity Phi Delta Epsilon (founded at Hahnemann in 1929), Il Circolo Italiano (founded 1928), and El Circulo Hispano (founded 1941). The 1944 yearbook was the first edited by a Jewish student, Irving Lester Lichtenstein, from Philadelphia, who would do his internship at Philadelphia's Jewish Hospital the following year.[78] Perhaps not coincidentally, the 1944 yearbook was dedicated to Grant Favorite, the school's first Italian immigrant department head, as "a research investigator of national note, a scholar, humanitarian and friend."[79]

Hahnemann's supporters and especially the faculty were aware that the school's image was changing, and it was easy for those dissatisfied with many of these changes to blame the admission of "a-typical" Hahnemann students. Hahnemann's relatively informal admissions system made this situation worse, for Dean Pearson was often the sole interviewer and his assessment of students drew from his knowledge of their backgrounds. Carl Fischer's father had graduated from Hahnemann in 1895 and was a member of the Alumni Association.

When Carl appeared at Pearson's office in 1924, Pearson said, "Oh, yes, you are Carl Fischer, John Fischer's son from Princeton. I thought you were coming in next year." This, Fischer later commented, "was my entrance examination."[80] Warren Landau, a 1945 graduate, recalled that he was able to get into Hahnemann because his family knew someone connected with Hahnemann's board of trustees. The importance of "pull," he later commented, "was probably true for most of the Jews there."[81]

Despite calls from orthodox medical leaders to restrict admissions, financial exigencies meant that the school's trustees continued to push for increasing numbers of freshmen.[82] Increasing the number of students was also made possible by physical changes, such as the razing of the 1886 college building in the late 1920s and the construction of a new multistory hospital; the college moved into the 1890 hospital building, which later became known as the "old college."

The increasing diversity of the student body did not mean that teachers and fellow students lost their prejudiced assumptions about the differences among students from nontraditional groups. In 1933, for example, the dean told his colleagues that the 153 entering class had 10 percent Jews, 41 Italians, and 96 "Americans."[83] In 1936 the Board of Trustees College Committee assured the rest of the board, in response to complaints by the AMA, that the "undesirable types" had been eliminated from the freshmen class.[84] And when Sidney Zubrow interviewed with Pearson in 1933 he was told quite frankly: "we have a 10% quota on Jews" and as "we're just about to approach it; if we take you we'll be just over it." Zubrow, who was subsequently accepted, was shocked not by the information but by the dean's frank admission.[85] Later, when he applied for a student loan he was told that "our experience with people of your kind has not always been the best." Zubrow recalled that some of the homeopathic doctors invited students to go out drinking and socializing, but they never invited Jewish students.[86] The extent of anti-Semitism faced by Jewish doctors was recognized by some of the school's Jewish students, who as graduates successfully petitioned the faculty to issue new diplomas in new names: in 1938 Shapiro became Shepard, and Leibowitz, Lee.[87]

The extent of anti-Catholic and anti-Semitic policies in American medical education has rarely been examined by historians. Perhaps exploring the "dark" side makes some historians too uncomfortable; perhaps, as historian Saul Jarcho argued some years ago, the evidence is too difficult to find even in this era of tremendous professional attention to the standards of medical education. "One may search through volume after volume of official publications and surveys of medical societies and universities," Jarcho commented, "without detecting a hint that the problem even exists."[88]

During the early and mid-1920s, if we are to judge by student yearbooks,

Hahnemann students seem to have been quite open and relaxed about their class-mates' ethnic differences. In 1921 Max Cohen, a twenty-seven-year-old Rus-sian Jew who had graduated with a B.S. from Central High School, was described fondly by his school nickname, "Bolshevik." Cohen's medical class had entered Hahnemann just as the Russian Revolution was completed, and British and American troops remained in what was then termed White Russia hoping for a return to czarist rule. During the 1920s many, perhaps most, American physi-cians were Republicans, and they supported the AMA's conservative policies re-jecting federal health insurance and its efforts to defeat the federal maternal-child health legislation, the Sheppard-Towner Act. At Hahnemann so rare were stu-dents who did not support the Republican Party that the few who described themselves as Democrats or socialists were seen as quaint rather than threaten-ing. "There is only one fault that we can find with Max," the yearbook editors wrote in a gentle and nonderogatory tone, "and that is, that nothing is modern except Bolshevism and nothing good unless it is sanctioned by the Soviet of Russia. Despite this, Max is a pretty good fellow. He enjoys study, raves over the opera, loves the women and is always ready for an argument. Never argue with Max. He always wins."[89] Jewish students remained uncommon for many years; among the sixty-three members of the graduating class of 1928, there was only one self-identified Jew and there were eleven Catholics. Morris Fiterman (known as Moish), the Philadelphia son of a cigar manufacturer, was an athlete and described himself as "a Hebrew and a Republican."[90]

The 1921 class also included Govind Saklaramji Hiwale, a thirty-two-year-old Indian missionary who had studied at the American Mission in Bombay, at Ursinus College, and at the University of Pennsylvania. His class nickname was "the Hindu Jew," and Dean Pearson had introduced him to the rest of his class as "a real Hindu missionary." His classmates commented with gentle mockery on his love of Indian music rather than jazz and on his performance on instru-ments that they termed his "Hindu pumpkin" and "native Indian banana," and they concluded that "Govind expects to return to India and show them how Homeopathy really works."[91]

Italian students, too, were seen as separate, and they experienced their years at Hahnemann in distinctive ways. Anthony James Di Marino, of the class of 1933, was nicknamed Philadelphia's Mussolini, in part for his constant champi-oning of "the Italian boys of the class."[92] Italian students soon developed a lively ethnic identity at the school and had their own fraternity and social activities. Sidney Zubrow remembers, however, that the sense of prejudice against the Jew-ish students was far less than the prejudice against the Italians, whom other stu-dents treated as "sort of second class."[93]

Although Hahnemann did not graduate an African-American student from 1912 until 1951, Hahnemann replied "No" when asked "Do you draw the color line?" during its application for membership in the AAMC in 1913.[94] During the 1920s, the list in its catalogs of YMCAs suggested as places for students to live included the "colored" southwest branch, at 1724 Chestnut Street. This listing disappeared from Hahnemann's catalogs after 1932. The choice to separate Hahnemann from the growing black community around it was to prove problematic in the 1960s, but the distance enabled students to perform an "old time Darky revival" in 1929.[95] The class of 1933 did include Livingston Chunn, a Pacific Islander born in Honolulu, who was described as "a sunny tan little man."[96] Chunn became a prominent dermatologist and member of Hahnemann's faculty. The college also accepted a few Asian students, usually from Japan or China, but a certain racism permeated the student body, a racism that was not surprisingly exacerbated by World War II. The 1945 yearbook, for example, used a racist metaphor to describe Japanese bombers: "over the horizon they came, like a swarm of Anopheles mosquitoes, their yellow bellies and red eyes gleaming in the blistering Pacific sun . . . from their probosci th[e]y unloosed the thunder that was Pearl Harbor."[97]

Many of these nontraditional students had gained entrance to Hahnemann through its School of Science. In 1928, of sixty-three graduating seniors, thirty-five had first graduated from the School of Science, including Richard F. Tomec of Germany; Boyden Waclaw Kowalski (known as Bob), the Polish son of a carpenter; and Mina Mandalon of Egypt.[98]

Students drawn from distant places were also more often interested in studying homeopathy than their American peers were, and indeed some may have sought out Hahnemann for its non-orthodox training. Like Govind Hiwale of Bombay, Keum S. Sohn of Korea, who had first gone to the School of Science, was described as "a strong supporter of Samuel Hahnemann."[99]

Hahnemann and the Depression

During the Great Depression Hahnemann's financial problems intensified. The trustees recognized that they could raise tuition only slightly, for many students were already struggling to afford to come. Sidney Zubrow recalls that when his acceptance telegram arrived from Hahnemann, he and his mother began to cry, both because they were excited he had been accepted and because they were terrified that they would not be able to afford it. Zubrow borrowed money from a family friend and worked in a delicatessen on weekends during his medical training.[100]

Increasing numbers of students unable to pay their tuition were forced to take a leave of absence, something the college's official policy did not permit, but which administrators sometimes allowed. Until 1940 Hahnemann required only two years of college, although it preferred three, and these admission

Figure 21. During the 1920s and 1930s, as a way to offset its growing debts, Hahnemann began to admit more students than its faculty and facilities could properly handle, as this crowded chemistry laboratory demonstrates. *Medic* 1930.

standards attracted some candidates who felt they could not afford to wait to complete the additional year of college before beginning medical school. Hahnemann benefited by being able to attract some students who would otherwise have attended more prestigious schools.

Economic struggles meant that the hopes of many students for a more prestigious college and medical school were curtailed. John Storer (1921–), a 1945 graduate, remembered that he had hoped to go to Bucknell University (as his father, an electrical engineer, had) and then to Jefferson Medical College, as his brother had. Instead Storer went to the University of Alabama for three years (with visions of playing football and saving money), which cost his family only one-third what a Bucknell education would have. In 1942 he began as a freshman at Hahnemann, which, unlike Jefferson, did not require a college degree. Storer commented that he thought the other factor that made him a likely candidate was that "I looked like a clean-cut American boy, and . . . I was a WASP." Hahnemann, he knew, took a higher percentage of Jews and Catholics than the University of Pennsylvania or Jefferson.[101]

Students in the 1930s began to protest the large classes, the low admissions standards, and the inadequate number of teaching faculty. In 1936 seniors mockingly stated that a reading knowledge of English was "not essential for admission."[102] Both the 1934 and 1935 yearbooks contained serious suggestions for improving the curriculum. Both classes wanted more selective admission policies, pointing out that "a large number of students is admitted and relatively few finish."[103] They wanted curriculum changes: less chemistry and less toxicology (the 1934 seniors felt that their toxicology laboratories were "a waste of time"), more anatomy, and new courses in medical economics and medical psychology, courses that would be introduced at Hahnemann only in the 1960s. More significantly, the students criticized the teaching methods, complaining about too many didactic lectures and about the teachers themselves: lecturers who "read off notes and put the class to sleep" and teachers who were theoreticians and "500X men" rather than "real practical Homeopaths like Dr. Boericke." The students also commented on the inadequacy of their clinical training, pointing out that in too many cases "only a few see what is going on and the rest sleep or talk."[104]

But such changes would have involved remaking Hahnemann into a different kind of institution; and until the late 1940s the college altered little of its curriculum or teaching methods, and the same men, whose teaching was modeled on that of their own teachers of the 1890s, continued to lecture, present patients in the amphitheater, and bring groups of twenty or more students to see ward patients. When in 1932 the sophomore class asked for less toxicology and more physical diagnosis, Harlan Wells explained to the faculty's executive committee that it was impossible to increase the number of clinical teachers because so many of them (all, of course, unpaid) were too busy with office hours.[105] Hahnemann students who criticized their medical training did so without much hope that things would change. The 1934 seniors prefaced their proposed improvements: "We present the following with no animosity on our part, but with a sincere desire to be of help to the future welfare of the college and with a faint hope that some broad minded executive or faculty member of Hahnemann may see the light and champion any or all of them."[106]

The Alternative Path Attacked

When Hahnemann joined the AAMC in 1913 the leaders of the college did not realize that trying to adopt national standards for education would prove fundamentally threatening to Hahnemann's simultaneous effort to define itself as a local institution producing general practitioners for a regional medical marketplace. When Carl Fischer wrote his brief history of Hahnemann, he called this period "The Threatening Thirties."[107]

The threat came from the AMA and AAMC's 1935 inspection, which was part of their national study published in 1939 as *Medical Education in the United States, 1934–1939*.[108] In November 1935 Herman G. Weiskotten, the report's main author and the dean of Syracuse University's medical school, came with an AMA representative to Philadelphia and visited Hahnemann and the city's four regular schools (they did not visit the Philadelphia College of Osteopathic

Medicine). To each school he visited he sent a private written report, but in the published document, unlike in Flexner's, no names were used.

Although Hahnemann was not put under private probation as the result of this inspection, as Temple's medical school was, the unpublished report on Hahnemann was scathing in its refusal to accept that Hahnemann could offer a satisfactory scientific education that was also homeopathic. The inspection came one month after a notice published in the *Journal of the American Medical Association* that the AMA's Council on Medical Education would no longer include institutions of "sectarian medicine" on its list of approved schools and hospitals. Weiskotten and his colleague urged the college to "make clear to the public the nonsectarian character of your institution." The report suggested that the college rewrite its catalog, saying that "the phenomenal advances of medical sciences" had "rendered obsolete the sectarian divisions among physicians which prevailed a century ago."[109] The report's authors took pains to ensure that these criticisms were not interpreted as themselves sectarian or prejudiced. The AMA's Council on Medical Education, they claimed, offered "no objection to the maintenance of a chair of a department of homeopathic materia medica and therapeutics, but it believes that with the exception of this department, in filling vacancies in your faculty selection should be made of the best teachers available without limitation or restriction to the graduates of particular schools."[110] The inspectors, in other words, recognized the parochial nature of the college and blamed it on the college's homeopathic identity, and especially on the college's tradition of hiring its own graduates—a tradition that was, of course, hardly distinctive to Hahnemann, or even to unorthodox schools in general. They wanted Hahnemann to teach homeopathy quietly, as a therapeutic specialty, and to present itself in the wider community as an institution that offered the same kinds of medical education as any other school rated Class A by the AMA.

In response to the 1935 report Hahnemann did begin to deemphasize its teaching of homeopathy; but it was unable to alter its reliance on didactic lectures and large group clinics. Organizing small group clinics and laboratories required a low faculty-student ratio, which the school could not afford. Nor was it easy to improve the quality of the faculty or students, for Hahnemann had long recognized that it could not attract the "best" students. Not only did Hahnemann hire its own graduates, often promising men with few other academic options, but it had no access to the kind of funding that would allow it to achieve the features that the AAMC saw as characterizing the ideal medical school: limited enrollment, substantial equipment and clinical facilities, full-time clinical teachers, and the possibility for in-house laboratory and clinical research.

The 1935 report implied that for the AMA and AAMC to leave uncriticized a school with too strident a homeopathic identity would be detrimental to or-

Figure 22. In the 1920s and 1930s most of the patients at Hahnemann Hospital were unavailable for student instruction, but outpatients who came to the hospital's dispensary were examined by college students anxious to try out their diagnostic and clinical skills. *Medic* 1930.

ganized medicine's broader vision for the American medical profession, a vision in which each physician, no matter what his or her private views, would present to the lay public an allegiance to the principles and practices of mainstream scientific medicine. Thus, Weiskotten and his colleagues asked the college to "make it unmistakably clear to the laity that in the teaching and practice of medicine all recognized schools stand upon common ground and that in opposing influences detrimental to the health of the people, the entire medical profession should present a united front."[111]

Hahnemann's responsiveness to some of these demands suggests that many of its trustees and faculty shared the feeling that an outspoken unorthodoxy was a sign of the past rather than of the future. The college's standing in the community as well as in the larger medical world, they contended, depended on its remodeling itself on the AMA's concept of professionalism and the AAMC's concept of a medical school, rather than choosing the separate path Hahnemann had taken in the 1910s and 1920s. Hahnemann was already in step with many of the AMA's cultural and political views, but the major changes involved in becoming a model AAMC school depended on money and visionary leadership, which Hahnemann lacked until the late 1950s.

The changes the trustees did institute in response to the 1935 report were mostly directed toward the ways Hahnemann represented itself to the public, prospective students, and professional organizations like the AMA and AAMC.

The 1936–1937 catalog used some of the ideas from the 1935 report, if not the exact language and tone, referring, for example, to "the remarkable advances" of medical science that had made sectarian divisions "unnecessary and undesirable."[112] It also boasted that there were now more beds available for clinical teaching: 386 of the 700 public beds at Hahnemann Hospital, an increase from the 370 listed in the previous year's catalog.[113] And although the students' course work remained unchanged, the catalog deleted a significant amount of prose extolling homeopathy, including an entire paragraph from its opening general statement. No longer did the college direct "special attention" to the Department of Materia Medica and Therapeutics or refer to the "materia medica of Hahnemann, Hering, Dunham and other noted investigators" and the ways "enthusiastic and experienced clinical teachers demonstrate the principles and efficiency of homeopathy in practical work."[114] Nor, in the description of Boericke's department, did the catalog describe the ways students would be "thoroughly drilled in the principles of Homeopathy and the teaching of [Samuel Hahnemann's] Organon" as well as in the process of drug proving.[115] Now there was a single sentence: "The courses of this Department are given in the first, third and fourth years and include the consideration of various forms of special therapy, such as homeopathy, roentgen and radium therapy, electro-physio- and mechano-therapy."[116]

The most significant change was the introduction of a new faculty member and a new department of pharmacology. This change, Provost Frederic von Rapp admitted in an article published in the *Hahnemannian Monthly* in 1936, was spurred by a recent critique of "sectarian institutions" in the *Journal of the American Medical Association*. The trustees, von Rapp claimed, "are hard at work on this very problem," and the new Department of Pharmacology would "meet every demand of the American Medical Association." It would "undertake more extensive biologic experiments" and would make "the training in this course second to none from the 'old school' standpoint." However, he added, conscious of the concerns of Hahnemann alumni, while "it was felt, in the light of recent developments that pharmacology should be on a par, as far as hours of instruction and importance are concerned, with the department of Materia Medica and Therapeutics, . . . the major concern has always been and will continue to be, the teaching of Homeopathic Materia Medica."[117]

In 1936 Reinhard Beutner became the head of Hahnemann's new Department of Pharmacology, with a salary of four thousand dollars.[118] Beutner had graduated with an M.D. and a Ph.D. from the University of Berlin and had previously been head of pharmacology at the University of Louisville.[119] It is not certain why Beutner was attracted to Hahnemann; but Berlin had become a center for homeopathy, and a few years after he came to Hahnemann, he began studying to obtain Hahnemann's homeopathic degree in order to take Maryland's homeopathic licensing exam.[120] In the *Hahnemannian Monthly* Buetner was described as "the representative of physiologic medicine . . . whose broad minded conception of drug therapy should aid and amplify our Homeopathic tenets rather than hinder them."[121]

In the 1930s, Hahnemann continued to be run pretty much as it had been in the 1910s and 1920s. Dean Pearson and other basic science faculty lost what little influence they had had, and the trustees and their representatives on the clinical faculty began wielding increasing power over academic affairs. Throughout the 1930s and 1940s members of the faculty tried to convince the trustees to more fully integrate a version of the AAMC model of the medical school. The faculty's executive committee, for example, warned (in vain) in 1934 that if the school continued to admit such large entering classes there was a danger of "de-classification."[122] But it was not until the mid-1940s, with the return of the AMA and AAMC survey committee, that Hahnemann was forced to abandon its alternative vision—a source of both its strengths and its weaknesses—and transform itself into an orthodox academic medical center.

Chapter 5   Turning Points

Hahnemann in the 1940s

Historians have pointed to World War II as a major turning point in the history of American medicine; it intensified the public's faith in scientific research and in specialization. Yet changes such as these did not come to Hahnemann Medical College until the 1950s; and the war had significant but not transforming effects: staff shortages, students in uniform, accelerated courses, and, as one graduate later put it, an enhanced "sense of purpose."[1]

What engrossed and disrupted Hahnemann during this decade were two other events: the admission of women students in 1941 and the decision by the American Medical Association (AMA) and the Association of American Medical Colleges (AAMC) to place Hahnemann on official probation in 1945. Perhaps because the probation years were so traumatic, the break in a ninety-three-year history of refusing coeducation seems to have been achieved surprisingly easily. Male and female students studied together, some dated, and some married each other. In the Baby Boom years, women requested and were granted maternity leaves. They also became faculty members at Hahnemann. In 1946, for example, Gladys Rosenstein, one of the first four women graduates of 1944, was appointed an assistant in the Department of Gastroenterology; Elizabeth Brown, a 1945 graduate, was appointed to the Department of Bacteriology and in 1958 headed the first allergy subsection in the Department of Medicine.

The probation, by comparison, resulted in a painful and abrupt process of change that shook the foundations of the institution. Hahnemann's response to the probation helped to transform the college fundamentally: from a local, parochial school with an affiliated community-based hospital to a major academic medical center, providing a range of academic courses and health care facilities and staffed by men and women whose teaching and research were oriented to

Figure 23. Most Hahnemann students served in the military during World War II, as can be seen by the number of uniforms in these photographs from the annual Blue and Gold Ball. The impact of the war at Hahnemann was overshadowed by the school's efforts to deal with academic probation during the 1940s. *Medic* 1944.

national and international standards. The 1910 Flexner report had forced Hahnemann's faculty, students, and supporters to decide what kind of school it was to become in the age of scientific medicine and what meaning its homeopathic heritage would have in this new order. The 1935 AMA/AAMC report had, likewise, proposed models of professionalism and of the ideal medical school,

Figure 24. "Lady M.D.'s of '44," composite from class photos in *Medic* 1944, designed by Barbara Williams for the fiftieth class reunion exhibit in 1994. In 1944 Hahnemann Medical College graduated its first five women: Beatrice Troyan, Laura E. H. Winner, Anna T. Onorato, Gladys Rosenstein, and Luisa M. Gonzalez- Quinones.

models that had pressured Hahnemann to choose which "alternative" elements it should preserve and which it should jettison. The survey conducted in April 1945 by Fred Zapffe, secretary of the AAMC, and Victor Johnson, secretary of the AMA's Council on Medical Education (and their private report issued a few months later) forced the school's trustees to listen and respond to dissatisfaction among students and faculty, and to try to bring the institution's mission in line with changes in medical education outside its doors. By the end of the 1940s Hahnemann had begun to institute changes that would cause it to shed much of its alternative heritage and bring it closer to the reigning midcentury version of a modern medical school and teaching hospital.

The Quiet Revolution: Women Students at Hahnemann

In December 1941 Margaret Giannini (1921–) was writing her letter of acceptance to Hahnemann Medical College. She had recently returned home to Haddonfield, New Jersey, from Boston where she was doing premedical studies at Boston University, to be with her mother who was ill. She knew that Hahnemann, which had already accepted its first class of women that fall, had made clear that it would accept no more than ten women a year. While she was writing, she heard the announcement of the Pearl Harbor bombing on the radio. She called the city desk of a local newspaper and asked if it was true. When she came to Hahnemann, she recalled later, "all the fellows were in uniform."[2]

Giannini and Beatrice Troyan (1922–), a 1944 graduate of the first class, recalled little overt discrimination, except from a few professors. Thomas Snyder, who taught histology, directed his comments on his slides of penises with lesions to the women in his class; Leon Ashcraft, professor of urology, dismissed the class when he was about to teach male physiology and arranged to meet the male students at another time; Ralph Bernstein of dermatology told lewd stories to shock the women and did succeed in upsetting Luisa Gonzales-Quinones, a student from a sheltered background in Puerto Rico.[3] Seth Fisher, who graduated in 1948, remembered that Jacob Crellin, who lectured on pulmonary diseases, made "the ladies sit in the front row" because "he believed that women could never be good physicians, and he wanted to keep an eye on them."[4]

But these examples were the exceptions. Giannini recalled men and women, all "wanting to absorb as much as we could," going together down to the pathology laboratory to watch autopsies "we were not required to do." She boarded at the Y on Arch Street, where a group of Hahnemann's women students lived on the two top floors and shared a drawing room where they could bring guests. It was "wonderful," she recalled. "We could walk to school," and "we'd meet at ten each night, have coffee and pie at Horn and Hardart, go for a walk, and go study again." Although it was later claimed that women were accepted by medical schools in groups of four so that they could be assigned a cadaver four to a table, Troyan commented that at Hahnemann two women and two men usually worked together in dissecting. After she had been at Hahnemann for about a month, some of her teachers stopped her in the hall and said they had voted against admitting women, but they seemed accepting nonetheless. Troyan got married the day before her physiology exam and recalled being called to the office by administrators worried that she would get pregnant. "I remember thinking what a nerve," she recalled, and, a few years after her graduation, while she was in labor with her daughter, she read cytology slides for the hospital's laboratory.[5] Student yearbooks in the 1940s and 1950s, while still edited by men, were also sympathetic, and in 1951 one remarked: "there were many skeptical eyebrows raised in those days [the 1940s], but the women proved equal to the tremendous task that lay ahead of them. . . . [in gross anatomy] it was many a football star who fainted while the little soprano from the glee club ran for water to pour over him."[6]

It is not clear why Hahnemann changed its policy in 1941, and while the approach of war suggests a ready answer, this explanation does not seem compelling. The public statement issued by Provost von Rapp argued that "the

Figure 25. Until 1974 Hahnemann had no student dormitories, but local cafés, automats, and delicatessens, like the Hahnemann Luncheonette, became places for students to congregate. *Medic* 1944.

decision was largely influenced by the realization that the heavy governmental demand is apt to bring about a shortage of physicians in civilian life." But, he added, "there was another reason. Women have entered, and have proven themselves in all of the professions, and we felt that they should have an opportunity at Hahnemann."[7] Perhaps the recent appointment of Harry Eberhard, a man who had consistently voted for the admission of women, as the college's first vice president for medical affairs might also partially explain the change in policy. Hahnemann's enrollment figures do not suggest a shortage of applicants: neither the number of freshmen nor the number of graduates had been declining, and three years earlier Hahnemann had built a new college building, the Klahr Building, which helped ameliorate the overcrowding in the school's laboratory and lecture rooms. What is particularly striking is that, in this instance, Hahnemann was at the forefront of progressive medical education. In 1941 fewer than a dozen private medical colleges were coeducational, although by the end of the 1940s only four schools in the country—Jefferson being one of them— did not accept some women students.

The women at Hahnemann were conscious of their role as path breakers and members of a minority professional group; in 1941 only 5.4 percent of the nation's medical students were women.[8] In 1942 the Hahnemann women formed the Women's Medical Society, a branch of the American Medical Women's Association, and in 1945 women students formed the Alpha Beta chapter of Alpha Epsilon Iota, the national women's medical sorority. By 1950 Hahnemann had women graduates working in gynecology, gastroenterology, medicine, anatomy, and therapeutics. It also began to hire women from outside the institution and in 1964 made cytopathologist Irena Koprowska Hahnemann's first female professor. Koprowska, born in Poland, was a 1939 graduate of Warsaw University's medical school and had come to the United States in 1944 to study with George Papanicolaou, the inventor of the Pap test. These women were courageous and determined; for example, Elizabeth Brown, who arrived in 1942, had responsibility for four stepchildren and two children of her own. And they were successful; Giannini, for example, became an expert in pediatric disability and was appointed the first director of the National Institute of Handicapped Research in 1980. This generation of Hahnemann women did not, however, self-consciously identify itself as feminist. In 1986, for example, as the speaker at Hahnemann's First Annual Lectureship and Recognition Award for Women in Science and Medicine, Koprowska said that after the two years she had spent at the New York Infirmary for Women and Children in the 1940s she had "lost [her] taste for all women institutions."[9] Only in the 1970s and 1980s did women students at Hahnemann form a group that focused on gender discrimination at the institution.[10]

Hahnemann on Probation

In June 1945, Joseph Conwell, the head of Hahnemann's board of trustees, received a letter from Fred Zapffe informing him that "in view of the situation existing in the Hahnemann Medical College [the Executive Council of the AAMC] could not do otherwise than recommend to the Association that the college be placed on probation."[11] Hahnemann's trustees protested: "the action taken by your board will definitely harm Hahnemann. You have criticized us for having a poor grade of medical student, but the action taken, *and the publicity given it*, will certainly not aid us in getting the kinds of students we should have."[12] Despite such protests, Hahnemann was placed on official probation by the AAMC, the AMA's Council on Medical Education, and the Pennsylvania State Board of Licensure. In the period of Hahnemann's probation—from 1945 to 1949—no other medical school in the country was reported as officially on probation.[13]

During the 1930s and early 1940s some members of the faculty had made clear to the trustees their discontent with the organization and direction of the college: its diverse and large student body, its inadequate funding base, the influence of a small cabal, and especially the power of the trustees over internal academic affairs. College administrative leaders also seemed to have lacked a vision of the future and to have had no sense of the professional and social changes affecting American medical practice and education. Hahnemann's building plan—halted after the construction of a new hospital building in 1928 and a new, not fully completed, college building in 1938—as well as the physical deterioration of the older buildings, only made this stagnation more obvious. Hahnemann faculty and staff also faced debts to vendors (which meant constant shortages of supplies and equipment) and low salaries. There was only a small group of full-time basic science teachers, a group that had altered little since the 1920s and had almost no influence in college affairs; and, with constant hiring and promotion from within, the faculty was mainly headed by Hahnemann graduates who had little interest in research or change. But shortages, low salaries, and peeling paint were not reason enough to spur trustee action. The trustees paid little attention to such complaints, ignored the financial and physical problems, and increased the numbers of students without increasing the size of the teaching staff. By 1941 Hahnemann had the second highest number of students in the city—only the University of Pennsylvania had more—fewer faculty than any other school but the Woman's Medical College, and its tuition, at $515 a year, was the highest.[14]

The report written by Zapffe and Johnson, like the 1935 AMA/AAMC report, was a private document intended only for the eyes of the board and senior administrators. But the act of probation was dramatic and public and was made visible in the June 1945 issue of the *Journal of the American Medical Association*.[15] The report criticized the organization of the college, the makeup and selection of faculty, the power of the trustees, the relations between the college and hospital, their leaders' lack of vision, and the institution's financial status. Targeting these factors was part of a larger effort by the AMA and AAMC to upgrade medical schools to make them conform to the new vision of a modern medical teaching institution. And by the late 1940s, as a result of a series of social and political changes, changes intensified by World War II, these bodies could provide schools not only a stick but also a carrot: government funding, especially for building construction and research projects. And the issue of Hahnemann's homeopathic identity no longer seemed so pressing as it had in Flexner's years, either for Hahnemann itself or for the AMA and the AAMC. Thus, Hahnemann, in theory, stood as good a chance to compete as more prestigious schools, as long as it appeared to be transforming itself into a modern institution. Increasingly, the measure by which medical schools were judged was less the caliber of their graduates or teaching faculty but the quality, quantity, and choice of their faculty's research projects. And in the 1950s and 1960s Hahnemann quickly came to recognize, under the guidance of Charles Cameron, where the money was.

Johnson and Zapffe had recognized what everyone in the college knew: that

Dean Pearson's replacement, William G. Schmidt, was a puppet of the reigning administration.[16] Johnson and Zapffe's report made clear that they had no confidence that anyone inside Hahnemann could supply the necessary leadership and vision to modernize the institution. During the few months after the AAMC's survey and report, and before the official announcement of probation in June, the college began swiftly reorganizing. In a series of letters to Johnson and Zapffe the trustees pointed out that they hoped these initial responses would stave off official public probation, something they knew had occurred in other schools. The college trustees and administrators tried to be both responsive and placating. As the report had urged, the trustees established a new three-person executive committee to function as dean while the college searched for a new dean. Johnson and Zapffe had directed that the committee should, for political as well as professional reasons, be made up of the acting dean, a preclinical faculty member, and a clinical faculty member, adding that "it is essential that the members of such a committee should be composed of those of the faculty who in the past have demonstrated an insight into the defects of the institution."[17] This committee included physiologist John Scott, who, one trustee pointed out to Johnson, "was reported by you and Dr. Zapffe to be the ablest of the preclinical professors and a member of the faculty group which has been critical of the management"; and oncologist Stanley Reimann, who like Scott was a graduate of the University of Pennsylvania and who was chosen because of "his high standing in the medical profession, his great interest in Hahnemann, and your recommendation that our institution has been too ingrown."[18] As for financial problems, the trustees claimed that the large debts enumerated in the report were exaggerated, for there had been "no borrowing" for the previous eleven years; moreover the mortgage debt had been reduced by $300,000 while the school's subsidy from the state had almost doubled.[19]

These protests were to no avail. Instead of reconsidering the probation, Johnson raised the level of professional threat by telling one trustee that "there was some discussion both by the Council and by the College Association group regarding the complete removal of Hahnemann from the list of approved medical schools," but they had decided that doing so was "unjustifiably drastic as an initial measure."[20] Perhaps Hahnemann's problems were sufficiently dire to warrant this response; perhaps the college's homeopathic heritage played an additional role in explaining the seriousness and inflexibility displayed by the AMA and the AAMC.

Preprobation Tensions

The notification of probation was a blow, but not an unexpected one. In the early 1940s a group of faculty had become dissatisfied with the growing power of a few men, especially Frederic von Rapp and Harry Eberhard. Von Rapp, a trustee who had been appointed provost in 1935, was administrator of Hahnemann Hospital, and he also had control of administrative affairs at the college. Eberhard was the only faculty member on the board of trustees, and he had been recently appointed as vice president of medical affairs, a newly created position. Both men had power over the dean. Johnson and Zapffe had noted disapprovingly how many committees von Rapp and Eberhard served on: Eberhard, for example, sat on the admissions committee, the faculty's executive Medical Council, the student grievances committee, and the college advisory committee, which provided a liaison between the Medical Council and the board of trustees. "It is undesirable that a member of the Board of Trustees serve on this rather considerable number of committees," Johnson and Zapffe warned, and they were especially concerned about his serving on the admissions committee, "in which the faculty should act entirely independently of any undue influence by the Board of Trustees."[21]

The faculty's dislike of these particular men and of the policies of the trustees they embodied played a major but not defining role in shaping events leading up to the survey and report. The appearance of Johnson and Zapffe in 1945 was the result of a series of thwarted efforts by faculty members to solve significant academic and administrative problems, especially interference by the trustees and a perceived decline in the standards and reputation of the institution. These problems were made more visible in the early 1940s by Hahnemann graduates' high failure rates on the state board licensing exams: in 1940, 18.2 percent, and the following year 18.3 percent.[22] The board failures became a potent symbol of hidden fissures within the institution. These public figures forced administrators and faculty to struggle to determine whose fault the failures were.

By October 1941 the faculty had organized an investigatory committee outside the Medical Council, and in April 1942 the committee wrote a report directed to the trustees, which laid out reasons for the failures and offered possible solutions.[23] In May 1943 the members of this committee met with Eberhard "for a discussion of the deficiencies of the school" and in June wrote him a letter laying out their recommendations, a letter that became known as the "petition of seven proposals."[24] The 1943 petition was signed by thirty-one faculty members, including John Scott (head of physiology), Reinhard Beutner (head of pharmacology), Bruce MacFadyen (head of gynecology), Newlin Paxson (head of obstetrics), Stanley Reimann (head of oncology), Garth Boericke (head of therapeutics), Russell Fisher (pathologist), and Carl Fischer (pediatrician and editor of the *Alumni News*). The petition placed the blame for the state board failures on two factors: first, they targeted the board's power in determining policy on the admission, promotion, and grading of students, and second, the faculty who supported those policies. The petitioners attacked the board's "system of selection of students," arguing that Hahnemann's large classes included "an increasing number of undesirable and unpromising students" and that their size led to a poor student-instructor ratio.[25] One suggestion involved using the first part of the examinations of the National Board of Medical Examiners as a prerequisite for admission to the junior class, and another urged comparing the scores on the state board examinations with the marks given by individual departments, so as to ensure "a critical study of the pedagogical methods in vogue at the present time in the various departments."[26] The petitioners criticized (but did not name) department heads who graded too easily and passed students because they feared "failing too great a proportion of the class," with the result that "the privilege of repeating a year at Hahnemann is prevalent and abused."[27]

The state board failures also gave this group of Hahnemann faculty an opportunity to address more serious structural problems. They suggested reorganizing the Medical Council, the faculty's executive committee, to include heads of departments, including the basic science departments. They also asked the board to eliminate von Rapp's position and to return to the position of dean "powers as recommended by the AMA's Council on Medical Education."[28]

At a meeting of the Medical Council to discuss the 1943 petition, Eberhard reported that the board would not authorize increasing the size of the council, arguing that including heads of all departments "would make too large a body." More than that, he explained, the board felt that "certain heads of departments, as they now function, would not afford proper material for Medical Council functioning." The Medical Council, whose members included Pearson, von Rapp, and Eberhard, agreed that while the new subcommittee on admissions had "done excellent work," nonetheless the "size of the class is entirely in the hands of the board of trustees." The council also agreed that there should be somewhat tighter rules for promoting students but that the board should have the power to make exceptions when there were "extenuating circumstances." Eberhard also dismissed the likelihood of any kind of professional probation; he told the faculty petitioners that he had "reliable information" from the AMA and the AAMC that the board failures "did not jeopardize the rating of The Hahnemann Medical College."[29] Throughout these discussions the faculty members were unable to represent their grievances formally, for, according to college bylaws they need 51 percent of the faculty present to have an official quorum. Because many faculty members were away on military duty and because the clinical men were, as Johnson and Zapffe later described it, carrying on "busy private practices in addition to their academic responsibilities," a quorum was impossible to assemble.[30]

When the trustees did not reply, faculty demands escalated. In October 1943 at the regular faculty meeting some of the petitioners suggested amending the bylaws "to be in accord with the intent of the founders and the tradition of Hahnemann specifically to allow for true faculty representation in academic management of the Hahnemann Medical College, and that it [the faculty] be given the right of self-determination."[31]

When the trustees did respond, they dismissed the seriousness of the demands and tried only halfheartedly to placate the faculty. In 1943 they requested the resignation of Hahnemann's longtime dean, William Pearson, and in January 1944 appointed a new man, William G. Schmidt, also from the chemistry department. Schmidt was an "interim dean," chosen to serve as a figurehead while Hahnemann selected a new, more reputable dean. Everyone recognized that his was an impossible position, and his complete lack of power made the emasculation of the dean's position all the more clear. Schmidt, for example, complained that Paul Correll, the representative of the State Board of Medical Education and Licensure, refused to direct "informal and official communications concerning academic matters" to him and sent them instead to von Rapp. As he told the Medical Council in August 1945: "Dr. Correll has purposely avoided or detoured the Dean's office because it was allegedly shorn of its conventional powers. . . . he has unceremoniously called me 'Smittie'. I yield to no man in a free expression of the democratic spirit of camaraderie, but I am disposed to suspect that Dr. Correll's informal appellation indicates contempt rather than good friendship."[32]

Schmidt, a chemistry and physics teacher with no medical training, had been teaching at Hahnemann since the 1920s, when he managed the School of Science, after which he was appointed an associate professor in the Department of Chemistry.[33] He seems to have had no support from any Hahnemann group whatsoever. He was not a Hahnemann graduate and had no connection with the Hahnemann alumni; he had no pull with trustees by way of patients or influential friends; and, worse, his having been sponsored by Eberhard, resulted, as he later admitted, in his becoming "personna [sic] non grata to a number of faculty members."[34] During his last year as dean, after he turned down the proposal of a full day's vacation for the junior class picnic, he was hissed as he began lecturing. And, he complained, "Evidence has come to me that students have been imbued with the thought that the Chairman [of the executive committee] is a puppet—a mere stooge or front for the administration—whose decisions can be set aside, whose regulations can be connived at and whose opinions are not to be regarded too seriously."[35]

Schmidt's marginality and his anger with his position meant that the letters he constantly wrote to alumni, to the trustees, and to Johnson and Zapffe were unusually candid.[36] Schmidt's one source of public influence was his position as editor of the *Hahnemannian Monthly*, a journal that had been under the sponsorship of the state homeopathic society since the 1910s. His editorials, like many of his private letters, were inflammatory and provocative. One referred openly to the school's "probationary status," calling it "a stigma—not to be erased with words, excuses or evasions." With a nasty edge, he commented that "chemists, engineers and business men are useful functionaries in their own way, but are scarcely qualified after all to set the pace, nor to inspire the cooperative response demanded by the complexities inherent in modern medical teaching trends," and he claimed his opponents exulted in "delusion, platitude and smug virtue." As a result he was telephoned by trustee Stauffer Oliver and told, as he later claimed to Johnson and Zapffe, "that I was 'to keep my mouth shut and not discuss Hahnemann with anyone at [the upcoming AAMC meeting in] Pittsburgh.'"[37] The state society also subsequently asked him to resign from his position as editor.[38]

In one of his letters to Johnson, Schmidt referred to the college's unfortunate "Drexler Affair," and this reference allows us to partially uncover this academic scandal that many of the faculty also saw as presaging the survey visit. At the heart of much faculty discontent was the feeling that college standards were constantly held subject to trustees' personal whims. The faculty were already frustrated, for example, with the board's policy of awarding honorary degrees to former and present trustees and local politicians rather than on the basis of scientific merit.[39] Leonard Drexler's case seems to have been part of the trustees' long-standing policy of allowing students to repeat exams they had failed or be promoted as probationary students, even when departments or individual faculty members objected. Leonard Drexler's name appeared in the minutes of a Medical Council meeting during a debate in 1944 about whether to allow him to be "declared in good standing" as long as he did not return to the college. The council decided to rescind a previous resolution that had permitted him to do so.[40] Carl Fischer, in his 1970 history of Hahnemann, offered his version of the event in a story about an unnamed student who is probably Drexler. According to Fischer, several students who failed an oral appealed to the trustees, who ruled that the students could not be failed without a written exam. Four were reexamined. One failed again, but the department was ordered to reexamine him reputedly because his brother was the secretary to an unnamed federal cabinet officer. Someone suggested that the student be provisionally passed provided he transfer to another school. The student was in the army, and after the army heard about the "provisional pass," the AMA, the AAMC, Congress, and the Pennsylvania state licensing board decided to investigate Hahnemann.[41] In March 1945, a month before Johnson and Zapffe's visit, one group of Hahnemann faculty wrote to them asking about the status of a freshman refused the right of repetition, aware that Hahnemann's policy of repeating exams was threatening its academic reputation.[42] It is clear from the 1945 report, although it does not discuss any case in detail, that various people talked to Johnson and Zapffe about the Drexler case. In the report Johnson and Zapffe commented at length on the board's recent policy of allowing written exams which its members could then reassess:

It is apparent that the Board of Trustees has concerned itself with questions of admissions of specific students, with promotions of such students, and with the manner in which examinations are conducted. The latter was evinced in a recent ruling of the Board that all final examinations are to be entirely written. The justification for this ruling is that written examinations are subject to review more easily than are oral examinations. This ruling is unsound both educationally and administratively.[43]

The faculty, they explained, "is responsible for determining whether a given student is qualified not only in his knowledge, but also in his character and personality" for the practice of medicine. These attributes could not be determined by a written examination, as was recognized by the use of oral examination by professional bodies such as specialty boards, medical schools, and licensing boards. "Few, if any, sick people would be willing to choose a physician on the basis of a written examination."[44]

The trustees' reluctance to respond to the faculty and the faculty's fervent welcome of the AMA/AAMC team can also be explained as the result of a personal vendetta against Harry Eberhard, a man with so many enemies that Schmidt described his support as "like the Kiss of a 'Judas.'"[45] Before the war Eberhard had identified as one of his major opponents the school's young associate professor in pathology, Harry Russell Fisher. Fisher, a 1928 Hahnemann graduate, had worked with Sappington in the Department of Pathology since 1930. In 1938, he had received a grant—one of the college's first grants for postgraduate education—for one year's postgraduate work "to Europe or another university."[46] In the early 1940s, according to one alumnus, Eberhard refused to certify that Fisher should be part of the college's list of "deferred" teaching faculty, and as a result Fisher was drafted for active service by the navy, ended up in China, and was seriously debilitated by amoebic dysentery. When Fisher returned to Pennsylvania in 1944 he went to the AAMC and suggested an accreditation survey as a way of attacking Hahnemann and Eberhard. He returned to the college, expecting to replace Sappington and be promoted to professor of pathology.[47]

Fisher's problems with the trustees continued even after the survey. Fisher and his supporters were incensed when the trustees refused to agree to his promotion. Fisher was proposed both by his former chief and by the new interim Medical Council that was established after the 1945 survey. When Sappington, who had come out of retirement to teach during the war, was asked his opinion about being replaced not with Fisher but with Lawrence Smith, a retired professor and head of pathology at Temple University, he replied: "the real need of the Department at the present time was not for another older department head whose replacement of himself would in no way increase the available teachers but rather a younger executive who could attract and train several young teachers of the caliber of the recent Residents in Pathology at Hahnemann." Sappington reported that he and other members of his department recommended "That Dr. H. Russell Fisher be returned to active service in the Department as soon as possible and that he be made Head of Department—a recommendation based upon his relatively young age, his proven ability as a teacher and his known interest in the welfare of the college and his popularity with the students." Sappington also pointed out that during the war the suggestion that Sappington would serve as acting head and Fisher would be designated as the formal head on leave had been "turned down by Dr. Eberhard," which suggested "that the Board of Trustees had already developed a prejudice against Dr. Fisher."[48]

In April 1945, the month of the AMA/AAMC visit, Joseph Conwell, the president of the board of trustees, wrote a formal letter to Harry Eberhard. It was a provocatively dismissive reply to faculty demands that the board give up its power over student admissions and promotions. Referring to "this unfortunate affair," Conwell wanted to "make it definitely clear that the administration and management of The Hahnemann Medical College and Hospital of Philadelphia rests entirely with the Board of Trustees." He did, however, believe that the board's policies were in line with modern professional thinking; the board did try to conform "in all respects" with the AMA's Council on Medical Education's latest guide to the 'Essentials of an Acceptable Medical School.'" But, arguing that "modern education is characterized by flexibility and a measure of liberality," Conwell rejected the idea of set rules for student promotion, for Hahnemann's were "adequate and in harmony with those prevailing in other medical colleges." The idea that the Medical Council should be made up of department heads was, he believed, a "principle . . . absolutely lacking in justification," for members of the board were "entitled to choose their agents in the Council with the utmost freedom and without any restrictions." He also rejected eliminating the position of provost and making any changes in the dean's powers. It was not, he made clear, the trustees' fault that Hahnemann graduates had failed the state board exams in such high numbers. "Neither the Board of Trustees nor the Medical Council is responsible for the State Board failures. These usually occur at the end of an internship one or more years after graduation. We cannot enforce study for the State Board Examinations under these conditions."[49]

The trustees recognized that American medical leaders believed that trustees, as trustee Burke Wilford wrote to the Medical Council, "should have nothing to do with the academic management of the institution, but should see that the money is available to carry forward and improve the teaching personnel and facilities." But, Wilford explained, while this might be "correct in substance," "there will be certain instances where personal ambition and pride of an individual might interfere with this general policy, and the Trustees must have the

final say in academic matters in order to keep the organization running." Wilford
blamed Hahnemann's problems on its finances and on the faculty conflicts. The
problem of raising a "satisfactory endowment" would be solved, he wrote, "if we
can get rid of small-mindedness, professional jealousy, and lack of confidence
in our own qualities," and he pointed to the importance of making Hahnemann
"less inbred with its own alumni."[50]

The alumni also pressed for reform. During the 1940s a small group of faculty alumni met regularly to discuss Hahnemann's problems. Carl Fischer, for
one, tried to use the upheaval to gain the ear of the AAMC to protest the
Alumni Association's lessening influence over college affairs. He told Zapffe that
he thought Hahnemann's probation was in part the result of the lack of representation of the alumni on the board.[51] In May 1942, the alumni's own board
of trustees had sent a resolution to the college's board "demanding a reorganization to be prefaced by the resignation of the Administration, the Board of Trustees and the Medical Council—to be followed by a Faculty election of the
successors at a special meeting." "Needless to say," Fischer later commented, "this
was rejected!" After this rejection, the eleven members of the faculty who had
been meeting "frequently" went to John C. Bell, a Philadelphia lawyer who later
became chief justice of the Pennsylvania Supreme Court. Bell told the group
that they had no rights and that Hahnemann's board was "self-appointing and
self-perpetuating," and he recommended that the alumni seek formal representation on the board "so as to secure a possible lever." Hahnemann's board agreed
to this, perhaps, Fischer later commented, "under the pressure of the accreditation agencies," and by the mid-1950s the Alumni Association was assured two
places on the board for its representatives.[52]

The Report

When Johnson and Zapffe came to the college in April of 1945, they saw their
task as fundamentally radical. They wanted to turn the school upside down, to
urge Hahnemann to rethink who should run the school, how students should
be selected and promoted, who was to be the voice of the faculty in determining faculty affairs and in speaking to the trustees, which departments in the college should have power, and what kind of institution Hahnemann Hospital
should be.

For Johnson and Zapffe, Hahnemann's lack of interest in research symbolized many of its larger problems. They argued that a modern medical school
needed to promote research not so much for research's own sake but to create
the right kind of academic atmosphere for teachers and students. At Hahnemann
there was little funding for research: in 1945 the Department of Surgery, for example, had twenty-five dollars for equipment and supplies and nothing for re-

search; and the Department of Pediatrics had seventy-five dollars for equipment and supplies and two hundred fifteen dollars for research.[53] Departments did not know how much was available to them for equipment and supplies either for the teaching program or research, and funds came from the administration "as each occasion arose" (21). In fact, as Johnson and Zapffe's report commented, there was "no budget in the ordinary sense of the word" (21). "A school cannot carry out its primary function of training physicians for the practice of medicine," Johnson and Zapffe argued, "unless research is stimulated and carried out in the school. A proper appreciation of medicine in the modern world cannot come to the student who fails to appreciate fully the spirit and place of research in this science and profession" (21–22). A student "will be a less competent physician unless he appreciates the full significance of the unknown and the role of research in its conquest"; and "no matter how excellently a teacher presents what is known, he is only partially a teacher unless he carries out some research as well" (22). With its limited resources, Hahnemann, they concluded, aimed "primarily at the training of physicians." It did not need "an elaborate research program" but must "stimulate research to the utmost of its ability and resources" (22).

Hahnemann clearly admitted large numbers of students, the report recognized, "for the purpose of obtaining funds for the operation of the school" (23). From 1939 to 1941 the number of freshmen averaged 148, and over the next three years around 156 (23). In October 1944 Hahnemann accepted an unprecedented 169 freshmen, a number exceeded only by the Universities of Illinois and Tennessee. In 1945, the freshman class had been reduced to 151, but "even this number is excessively large for an institution with the resources and facilities of this school." In 1943 there were only four medical schools with larger enrollments; and first-class schools like Stanford, Yale, Chicago, and Vanderbilt accepted only sixty to seventy freshmen that year. Hahnemann would not be able "to maintain satisfactory educational standards" unless it admitted markedly fewer students or increased the size of its facilities "particularly in the clinical years" (23).

Johnson and Zapffe also argued that the students were not of good quality. The clearest evidence of this, they suggested, was the results of the recent state board exams, and they included a table to demonstrate the problem (24–25).

Year	% Hahnemann Failures	Overall % in Approved Schools
1939	10.7	2.8
1940	15.9	5.1
1941	18.2	4.6
1942	18.3	2.4
1943	6.0	1.5
1944	9.9	2.9

Johnson and Zapffe added that the drop in failures in 1943 was probably the result not of changes at Hahnemann, as all failures dropped in that year, but of "increased leniency on the part of State Examining Boards during the war" (25).

They blamed these failures on the poor quality of students, pointing to the high numbers of in-state students suggesting the school's lack of national competitiveness. They explained the twelve members of the 1945 freshman class who were from California, "perhaps because of an interest in Homeopathy in California" (23). Johnson and Zapffe reported that the faculty frequently said that "a goodly proportion of the class should not be in medical school at all" (23–24). Standards at the school suffered because "better students are likely not to extend themselves" to outperform inferior students, who were "very easy to beat scholastically" (24). In their survey of the academic records of successful candidates, Johnson and Zapffe found many freshmen whose scores were below fifty on the Medical Aptitude test, and reviewing thirty-two of the (already culled) sophomore class, they found an average score of forty-nine (24). But Johnson and Zapffe not only blamed the failures on the state boards on the admission of too many students with "extremely poor" academic records but also found "evidence of irregular practices in the admission of certain students" and found that the selections of the admissions committee were not always made "on a democratic basis with the majority rule obtaining" (24a).

Johnson and Zapffe were also critical of the content and style of Hahnemann teaching. There was, they concluded, too much time spent on anatomy (633 hours), chemistry (290 hours), pharmacology and prescription writing (232), and pathology (436). In fact, there was too much prescribed time. "Apparently, the instructors attempt to cover every minor detail in their courses including much that is insignificant or irrelevant, and leave little to the student to acquire for himself" (33). The selection of courses was standard, and the report briefly and neutrally mentioned the homeopathy taught to juniors and seniors, which was, by 1945, a general course on therapeutics: "the treatment of disease by all forms of therapy is presented. Homeopathic theory is not stressed and there seems to be no compulsion upon the students to favor Homeopathic therapy" (46). But in 1946 Zapffe did write to the trustees to suggest that Hahnemann rethink the status of homeopathy in the curriculum and become a regular school.[54]

Even more serious than the deficiencies of the preclinical program were the problems in Hahnemann's clinical training. According to Johnson and Zapffe's report, the third-year clinical curriculum was "entirely obsolete . . . the kind of program which was in operation in our medical schools 25 years ago before the advent of well organized clerkships" (34). At Hahnemann, juniors and seniors were taught mostly through classroom work and group work. The classes were too large to permit ward rounds, "so that practically all the experience the students gain with patients in the third year is in the display of patients by staff members in large clinic demonstrations." "This method of instruction no longer has a place in a modern medical school" (34). In order to introduce the proper teaching method—the case method—Hahnemann needed to either decrease its class size or increase its clinical facilities by affiliating with other hospitals. Affiliation, was, however, less desirable, as "it is nearly always difficult to control an educational program and maintain it at a high level in a hospital not completely controlled by the medical school" (35).

Johnson and Zapffe felt that the clinical program suffered because Hahnemann Hospital was both poorly managed and poorly designed. It had been, they argued, "constructed in complete disregard for the requirements of a teaching hospital." "Apparently, the major thought in planning this hospital was to provide as many beds as possible with a complete disregard for other facilities which must be included in a medical school" (28). There were so few offices for teaching staff that student conferences were held on benches in corridors or in clinic cubicles. There was virtually no space for research or staff laboratories, and that the students' laboratory was a small, ill-equipped room meant that most students needed to go to the medical school "at an inconvenient distance from the wards" (28). And there was little space for students or house staff to do their clerical work: "students were seen sitting on benches in the corridor or even standing beside the nurse's desk, writing histories on their patients" (28).

Worse, relations between the college and the hospital were such that despite the large college classes, only 350 of the 500 beds were available for clinical teaching, and of those, up to 100 were sometimes not filled. "The major, purely academic difficulty of this medical college is the inadequacy of the clinical facilities" (31). Thus, there were only two beds (rather than the standard four) for each Hahnemann junior, and often two students per patient; so students were unable to do real clerkship work on the wards (32). The outpatient service was also too small, and seniors also had to share a patient (37–38).

What was crucial about Johnson and Zapffe's criticisms was their conception of the character of medical education and the place of a teaching hospital, their conception of the proper relationship between junior and senior students and the hospital staff and patients (a conception that would be fundamentally challenged in the 1960s and 1970s). Johnson and Zapffe saw that Hahnemann juniors and seniors were treated as students rather than as apprentice physicians and given little responsibility or respect. The AMA and AAMC clearly saw the role of the physician-in-training differently. "Beginning in the junior year," Johnson and Zapffe argued, "the student should look upon himself and be considered by everyone as a junior physician, having the responsibilities of a physician in charge and carrying out the various procedures starting with the history" (32). And they spelled this philosophy out clearly:

> Students are not considered as student physicians. They are not ad-
> dressed as doctors either by the instructors or by the nursing and other
> hospital personnel. It is essential that students at this level be regarded as
> physicians under supervision and that they be called "Doctor". If this is
> not done, the student is at a decided disadvantage with the patient from
> the outset. The student should introduce himself as "Doctor" to the
> patient and explain to the patient that the history and examination will
> be made more than once by several individuals and that this system has
> served to the best interests of the patient in the experience of this hospital.
> There can be a dignified relationship of this kind between the student on
> the one hand and the physician and patient on the other hand (36).

Students, thus, were to present themselves as ambassadors of the teaching hospital, a major shift from the voluntary hospital where trustees still largely saw
their role as protecting patients from unfettered clinical instruction.[55]

Johnson and Zapffe's complaints about clinical training had been preceded
by similar complaints from Hahnemann students in their yearbooks. The 1940
seniors satirically described their work at the surgical dispensary, where students
"may learn to do things which any Boy Scout could do with much less fuss."
The duties of a student assisting at a sebaceous cyst removal were "(a) To hold
the patient's coat, (b) To move the light around for the staff man, (c) To keep
out of the staff man's way." Seniors in 1945 reported that they all agreed "the
amphitheater was only built for an audience of three." "Perhaps someday, some-
where, someone will discover a few of the more obvious flaws in the teaching
methods at Hahnemann, and of special import, the mass clinics in which little
if anything is gained." Margaret Giannini recalled that much of her clinical experience involved "going as a group and looking at a patient." And with a sharp
awareness of the politics of academic status at Hahnemann, the 1936 class had
described the "Requirements for Promotion":

1. Make friends with the Dean, or
2. Must have a friend on the Board of Trustees, or
3. Must clean Chandler's test tubes, or
4. Must stooge for Bernstein, or
5. Must crib the exams, or
6. Must study like hell and finally, when the four years are completed, be too
   damn tired to enjoy life.[56]

Johnson and Zapffe's 1945 report was more reticent about the Hahnemann
faculty than it was about the students, the curriculum, and the organization of
the school, praising only the physiology department (the "strongest of the preclinical departments") and the pharmacology department, headed by Reinhard
Beutner, "an outstanding Pharmacologist with a national reputation" (42). It

targeted chemistry, with its four full-time faculty (including one former and one acting dean), all over fifty, and suggested it needed instead "young and promising men" (41). There should be one full-time faculty member in the basic sciences for every twenty-five students (43). It also criticized the large number of departments, clearly identifying them as personal fiefdoms granted by the trustees as favors to individuals over the previous few decades.[57] The AAMC and AMA representatives wanted to give Hahnemann faculty more power in their institution, and the only model they felt would accomplish this goal was a research-oriented, full-time faculty.

The 1945 report indicated that Hahnemann had too many clinical departments, some of which seemed to have been established without consideration of "educational or administrative desirability" and to "have no justification for existence as separate departments in any medical school" (44, 53). And the vast majority of teachers were Hahnemann graduates: "A faculty of this kind is far less desirable than one containing graduates of other medical schools who can bring to the clinical departments new ideas and methods. Every effort should be made by the school to obtain more men from other institutions" (44–45).

Thus, Johnson and Zapffe concluded that there was "an acute need for a reorganization of the administration of the medical school" (53). They sympathetically retold the story of the efforts made by faculty members over the previous three years to have their complaints heard. "At times the administration has interfered unduly in the academic activities of the faculty" (55). Faculty committees, they agreed, needed to have greater representation of preclinical departments, and their governing body, the Medical Council, needed more authority "in the academic affairs of the medical school." "The faculty as a whole should be permitted a more active part in the conduct of the educational program" (53).

The Response

Although Johnson and Zapffe had urged Hahnemann's administrators not to publicize the report, by July 1945 Dean Schmidt reported to the trustees about "the many anxious inquiries by current and prospective students, alumni members, sponsors, and parents as to the probable outcome of pending conditions." Schmidt and Scott, as members of the new executive committee acting as dean, urged the board to "invest the Executive Committee . . . with adequate powers— educational, administrative, and fiscal—to meet all of the requirements of the current emergency" and to ensure "a well-defined partition between the jurisdictional powers of the officers of the Provost and the Dean" to avoid "even the suggestion of frictional contact." They asked that "all of our policies, acts, and decisions be not influenced, directly or indirectly, by any trustee in his individual or official capacity."[58]

The Alumni Association also played an important role in pressuring the trustees. The report was "for several months," according to Carl Fischer, "kept from the Faculty and Alumni Board." As the alumni faculty became frustrated with little initial response to the 1945 report, the association decided to send to all Hahnemann alumni a brochure entitled "Hahnemann and Its Future." The brochure—which was directed mainly at Stauffer Oliver, the new head of the board and a judge on the state's Court of Common Pleas—was, Fischer claimed, "much to the Judge's dislike." In September 1945 there was a joint meeting of the alumni board of trustees and the Hahnemann board's college committee, at which "Acting Dean Schmidt and Judge Oliver spoke at great length and frequently at odds." After this meeting, the alumni board publicly endorsed the survey report.[59]

In response to the 1945 report, the subsequent probation, and its impact on the school's reputation, Hahnemann's trustees restricted the number of freshmen to just over one hundred and began to apply stricter guidelines for the admission and promotion of students. They established classrooms on the hospital's ward floors, opened a new outpatient clinic, and gained additional hospital affiliations.[60] They tried to use the National Board exams as a neutral way of assessing and promoting students but found that students still pressured the faculty and the trustees to make exceptions.[61] They also organized a special committee consisting of the heads of medicine, surgery, obstetrics, gynecology, and pediatrics (the only clinical departments that the report's authors had argued deserved the standing of "department") to "overhaul and to revise thoroughly our curriculum for the clinical years."[62] But, as Schmidt warned Zapffe privately, instituting such changes would be "much more difficult than [reorganizing] the curriculum for the preclinical years in view of the long established and difficult-to-change traditions."[63] In response to Johnson and Zapffe's criticism of the makeup of the main faculty committee, a new Medical Council was set up which included, as trustee Stauffer Oliver pointed out to Zapffe, "critics of the administration" such as physiologist John Scott, gynecologist Newlin Paxson, pathologist Hunter Cook, and pediatrician and alumni representative Carl Fischer.[64]

However, it quickly became clear that this new Medical Council was not considered by the board to be a truly authoritative body. In December 1945 the Russell Fisher supporters on the interim Medical Council—Paxson, Scott, Hessert, Reimann, Martin, and Wells—threatened to resign. They were angry about the trustees' decision not to promote Fisher: they declared that there was "no satisfactory academic or scholastic reason for this action."[65] They also pointed out that the council was still not organized "in accordance with the American Medical Association Survey recommendations." They suggested abolishing both von Rapp's and Eberhard's positions, appointing two alumni members to the board, and procuring "a competent, medical dean." The Medical Council, they told the board, needed "to exercise its academic prerogatives entirely free of co-ercion, interference or unjustified supersedence by any other college authority."[66] Later the faculty complained that "it is the opinion of the Medical Council that it should have the power to appoint its own Hospital Advisory Committee from its own membership."[67] Schmidt had already pointed out that "the Provost con-tinued to retain his status as the chief academic officer," which led to conflicts of "jurisdictional authority." And he noted that a member of the admissions com-mittee had been appointed by one of the trustees, which was "contrary to the existing by-laws," and another member was "not among those approved by the Medical Council."[68]

A central decision was who should be appointed as the new dean, a deci-sion that Johnson and Zapffe made clear would send a signal to outside profes-sional bodies about what kind of institution Hahnemann wanted to become. As trustee and new board head Stauffer Oliver described it to Carl Fischer, his reading of the 1945 report suggested that the right dean for Hahnemann would need "a medical degree, distinguished teaching experience, a good knowledge of modern trends in medical education, pronounced executive ability, and a good personality."[69] Schmidt told Oliver that it was tempting to think that finding the right man, perhaps an outsider, would solve all Hahnemann's problems, as if Pearson had been their cause. But he thought it more important to find a man "thoroughly conversant with *our unique local problems*." Such an appointment would not be a "panacea" nor would it "magically transform the situation at Hahnemann, unless certain fundamental issues are also completely resolved. It is a fatuous reflection for us to repose hope and salvation in a palliative course of action that will not touch on the basic problem of 'ultimate control.'"[70] More crucially, he argued, the administration was "still exceedingly reluctant to con-cede certain profound reorganizational changes that would affect its ultimate power and control."[71]

The appointment in October 1946 of Charles Brown, the former head of the Department of Medicine at Temple University, was the first of a number of major administrative and personal changes at Hahnemann.[72] Schmidt returned to the chemistry department but remained on a number of faculty committees.[73] A number of senior faculty retired in the late 1940s, including surgeon Gustav Van Lennep, obstetrician John E. James Jr., ophthalmologist Frank Nagle, and hospital director Ralph Plummer.[74] In 1947 Frederic von Rapp resigned and was replaced by Raymond Leopold, as an alumni representative on the board of trust-ees and as administrator of the hospital.

Russell Fisher was not appointed head of pathology, but another of Sappington's candidates was: John Gregory from Johns Hopkins.[75] By 1946 the newly reconstituted and renamed faculty College Council included the heads of all the major departments: Sappington (pathology), Pearson (chemistry), Wells (medicine), Phillips (anatomy), Beutner (pharmacology), Scott (physiology), Martin (surgery), Hessert (obstetrics), and Fischer (pediatrics). It did not include Eberhard or Boericke. By 1949 a change in bylaws specified that the council must include the heads of nine major departments and that the majority should always be preclinical faculty, a ruling that remained in effect until the 1960s.[76] The alumni also gained two seats on the board, and the first two alumni representatives were Raymond Leopold (class of 1906) and Harold Taggart (class of 1919), both of whom played major administrative roles during the 1950s.

Brown needed to unify the institution, gain the respect of the faculty and power from the trustees, and design an acceptable plan for the future. It was an impossible task. He saw one of his first jobs as defending the institution to Johnson and Zapffe and demonstrating that the changes being made were a significant part of the long process of getting off probation. Brown attended the annual meetings of the AAMC and also met regularly with Johnson and Zapffe. They discussed finances, additional hospital beds for clinical teaching, additional full-time preclinical and clinical teachers, the students' clinical teaching, and scheduling a time for a resurvey.[77] He especially sought to defend the college's budget.[78] By 1947 it was clear that Johnson and Zapffe's "desirable formula" of spending two dollars from nontuition sources for every dollar from student tuition was a goal that was "obviously . . . impossible for us to reach . . . at this time." Hahnemann was spending one dollar for every student tuition dollar, and expenditures had increased from 20 percent in 1944 to nearly 50 percent in 1947, the result of an increased amount of state aid. "I believe the Survey Committee will be impressed with the increase just mentioned," Brown told the trustees, "and the progress along the line mentioned by Dr. Johnson, and this in spite of greatly reduced student enrollment."[79]

Most significantly, the trustees began to take an active responsibility for Hahnemann's problems: not just in agreeing to reorganize the college curriculum and administration but in demonstrating their commitment by organizing a major fund-raising drive and contributing personally. Johnson wrote to Brown in 1947 arguing that "one of the most serious difficulties responsible for the action of the Council in placing the school on probation was the inadequacy of the financial support of the institution."[80] And Brown reported to the trustees that "it has been apparent that the responsibility for our troubles at Hahnemann has been laid directly at the door of the Board of Trustees."[81] In 1948 the AMA representative told Brown: "I hope that the Trustees will take the opportunity that will be afforded by the forthcoming drive to demonstrate their confidence in you and your school. If this drive is successful in raising sufficient funds to stabilize the school's financial status and to make possible its continuing development, it will be tangible evidence to all concerned that the Trustees are serious in their determination to complete the rehabilitation of the medical school."[82] The trustees' fund-raising effort, which began in January 1949, raised more than forty-three thousand dollars for college improvements and also twenty thousand dollars for general college and hospital improvements through direct contributions of the trustees themselves.[83] And in April 1949 probation was lifted.

A few of the changes at Hahnemann during the late 1940s suggest that some Hahnemann supporters blamed the school's difficulties on its continuing association with homeopathy. As part of Hahnemann's effort to appear closer to the reputable mainstream, its 1946–1947 catalog no longer referred to the school's degree of homeopathic medicine and mentioned only the degree of "Doctor of Medicine," although diplomas contained both degree titles until the early 1950s.[84] These changes were spurred by comments like those of Dean Brown, who discussed at length with the faculty and trustees "his efforts in securing additional facilities for clinical teaching and additional full-time teaching and the bearing of the required teaching of homeopathy on these two problems."[85] The faculty and the trustees agreed in 1947 to make homeopathy an elective course starting in September 1947. Of the freshmen that year, the dean reported, 79 of 105 chose the elective.[86] The faculty's homeopathic committee, chaired by Boericke, recommended a postgraduate course and a certificate for proficiency in homeopathy, but it is not clear that this recommendation was ever put into practice.[87] Boericke continued to teach his homeopathic therapy course until his retirement in 1959.

By 1948, even before the end of probation, Hahnemann was forced to confront the meaning of the upheaval with its celebration of the school's centennial. In 1947, the trustees asked William Pearson, former dean and still head of chemistry, to write a history of the college and hospital that continued Thomas Lindsley Bradford's history, which had ended in 1898. Pearson tried to frame his story (told in a series of brief articles in the *Hahnemannian Monthly*) as one of progress out of darkness. It did give him an opportunity to assign blame: to the trustees and not the faculty. "The Board of Trustees insisted on increasing the number of medical students," he wrote, which led "to the maximum limit of our facilities, with the inevitable result that high scholastic standards could not be maintained and a disgraceful proportion of our graduates failed to pass examinations for licensure." But Pearson also hinted at the complexities of the story: "It would be improper to relate the many factors which were responsible for these dark days. Rumors of war and the obvious need for many young physicians may be given for the continence of this unwise policy."[88]

In 1949, the year after the publication of Pearson's history, at the most significant faculty meeting of the whole period, Schmidt resigned from the faculty, and Eberhard retired. At the same meeting the faculty discussed a recent AMA/AAMC survey that had found "marked improvements," and they congratulated the administration and themselves "on the progress that has been made" and announced the end of probation.[89] In the 1949 yearbook, the seniors at Hahnemann bid William Schmidt farewell. They praised him as "the hub of a bogged down wheel [in which] . . . some of the spokes were broken, others twisted, and still others strong and ready." Hahnemann they described as "a proud institution beginning to crumble as a result of slow decay." In a spirit of optimism, this class, which Schmidt himself had termed the "Children of the Storm," lauded their acting dean: "a firm believer that dead issues are for dead minds only, he dealt with real issues. He was instrumental in formulating the solution of the problems which have now ceased to trouble Hahnemann."[90] Although by 1949 Hahnemann was no longer on probation, it would find putting into practice the model of an "acceptable" medical school outlined by the AMA and AAMC far more troublesome than anyone had envisaged.

Part III

The Final
Fifty Years

*Re-creating a School
and an Identity*

Chapter 6   Embracing Orthodoxy

The 1950s and 1960s

Hahnemann celebrated its centennial quietly. In 1948 the school was in its third year of the probation imposed by the American Medical Association (AMA) and the Association of American Medical Colleges (AAMC) and was still in the throes of internal conflict now overseen by a new dean, Charles Leonard Brown (1899–1959), the former head of Temple University's Department of Medicine.

By the end of the 1960s Hahnemann had experienced the most profound transformation of its history. Under the direction of Charles Brown and his successor, Charles Sherwood Cameron (1908–), Hahnemann's medical school and hospital began not merely to adopt but to embrace the midcentury orthodox model of medical education, as articulated by the AMA and AAMC, within the context of Philadelphia medicine and Hahnemann traditions. Hahnemann dropped its homeopathic links, including its homeopathic degree, and alumni began organizing social events, like a Hahnemann Smoker, at AMA annual meetings. Its new full-time senior faculty reorganized the curriculum in accordance with modern teaching methods and served as examples for their students by directing laboratory and clinical research programs. Hahnemann Hospital began to integrate teaching and research activities, lessening its long-standing role as a community health facility, and for the first time began to use private patients systematically for teaching and research purposes. Hahnemann's technical training programs, previously hidden in hospital departments, were institutionalized in 1968 into a new body, the College of Allied Health Sciences. In 1949 Hahnemann created the Graduate School of the Basic Medical Sciences, which was renamed the Graduate School in the early 1970s. The graduate school allowed Hahnemann to include graduate and postgraduate students in its faculty members' expanding research programs and by the mid-1960s helped to justify a growing feeling among basic science faculty that Hahnemann should become a university, which it did in 1981.[1] The transformation of Hahnemann's physical plant provided the laboratories, clinical facilities, and modern appearance that would help make Hahnemann function as an integrated academic health center. Hahnemann took over adjoining buildings and renovated and then tore down most of its existing physical plant; by the end of the 1960s, of "old Hahnemann" only the 1938 Klahr Building and the 1928 hospital remained.

The 1950s and 1960s saw not only a remaking but a resurrection of Hahnemann. The problems Hahnemann had faced in the 1940s were so serious that we need to try to understand how Hahnemann managed to survive, and even flourish, in later decades. The poor decisions of a few powerful men were not the only cause of Hahnemann's probation: the college had admitted too many students and had not increased its faculty or improved its facilities because it was considered by the trustees a burden and appendage to a financially ailing hospital. Hahnemann's supporters, especially its alumni, had recognized the school's decline. But, with the corporation's financial problems worsened by the Depression, the school had had no way to raise funds other than increasing tuition or appealing to individual trustees and the alumni. Yet the changes demanded by the AMA and AAMC in the 1940s and 1950s were even more expensive: more full-time faculty, fewer students, more and better equipped laboratories, and a budget committed to research and curriculum development. After surveying Hahnemann at the end of Brown's tenure, AMA/AAMC representatives warned the trustees in a private report: "Without success in acquiring adequate funds it is apparent that the future of this institution, important as it is to medical education, will be in jeopardy."[2]

Providentially, in the postwar decades, Hahnemann medical school's financial prospects changed dramatically. In this period a combination of social and scientific factors helped to provide Hahnemann with access to private and government funds that enabled it to fulfill the hopes of those who with such difficulty had supported professional probation. These were decades in which American society placed special value on medicine, science, and education. Partly as a result of veterans' experiences during World War II, and partly in response to the postwar economic boom, medical schools received private and government funds and immense public interest.

Medical schools like Hahnemann were able to fashion themselves in the AMA/AAMC image because American society came to value scientific research more than it ever had in the past. The American public, already impressed with the scientific achievements made during the war—penicillin, radar, the atom bomb—saw research as exciting and as possessing the potential to improve both the world and everyday lives. World War II, as one historian described it, "en-

Figure 26. In the Baby Boom years, many male Hahnemann students arrived funded by the G.I. Bill and were also helped through school by their wives, who, during the 1950s and 1960s were the recipients of a mock degree from Hahnemann: a Ph.T. (putting hubby through). *Medic* 1946.

hanced public belief that scientific research offered an endless frontier on which a happier, healthier life could be built."[3] Particularly important was the therapeutic revolution of the 1950s, an explosion of new drugs that seemed to promise to conquer all diseases, both the infectious diseases that were seen as problems of past generations and the chronic diseases that were of present and future concern. American veterans had also come home impressed with the power of modern medicine, and they began to demand new technologies and especially modern hospitals in their own communities. Congress responded by passing the 1946 Hill-Burton Act, which provided funding for hospital construction and renovation.

Further, this was an era when higher education was suddenly made accessible to a wide swathe of Americans by the 1941 G.I. Bill. A generation of veterans was offered the financial means to attend college and professional schools; the G.I. Bill thus became a major source of funding for medical schools. The veterans who entered medical school were older, more mature, and often married, and they approached their study seriously, as a way of achieving a secure position in the middle class. The more ambitious, seeking the cutting edge of medicine, saw the opportunity to study specialties and subspecialties. Higher education opened the door to a better life and a respected professional career. School traditions that had been reinforced by generations of students and faculty alumni, such as singing bawdy songs before lectures and fighting for the right to sit in the front seats, seemed irrelevant to the new, more serious postwar generation, many with spouses and children, who felt lucky to be able to attend college and medical school and who were determined to enter a profession that would give them financial stability and public respect. In the fields of science and medicine, this was an era of youth: old ways and old knowledge seemed not only out of place but also reactionary. "The physician who did not read Time Magazine," the editor of Hahnemann's 1950 senior yearbook remarked, "was apt to feel left far behind in the rapid advance of medical science."[4]

As scientific research gained new prominence and prestige, so did efforts to support it. As one contemporary historian noted, "research was glamorized in novels, plays, and radio broadcasts, whereas teaching was usually ignored as uninteresting or spinsterish."[5] Philanthropic groups began to offer money for laboratories or specific research projects. The massive expansion of public philanthropy around medicine and science in this period has not been explored by historians, but, as Hahnemann's experience demonstrates, the 1950s and 1960s saw not only new targets for giving but a profoundly altered demography of philanthropy. Before the 1940s Hahnemann Medical College had had little access to funding from private foundations, the major sources of medical funding for education and research, and had attracted few individual donors. But the groups that were newly organized or newly energized in the 1950s and 1960s looked very different from those on which medical schools had depended (in vain in

Hahnemann's case) for funding before the war. Middle-class American society now included the children and grandchildren of immigrants, and some, like American Jews, had developed since World War II a more pronounced sense of themselves as ethnically distinct and as having a special role to play in American life.

These new groups began to organize fund-raising efforts in areas that were previously seen as the province only of elite WASPs, an appellation coined in this era by a University of Pennsylvania sociologist. Medical philanthropy became democratized and somewhat pluralistic as lay Jewish and Catholic donors no longer targeted only the hospitals and charities of their immediate communities. Colleges and universities, and especially medical schools, became popular spheres, in part because of the high public esteem for science and the idea that funding scientific research was a powerful and patriotic way to help conquer the world's ills and to demonstrate one's social conscience. Wealthy non–Anglo Saxons began funding and creating laboratories—sometimes hidden on the top floor of a hospital—as memorials to themselves or to their parents. But these gifts had a purpose beyond personal aggrandizement. Philadelphia Jews in particular had long resented the quota system that they and their children faced when applying to the city's medical schools. They hoped that this new philanthropic role would shame and pressure medical school administrators to rethink the anti-Semitism that still existed—as Laura Z. Hobson's popular novel on anti-Semitism, *Gentleman's Agreement* (1947), had shown—in middle-class America.

Medical schools also benefited from the American public's fascination with new drugs, especially antibiotics, developed during and after the war. Pharmaceutical companies began to provide research funding to medical schools to test these drugs, for they needed the distinctive resources a medical school and teaching hospital could provide: well-trained investigators and, more important, access to patients as research subjects. American physicians as well as the lay public intensified their faith in the power of pills to solve long-standing medical and social problems. Thus in the early 1960s, when Hahnemann organized a research symposium entitled "Psychosomatic Medicine," it was to discuss the role of the new tranquilizers and antidepressants for mentally ill patients.

Organized medicine recognized the importance, the prestige, and the cost of the research-oriented medical school. The AMA began to organize its fund-raising on a professional and national scale, employing public relations consultants, and in 1951 it established the National Fund for Medical Education to coordinate fund-raising. The AMA also established the American Medical Education Foundation to encourage and coordinate donations from physicians, which would be distributed through the fund. Within four years the fund had distributed more than nine million dollars.[6] At the same time the Ford Foundation provided ninety million dollars to help private medical schools expand their facilities to provide the basis for modern research programs. By the mid-1950s Hahnemann had received five hundred thousand dollars from the Ford Foundation.[7]

As a consequence of and a spur to these changes, the federal government dramatically expanded its funding of medical research and health care facilities. Medical research, historian Victoria Harden has argued, became "the principal way by which congressmen could vote to improve their constituents' health."[8] Caught up in the excitement of the wartime achievements and the competition of the Cold War, Congress expanded the National Institute of Health (NIH) by adding to its National Cancer Institute (formed in 1937) the National Heart Institute in 1948 and the National Institute of Mental Health in 1949. In 1950 Congress established the National Science Foundation. The total NIH budget grew from $29 million in 1948 to $1.4 billion in 1967.[9] These institutes reflected public expectations that scientists could not only defeat major infectious diseases but also develop new methods to explain and cure chronic disease. Medical schools now could apply for government grants not only for individual researchers but also for doctoral and postdoctoral fellowships, for new equipment, and for new buildings. Pennsylvania, like other states, also began expanding its medical school funding. In 1955 the state legislature altered its method of funding, so that instead of making separate grants to individual schools the state based its funding on the number of students enrolled.[10] As a result Pennsylvania's medical school deans had a new incentive to work together to demand more money from the state rather than to feel that one school's gain was another's loss.[11] Further, during the 1950s, industrialist Pierre du Pont, through his Longwood Foundation, provided grants to every medical school in Pennsylvania.[12]

World War II has been considered by many medical historians as the great turning point in twentieth-century American medical history. But for Hahnemann it was the decades after the war—with these social, political, and professional transformations—that forced the institution to remake its identity in order to survive and expand. To a great extent, more than any other time in its history, Hahnemann adopted the model of the midcentury orthodox model for medical schools and teaching hospitals, the model put forth by the AMA and AAMC. This model of medical education was distinctive in its assumption that funding for building expansion and for research would be available; and the assumption was correct. At the heart of this model, too, was the notion that "practical" schools producing general practitioners were out of place in modern American society. Veterans' experiences during the war had intensified the respect for specialists and for specialty training. As one 1945 Hahnemann graduate described it, "after the war, it became very stylish for patients to go to specialists."[13] In 1963, Hahnemann's dean argued that "The title, General Practitioner, is no longer appropriate and should be abandoned." Speaking at the inauguration of the second Hahnemann graduate to serve as president of the Philadelphia County Medical Society, the dean noted that less than one-quarter of the members of the society considered themselves general practitioners, and he urged the society "to divorce ourselves from emotion—particularly the emotion which tempts us to turn to the past. The horse and buggy doctor is dead. He will never be resurrected. Furthermore, he would be out of place if he were."[14]

After rejecting both homeopathy and its interwar parochial character as an institution that hired its own graduates and tended to its local community, Hahnemann had to decide what would define its new identity. Through regular professional reports and unpublished surveys, AMA and AAMC representatives had told Hahnemann that it could not educate modern physicians without integrating an active research program into the curriculum. Unlike the 1930s—during which medical schools' already limited funds were supposed to be used for nonexistent faculty research projects—the 1950s and 1960s were a research-funding bonanza. As Hahnemann's insightful deans quickly discovered, Hahnemann needed respected research teams and projects to attract this money.

To attract research funds Hahnemann needed first to lure prominent researchers, which was not an easy task. Being on probation had hurt the already ailing school. By the 1940s Hahnemann had virtually no national reputation, which was made brutally clear when it first tried to hire outsiders; one candidate remembers receiving a letter in 1950 inviting him to apply for a senior position: "I almost threw the letter away as I had never heard of Hahnemann before."[15] Locally, Hahnemann's reputation had fallen far below that of prestigious schools such as the University of Pennsylvania and Jefferson. Hahnemann was able to hire young researchers by promising a senior position and, even more enticing, a high salary. As Dean Brown warned Hahnemann's trustees in 1947, "to get new faculty we have had to pay somewhat higher salaries than are paid to some of our older faculty."[16]

What Hahnemann was seeking in these difficult decades was more than academic respect. The AMA and AAMC argued that a transformed commitment to modern teaching and research efforts would enable the institution to improve its professional standing, but Hahnemann's leaders wanted more. They wanted a spectacular renewal—faculty who were pacesetters, gleaming new buildings full of the latest technology—so that Hahnemann could grab the attention of the national media and the medical press. Unfortunately, as Hahnemann's administrators and trustees soon discovered, these goals were not always commensurable with what could actually be achieved. Hahnemann's pacesetters were sometimes less enthusiastic about the changes that came along with a commitment to a modern academic health center, especially if they felt their own power in the institution threatened.

Research as Survival and Recovery

In the postwar decades the American public was excited to see scientific research eliminate frightening epidemic diseases such as polio and tuberculosis. Public interest began to center around newly prominent chronic diseases; by the 1950s the major causes of American morbidity and mortality were heart disease and cancer.

Reflecting the widespread faith in science as the conqueror of disease, old and new medical fund-raising organizations began to channel their funds toward research, many for the first time. In 1944 the American Society for the Control of Cancer, an organization largely devoted to public education—later renamed the American Cancer Society—for the first time began to spend its funds for cancer research. In 1945 the New York Memorial Hospital received money from the city and from General Motors to establish the Sloan-Kettering Institute for Cancer Research, which became the largest private cancer research center in the world. A year later Sidney Farber, a Harvard pathologist, established a children's cancer research society known as the Jimmy Fund; and reporter Walter Winchell created another cancer research philanthropy, the Damon Runyon Memorial Fund for Cancer Research, named after a Broadway reporter, and used his connections to movie stars like Bob Hope and Frank Sinatra to give cancer research a high profile.[17] When Hahnemann was considering candidates for dean, Charles Cameron's foremost attraction was probably his national reputation as the medical and scientific director of the American Cancer Society and as the author of a best-selling book entitled *The Truth about Cancer*.

Heart disease also gained a special aura. Voluntary societies across the country organized benefits to help patients receive expensive heart treatments and to help hospitals build the facilities needed for heart surgery. The field was exciting and expensive, and its human drama made wonderful headlines when patients, especially children, were saved by a courageous surgeon using the latest technology. Heart disease philanthropy came to be high-prestige giving, and, like cancer societies, groups like the American Heart Association raised money not just for equipment and medical care but for research as well.[18]

Throughout this period Hahnemann's strength lay in heart disease research rather than in cancer research.[19] Even before the war Hahnemann had developed a strong tradition of cardiovascular research. In 1939 Hahnemann cardiologist George Geckeler (1894–1989, Hahnemann M.D. 1919) was one of the first to record human heart sounds on long-playing records and use them with his specially developed "stethophones" for group teaching. His distinctive voice became familiar to a generation of medical students who learned to distinguish cardiac sounds from the records produced and distributed by Columbia. He became nationally recognized as a cardiology educator, and in the 1950s he received a grant from the newly established National Heart Institute for his cardiac teaching project.[20] Geckeler's student William Likoff (Hahnemann M.D. 1938) became a well-known cardiologist, and in the late 1970s his appointment as Hahnemann's executive president was a sign of Hahnemann's respect for his skills as a researcher, practitioner, and academic.[21] The work of thoracic surgeon Charles Bailey (Hahnemann M.D. 1932) particularly won popular attention, and Hahnemann Hospital recognized the power of heart surgery to attract public support and encouraged the local press to feature stories of its recovering patients.

At Hahnemann a group of clinicians and basic scientists on the faculty began to organize in ways to benefit from the new social prestige of heart research. In 1948 they formed the Cardiovascular Institute (CVI), a grand name for what was initially simply an interdisciplinary working group. The early members included George Geckeler, its first director; Charles Bailey; pulmonary specialist Jacob Crellin; pathologist John Gregory; radiologist Stauffer Lehman; physiologist John Scott; anatomist Raymond Truex; cardiologist William Likoff; and pharmacology researcher Joseph DiPalma, almost all of whom headed departments or sections at Hahnemann.[22] This group saw itself in the vanguard of research in heart disease and heart surgery. As Likoff later reflected, they "wanted to be released from the slowing influences of the remainder of the institution and strike out as a closely knit co-operative group working in the field of research."[23]

The group became one of the first at Hahnemann to tap into the newly diversified philanthropy in their city. And they were chagrined to discover that it came with a price. Their first task was to find funding for their research and a separate building to make the institute more than just a name. When CVI applied as a group to the NIH it was initially turned down, although its individual members were successful; finally in 1961 it received a two-million-dollar grant. Its greatest success came from the financial support of private donors. Initially Charles Bailey approached Joseph Ehrlichman, a prominent Jewish philanthropist who was in the process of transforming Deborah Sanatorium, a defunct tuberculosis sanatorium, into a cancer and heart research and therapy facility, but there was some concern at CVI. In 1949 Bailey reported to the group that "Mr. E[h]rlichman discussed the question of the admission of Jewish students to Hahnemann Medical School and Dr. Bailey showed Mr. E[h]rlichman that we had quite a number of Jewish students. Dr. Bailey stated that Mr. Stealman and Mr. E[h]rlichman showed no evidence of requiring any commitment re any increase in Jewish students." The CVI group after "much discussion regarding this question" decided that "there should be no definite commitment, re Jewish students at Hahnemann for any help that the Deboria [sic] Group might provide. Unanimously agreed that the cooperation would be under no obligation and that we could make no commitment re college admission."[24]

Bailey was more successful in approaching former patients, a few Hahnemann trustees, and some prominent Philadelphians, such as Richard Slocum, the editor of the *Evening Bulletin,* and John Wanamaker Jr., the son of the department store founder.[25] This group formed the Mary Bailey Foundation for Heart and Great Vessel Research (later the Mary Bailey Institute for Cardiovascular Research) to raise money for cardiac research. The foundation, established in 1950, was named in memory of Charles Bailey's daughter, who died in December 1949 of infectious hepatitis.[26] CVI was also able to attract additional supporters, like Charles and Fanny Zeitz and the National Council of B'rith Sholom Women, who helped CVI open the Clinical Physiological Laboratory for Cardiovascular and Pulmonary Research on the fifteenth floor of Hahnemann Hospital in 1951 and later funded a laboratory for cardiac catheterization.[27]

In 1961 the Bailey foundation enabled CVI to open its own building, a former automobile showroom on Board Street. The institute became a public showpiece. In 1962, Joseph DiPalma, its second director, warned fellow researchers of "the desirability of keeping the C.V.I. Laboratories in an especially good condition" since these rooms are frequently shown to distinguished visitors."[28] The institute, like other research facilities, also attracted critical attention from antivivisection groups, which, while less influential than they had been in the 1920s and would become in the 1980s, were nonetheless a force in shaping medical research facilities. DiPalma warned all CVI staff to be careful to lock their doors as "unauthorized individuals have on occasion observed the experimental dog work going on in the laboratories," and "unknown persons have complained to the Society for the Prevention of Cruelty to Animals." The CVI members decided to have their locks changed.[29]

Hahnemann trustees worried that the CVI group might become so discontent with Hahnemann's lack of support that it would look for a separate medical facility for its clinical work and take patients from Hahnemann Hospital. Thus in 1953 Stauffer Oliver, the chairman of the board of trustees, wrote an "Important and Confidential" note to his fellow trustees warning that, although "our surgeons are leading the world in this dramatic field of alleviating and correcting heart disorders, . . . we have been slow to realize the public relations value of the great work in Cardiovascular research and surgery which has been developed at Hahnemann." Oliver quoted "one of the M. B. Foundation enthusiasts" who had claimed that "Hahnemann is far better and more favorably known through the world than it is in Philadelphia." Oliver noted that more than five hundred American and foreign doctors and surgeons had visited Hahnemann in the previous two years and that the American Heart Association was "raising large sums of money throughout the United States by hammering away on 'Mitral Stenosis' and other operations, which were either originated or perfected at Hahnemann."[30] Heart research and heart surgery, Oliver argued, could be used to enhance Hahnemann's image and its solvency. He reminded the board of "Dr. Blalock, a surgeon at Johns Hopkins" who "is reputed to have been largely responsible for pulling an insolvent institution out of the doldrums, by his famous 'Blue Baby' operation—which is . . . now no longer used," and he compared Alfred Blalock's work "to the thrilling work being done today, right in our own institution . . . upon which to capitalize on our fund raising efforts. I am fearful we are too lethargic and that others will reap the benefits which should come to Hahnemann. . . . I believe also we should have a first-class publicity man or public relations expert, and that we should, in every legitimate and ethical manner, arouse our Philadelphia public to the accomplishments of Hahnemann and its great value to our community." Hahnemann had not "awakened to the value of what it has, especially from a public relations standpoint and the attraction of gifts and legacies."[31]

While most histories of medical education in this period have focused on the ways the scientific establishment supported and shaped the research programs of American scientists and physicians and spurred the growth of American medical science, Hahnemann's experiences also remind us of the central role of the lay public, especially patients, in directing and supporting scientific research as well as medical education. As we have seen, in the nineteenth century Hahnemann had long depended on gaining public support; it had always been run by a lay group and to a large extent was responsive to the demands of the local community. In the 1950s and 1960s the public, especially former patients, politicians, and city industrialists, played an important role in directing Hahnemann's policies.

The choice of Charles Brown as dean is a good example of the hidden side of academic hiring. Brown had solid academic credentials and had demonstrated his administrative skills at Temple. But his added strength was the financial support he could bring to Hahnemann through his wealthy patients. One particularly prominent supporter was William Goldman, Brown's friend and patient, who left Temple's board of trustees when Brown came to Hahnemann, and joined Hahnemann's board, becoming one of its first Jewish members. When Brown left Hahnemann in 1955, Goldman left with him and returned to Temple. Described as "the most active and aggressive member of the board," Goldman made a series of generous donations to Hahnemann during the 1950s, including money given specifically to Brown designated as the "Dean's Fund."[32] Goldman brought not only money but also welcome color to Hahnemann. The owner of a chain of movie theaters along the East Coast, he provided faculty and students with free tickets to the latest movies and sometimes invited faculty members to have lunch with visiting movie stars.[33] Goldman was able to tap into his Hollywood connections to help Hahnemann's researchers. In 1954 he arranged for Mr. Sidney, an MGM representative, to talk to George Geckeler about the possibility of a heart film, and he told the CVI group that Sidney and "a friend of his Mr. Cohen" would "make a generous contribution next year." Goldman also assured Hahnemann of its "favorable position . . . with respect to medical publicity through the MGM Studios."[34] The renovation of the college's histology laboratory was completed with the "administrative efforts and generous financial aid of Dean Charles L. Brown and William Goldman" and was renamed the William Goldman Laboratory of Microscopic Anatomy.[35] In 1949, at a meeting of the AMA's Council on Medical Education and the AAMC, Donald G. Anderson noted approvingly that "Mr. William Goldman of Philadelphia . . . had been elected trustee of the Hahnemann Medical College of Philadelphia . . . and has shown a great interest in the school and will be of great value in a business advisory capacity."[36]

Academic Medicine Comes to Hahnemann, 1946–1955

Hahnemann's administrative upheavals, although clearly prompted by the special circumstances of probation, were in other ways typical of medical schools across the country in this period. In 1946, for example, fourteen of seventy-eight medical schools had new deans.[37] At the University of Pennsylvania, William Pepper, who had been the medical school's respected and influential dean for over thirty years, retired in 1945 and was replaced by Louis Starr, a 1920 Pennsylvania M.D. and a pharmacology researcher.[38]

By 1949 there were only seven men on Hahnemann's board of trustees who had been there in 1945. New members such as Frederick Strawbridge continued an earlier pattern of paying for individual pieces of equipment; in 1954, for example, Strawbridge provided money for a "gas-fired anatomical incinerator to eliminate several unnecessary health and public relations hazards" when Hahnemann researchers cremated "materials used in scientific study."[39] Stauffer Oliver remained chairman of the board until 1955, when the board chose first an interim chairman to deal with a financial crisis and then Watson (Pat) Malone III, a lumber industrialist, who led the board until 1971. In 1954 the Alumni Association, which saw itself as having been a major force in bringing Hahnemann out of the darkness of the 1940s, gained two formal representatives on the board, with the proviso that neither could be active members of the faculty. One of the first representatives, Harold Taggart (Hahnemann M.D. 1919), left the board when he was appointed acting dean after Brown left, and, under Dean Cameron, he remained a Hahnemann administrator as assistant dean and medical director of the hospital. Memories of probation began to fade as the major figures involved resigned or retired; by 1952 Frederic von Rapp, William Schmidt, Harry Eberhard, and Russell Fisher had all left Hahnemann. By 1955, when Brown left, Hahnemann had a number of junior faculty on salary, and its departments of anatomy, chemistry, pharmacology, and bacteriology all had new full-time chairmen, none of whom were Hahnemann graduates.

Charles Brown was not the trustees' first choice for dean, but their other candidates, including an assistant dean at Harvard, were not interested in trying to lead a school in so much trouble and with such internal division.[40] Brown was a respected internist, and some of his patients were influential businessmen. He was not a Hahnemann graduate and had out-of-state training; his outsider status was appealing, yet he had lived in Philadelphia for thirteen years. Brown was born in Illinois and had graduated from the University of Oklahoma (B.S. 1919, M.D. 1921). He was part of a new generation of physicians seeking a career in academic medicine. After a year of private practice in Oklahoma City he had worked as a house officer and then a pathology resident at the Peter Bent Brigham Hospital in Boston. During that time (between 1923 and 1928) Brown also taught at Harvard Medical School as an instructor in pathology and a teaching fellow, and he worked with internist Henry A. Christian, a pupil of William Osler, who was engaged in revising Osler's textbook. In 1928 Brown left Boston for Ann Arbor and became an assistant professor in internal medicine at the University of Michigan; he was promoted to associate professor a year later and remained there until 1935, when he came to Philadelphia at the age of thirty-six to take up the position of professor of medicine and head of the Department of Medicine at Temple University, where he established the full-time system.[41] In 1944 he became president of the Philadelphia County Medical Society, a position that was not held by a Hahnemann graduate until 1952. This background seemed to fulfill the 1945 AMA/AAMC report's demand for someone who could provide Hahnemann "with the kind of leadership which is based in part upon a thorough-going knowledge of the problems and trends in modern medical education."[42]

Brown was to be a new broom with no previous Hahnemann connection. His experience as a Philadelphia physician and as an academic administrator suggested he would be sensitive to local medical politics. His medical background gave him a seniority that the two previous chemist deans had lacked, and it was hoped that this background would help restore the power and respect of the dean's position among the other faculty and with the trustees (the dean's lack of power had disturbed the 1945 AMA/AAMC committee). Brown's appointment in 1946 also showed the ways Hahnemann's trustees had interpreted the 1945 AMA/AAMC's report on how to best help their institution gain professional respect. As one of the trustees put it in 1947, "excellent organization and efficient administration, although indispensable to a school, are not sufficient in themselves to give it tone or preeminence. What Hahnemann has lacked throughout many years is medical leadership of the inspirational type to keep its name and activities in the forefront of medical education." But it was not "inspiration" that most impressed the trustees about the new dean; it was his personal style and character:

[Brown] is admirably qualified by education, experience, personality, and ability to thus represent Hahnemann in a gracious, dignified, and wholesome manner which no one in or out of the school could possibly emulate. Through his easy entree and immediate acceptance into the most exclusive and demanding medical circles, Hahnemann will quickly come to an unreserved recognition and an intimate appreciation which have elusively escaped the school for many years.[43]

Brown's policies closely followed the recommendations of the 1945 AMA/AAMC report and the subsequent surveys in 1948 and 1949. All had pressured Hahnemann to expand its Department of Neurology to include psychiatry, and under Brown the school received a government grant for "the teaching of psychiatry."[44] The college also created the Department of Public Health and Preventive Medicine; public health and preventive medicine had formerly been taught as occasional lectures and field trips by the Department of Pathology and Bacteriology. Neither of these two departments was headed by a full-time professor. Edward Steinhilber continued as head of a joint neurology and psychiatry department until 1951 and was replaced by Van Buren Osler Hammett (1908–1980), who was head until 1973. Pascal Francis Lucchesi (1903–1973) juggled his position as head of Hahnemann's new public health department with his other jobs as superintendent of Philadelphia General Hospital and member of Philadelphia's Department of Health.[45]

With the respect of Philadelphians and with some national connections, Brown was able to convince a small group of young research-oriented faculty to join Hahnemann as full-time members of the basic science departments. The faculty who came to Hahnemann in the postwar years were men whose backgrounds, loyalties, and conceptions of medical academia were significantly different from those of most Hahnemann faculty in the 1920s and 1930s. They had orthodox training and no association with homeopathy or other unorthodox medical systems. They were recruited to an institution with an admittedly poor reputation with the promise of power and money: a good salary, a position as department head, and a say in the running of the institution. Most had few connections with Philadelphia and none with Hahnemann's alumni or its past traditions or heritage. Some were graduates from the University of Pennsylvania's medical and graduate schools, an uncanny reflection of the first faculty of Hahnemann Medical College in 1848, in which six of the first seven had had a Pennsylvania medical degree. Brown's appointees also brought to Hahnemann a model of medical education that the institution had largely been able to ignore until the 1940s. They were hired to try to overcome what was not made explicit at the time, but what Margaret Giannini, a 1945 graduate, later recollected was the main problem with what she had felt was an otherwise good education at Hahnemann: that there was "no one there to make you get excited at anything." Giannini remembered that both she and other female and male students found no professor inspiring enough to be an ideal, no one who made students say "I want to be like you."[46]

Physiology was the only basic science department that continued to be led by its pre-war chairman. John C. Scott, a 1929 Ph.D. from the University of Pennsylvania, had come to Hahnemann as an assistant in the School of Science in 1923. He later joined the physiology department, becoming its head in 1939 after the death of Frank Widman. By the late 1940s his department had two research grants from the new National Heart Institute.[47] Scott retired in 1968, after almost thirty years as head of the department, and was replaced by Evangelos T. Angelakos (1929–), who had a 1956 Ph.D. in physiology from Boston University and a 1959 M.D. from Harvard; and the department was renamed physiology and biophysics.[48]

Brown had great hopes for invigorating Hahnemann's pathology department, which had been led for more than thirty years by Hahnemann alumnus Samuel Sappington. In this period pathology was considered, according to a contemporary, "the pivotal subject in medicine and the pathologist had the final word on the diagnosis and criticism of the clinician [and could] . . . determine if diagnosis and therapy [were] being done according to acceptable standards. Thus, the pathologist was a respected figure although he may not have been well liked."[49] In 1947 Brown managed to hire John Gregory as head of the department. Gregory (1909–1990) was intended to be the "star" of the basic science chairs and was supposedly hired with special money Brown had received from the state. During the 1940s and 1950s he was often described as a "Hopkins graduate," but in fact his 1940 M.D. was from the University of Cincinnati. He had worked as a resident in pathology at Johns Hopkins Hospital and as an instructor at the medical school.[50] In 1950 Gregory was made head of a new division of pathology, which included sections (known as departments) of clinical pathology and bacteriology. Gregory was not a success at Hahnemann; a diffident man, he was seen as a loner, and he left after a few years. He was replaced briefly by George Tedeschi, who was succeeded by Joseph E. Imbriglia (1912–1997), a 1938 Temple M.D. and a 1949 University of Pennsylvania D.Sc. who had been head of Hahnemann's section of clinical pathology since 1950.[51]

To head the bacteriology section, Brown hired Amedeo Bondi (1912–), a 1942 Ph.D. from the University of Pennsylvania who had worked as an assistant professor of bacteriology at Temple. Bondi came to Hahnemann in 1947 and remained head of bacteriology until his retirement in 1979.[52] In anatomy, Thomas Phillips (1887–1975), chair since 1936, retired in 1949 and was replaced by Raymond C. Truex (1911–1980), a 1939 Ph.D. from the University of Minnesota, the first non-M.D. head of that department.[53] In 1949 Hahnemann appointed J. Stauffer Lehman (1906–1974) to its new Department of Radiology;

Stauffer was a graduate of Hahnemann's School of Science and medical school, and he headed the department until 1970. In 1948 former dean William Pearson retired as head of the chemistry department, later renamed the Department of Biological Chemistry, and Brown chose Milford John Boyd (1902–1986), a 1932 Ph.D. from the University of Cincinnati's medical school who had been teaching at Cincinnati's biochemistry department. Boyd remained head until 1967 and was a major force behind the development of the graduate school and became its first director. He was replaced by Thomas M. Devlin (1929–), a 1957 Ph.D. from Johns Hopkins and previously the director of enzymology at the Merck Institute for Therapeutic Research in New Jersey.[54]

One of the centerpieces of this aspiring research-oriented medical school in these decades was its Department of Pharmacology. Pharmacology was able to attract government, philanthropic, and industrial funding and to command public interest. After Reinhard Beutner retired, the new head, appointed in 1951, was Joseph R. DiPalma (1916–), a 1941 M.D. from the Long Island College of Medicine, who remained head until his promotion to dean of the medical school in 1967. DiPalma was trained as an internist but had become involved in pharmacological research. DiPalma decided to take the position, he later recalled, because he had recently married and had a child, and he and his wife were impressed with Philadelphia's suburbs: "spacious, well maintained, with excellent schools and easily accessible from center city."[55] DiPalma, the son of Italian immigrants, also recognized that he had little chance of getting a chairmanship at the medical college in New York where he was teaching, and he was swayed by the impressive salary (twelve thousand dollars) Hahnemann agreed to and by the opportunity for the kind of high academic position that he knew was "rarely offered to Italian Americans." He was then thirty-four. Nobody mentioned to him that Hahnemann had just emerged from probation.[56]

During Brown's tenure, for the first and perhaps the only time in Hahnemann's history, basic science faculty had true power in the institution: they outnumbered clinical heads in the College Council; theirs were the only departments with full-time senior faculty; and, unlike those of Hahnemann's senior clinical men, their educational and research programs were consistently praised by AMA/AAMC surveys.[57] In 1956 an AMA/AAMC committee, for example, saw the new heads of the basic science departments as representing "a fine example of the high ideals of university education," providing "the stimulus which accounts for much of the progress that has taken place at Hahnemann," and saw them as exhibiting "a vital concern for the affairs of the total institution."[58] These men also received increasing amounts of outside funding. In 1954, for example, Truex's Department of Anatomy received money from the U.S. Public Health Service and from the Damon Runyon Memorial Fund for Cancer Research; Bondi's Department of Microbiology received grants from Smith, Kline and French, the American Cancer Society, the Office of Naval Research, and the U.S. Army.[59] Further, until the mid-1960s, the basic science departments had control of the teaching material for first- and second-year students, including the power to tell members of the clinical departments what information they needed to cover in their own lectures.[60]

Perhaps the most innovative research at Hahnemann came out of the participation of Hahnemann senior faculty in CVI. The CVI group had felt that changes under Brown were too slow and had gone outside the institution for financial support. They had also sought to bring together their mutual interest in cardiology research and to practice as a team, in a manner reminiscent of the highly regarded military efforts during the war. "The idea," DiPalma recalled, "was to establish a laboratory and research group of all these workers in cardiovascular diseases so that mutual cooperation could be engendered for the solution of major problems."[61] This unusually integrated group of cardiology surgeons and basic scientists doing cardiology research made important scientific contributions, including the establishment of the first cardiac nurses' training program in 1949, the use of lidocaine in cardiac anesthesia, and the experimental development of coronary bypass operations.

In 1948, after Brown had been at Hahnemann for two years, G. Harlan Wells, a 1902 Hahnemann alumnus and respected homeopath, retired as professor and head of the Department of Medicine. When Brown was appointed as Wells's replacement he became the first full-time salaried senior clinical faculty member at Hahnemann and the first non-Hahnemann graduate to head one of its important departments.[62] Brown's fervent effort to improve Hahnemann's laboratory facilities and attract young scientists brought him into administrative peril, however. In the mid-1950s it was discovered that Brown's financial officer had been using for the school's expanding academic budget money that should have been set aside to pay federal income taxes. The board appointed a new chief executive, Madison Brown, and Charles Brown became a "lame duck Dean." Brown left Hahnemann in 1955 to help organize Seton Hall, a new medical school in New Jersey, but he died in December 1959 without seeing the graduation of its first class. In 1956 Cameron described his predecessor using the language of Cold War scientific assurance: "He was a kind of quiet Atomic explosion at Hahnemann—the chain effects of which are even now being felt."[63]

Cameron's Full-Time Plan: The Trouble Begins

Charles Cameron was the first of Hahnemann's deans born in the twentieth century. With a college degree from the University of Pennsylvania, he graduated from Hahnemann in 1935, at a time when Hahnemann was still considered "sectarian," as he later termed it. Nonetheless, he became the first Hahnemann

Figure 27. In 1956, as part of its effort to remake itself into a modern academic medical center, Hahnemann hired Charles Sherwood Cameron (1908–, class of 1935) as its dynamic new dean, and he continued to lead Hahnemann until 1972. *Medic* 1959.

graduate to intern at Philadelphia General Hospital (PGH). Cameron worked alongside graduates from Duke and Yale at PGH and recalled later that he had not felt inferior to them; indeed he was often called on to help with technical procedures such as phlebotomies.[64] At PGH, after working in the men's and women's cancer wards as an intern and surgical resident, he developed an interest in cancer.[65] From 1938 to 1942 he held a Rockefeller Fellowship at Memorial Hospital in New York (later known as Sloan-Kettering) and then spent four years in the navy. In 1946 he joined the American Cancer Society as its medical and scientific director, and while there he emphasized public education on early detection, including trying to educate women and their doctors about the importance of the Pap smear, then not a standard diagnostic test.[66]

Cameron was chosen as dean partly because of his background—his connections to Hahnemann and the Main Line—and also because of his national presence.[67] He understood the workings of national academic and government funding: before he came to Hahnemann he was already a study section member of the National Cancer Institute and was subsequently chosen as a member of the AMA's National Fund for Medical Education and the National Board of Medical Examiners. He had no administrative experience in academia, but the trustees were clearly looking for someone more like a senior executive, someone who could help not just improve Hahnemann academically but also raise its regional and national presence. Cameron was an impressive and elegant figure, well spoken and charming, and his best-selling 1956 book, *The Truth about Cancer*, had been widely translated.[68] As a leader he brought vision and vigor, and within a few years he had presented the trustees with a twenty-five-year plan. His building program enabled Hahnemann to expand its educational and research facilities and had as its assumption the gradual expansion of a full-time faculty committed to the same vision. The basic science men hired by Brown, Cameron later recalled, were especially skeptical of his lack of academic background, but "in the end when the buildings went up they came around."[69]

Before Cameron's time Hahnemann's clinical faculty members were a typical mixture of first-rate clinicians and mediocre teachers. All the major clinical departments were chaired by men who also had private practices, and, like most private medical schools, Hahnemann never had enough money to match the income of specialists.[70] (Basic science faculty were cheaper, although not as cheap as they had been before the war.) The clinical chairs were powerful figures at Hahnemann, as they were at many medical schools, because of their influential patients and especially their ability to bring private patients to Hahnemann Hospital, which, like all inner-city hospitals, was suffering under the financial burden of ward patients admitted for the justification of state and city appropriations and as teaching material.

As the status of clinical research soared, it became easier to convince both admitting clinicians and their patients to accept middle-class men and women as teachers and as research subjects. John Moyer, the new head of the Department of Medicine, later claimed that he had convinced Cameron of the importance of having access to private patients in Hahnemann Hospital, as almost two-thirds of the hospital's patients were private patients of the staff clinicians. Cameron initially had "grave reservations": he feared that the patients would resent being cared for by students and residents, even if the residents were supervised by the patients' private physician, and that the clinicians would resent the encroachment of the private physicians. But the change was a success and became standard in most teaching-community hospitals.[71] Still, many middle-class families were moving to the suburbs outside Philadelphia's inner city and going to suburban hospitals that looked more modern than thirty-year-old Hahnemann Hospital.

Most of Hahnemann's clinical teachers were alumni who had donated significant time and energy to the institution, especially in teaching students, interns, and residents, but education and research were not their first priority. It became clear during some of the later struggles over the introduction of full-time clinical staff that many of these clinicians were not convinced that "academic" men were better suited for their position than they were. By the mid-1950s most clinical departments at Hahnemann had a number of part-time members and a few full-time members, all of whom were junior physicians with the rank of assistant or associate or, more often, "instructor." These were the young physicians who walked Hahnemann students through the wards, taught them basic techniques, and introduced them to patient care. In 1956, for example, Hahnemann's Department of Medicine had eighteen part-time faculty members, with annual salaries ranging from three hundred to five thousand dollars; the Department of Dermatology had eight part-time members; oncology six part-time; psychiatry six part-time and a full-time fellow; and public health six part-time. The Departments of Gastroenterology and Neurology were staffed only by volunteers.[72] The head of the Department of Surgery was William Lemmon Martin (1891–1989, Hahnemann M.D. 1915), who had been on the faculty for thirty-five years and received no salary.[73] The head of gynecology, Bruce Vischer MacFadyen (1904–, Hahnemann M.D. 1928), had held that position since 1948 and was also not paid a salary; and obstetrics was led by Newlin Fell Paxson (1895–1982, Hahnemann M.D. 1919), the well-known obstetrician who had delivered Grace Kelly and the other Kelly children. The Department of Pediatrics was headed by the eminent Carl Castle Fischer (1902–1989, Hahnemann M.D. 1928), who was paid a part-time salary.[74] These men were committed supporters of Hahnemann, had a deep knowledge of its traditions and heritage, and played a critical role in its financing.

When Cameron began gradually to introduce the notion of full-time clinical faculty to Hahnemann, he did not recognize the serious disruption this innovation would cause. AMA and AAMC reformers had optimistically believed these changes would create a complementary system, where "volunteer" faculty would work alongside salaried clinicians, each benefiting from the other's strengths, the volunteers able to avoid the burdens of pedagogic organization, the salaried faculty able to use the time they were not spending in developing a private practice in teaching and especially in research. This rosy-colored vision lacked any awareness of the ego invested in academic clinical positions, and money questions complicated the situation. While volunteer faculty did not want to trade in their high incomes for an academic salary, they did value highly their academic posts, as well as the status (and consultations) those posts brought them.

When Cameron arrived at Hahnemann his commitment to the full-time system was backed by a recent survey of the medical school by five AMA/AAMC representatives. Their 1956 unpublished report had strongly urged Hahnemann's trustees to hire full-time senior clinical faculty, who would provide "new, vigorous, intelligent leadership" in "the areas of administration, investigation, and teaching." Full-time faculty were, they assured Hahnemann's trustees, the backbone necessary for the creation of a modern medical institution. "Part-time and voluntary faculty personnel certainly can always play an important role in the teaching program, but the complexity of modern medicine requires the full time and efforts of a nucleus of capable career teachers and investigators who do not have the physical and intellectual distractions imposed by an outside practice."[75]

The 1956 report criticized the quality of Hahnemann's clinical faculty. While acknowledging that "board certification does not represent the ultimate measurement of any individual's ability to serve as a member of a medical faculty," the AMA/AAMC representatives felt nonetheless that "it was highly unusual" for major clinical departments to have so few board-certified faculty. They pointed out that in the Department of Medicine of the fifty faculty members (thirty-five of them Hahnemann graduates), only nine were board certified; and of the forty-seven in five other clinical departments within the division of medicine (dermatology, gastroenterology, neurology, oncology, and therapeutics), only seventeen were board certified.[76] Not surprisingly the report also found little evidence of clinical research.[77] The Departments of Obstetrics and Gynecology, for example, had "only one small research laboratory."[78] The report's authors calculated that between 1954 and 1956 of almost one hundred faculty members in the division of medicine only sixteen had published; thus, "the large majority of the faculty is not contributing to what should be one of the major obligations of the medical college."[79]

Cameron may have believed that hiring full-time clinical faculty would simply be a continuation of Brown's policies; but it turned out to be far more expensive and involved a serious reallocation of the institution's resources. As the trustees soon discovered, putting this policy into practice also struck a blow at the traditional structure of the hospital and its relationship with the medical school. Hahnemann's volunteer clinicians recognized the vital role they played in attracting private patients to the hospital, and they made sure the trustees were aware of it too.[80]

Cameron's first major appointment was a success. In 1957 he hired John H. Moyer (1917–), an academic clinical researcher who remained professor and head of the Department of Medicine until his promotion to vice president for academic affairs in 1970. Moyer was in his forties, and he had a Penn background and respected research abilities. Born in Philadelphia in 1917, he had studied at Lebanon Valley College and received his M.D. from the University of Pennsylvania in 1943. He then took a fellowship there in pharmacology and medicine and later taught at the Baylor University College of Medicine in Houston. He became well known for his work at Baylor on antihypertension drugs; he said later, "I was just in a golden era for new drug development, and almost everything we touched came out with a positive result."[81]

Before Cameron's invitation Moyer had turned down offers to head a section of clinical pharmacology at Louisiana State University, the Department of Internal Medicine at the University of South Carolina, and the Department of Pharmacology at Yale.[82] Cameron flew to Houston to recruit him and admitted to Moyer that he was having great difficulties "getting a good academic institution moving along," that there was little basic research, and that there were no local funds to support a research program. But he said he would find some money to support research at the college. However, as Moyer remembers it, when Cameron saw Moyer's research setup at Baylor—which included a hypertension clinic, a laboratory that Moyer directed—and Moyer's access to patients at two hospitals for clinical research, Cameron said "he would feel guilty if he encouraged me to accept such an impossible job as existed at Hahnemann."[83] Moyer, however, became intrigued; he remembers telling his wife: "that son of a gun thinks that I would not be capable of setting up and running a department of medicine." Moyer was also drawn to Philadelphia because his children would be closer to their grandparents in Hershey and because, as he later commented, of his "continuous yearning to get back to my roots of origin."[84]

Moyer found the Department of Medicine "completely disorganized and without any administrative structure of which to speak." Forty years later he wrote, "as I reflect on my initial years at Hahnemann, Dean Charles Cameron had indeed described the situation quite clearly and, if anything, it was worse."[85] Before Moyer arrived the Department of Medicine had, for example, only forty-four ward beds and twenty-one semiprivate ones available for teaching purposes at Hahnemann Hospital, and its only access to a research laboratory was at CVI.[86] The trustees supported Moyer's effort to establish a strong research program; in 1958, for example, they provided ten thousand dollars of Longwood Foundation money to set up a laboratory specifically for his department.[87] Moyer demonstrated an impressive talent for administration—both in inspiring others' research programs and in organizing curriculum. At Hahnemann he began to integrate clinical lectures with clinical instruction. He hired some board-certified, salaried junior faculty members and was able to have them direct the medical services, without offending senior clinicians, by calling them "administrators." As Moyer later explained, "this came off without a ripple, since the chiefs of service did not want to be designated as administrators, and they retained their title while the younger salaried faculty progressing [progressively] took over the organization and administration of the services."[88] Moyer expanded the medical department's subspecialties and attracted bright young researchers with new postdoctoral fellowships. He established a residency in internal medicine and began to reorganize Hahnemann's clinical services, most significantly turning the outpatient service from the least desirable rotation (seen by some as a "medical academic Siberia") to the most desirable by appointing section heads to all its departments and by giving students direct responsibilities for individual patients.[89] Wilbur Oaks (1928–, Hahnemann M.D. 1955) applied to Hahnemann Hospital for his residency to work with Moyer and was flattered when Moyer involved him as a resident in research projects on hypertension and renal disease. With Moyer, Oaks recalled, young faculty felt "that thrill of building something new" and felt what he later described as "a spirit of togetherness." Moyer also became, Oaks commented, "a bit of a father figure" and was not happy when Oaks replaced him as chair of medicine in the 1970s.[90]

Moyer also recognized that Hahnemann's reputation depended not only on internal reorganization but also on being seen as a research-oriented institution. He tried to give Hahnemann a regional and national presence, both by encouraging a strong research program and through what he called "continuing education." He organized what became regular research symposia sponsored by Hahnemann, the first in 1958 on hypertension, his own research interest. It had 431 paid registrants and was, the trustees commented, an "outstanding scientific activity" and a "tremendous success."[91] The proceedings published from these symposia, as well as from the research seminars and specialized courses Moyer's department arranged for community hospitals and local medical societies, added, as DiPalma later commented, "to the growing prestige that this endeavor brought to Hahnemann," and were part of the impetus for the establishment of Hahnemann's School of Continuing Education.[92]

Cameron's next appointment was far more freighted, and it indicated, among other things, the great influence that surgeons had at Hahnemann in this era. In 1958, with the retirement of William Martin, Cameron proposed John Howard as the new head of the Department of Surgery. John Malone Howard (1919–) had an M.D. from the University of Pennsylvania and had worked at Emory. He was an academic surgeon whose slow hand was looked down on, so the story goes, by traditional Hahnemann surgeons who had always boasted of their speed, a skill most useful in pre-antibiotic days. A surgical resident at Hahnemann who worked with Charles Bailey recalled Howard as "a laboratory surgeon" who had "written papers" but could "not cut the mustard in the operating room."[93] That Cameron chose another senior man from outside the faculty raised hackles, and the uproar threatened to undermine the remaking of Hahnemann.

When they heard about Howard's appointment, the Alumni Association and a number of hospital clinicians began to try to pressure the board of trustees to reverse Cameron's decision. They knew that the trustees depended on them to admit private patients to try to make up the debt Hahnemann Hospital faced, even with its state and city subsidies, as a result of the financial drain of ward patients, a major concern in the era before the introduction of Medicare and Medicaid in the mid-1960s. The Alumni Association sent the board a letter "concerning the advisability of appointing Hahnemann graduates to positions of importance."[94]At a difficult meeting of the board in early 1958, Lee Thomas, a trustee and a firm friend of Theodore Geary (Hahnemann M.D. 1924), a senior hospital clinician, read a prepared statement warning that, with the board having gone "outside the faculty" for the dean and the chair of the Department of Medicine, "there is reason to believe that we are building up a good deal of faculty resentment." "In carrying out our long range program the feelings of senior personnel must be seriously considered," Thomas argued. He saw the Alumni Association's letter requesting that the next appointment be made from within the faculty as perhaps "a symptom of a movement which could be very dangerous." Thomas made clear that he felt the board's long-standing policy of subsuming college concerns to the hospital should continue. The alumni's letter, he noted, "contained some implications which might conceivably lessen the bed occupancy of the hospital. Such an implication is so serious that it should be evaluated by the whole Board." Thomas proposed delaying the appointment of the head of surgery until "the Board can determine whether we are not proceeding in dangerous haste with an over-all re-organization of the staff." The board debated this suggestion but "after detailed discussion, in executive session" accepted Howard's appointment, with Thomas dissenting.[95]

Rumors spread through Hahnemann that this appointment was the beginning of a plan to force every department and section head to accept a full-time system. So tense was the situation that in August 1958 Cameron issued a statement on the board's policy on the full-time system, a statement that was published in Hahnemann's new internal newsletter, the *Medical Staff News*. The statement was prefaced by an introduction from Watson Malone, the board's chairman, urging a "careful reading of this statement by every member of the faculty" to "allay much of the apprehension which has apparently resulted from misunderstanding."[96] Cameron attacked "the rumor mill" that had created "baseless fears and false prognostications," and he reminded Hahnemann that he had already said that "practical considerations prevented any general extension of the full time system at Hahnemann, regardless of what merit it had." Nonetheless, he explained, his administration, supported by the trustees, "subscribes to the principle that it is advantageous and desirable for Department Chairmen (including clinical departments) to be on full time status." The principle "has not been established hastily nor capriciously," and he quoted from the 1956 report: "Almost all medical schools in the United States have accepted and implemented the principle that a nucleus of competent full time faculty members in the major clinical departments is fundamental to the successful operation of a medical school." Cameron reminded readers that only 2.7 percent of clinical faculty, "a micronucleus," were full-time. He argued:

> I do not think it appropriate to argue for the full time philosophy in this
> statement. I happen to believe in it, but if I did not I would still hold it
> undesirable to continue in the position of being out of step with the
> vanguard of modern medical education. . . . [Having] the clinical
> departments headed by full-time Chairmen . . . is not going to be
> accomplished soon, nor will anyone be coerced into it, nor will it affect
> the normal tenure of anyone now holding a Chair.[97]

Yet Cameron acknowledged that Hahnemann traditions, especially the right
to groom a protégé as one's successor after retirement, would be eliminated under his new system. The right to succession of a departmental chairmanship, he
explained, "must be replaced by a merit system," although "precedence will remain an important consideration." "The extension of the full time principle to
all heads of Sections is even more remote, and, indeed has never been considered as a practical problem," although it was more likely for those sections "which
bear a large burden of teaching and investigative responsibility." He assured the
faculty that "nothing was contemplated in our plan for the future which could
conceivably threaten the position of anyone presently a member of the faculty."
Implicit was a criticism of the goals of the old Hahnemann that had emphasized producing a practitioner and teaching students through lectures and somewhat informal preceptorship by visiting clinicians. "What we are trying to do is
to preserve the best of our heritage but at the same time to move forward. As I
see it, our great need is to instill a reasonable measure of ideation and creativity
and basic science into a clinical milieu which has been essentially pragmatic."[98]

Cameron's most serious failure, one that was brought up a decade later to
justify why Hahnemann's medical school needed new leadership, was the departure of Hahnemann's most famous faculty member, cardiac surgeon Charles
P. Bailey, as a direct result of Cameron's policies in general and his appointment
of Howard in particular. Bailey, head of the Department of Thoracic Surgery established especially for him, disliked Howard. But his anger was not simply a
response to a personal feud. As Bailey himself noted at the time, his department
was part of volunteer clinicians' struggles over the full-time system and their
role in a new Hahnemann.

Charles Philamore Bailey (Hahnemann M.D. 1932) had been working at
Hahnemann as a hospital clinician and teacher since 1940. Bailey found
Hahnemann a welcome environment for his work, which involved dangerous
and often innovative and experimental procedures. Bailey was part of an early
group of heart surgeons who learned to operate before the widespread use of the
heart-lung machine and before open heart surgery. Bailey's dramatic heart operations gained international attention, especially after his pioneering work in
1948 on the world's first successful closed-heart surgical repair of stenosis of the
mitral valve, an operation he called a "mitral commissurotomy."[99] William Likoff,

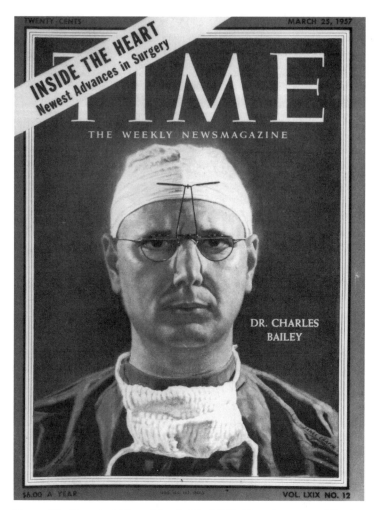

Figure 28. Cover of *Time*, March 25, 1957. Noted surgeon Charles Philamore Bailey (1910–1993), a 1932 Hahnemann graduate, was professor of thoracic surgery at Hahnemann from 1940 to 1958. His innovative work in cardiac surgery earned him the cover of *Time* magazine in 1957. (© 1957 Time Inc. Reprinted by permission.)

who became Bailey's partner, recalled his ability to "insert a finger within the still beating human heart and make necessary repairs."[100] In 1950 he was appointed head of Hahnemann's new Department of Thoracic Surgery. He was one of the founders of the American Board of Thoracic Surgery, and in 1955 his status as a cardiology expert was solidified with his text *Surgery of the Heart*, which summarized the current work in cardiac surgery.

Bailey was a flamboyant character, deliberately shocking. He cursed in the operating room; he worked himself and everyone else days, nights, and weekends. Bailey openly competed with other surgeons for original and first procedures, and the drama and excitement of his work attracted many followers.[101] He was, George Geckeler later commented, "not a conformist."[102] John Moyer believed that "his personality was typical of cardiac surgeons . . . being aggressive and almost ruthless in the development of new technology and cardiac surgery procedures."[103] John Storer, a freshman who later became the first Hahnemann graduate Bailey accepted as a resident, remembers first meeting Bailey in 1942 outside Horn and Hardart. Bailey was lolling on the wall, with a toothpick in his mouth; Storer thought to himself, "if this guy can get through school, I can too."[104]

By the mid-1950s Bailey's cardiology service was the largest clinical service at Hahnemann Hospital, and the largest in Philadelphia.[105] When Cameron first hired Moyer, the dean described the service as having "completely overrun the entire hospital" and having become "the tail that wagged the dog."[106] Bailey's patients came from across the United States and from all over the world, desperate for his help, and they were housed in hotels all around the city. In these days before institutional review boards, when heart surgery was still in its early stages, Bailey would "try anything."[107] DiPalma later thought that "Bailey's talent resided in a great drive and guts to explore where others feared to tread."[108] In the early 1950s Bailey asked DiPalma to do some animal research to test techniques for hypothermic surgery, and although the dog experiments still had what DiPalma considered an unacceptable risk of failure, Bailey decided to operate on a patient, saying, as DiPalma remembered it: "I'm going to beat Swan [another cardiac surgeon] to the punch. I have a female patient who needs a difficult heart repair which can't be done with the available technology."[109] Bailey's work on "deep freeze" surgery was covered in *Life* and *Modern Medicine*, and in March 1957 Bailey made the front cover of *Time* magazine.[110] "There is little doubt," DiPalma reflected, "that Bailey by his daring and brilliant exploits put an obscure homeopathic medical school on the map."[111] In 1951 Hahnemann seniors dedicated their yearbook to Bailey, "a man whose enthusiasm, both as a teacher and investigator, has inspired all those who have come in contact with him . . . [and] whose scholarship, initiative and manifold abilities personify the new spirit of Hahnemann."[112]

In 1958 Bailey heard that John Howard, whose position as surgery chair Bailey had wanted, was claiming to be head of all surgical services and that Howard had operated on a patient that Bailey had considered a thoracic case.[113] This incident was a factor in Bailey's departure, but Bailey did not leave simply because of a personal disagreement, as he himself indicated in a long letter to the chairman of the board. At issue was the power of the new full-time faculty in dealing with volunteer clinicians, especially in scheduling operations and in teaching students. Instituting a full-time system, Bailey believed, would lead to a "fundamental alteration in Hahnemann's structure and character." He was unhappy with Cameron's "clearly evident policy of accentuation of the prominence of full-time physician teachers, to the detriment or even suppression of the clinical or voluntary staff." His partner William Likoff, for example, was being pressured by Moyer to accept a full-time status, "the basis being (so stated in a letter) that it is Dr. Cameron's intention that all heads of sections shall be on full-time status. Such a concept is anathema to me; yet, obviously, it is but a matter of time until a similar proposition will be broached to me personally? What will we say when the medical fashion changes or reverses itself within a few years?"[114] Bailey described himself as "being psychologically incapable of adjusting to the present 'New Order' at Hahnemann" and in his most telling words declared: "While I have no fundamental brief against full-time teachers as such, neither do I hold the exaggerated opinion of them to which so many adhere. While some full-time men produce well, the majority of them fail to measure up to their opportunities, as well they might since all their natural incentives which spur a man on have been eliminated from their professional life."[115]

Bailey resigned from the medical school but, at least at first, remained affiliated with Hahnemann Hospital. The trustees and the hospital administrators tried desperately to keep him linked to the hospital and met with him a number of times to see if they could placate him enough to stay. The trustees did make it clear that as part of their support of Cameron's efforts to transform Hahnemann into an academic center, "no restrictions are to be applied to Dr. Howard in his efforts to establish an academic program, including a service of thoracic surgery which shall be complete and balanced and, therefore, accredited for two years of residency training."[116] Charles Paxson, the hospital administrator, pointed out that if Hahnemann could avoid a complete break with Bailey, "the Alumni would feel better about our retaining our affiliation with him" and "his staying would not precipitate misunderstandings on full time." In confidential notes Paxson calculated that in 1958 Bailey and his staff brought to the hospital 1153 cases charged at about 125 percent of the cost of an average medical or surgical case—a total of about $800,000 annually—and that the hospital would need 1500 new admissions to "offset the loss of Dr. Bailey's work," or a 25 percent increase of admissions from the rest of the staff.[117] But Bailey stayed only until 1959 and then went to the (formerly homeopathic) New York Medical College and later attended Fordham Law School, where he received a law degree and became an expert in medical malpractice, both as a practicing attorney and as a medical educator.

By the early 1960s Cameron had begun a different policy, appointing full-time junior faculty as section heads, as John Moyer was doing in the Department of Medicine. Both he and Moyer pressured existing clinicians, as Bailey had foreseen, and waited out the stalwarts. By 1966 all but one of the major clinical heads were full-time faculty, and Carl Fischer, the last remaining old guard head, retired in 1968. The trustees had to keep reiterating, as they did in 1966, that "the volunteer faculty is an essential part of the faculty. There will always be a need at Hahnemann for the practicing doctor to hold a faculty appointment."[118] But increasingly the new Hahnemann was growing larger and more distant from the immediate community, and its faculty had less and less interaction with local physicians.

A New Face: The Building Plan

Brown and especially Cameron recognized that attracting good students and faculty meant offering an appealing physical plant. Indeed, after the completion of the Klahr Building in 1938, which was one part of what was supposed to be a multistory new college complex, the architect's drawing continued to grace the college catalog for some years. Karl Koiwai, a Japanese-American who left a relocation camp in California to study at Hahnemann in 1944 and who later became a pathology professor there, remembers being shocked by the difference between the catalog picture and the school he encountered on Fifteenth Street.[119]

Brown continued Hahnemann's long-standing policy of renovating existing buildings and gradually acquiring surrounding buildings, conscious that the 1945 AMA/AAMC report had pointed out that to attract full-time faculty Hahnemann needed not only money but also "physical improvements to provide office and laboratory space as well as equipment."[120] In 1945 Hahnemann bought the former Northwest Grammar School on Race Street from the city of Philadelphia and moved its outpatient facilities there from out of the hospital basement; later the college rented rooms at the nearby Hotel Philadelphia (the former Elks' Club) and the Schaff Building (later renamed the Bellet Building) for psychiatric outpatient care. Nurses lived in parts of the 1928 hospital building and in a former firehouse; a former caretaker's apartment became a cytology laboratory; storage area became an institute for biochemical studies in cancer; and a stable that housed animals for experimental purposes was called the biological research building. CVI, as we have seen, began operating in a renovated automobile showroom.[121]

Hahnemann leaders recognized that this makeshift setup was inadequate; Hahnemann needed new buildings to make convincing its transformation into an orthodox academic medical center. Vincent Zarro (Hahnemann M.D. 1962), remembers taking prospective faculty members into the old hospital building, which had no air-conditioning; "they would come, look around, and leave."[122] In 1956, in his first speech to the Alumni Association as dean, Cameron

Figure 29. A view from Broad and Vine streets (ca. 1965) showing the 1963 nurses' building, the 1928 hospital, and the 1938 Klahr Building. During the 1960s, Hahnemann took part in Philadelphia's construction boom. At the upper left corner is City Hall.

commented: "Converts may make the best church members, but they are not first choice in the creation of a top drawer medical center," and he warned alumni of the attitude of "newcomers and of visitors from the Joint Accreditation Board."[123] AMA/AAMC representatives observed in their 1956 survey report that "rather extensive renovation has prolonged the useful life of much space that would under other circumstances have been obsolete long ago. Effective as these improvisations have been, however, the old college building is qualitatively and quantitatively inadequate for the purposes it is designed to serve and should be replaced in the near future." Full-time clinical faculty members, they noted, would need "adequate office and research space."[124]

Cameron's twenty-five-year plan, which he outlined in 1964, centered mainly on new construction. He proposed an ambulatory services building for the "usual clinical patients" and also for the "private patients of the staff." It was to be "a twin house, with separate entrances for private and clinic patients but common X-ray and laboratory facilities." He also proposed a new basic science building to replace the 1890 college building.[125] Cameron was impressively effective in finding ways to finance this plan. He was able to supplement

Hahnemann's building drive, for example, with $882,000 from the NIH and $100,000 from the Pew Foundation for the construction of a clinical research institute.[126] He continued this plan during his years as Hahnemann's president. He dedicated the opening of Hahnemann's first new buildings since 1938: in 1963 a nurse's building to replace the 1906 building, and in 1967 the Elmer Holmes Bobst Institute of Clinical Research, described by the alumni magazine as "designed to accommodate Hahnemann's rapidly enlarging research enterprise." One of its floors was named for Charles Brown.[127] Student yearbooks throughout the 1960s are replete with pictures of scaffolding and cranes. The construction, although exciting, was disruptive. In 1966, during the building of the new college Hahnemann moved students into the former Eccles College of Mortuary Science on North Sixteenth Street, a four-story building that had so little heat that students wore overcoats in bad weather and, as there was no gas, used propane torches.[128] But most of all, the construction foreshadowed the true and profound transformation of the old Hahnemann into the new. Memories of both faculty and students before the completion of most of this work in the 1970s are of the poor physical plant of both the college and the hospital: dark interiors, unpleasant bathrooms, uncomfortable chairs, inadequate classrooms, limited laboratory space, and dirty patient waiting rooms. Even in the 1930s, one graduate recalled, the school was a "small place" with old buildings and no cafeteria.[129] But after the new buildings went up there were still problems: one faculty member remembers being most impressed by Wharton Shober, who replaced Cameron as president in 1971, when he promised elevators that worked.[130]

In the summer of 1968 the old college building closed and was demolished. It had been Hahnemann's oldest building, built in 1890 for the then new hospital. Administrators consistently got the date wrong in describing it, and when it was memorialized on canvas it came to seem even more a part of the distant past. In 1967 E. R. Squibb and Sons, the pharmaceutical company, presented Hahnemann with a painting of the building as part of the company's series of original oil paintings of the United States' eighty-six medical schools, a project known as "Collegia Medica." Hahnemann's painting, entitled "The Old College," was the twenty-sixth in the series and was painted by Philadelphia artist Jack Bookbinder. Both Cameron and William Kellow, his successor as dean, were present at the dedication.[131] At the dedication, Kellow, who had a 1946 M.D. from Georgetown University, turned more of old Hahnemann's history into the mists of time.

> It is particularly appropriate that we receive this painting at this
> particular time because . . . this grand old building is going to be
> destroyed before this date comes by again. . . . I'm a real old fashioned
> fellow. . . . When I look at this old Victorian structure, with its peaks
> and cornices, I like the grandeur and I feel a great deal of magnificence

somehow . . . in the past [and] a great deal of grandeur and magnificence in the profession of medicine in America today.[132]

Hahnemann used the dedications of its new buildings as public relations exercises, as occasions to demonstrate its social and political connections. Of all of the speakers at these events, one of the most prominent was Richard Nixon, who was then a former vice president and had not yet begun his run for the 1968 presidency. Nixon was the keynote speaker at the opening of the Elmer Holmes Bobst Institute of Clinical Research in May 1967, held at the Sheraton Hotel for over a thousand guests, including alumni and business and civic leaders. Bobst, who had once worked in Charles Cameron's father's pharmacy, was now head of Warner-Lambert, a pharmaceutical firm and a major contributor to the Republican Party.[133] Nixon directed his speech to the Hahnemann seniors present, urging them to engage in "a broader participation in public affairs . . . [for] in the last third of the 20th century, the decisions that America will be making are so important that they need the best thinking that America can produce," a suggestion that subsequent Hahnemann classes would take to heart, although to a different end than Nixon intended.[134]

These buildings were intended to reinforce Hahnemann's profound reorganization and also to placate the unsettled and displaced. Perhaps the most significant was the Myer Feinstein Building, which institutionalized Hahnemann's commitment to a full-time clinical system on a geographic basis; thus Hahnemann clinicians could continue to see private patients, but in a Hahnemann facility and with a set amount of their income returned to the institution. This arrangement did not resolve the problem of volunteer clinicians, and in the late 1960s a group of Hahnemann faculty expressed their increasing sense of alienation from the Hahnemann full-time faculty by founding the Hahnemann Physicians Society. In the early 1970s the society's president, William Likoff, pointed out to the trustees that "the preclinical and clinical categories are anachronistic and hardly representative of the sole, critical line of cleavage between segments of the faculty." "By far a more natural and meaningful division," he argued, "exists between voluntary and employed faculty."[135] By 1976 this society had around one hundred members, and at a meeting on the relationship between volunteer and full-time faculty—a meeting at which, typically, all of the volunteers and only two of the full-time physicians showed up—the former complained that they were "considered step-children and not treated equally by the GFT [full-time] staff." They held lower academic appointments and were rarely section or division heads. Opportunities for academic participation were "unfairly distributed"—for example, volunteers were "passed over for Grand Rounds"—and these inequities contributed to "injured feelings among volunteer staff."[136]

The Last Hahnemann Homeopath:
Redefining Research and Hahnemann's Identity

In 1948, as we saw in chapter five, former dean William Pearson prepared a history of Hahnemann that continued Thomas Lindsley Bradford's history up to 1948.[137] The series of brief articles that Pearson published in the *Hahnemannian Monthly* were highly charged documents, full of the bitterness of the probation years in which they were written, full of his sorrow that Hahnemann's homeopathic identity was fast disappearing. Pearson urged everyone to read Bradford's history "so that all may appreciate the trials, tribulations, sacrifices and devotion of hundreds of loyal Homeopathic physicians to provide the rich heritage we enjoy. We will not sell our birthright for a mess of pottage if we are loyal to those who presented to us The Hahnemann Medical College."[138]

That Hahnemann was no longer a homeopathic school was the result of pressure not just from outside bodies like the AMA but also from both Hahnemann faculty and students, who were demanding to purify their past and make orthodox their future. As early as 1939 students had presented the faculty Medical Council with a petition, signed by 411 out of 448 students, requesting two diplomas, one with an M.D. and one with an H.M.D.[139] The council had refused. But in 1946, during probation, when the Student Institute told the dean that the majority of seniors were even "willing to pay an extra diploma fee" for two diplomas, the faculty executive agreed, despite the dissent of Pearson and acting dean William Schmidt, and in 1947 the school's homeopathic courses became electives. By 1951 the commencement program reported seniors graduating with only an M.D., although the memory of graduates about the exact date the H.M.D. disappeared conflicts.[140] Hahnemann's faculty, as well, no longer sought to portray themselves as leaders of homeopathic education. In 1940, members of a homeopathic society in Mexico sent the college a diploma that they had issued posthumously honoring Constantine Hering as "a benefactor of medicine." Hahnemann's faculty executive agreed to frame it, but it was hung in the college vault.[141]

The impact of Hahnemann's homeopathic past persisted longer than its training, and many graduates of the 1940s and 1950s were forced into less prestigious medical careers. Wilbur Oaks, who graduated in 1955, remembered feeling that Hahnemann students had to work harder and study more than other Philadelphia medical students, and he summed up his notion of Hahnemann as being "second-best, not second rate."[142] John Storer, who graduated in 1945, remembered that Hahnemann graduates were "really looked down upon by the medical community at large." Storer's brother had graduated from Jefferson and interned at Cooper Hospital in New Jersey, and he told Storer that Cooper Hospital wouldn't "take a Hahnemann man." Because Storer was friends with the son of neurology professor Edward Steinhilber, he was able to go to the former homeopathic Huron Road Hospital in Cleveland, part of the fading homeopathic network. Storer also recalled that in the army he felt an intellectual equal to Temple and Penn graduates, but they tried to "dig it in." Near the end of his senior year, as part of the Army Specialized Training Program (ASTP), all Philadelphia medical students had to attend an army film. When the Hahnemann students went by the other students chanted "quack, quack, quack." As Storer remembered it: "I felt like charging into the ranks and taking them on."[143]

During the 1940s and 1950s Hahnemann tried to overcome the stigma with surprisingly speedy admissions policies. Oaks, for example, went to Hahnemann, although his father had studied medicine at Pennsylvania, mainly because at Hahnemann Oaks was told he was accepted immediately after his interview; five days later he found out that he had also been accepted at Pennsylvania.[144]

Homeopathy left Hahnemann after the war, for, in the embrace of the modern academic medical center, it had little place. But homeopathy's disappearance was not just the result of sectarian prejudice: the therapeutic revolution made homeopathic therapies seem irrelevant; the new faculty had no interest in or tolerance for homeopathy; and, most significantly, American homeopaths in and outside of Hahnemann had, in the previous few decades, been unable to capitalize on the growing prestige of science and especially scientific research.

In this era of therapeutic revolution, penicillin, aureomycin, streptomycin, chloramphenicol, and cortisone became the symbols of a new era in medicine. These agents, a number of Hahnemann graduates from the 1930s and 1940s later reflected, put the last nail in the homeopathic coffin. Hahnemann faculty in the post-Flexner years had promulgated the idea of homeopathy as a therapeutic specialty, as good as if not better than orthodox therapies. But that argument and those practices now seemed like a remnant of nineteenth-century medicine, like leeches and bloodletting, not the practice of a modern clinical practice. When chemotherapy and antibiotics arrived, Herbert Harkins (1912– , Hahnemann M.D. 1937) recalled, "all homeopathic and dominant therapies went out the window—it was a new era."[145] Homeopathy had seemed especially effective in the prevaccine days of virulent infectious diseases. One 1948 graduate remembered being impressed by hearing of the lower death rate among the patients of homeopaths during the 1918–1919 influenza epidemic. He and other homeopaths, however, "yielded to the dawn of antibiotics," as "for the first time [there was] something equal or superior."[146] Even Garth Boericke admitted in the early 1940s that "the progress of modern surgery; the lessening of infections and contagious diseases; the discovery of new drugs such as sulfapyridine, sulfanilamide, liver extract, and insulin, and the host of efficacious anodynes of the barbituric group all tend to detract from homeopathic prescribing . . . and have rather severely shaken the appreciation of symptoms per se in a young man trained according to modern methods." In vain he urged students: "it is essential not to over-valuate biologic and laboratory aid, or draw false conclusions, such as from minor changes in blood chemistry or blood counts, or too dogmatic deduction from an E.K.G., or too literal interpretations of liver and kidney function tests, x-ray readings, and statistical conclusions."[147]

The new basic scientists and clinicians saw getting rid of Hahnemann's homeopathic remnants as part of their job. By 1949 Reinhard Beutner's pharmacology department stopped teaching "all experiments relating to pharmacy and the chemical and physical properties of drugs."[148] Buetner's successor, Joseph DiPalma, recalled throwing out old homeopathic drugs in his laboratory and sitting in on the lectures on prescription writing by two practicing homeopaths—Ray Seidel (Hahnemann M.D. 1935) and Joseph Messey (Hahnemann M.D. 1933)—and then canceling them. "They were both fine gentlemen," he later commented, "and took this graciously."[149] John Moyer remembered that the basic science heads protested when he initially retained the Department of Therapeutics, but he told them, "I thought it was worthwhile as it had lasted so long."[150]

Most striking was the intellectual and professional isolation of Hahnemann's last homeopathic teacher, Garth Boericke, in this last decade of his thirty-year teaching career. His isolation is powerfully illustrated in the annual reports that department heads were now required to write. In his 1954–1955 annual report, Boericke tried to use the language and modes of his new research-oriented colleagues. Members of the department, he wrote, had attended the annual meeting of the AMA in Atlantic City and also of the state homeopathic society in Wernersville. His department's research during the previous two years had continued the "study and application of our lipoid flocculation test for selection of homeopathic remedy" as well as "spectroscopic studies on seven homeopathic drugs." For grants he could list only the Pender Fund, which had been designated especially to Hahnemann's Department of Therapeutics. Somewhat pathetically, under the heading "recommendations," he argued that "personnel of the department would be glad to cooperate in the teaching curriculum of the Out Patient Department if solicited."[151]

In the 1950s Boericke's influence as a teacher and clinician faded. Even before Boericke's homeopathy courses became electives, a 1945 graduate remembered that a homeopathy lecture once a week "was just a course we had to take" and that homeopathy "was not practiced at Hahnemann," except by Boericke.[152] In 1950 the college catalog listed—along with its school of nursing, school of medical technology, and school of X-ray technology—a "course in Homeopathic Therapy," which was available to graduate physicians, but even this reference disappeared the following year.[153] By 1945 the Garth W. Boericke Society of Therapeutics organized in 1936 for the study of homeopathy had been renamed

Figure 30. Garth Wilkinson Boericke (1893–1968), head of the Department of Materia Medica and Therapeutics from 1926 to 1959, was
Hahnemann's last teacher of homeopathy. Homeopathy was made an
elective in 1947, and the department disappeared in 1958. *Medic* 1946.

the Undergraduate Research Society, and its declared purpose was now to stimulate "further interest in the treatment of conditions the physician meets in everyday life."[154] In 1958, a year before Boericke retired, his Department of
Therapeutics, which had been the centerpiece of Hahnemann Medical College
in the nineteenth century, was renamed the Department of Clinical Pharmacology, and therapeutics as a title disappeared.[155]

Boericke was increasingly praised not as a homeopath but as a clinician.
Throughout the 1940s student yearbooks stressed that he taught both homeopathy and orthodox medicine: "an authority on therapeutics, whatever the

school."[156] By this time a medical school with a department of therapeutics sounded old-fashioned. Before probation the department was a mishmash of pharmacologists, radiologists, and physical therapists (that is, a kind of therapeutic eclecticism). But by 1946 the college had taken most of the members out of the department and reassigned them to the Departments of Radiology and Pharmacology. Boericke's homeopathy lectures, which had also become standardized, offered an almost stereotypical presentation of homeopathic individuation. According to seniors in 1946: "[Boericke] presented each drug as living persons, the pulsatilla blond, the indolent lazy sulphur, the high pressure nux, etc. Many a student found his type during these discourses."[157] And a laconic poem entitled "Tuesday at Three in Room 'B'" described students there for roll call: some were sleeping, others were looking at their watches, another was reading an article on sulfa drugs while "The front row students smile with poise, / Others laugh to make some noise." After the lecture has ended and the classroom is empty:

A shadowy figure rises late.
Straight and tall, yet dim and wan;
It's Samuel Christian Hahnemann.
These words are heard from the creator
As he ascends the ventilator;
"So this is called my therapy;
So this is Homeopathy!"[158]

The power of the new orthodox drugs and the public fascination with research accentuated the weak connection between homeopathy and scientific research. When Garth Boericke retired in 1959 he left no legacy because he had been unable to tap what was valued most highly in 1950s and 1960s medical education: pharmacological research, an endeavor that was believed to have the potential to conquer all diseases and to which, ironically, homeopathy did not seem, to the postwar public, to have contributed. In 1969, in a speech to the alumni entitled "Hahnemann and Rush: A Re-Evaluation," Cameron cleverly reassessed Samuel Hahnemann's legacy by asking the question "Why is one more lustrous while the other is tarnished?" Homeopathy, he argued, drawing on Morris Fishbein's *Medical Follies*, had been better than Benjamin Rush's system of purging and bleeding: it had provided medicine with new drugs and tested the effects of drugs on "the healthy organism"; and the idea that it allowed the patient's defense mechanisms to operate suggested an early notion of immunity. In fact, Cameron argued, conscious of his audience's now largely sentimental ties to homeopathy, the only reason homeopathy was not valued higher was that it, unlike Rush's work, had been "carried into the era of scientific medicine."[159] Cameron also began proposing that Hahnemann's name be changed. "Homeopathy served its day well and it pointed toward future directions which were right," he told the editor of the *Evening Bulletin*, writing in 1962 to protest a news item that had suggested that Hahnemann was still homeopathic. "Thus, it is respected and interred."[160] And to the board of trustees in 1970, he described the disappearance of the other homeopathic schools in the United States: "We are left alone, still stigmatized with the burden of error which is the legacy of an 18th century physician who died before the first disease-causing bacterium was discovered . . . the founder of a system of medicine which at worst is ridiculed and at best is dismissed as a passing fancy. We have made our break with the system and I am suggesting that . . . we proclaim that break by a change of name."[161]

Even before the old building was razed, concrete expressions of the school's homeopathic past were dismantled. The school's museum, now named the Rufus B. Weaver Museum of Anatomy, was still mentioned in college catalogs through the 1940s, but by 1949 it was in ruins. Some of its space was being converted into a laboratory for the Department of Anatomy, and the rest was used for storage and, the AMA/AAMC representatives noted, "will be put to other use as the specimens can be sorted and disposed of."[162] Weaver's "Harriet" found her way into the library, where she became an exhibit rather than a research tool.

Hahnemann, and indeed American homeopathy at large, had never been able to capture and build on a concept of scientific homeopathy. Around 1900 homeopaths had debated the idea of using laboratory and clinical research methods to study homeopathic drugs and therapeutic modalities. But homeopathic research never developed. It could not get foundation funding, although, in the early decade of the twentieth century, the lay community, at least in Philadelphia, showed some interest in homeopathic research and some recognition of its costs. In 1910 Walter Hering, Constantine Hering's son, set up a fund to provide scholarship funds for poor boys to attend the college, to endow a chair in homeopathic materia medica and therapeutics, and to establish the Hering Research Laboratory. Oliver Haines, its first recipient, was therefore in a sense Hahnemann's first salaried clinician, but of course he was hardly full-time. He continued his private practice, as did his successor, Garth Boericke, who also became the director of the laboratory.

The Hering Laboratory became part of the college's promotional literature, mentioned in numerous catalogs. It was promoted in the post-Flexner years as "a laboratory of pharmacology and therapeutics which shall be devoted to scientific research in drug action according to the most modern methods, the ultimate object of this department being the systematic study and teaching of homeopathy."[163] In the 1932 yearbook students included a photograph of the laboratory with a caption describing tests where the blood of patients was brought in contact with a "saline solution" containing a special dilution; "in cases where the similimum is in doubt, dilutions of all drugs indicated by repertory work are

Figure 31. The Hering Laboratory, ca. 1918. Research at Hahnemann before the 1940s was neither supported nor encouraged; Hahnemann had few full-time faculty and could attract no money for research other than for its homeopathic Hering Laboratory. The laboratory's lack of equipment as well as its books and portraits of homeopathic figures suggest remnants of a nineteenth-century research culture.

placed in separate vials, and allowed to come in contact with specimens of the patient's serum." According to the yearbook, the work was "yet in its infancy" and suffered from "lack of adequate facilities," but the clinical results "so far obtained are quite encouraging."[164] A few years later students, in praising their college's "department of roentgenology" (housed in seventeen rooms on the hospital's third floor) mentioned radiology practices that also seemed to incorporate the ideals of a scientific homeopathy: "Fractional therapeutic doses of the X-ray according to homeopathic principles have resulted in a high degree of success."[165] By the 1950s student yearbooks made no mention of the laboratory.

There were two main reasons for the failure of homeopathic research to properly develop at Hahnemann: the lack of funds to develop modern research programs with well-equipped laboratories and the traditions of the Hahnemann-trained faculty, whose notions of research and its place in orthodox medicine were shaped by their continuing loyalty to Hahnemann's homeopathic past.

In the 1880s and 1890s, some homeopaths—at Boston University and the University of Michigan—had dreamed of an alternative research program, in which young homeopathic physicians, with training in the latest clinical specialties and laboratory techniques, would demonstrate the scientific efficacy and veracity of homeopathy. But Michigan had lost its homeopathic department in 1895, and Boston turned orthodox in 1918. Hahnemann Medical College, one of the last homeopathic schools remaining after 1920, did not pursue these research plans, but in the late 1920s it did have its students involved in a "proving squad," although these provings were not as systematic as Michigan's earlier trials.[166]

The one man who tried to encourage scientific homeopathic research at Hahnemann was Harry Eberhard, Hahnemann's gastroenterology professor, who was a wealthy practitioner and a powerful force within Hahnemann. In 1937 Eberhard invited Ehrenfried Pfeiffer, a Swiss chemist and crystallographer, to come to Hahnemann to pursue his research work on seeking a blood crystallization pattern for cancer, and later arranged for him to receive an honorary doctor of civil laws degree. In 1939 Eberhard gathered a group of eminent homeopathic supporters from Hahnemann's board of trustees (probably many of them his patients) and formed what he called the Hahnemann Research Foundation, modeled on the Wisconsin Research Foundation.[167] Throughout the 1940s Eberhard remained convinced that the modern research could encompass homeopathy. He urged homeopaths to pursue a research program to place the law of similars "in its proper category" by getting rid of "obsolete remedies" and to help resolve long-standing homeopathic debates about therapies and theories, showing a faith in science as beyond sectarianism.[168] He also wrote a series of articles, published in Hahnemann Hospital's promotional magazine *Hospital Tidings*, boasting of the research being done by Hahnemann faculty, including research on cancer and on the function of the thyroid and the recording of heart sounds, as well as the "modern reinvestigation of Homeopathic remedies."[169]

But other than the cardiology work Eberhard praised, none of this research lasted into the 1950s. During the 1930s and 1940s the heads of most of Hahnemann's departments were men in their fifties and sixties, noted more as "characters" than as engaged clinical or laboratory researchers. Their research was not something students were welcome to share. Samuel Sappington's pathology laboratory had a sign warning students away; one graduate remembers a red line that could not be crossed.

Nationally oriented research had not been part of the school's vision of itself since the 1890s. In the nineteenth century, homeopathic drugs, therapies, and theories of disease could command a national audience. At that time, Hahnemann's faculty were the authors of respected homeopathic textbooks used in the nation's many homeopathic schools, and amid numerous American homeopathic journals, the college's *Hahnemannian Monthly* was a well-respected and frequently cited example, publishing research, programmatic, and philosophical articles as well as news of the college and Philadelphia's homeopathic world. But during the twentieth century the school had narrowed its expectations for both students and teachers as its graduates were denied by their homeopathic heritage and training access to academic research positions in prestigious orthodox schools or research institutes. In Trites's 1929 novel, *Paterfamilias*, the father, a committed homeopath and college faculty member, acknowledges that his son's decision to study regular medicine will enable him to gain fellowships to pursue scientific research, that his decision will open doors that homeopathic training would not have opened.

Until the mid-1950s the faculty publications listed in Hahnemann catalogs reflected this marginality and lack of coherence. Research—either orthodox or homeopathic—clearly did not define Hahnemann's identity. That the catalog's lists included commencement speeches and philosophical musings reflects an older tradition of physician as thinker rather than as scientific expert, a traditional that rejected the vocabulary and technologies of orthodox research. Further, Hahnemann faculty found it more and more difficult to publish in mainstream journals. During the 1930s and 1940s most of the faculty's research publications—philosophical and investigatory—appeared in the *Hahnemannian Monthly* and the *Journal of the American Institute of Homeopathy*, the organ of the national homeopathic association. This trend suggests not necessarily poor research but the continuing discrimination faced by homeopathically identified physicians. During 1938–1939, for example, of seventy-eight listed publications by forty-seven writers, fifty (64.1 percent) were in the *Hahnemannian Monthly* and nine (11.5 percent) in the *Journal of the American Institute of Homeopathy*. One group of Hahnemann pediatricians did publish an article on "adrenal neuroblastoma" in the *American Journal of Diseases of Children*, and John Scott of the Department of Physiology published two research pieces in the *American Journal of Physiology*. More typically, Reinhard Beutner, head of the new Department of Pharmacology, published a book entitled *Life's Beginning on the Earth* (1938). The most prolific faculty member was Montague Francis Ashley Montagu, an anthropologist who began teaching anatomy as an associate professor in 1939. The 1938–1939 catalog boasted of his recent publications: a book on the Australian Aborigines, a piece on "social time" in the *American Journal of Sociology*, and two pieces in *Science*, "The Concept of Atavism" and "Climate and Reproduction." The following year some of his sixteen publications appeared in *Science*, and three pieces appeared in the *American Journal of Physical Anthropology*; and in the 1942–1943 school year he published more than twice as often as any other faculty member. That he had a social science rather than a basic science background, however, made him an outsider in the new Hahnemann, and he left in 1950.[170]

Hahnemann graduates before World War II were groomed for private practice and became clinicians in communities where homeopaths, or homeopathically oriented physicians, were an accepted, sometimes traditional part of health care, especially parts of rural and eastern Pennsylvania.[171] This orientation—toward developing clinicians rather than researchers—has in the 1990s been described as the "Hahnemann tradition." Boericke himself was highly respected as a clinician, and while it is hard to pin down, perhaps the notion of a Hahnemann physician as foremost a practicing clinician is the one part of the old Hahnemann that lingered past Boericke's retirement into the 1980s and 1990s. Seth Fisher, for example, who graduated in 1948, praised the Hahnemann physicians he worked with at the hospital who were involved in "taking care of patients not in writing papers."[172] Karl Koiwai thought that Hahnemann graduates were considered good clinicians: "wherever they go they are appreciated"; and according to John Storer, a Jefferson professor once said: "if you're in a town with a Hahnemann man, he'll be the most successful general practitioner in the town."[173] In 1970 this clinical orientation was institutionalized in a new curriculum, known as the Core Curriculum, which introduced clinical subjects to students in the second year. Ana Nuñez, a 1986 graduate, remembered that she was taught "if in doubt, examine the patient. If you're smart enough and listen hard enough, the patient will tell you what's wrong."[174]

Nevertheless, when homeopathy was "rediscovered" by American physicians and the lay public in the 1970s and 1980s, the flowering occurred not at Hahnemann or in Philadelphia but in California and Oregon. Philadelphia's marginality was completed when in the 1980s the long-standing homeopathic pharmacy Boericke and Tafel moved to San Francisco, although John Borneman's firm, now owned by Boiron, remained in the city.

More Than Orthodoxy

Hahnemann not only embraced orthodoxy in this period but made it a distinctively rigid ideal. Being seen as an innovator was too dangerous for a school so recently on probation, and Hahnemann's leaders were concerned not to alienate the public. Thus in 1948, during probation, when the heads of obstetrics and gynecology suggested establishing a contraceptive clinic in the hospital they found little support, even though birth control had gained significant public respectability since the war and even though President Harry Truman had become a patron of Planned Parenthood. Hahnemann's hospital staff asked Charles Price, the hospital administrator, to investigate "the legality and ethics of such a clinic." Price reported that although it was not illegal under state laws, it "would set a precedent in that it would be the only Contraceptive Clinic associated with a Medical College in the State of Pennsylvania." Considering the "prejudices in certain quarters which might mitigate against the College and Hospital in a financial way," the Hospital Council decided to postpone the idea "until a more appropriate time."[175]

Hahnemann's policies on abortion were similarly cautious. During the 1950s Hahnemann physicians began to more openly acknowledge that they and their colleagues were performing abortions in their private offices and at the hospital. They were mocked in a satirical poem entitled "Obstetrics" in the 1950 yearbook:

I am the very model of a modern obstetrician . . .
I vehemently stand opposed to abortion
But don't you dare to question me on where I made my fortune.[176]

In the late 1960s Hahnemann Hospital was "quietly picketed" by a group seeking liberalization of abortion laws. Cameron explained to the trustees that the group had selected Hahnemann because of "its downtown location, the fact that is a major resource in an area of the city where the illegal abortion rate is high, and because Hahnemann is about as rigid an institution in following the usual prohibitions against abortion as can be found."[177] By 1971 the hospital agreed to require only one psychiatric consultant to authorize a therapeutic abortion instead of two, but nonetheless, obstetrics head George Lewis assured his colleagues, "the Department is still taking a conservative approach."[178]

Another sign of Hahnemann's conservative interpretation of orthodoxy during this period was its attitude toward alternative practitioners. Osteopaths had been campaigning for admission to residencies and hospital staffs since changes had been made in AMA membership policies in the late 1950s. Hahnemann's physicians expressed unhappiness with what one in 1963 called "a major force [that] is beginning to exert pressure to allow these physicians to be added to the existing hospital staffs."[179] During the 1960s Hahnemann resisted developing any general policy, despite rulings by the Pennsylvania state medical society that osteopaths could be admitted to hospital staffs and participate in teaching programs. In 1969 the AMA urged medical schools to develop "reasonable curricula" at the postgraduate level for awarding an M.D. to qualified osteopaths, and in 1971 Hahnemann altered its bylaws to require that all members of its medical staff be "graduates of approved medical schools, dental schools or schools of osteopathy."[180] In 1972 an osteopath resident at Hahnemann Hospital, one of about twenty, asked for such a program through Hahnemann's medical school. DiPalma, who had become medical school dean after the departure of William Kellow for Jefferson in 1967, pointed out to the faculty executive that a committee of the Philadelphia County Medical Society was considering this issue and that deans of all the city's schools thought it should be solved "as a unit." DiPalma believed, however, that the deans would "probably not do anything" and that "some individual school will have to start the program." Charles Paxson, the hospital administrator, commented that Hahnemann "could get osteopathic residents for free if we gave them an M.D." and that doing so would solve some financial problems. But physiologist Evangelos Angelakos, the head of Hahnemann's curriculum committee, warned that Hahnemann would get a large number of candidates for the first year, "but once we got a national reputation, no good students will come. It would be like the situation of the community hospital reducing costs by hiring foreign graduates." The idea was tabled.[181]

Remaking Hahnemann Hospital

The 1945 report had taken the trustees to task for not pulling their weight as influential philanthropists and for relying too heavily on student fees to finance the running of the medical school, and the 1949 report had used as a critical reason for taking Hahnemann off probation the reduction in "overhead charges to the medical school" by its trustees and had praised the fact that "none of the funds which properly should be available to the medical school for operating its educational program are now being diverted to the hospital."[182] The 1956 report more explicitly said that the hospital would have to rethink its relationship with the school. "Hahnemann's financial difficulties," it said, "have been almost unprecedented in chronicity and degree." "The primary objectives of Hahnemann Hospital," the AMA/AAMC representatives commented, did "not appear to have been clearly defined"; yet "the transmittal, preservation and advancement of knowledge must be considered the primary objectives of not only the medical college but also the hospital." While the hospital could continue to provide "a community service," "its policies must be determined in light of its primary educational goal."[183]

Hahnemann Hospital always remained the major financial motor of Hahnemann, and the trustees never stopped seeing student tuition as a simple way of increasing revenue. During the 1950s and 1960s Hahnemann was under strict restrictions by the AMA and AAMC not to increase the numbers of medical students admitted without permission, so instead the institution raised tuition. By the early 1960s, Hahnemann was one of the most expensive medical schools in the United States. In 1957 Cameron hired a new hospital administrator, Charles S. Paxson Jr., to replace Madison Brown. Paxson had been associated with Hahnemann in the 1930s and had been president of the Philadelphia Hospital Association, and he had a clear understanding of the new hospital culture and financial context that Hahnemann faced in postwar Philadelphia.

A major factor underpinning problems in both the college and the hospital was money. The institution had a large mortgage and significant vendor debt. During the 1940s and 1950s, as various alumni later recalled, skeptical Philadelphia vendors would only supply the hospital with equipment if administrators claimed it was an emergency. State and city appropriations for the care of indigent patients kept the hospital afloat, but this money was premised on the hospital's functioning as a community facility, maintaining a high number of free beds. While the hospital did have private beds and had introduced semiprivate rooms, it was known in the local community as a "soft touch" and therefore had numerous unpaid bills from private patients.

The American hospital was in the midst of a profound change, and Hahnemann Hospital would have been affected by these changes irrespective of its postprobationary policies. World War II had altered the prospects and expectations not only of doctors and nurses but also of hospital employees. Working-class veterans came back to Philadelphia with hopes that were similar to those of their middle-class compatriots; they were looking for a better life: a house, a car, a family in the burgeoning suburbs, and a job with wages high enough to pay for this Baby Boom–era dream. For many this dream was translated into a demand for a minimum wage and job security, and union activity blossomed among hospitals' janitorial, technical, and secretarial workers, who were increasingly female and nonwhite. Typical of many teaching hospitals based in the inner cities of the United States, racial segregation in the hospital became even more striking when, as a result of shifting demography of the neighborhoods around Hahnemann, almost all the ward patients were black or Puerto Rican while private rooms were filled with white middle-class patients. This situation was also the result of segregationist policies. Lonnie Fuller (Hahnemann M.D. 1960), Hahnemann Hospital's first black medical resident, recalled that black patients were always automatically admitted to the wards unless there happened to be a semiprivate room that already had a black patient.[184] Hahnemann's senior yearbooks began to feature photographs of white students with nonwhite patients, a dichotomy that would become the source of great dissension in later, more radical and more liberal decades.

The appearance of unions within hospitals was a sign that many working-class Americans no longer saw hospitals in their nineteenth-century guise: where service was either voluntary (by physicians) or low paying and compensated for by paternalistic policies and a feeling of altruism. As early as the 1950s Hahnemann administrators watched uneasily as newly militant unions began to try to organize workers in nearby hospitals.[185] Until the late 1960s Hahnemann's policy, which was backed up by public statements by its board, was "to oppose granting recognition to any union" but at the same time to raise wages. In 1965, during a strike at Cooper Hospital in Camden, Hahnemann raised its minimum wage from sixty-five cents an hour to one dollar an hour and told employees that wages would probably go up to $1.10 an hour soon.[186] After a series of walkouts in the early 1970s, however, Hahnemann Hospital did negotiate with union leaders and used the hospital's contracts with Blue Cross and the state to ensure that, as the trustees were assured, "the problem of union demands will land in the Governor's lap for solution."[187]

Perhaps the most striking new feature of the postwar hospital was the sudden appearance of assertive and demanding nurses. A widespread awareness of a nursing shortage led both graduate and student nurses to begin to demand higher wages, and hospital administrators had to seek with alacrity alternatives such as nursing aides. Despite protests from hospital clinicians, some wards and floors were closed.[188] One hospital administrator suggested hiring "more aides, orderlies and intelligent nursing helpers, such as high school girls for errands, telephones, supply trays and fluids for the patients."[189] Hahnemann expanded its nursing school, responding finally to the calls for improvement by Pennsylvania professional nursing reformers, and began a public relations campaign to attract its own graduates and other hospitals' nurses to Hahnemann. It also raised nursing salaries.

In his 1910 report Flexner had proposed that the hospital be "itself in the fullest sense a laboratory."[190] But, like other hospitals attached to private medical schools, until the 1950s Hahnemann was two hospitals in one: a teaching hospital for patients in the wards and a health care facility for patients in private rooms. During the 1950s and 1960s Hahnemann began to expand the concept of the teaching hospital to all parts of the hospital, and for the first time medical students regularly entered the sanctuary of the private room. The contract that all poor patients had implicitly had to agree to—to act as clinical material for teaching and research—was extended to middle-class patients as well. In 1966, Charles Paxson told the trustees, 90 percent of the hospital's private patients were "available to our students."[191] The AMA/AAMC representatives had been assured that "all private patients may be used for teaching," but until hospital services were overseen by full-time clinicians it was in fact impossible to ensure this.[192] It is not surprising that it was during these decades that Congress first began to develop legislation to enforce the proper use of informed consent forms and institutional review boards.[193] In considering an expansion of the hospital in the mid-1960s, Dean William Kellow told the trustees with rare candor, "if we were to eliminate either clinic or private patients, it would be undesirable. The lower social and economic classes are far less communicative but far more available to physical examination. The reverse is true for the upper social and economic groups. Thus the availability of each group to student training is desirable."[194]

Before the 1940s Hahnemann Hospital had cobbled together funding from individual and industry subscribers who had endowed a bed, a room, or a ward and from a few donors who had enabled the hospital to buy equipment. Medical school alumni did not see the hospital as part of their responsibility; they thought, as one alumnus admitted ruefully in 1957, "that they have their own hospital to support, why help Hahnemann?"[195] During the 1920s and 1930s Hahnemann had increased the number of paying patients by promoting its scientific expertise and dramatic technology. In the late 1940s Philadelphia hospitals accepted the Blue Cross system, and in the mid-1960s, the federal and state programs of Medicare and Medicaid, which helped to pay for two growing groups of hospital patients: the elderly and the poor. Having a predictable amount of income each year enabled hospitals like Hahnemann for the first time to plan a little, but the money did not come without strings.

Blue Cross placed Hahnemann under even greater pressure than the AMA/AAMC accreditation committees had. Blue Cross was never a silent third party. By the 1950s it was demanding that Hahnemann bring down its average patient stay from eleven days to closer to eight, although it remained at eleven days more than a decade later.[196] In 1971, some years before the Congressional mandate on funding by Diagnostic Research Groups, Blue Cross gave Hahnemann administrators a list of disease categories and asked them to calculate for the previous three years "the average length of stay for each Medical and Surgical category."[197] Blue Cross was aware of the costs of running a teaching hospital and saw itself as a guardian against unreasonable expansion. In the early 1970s it insisted on an 8 percent reduction of resident and intern staff and a gradual elimination of residents and interns subsidized by patient care. "Funds to support the program must be obtained from other sources," the hospital staff was informed.[198]

The struggles that Hahnemann Hospital faced in becoming an integrated teaching hospital can only be touched on here, but its constant problem with autopsies during the 1950s and 1960s suggests both a lack of commitment to teaching and research on the part of the hospital staff and also a suspicion of the newly expanding mission of the hospital by patients and their families. The Joint Commission on Accreditation of Hospitals, established in 1952, had stated that a hospital must maintain a 50 percent autopsy rate in order to remain in good standing.[199] For most of this period Hahnemann Hospital was unable to achieve this. In 1968, after learning of the 41.3 percent rate of the previous year, which was a decline from the year before, Hahnemann's Hospital Council noted that "there were two important issues in obtaining autopsies: 1) it was important for accreditation, and 2) it was a fine educational function." The council again urged the heads of services to talk to their staff.[200] Similarly, hospital administrators found it almost impossible to ensure up-to-date medical records, a difficulty that was a reflection of the practices of volunteer clinicians who had little incentive to contribute to Hahnemann's teaching or research program. In one exasperated annual report John Moyer described the condition of records in his department as "deplorable," and he complained that the hospital had no "administrative policy" on record keeping.[201] Faculty and administrators tried in vain to enforce timely records, even at one stage threatening hospital staff that they would be "deprived of registering private cases in the hospital until such time as they have completed their unfinished hospital records."[202]

Orthodox Integration

The transformation of Hahnemann was gradual but significant. Hahnemann graduates and especially Hahnemann faculty (no longer always alumni) began to integrate themselves in the orthodox medical community, both in Philadelphia and nationally. In 1957 three Hahnemann graduates became presidents of local specialist societies: Robert Hunter (1921), of the Philadelphia Obstetric Society, Horst Agerty (1934), of the Philadelphia Pediatric Society, and Horace L. Weinstock (1927), of the Philadelphia Urological Society. A powerful symbol came five years earlier with the election of Joseph Post (1909) as president of the orthodox Philadelphia County Medical Society, and then Charles Thompson (1931) in 1963. Thompson was Harry Eberhard's successor as head of Hahnemann's gastroenterology department, and he also headed a medical service at Philadelphia General Hospital providing Hahnemann students better access to this important institution. In 1961 Carl Fischer became president of both the American Academy of Pediatrics and the Philadelphia Pediatric Society, and in 1967 William Likoff was elected president of the American College of Cardiology.

In embracing orthodoxy Hahnemann also began to alter its policies on student admission. It retained a quota on women students—around 10 percent of the entering class—which did not change until the early 1970s. But Hahnemann's restrictions on Jewish and Catholic students began to ease, and eventually, according to a 1967 statewide report, Hahnemann had the highest percentages of these students of any medical school in the state.[203] DiPalma recalled as a member of the admissions committee in the early 1950s seeing the "green" files indicating the applicant was Jewish. In his recollection Hahnemann's Jewish quota ended with Cameron.[204]

A striking change in the 1950s was that Hahnemann, like other Philadelphia medical schools in this period, admitted a small number of male African-American students (not until 1973 did the first black woman graduate). No black student had graduated from Hahnemann since 1912. Perhaps administrators were prompted by an anonymous offer of a scholarship for black students; perhaps the growing civil rights movement made a difference, with, for example, the acceptance in 1948 of the first black student in a Southern medical school, the University of Arkansas.

African-American men and women played crucial roles in the college and hospital, roles that are, however, largely invisible in Hahnemann documents. Graduates in the 1940s and 1950s recalled a woman named Viola who worked in the terrible heat of the hospital basement washing glassware for the laboratories and cooking the tissue media.[205] Black women were accepted as students in Hahnemann's small technical programs, and they appear in pictures of cytol-

Figure 32. In February 1968 Martin Luther King Jr. developed laryngitis while in Philadelphia organizing an anti-Vietnam campaign; he was treated by Walter P. Lomax Jr. (1932–, class of 1957). Courtesy of the Lomax family.

ogy technicians in the late 1950s. The 1947 yearbook featured a picture and biography of a man named George who headed the dissection "Green Room." After working as a valet and then in the laboratory at Medico-Chirurgical, George came to Hahnemann in 1917; and he recalled working for Rufus Weaver, whose "prize dissection" would, he believed, "always linger in the hearts and eyes of thousands."[206] In 1956 DiPalma hired Robert F. McMichael, a biology graduate of Lincoln University. McMichael became not only DiPalma's technical assistant but also his research associate, and DiPalma listed him in joint publications, as did other members of the pharmacology staff. McMichael directed a program organized by the American Foundation for Negro Affairs that brought high school and college students to work in laboratories so that they could gain some experience and find some role models that would aid them in applying to medical school. In 1969 McMichael was honored as employee of the year.[207]

A number of the early black medical graduates became teachers at Hahnemann. Edward Murray (1951) taught endocrinology, and Warren E. Smith (1957) taught psychiatry in the Department of Mental Health Sciences. Smith (1922–1990) was a civil rights supporter and a member of the Congress of Racial

Equality (CORE), the NAACP, and the Medical Committee for Human Rights (MCHR). Hahnemann's mental health department was unusually open to black psychiatrists, partly because during the 1960s it encompassed five satellite community mental health centers and partly because its senior faculty such as Israel Zwerling were especially interested in civil rights issues.

One of the most intriguing early black graduates was Walter P. Lomax Jr. (1932–). A LaSalle College graduate, Lomax graduated from Hahnemann in 1957 and began a private practice at Eighteenth and Wharton in South Philadelphia, near where he had grown up. Lomax was able to take advantage of federal money for disadvantaged city areas, and he formed a small group practice with support from the 1970 Emergency Health Personnel Act, which placed on government salary physicians who won exemptions from military service during the Vietnam War. By 1973 he had a health center with eight treatment rooms.[208] In February 1968 when Martin Luther King Jr. was in Philadelphia organizing against the war Lomax was asked to come to his hotel room to help him with his laryngitis. Lomax became an early health care manager, and in the 1980s his Lomax Company gained contracts to provide care to welfare recipients and prison inmates in Philadelphia and in Boston.[209]

HAHNEMANN'S embrace of orthodoxy was committed but awkward. Remaking the school and hospital was seen as part of a modernizing process that involved discarding Hahnemann's past—both its achievements and its failures. So successful was the transformation of Hahnemann Hospital into a standard teaching hospital that the Hahnemann students who arrived in the late 1960s saw it as a typical institution that needed to gain an awareness of and sensitivity to community needs. Similarly, major players at the medical school seemed to offer students models of laboratory and clinical researchers rather than clinicians. Hahnemann integrated itself so firmly in local and national medical culture that its internal and external critics in the late 1960s and 1970s attacked it as exhibiting typical problems of orthodox American medicine, a world, ironically, that Hahnemann had only just begun to enter.

Chapter 7   Radical Alternatives
1968–1972

BY THE LATE 1960s Hahnemann had successfully remade itself into an ortho-dox, research-oriented academic medical center. Hahnemann had become in-creasingly responsive to pressures from outside professional bodies like the AMA and AAMC, to financial incentives from government and from pharmaceutical companies in encouraging certain kinds of basic and clinical research projects, and to the demands of a new group of salaried faculty from within the institu-tion. But just as this transformation was achieved, Hahnemann came under at-tack by critics with a radically different vision of medical education, health care, and relations between American physicians and society.

This period in Hahnemann's history is filled with ironies. Attacked for so many years as too different and distant from orthodox American professional-ism and the ideal American medical school and teaching hospital, Hahnemann institutions were now attacked for being too mainstream, too integrated into the structure and ideology of organized medicine. Critics held new ideals: hu-mane health care, a hospital responsive to community needs, especially those of minorities and the poor, and a new kind of physician trained to practice a new kind of medicine.

The source of these attacks was also new. In the 1930s and 1940s a group of faculty had used the standards of outside professional organizations to try to alter Hahnemann's administrative and academic structure. But in the 1960s and 1970s, the new agenda for Hahnemann was defined not by administrators or, largely, by the faculty, but by the federal government and by a group of Hahnemann students. Hahnemann since the early postwar years had tried to follow federal guidelines in reorienting its research programs and curriculum. But now a new liberal agenda pushed Hahnemann to restructure its admissions policies, teaching methods, and relations to the community.

Radical students urged not just these changes but many more, and their criticisms profoundly undermined Hahnemann's entire mission as a teaching and research institution. These young men and women drew their intellectual and moral force not from professional medical standards—indeed they scorned such values—but from an ideology and vision gained from outside bodies, especially the civil rights movement, the antiwar movement, and the counterculture and antiestablishment youth movement. Their new vision reconceptualized the place of the medical school, the hospital, and physicians in American society. Students called for greater responsiveness to the local Philadelphia community. They urged Hahnemann to admit more minority students, to restructure its curriculum to reflect a broad environmentalist view of health care, and to institutionalize the voices of students in the running of Hahnemann itself.

In the 1960s and 1970s American medicine became an important target for those who sought to transform American society; medicine was seen as epitomizing the worst of mainstream American values. A variety of social critics, including consumer and patient advocates, feminists, and environmentalists, attacked organized medicine, hospitals (especially teaching hospitals), practitioners, and medical academics, especially those who selected and trained doctors. American physicians, according to this critique, had neglected those Americans who could not afford and did not have access to proper health care. America's health care system was not only inequitable but paternalistic, racist, and inhumane: authoritarian doctors ignored patient concerns and dignity and paid attention only to tissues and organs rather than to the "whole" person, either in sickness or health, in his or her social environment. Demonstrations became commonplace outside the AMA's annual meetings, and the demonstrators protested, among other things, the AMA's policies on contraceptives and abortion, its acceptance of racially segregated medical societies as AMA members, and the use of homosexuality as a standard psychiatric diagnosis. The revelations in 1972 of the Tuskegee syphilis experiments, which had been carried on for forty years by respected U.S. Public Health Service physicians, only invigorated the debate and the critique of the medical establishment.[1]

Reinforcing these criticisms, and spurring a significant responsiveness from many medical institutions, were larger social and political changes during the 1960s, especially Lyndon Johnson's Great Society (1963–1968). Because they were made during a period of political liberalism, the attacks on American medicine were more than simple moral critiques, and they carried great weight. Great Society programs provided the foundation and funding for a new welfare infrastructure. Programs such as Medicare and Medicaid (both established in 1965) and other health services funded by the Office of Equal Opportunity were significant in inner cities like Philadelphia's, where hospitals especially affected the lives of the poor and minority groups who depended on them both for employment and emergency care. Great Society programs, spurred partly by growing activism among minority groups, began funding community-based health services such as mental health clinics and began encouraging hospitals and medical schools to staff such facilities and teach community health to their students. Even with the election of Richard Nixon in 1968 little of this liberal ideology or the welfare infrastructure was initially dismantled. Medical school and hospital administrators began to recognize that remaking their institutions, at least in some ways, in this liberal vision of the world could be financially rewarding.

Demands closer to home also forced Hahnemann to listen and respond to its immediate community. The college and hospital on Broad Street were no longer surrounded by the middle-class physicians and patients of earlier generations; instead, the patients of the public wards and outpatient clinics made up the neighborhood. With the help of sympathetic state and national officials, local communities became more active: they created organizations to reform housing, working conditions, and discrimination, and they gained political influence in city and state government. Hahnemann Hospital employees began to press for better working conditions through union activity, and they found the state's governor supportive. Philadelphia's black community, increasingly radicalized after the assassination of Martin Luther King Jr., demanded a more responsive city government. Pressure from Washington and Harrisburg meant that some city institutions, fearful that they would lose both funding and popular sympathy, became responsive to welfare and civil rights issues. Civil rights activists' demands for medical institutions had special power in Pennsylvania because the state had somewhat blurred the distinction between public and private by funding all its major hospitals and medical schools, a situation that created an especially politicized environment in which organized medicine was an easy and visible target. A newly activist student body saw itself as being able to speak for the local community. As Hahnemann students became more aware of the racial and class divisions separating them and their teachers from residents of Hahnemann's neighborhood, their critical voices sharpened.

The most significant source of Hahnemann students' activism came from the new radical health movement. Inspired by the social upheaval of this period, a number of physicians, nurses, medical students, and other health professionals began to organize themselves into medical civil rights groups. In 1968, Physicians for Social Responsibility—organized in 1961 to protest against nuclear testing and then chemical and biological warfare, including the use of tear gas and pesticides in Vietnam—issued a manual discussing alternatives to the draft for doctors.[2] Members of medicine's New Left included pediatrician Benjamin Spock, who was arrested for antiwar activities in 1968, and Howard Levy, an army dermatologist who was court-martialed after refusing to teach Green Berets dermatology so that they could win the "hearts and minds" of the Vietnamese.[3]

The Medical Committee for Human Rights (MCHR) was founded by physicians, nurses, and medical students to provide money and medical assistance for the civil rights activists during the 1964 Mississippi Freedom Summer, and in 1965 the group helped those protesters wounded during the Selma march who were denied care by segregated hospitals. MCHR criticized the AMA, organized model health clinics, and developed a broader political ideology that argued that American society needed to rethink its use of resources, to reorganize its health care and training institutions, to demystify medical knowledge, and to give health care workers and patients more control of health care institutions. MCHR members regularly attended antiwar demonstrations, and, according to one commentator, it became common to see "young, long-haired medics, often wearing motorcycle helmets and laboratory coats with the initials MCHR on their sleeves."[4] The group organized legal help and physical examinations for young men eligible for the draft, and it also supported the patients' rights movement, handing out brochures, such as one that read "The doctor and the hospital are *not* doing you a favor to see you," and providing patients with a list of questions for their doctor, including "Is this treatment for my benefit or for research?"[5]

The radical group that played the most significant role in politicizing Hahnemann students in the late 1960s was the Student Health Organization (SHO). SHO was founded in 1965 by medical students working with California migrant agricultural workers. These students set up health clinics and research projects looking at the health of neglected minority groups, and they used their experience to develop a political philosophy that reflected the radical critiques of Students for a Democratic Society (SDS) and the Black Panthers. They also turned their attention to medical school admissions, curricula, and structure.[6] They were able to gain federal grants for summer health projects among the poor, which drew already concerned student health care professionals and helped to further radicalize them. Peter Eisenberg, a 1971 Hahnemann graduate, recalled that he and a small group of Hahnemann freshmen were sent by the local Philadelphia SHO chapter into the Ludlow area, north and east of Hahnemann Hospital, on a federal project to convince residents to donate blood because so many were shot or stabbed on Saturday nights that the hospital frequently ran out of blood. The project made him and his friends angry, he recalled, for "what they [the residents] needed was not more blood but a home, job, food." After the summer the group rushed into the college dean's office and demanded that he "fix it." "They had a fit," Eisenberg commented.[7] Later that fall SHO held its national meeting in Philadelphia, further inspiring medical and nursing students in the city to radical action.

Students Redefine Hahnemann's Mission:
A New Kind of School

Hahnemann, like many medical schools, had not felt the need for student representation in its formal organization. During the 1920s and 1930s the school had been small enough to allow its faculty members personal interaction with most students. Teachers often acted in a paternal way, advising students on professional and personal affairs; and Hahnemann students, at least in the interwar period, were often young, around twenty or twenty-one, for they could enter Hahnemann with only two and then three years of college.

Until the 1960s, most Hahnemann students had not concerned themselves much with the running of the school or hospital. When students did organize themselves it was more likely into fraternities and research societies, which allowed greater involvement with their faculty sponsors. Many students were active in college social life. Some of the traditions of Hahnemann had faded: the arrival of women students in 1941, for example, meant the end of singing risqué songs before school lectures. Other traditions, like student music groups and the annual Blue and Gold Ball flourished in the immediate postwar years.

A group of seniors each year produced Hahnemann's senior yearbook. The yearbook (which had been published annually since 1928) helped to shape the remembered experience and the public face of seniors for the students, their families, the faculty, and the alumni. It became a memento and a kind of guide to student thinking and the direction of each generation of Hahnemann graduates. These yearbooks reflected, in a selective way, students' experiences of medical training and their social lives. The yearbooks often included quite detailed discussions of college departments and faculty members. With the growing activism of Hahnemann students, however, yearbooks lost their multipage prose commentaries that had conveyed a sense of cohesive community, and by the 1970s they were made up largely of pictures.

Before the 1960s there is some limited evidence in these yearbooks of petitions from individual classes dissatisfied with a particular course or teacher, and in 1934 and 1935, as we have seen, the senior yearbooks listed a series of demands, complaining, in effect, that Hahnemann was not close enough to the AAMC's model of a modern medical school. During the 1930s the Student Institute had become the major student body, and it was an internally focused political group made up of elected class representatives who met occasionally with the dean or other administrators. Most complaints centered around the educational facilities. In 1946, for example, the officers of the Student Institute complained to the dean about the unsatisfactory student health service, the commencement exercises, and the inadequate library facilities.[8] There were occasional comments on curriculum decisions. In 1947 the faculty sympathetically heard complaints from the sophomore class that the National Board exams had been made too central a requirement for promotion to junior year and that their centrality resulted in the "basic inequity of the situation wherein a student's physical and mental health in a given three days are made the basis of his entire future career."[9]

In the decades before the 1960s, demands for change from both faculty and students reflected the issues raised by the AMA and AAMC both in their private reports and in their public surveys of American medical education. Hahnemann faculty and students alike were consciously seeking to participate in the mainstream medical culture and to repudiate their alternative, unorthodox heritage and reputation. There is little evidence that medical students here or at most other schools questioned the mission of their institutions before the late 1960s.

At Hahnemann only briefly during the 1940s did a few yearbooks, especially during the war, concern themselves with social problems and urge broader conceptions of health. The 1944 *Medic*, for example, was, as we have seen in chapter four, dedicated to the professor of bacteriology and preventive medicine, Grant Favorite. Favorite, "more than any other faculty member," the seniors claimed, "made clear to us . . . the inevitable effect present day governmental trends must have upon medicine" through his "rare, basic appreciation of the true purpose of a physician; he believes in and has taught us the scientific not the artistic approach to medicine, the social and not the economic approach to man."[10] The 1944 yearbook editor, Irving Lichtenstein, reflected on the function of yearbooks when he commented in his foreword that "in days when men lose their lives for a belief and countries are obliterated for a cause—a Year Book is inconsequential," but "if this record has served, though imperceptibly, to foster a mutual tolerance and respect for individual beliefs and convictions, even in this small but heterogeneous group of varied races and religions—then it *has* accomplished a *fundamental* purpose."[11] The 1948 edition of the yearbook was a particularly powerful one. The cover superimposed the physician's serpent and staff over a sketch of an atomic bomb explosion. In the yearbook's opening statement the seniors commented that "in a world of atom-bombs, minorities, tidal waves, and above all, people, predictability doesn't exist." Graduates would need to rely not just on each other and the medical profession but also on "the vast, interwoven complex of non-medical society."[12] By the early 1950s, however, such comments were rare. Hahnemann yearbooks showed student life revolving around family and career, with pages on the young children and spouses (mostly wives) of Hahnemann students and on the students' music and social groups.

In the late 1960s, however, Hahnemann students, reflecting concerns of young Americans around the country, especially those at universities and colleges, began to critically analyze the function of their education, the structure of their society, and the policies of their government. Such debates took place within the context of profound social and political unrest: the anti-Vietnam movement, the rise of radical student rights and civil rights groups, and the hippie counterculture. Many students angrily attacked urban medical schools and hospitals as part of a health care system that trained doctors inadequately and provided limited and inadequate health care to the urban poor, who nonetheless were expected to participate willingly as research subjects for medical students and clinical researchers. This sense of alienation from mainstream medicine and American culture was expressed through students' provocative dress and long hair and increasingly strident protests. Theirs was a new alternative vision of American medicine. They rejected the commercialism of American physicians and the AMA's model of professionalism, and they applied their new values of participatory democracy and affirmative action to the running of their own educational institutions.

Social pressures on Hahnemann students began forcing many to rethink their role as American citizens and potential physicians. They began to demand a voice in the running of the institution that they saw as defining their identity. Crucial for understanding many of the radical demands Hahnemann students made of their teachers and institution was the constant awareness of the Vietnam War, the terrible conflict that was splitting apart American families, communities, and generations. Medical students, like other American young men, could not distance themselves from the war and its meaning for their own lives as well as its social and political implications.

Graduating from Hahnemann meant becoming reclassified by one's local draft board and a high likelihood of being sent to Vietnam. Thus it is not surprising that Hahnemann's radical student paper published an article by Philip Scranton, a draft counselor at the University of Pennsylvania. According to Scranton, "the attainment of the MD degree is the magic wand which transforms an otherwise quiet 2–S, 1–C or 1–Y into a trembling 1–A." He discussed the options for graduating medical students. A medical graduate could try to become a conscientious objector, for "a physician might rationally oppose his Hippocratic commitment being used for feeding the death machine." The graduate might ask for "non-combatant alternative service" in the military or civilian world, but because of the "extreme resistance on the part of local boards to granting job deferments to already much deferred medical graduates," he was not likely to get permission to do an internship or residency. A graduate could try to join the U.S. Public Health Service but should be aware of the strict physical requirements. Or he could think about illegal alternatives like going to Canada or "dropping out of sight." However, Scranton warned, "the underground for doctors has little career future."[13]

Students viewed their involvement with the war as part of a larger relationship with the American establishment. With a special sense of the importance of living one's political convictions ("the personal is the political") all aspects of medical training—the kind of institution, training, fellow students, and relations with teachers and patients—became problematized. During the late 1960s a small group of Hahnemann sophomores and juniors renamed *Impulse*, the student paper, *Grand Mal*. *Grand Mal* was deliberately provocative and brought Hahnemann issues into broader political and cultural concerns. One issue, for example, was dedicated to the Beatles' "Maxwell Edison," a murderer who was "majoring in medicine." Using this paper as a public forum, the students demanded greater representation on major committees, including the promotions and admissions committees, the faculty's College Council, and the board of trustees.[14] But first they wanted to be accepted as political, liberated individuals with their own distinctive youth counterculture.

Dress

Social change first began to make itself felt at Hahnemann Hospital when the dress and personal appearance of medical students, residents, and employees became a problem. Dress symbolized the entry of a youth culture, with which many older doctors had little sympathy, into the hospital and the medical school. By the late 1960s dress and especially hair had become increasingly politicized emblems of the antiestablishment and antiprofessional culture, although it was not until the mid-1970s that Hahnemann yearbooks displayed a majority of students with mustaches, beards, or long hair. Dress at medical schools excited student unrest, just as it did in many high schools and other educational institutions.

Initially the changing dress among physicians-in-training reflected a more medicalized hospital culture, one less concerned with traditional propriety. In 1965 Hahnemann Hospital staff noticed with disapproval the "increase in the use of scrub suits without white coats in the hospital" and warned that "this practice should be discontinued immediately."[15]

Students and young physicians at Hahnemann began dressing with even less traditional propriety: long hair and untrimmed beards, jeans and a shirt rather than the jacket and tie considered an accepted part of professional culture. While many teachers resented these changes and their implied criticism and tried to discipline their unruly charges, medical school educators were particularly incensed. Senior physicians saw a student with jeans and long hair as an explicit, disrespectful, and public rejection of professional culture and standards. But, worse, such changes threatened to undermine the special place of medicine as the premiere emblem of professionalism. The medical profession had become such a model of professionalism for American social scientists that there was a special field called medical sociology. The 1940s and 1950s were perhaps the high point of American medicine's golden age: physicians enjoyed unprecedentedly high incomes and a high status among the public, and they were glowingly portrayed in radio shows, movies, and the new medium of television.[16]

Numerous groups in the 1960s and 1970s attacked the status of physicians and the basis for it. Horrified professional leaders and medical school administrators regarded students' appearance as not just unaesthetic and unprofessional but antiprofessional. Hahnemann traditionalists tried to phrase their dislike of long hair as concern with the public face of the institution and its effect on patients. In 1969 the vice president and administrator of the hospital, Charles Paxson, condemned long hair for its connection with dirt and disorder. In an impassioned open letter printed in *Grand Mal*, Paxson asked, "Does an unkempt appearance—a total lack of basic cleanliness—really help your protest against the establishment, the organization, the government, war, poverty and the like?" He continued:

> How can a young man who is sincerely interested in providing better
> health care to disadvantaged people and a better world for all people
> believe that he is doing anything positive by wearing dirty clothes,
> unwashed and uncombed hair and an untrimmed beard? . . . As a
> medical student, you are preparing for a professional career . . . in which
> traditionally the community in general and your patients in particular
> will want and need to look up to you. Your white coat is a symbol of
> your profession. . . . The person in the coat must be clean . . . clean in
> mind, spirit and body, to meet the implied lofty goals.[17]

As a senior administrator Paxson continued in a stern but paternal tone: "While we at Hahnemann will remain permissive and understanding (if not always sympathetic) to your political concerns and activities—we will not continue to tolerate sloth, filth, slovenliness."[18] Peter Eisenberg recalled that he had a beard as a student ("it was a straggly, not very attractive beard") and "everyone gave me hell."[19] Stephen Baer, a 1972 graduate who was not a student radical, also recalled students who came to class "in shorts and ripped T-shirts, with long hair and sandals." The teachers were "appalled," he said, "but what could they do?"[20]

Opposition to the counterculture was not limited to verbal disapproval. By the early 1970s both the college and hospital were initiating disciplinary action against students and staff who were "inappropriately attired." Hospital staff asked that "medical students working in the Hospital look as professional as possible" and warned them "to wear a clean white coat and necktie while in the Hospital . . . [although] during the warm summer months, the necktie could be considered optional."[21] At an earlier meeting the staff was concerned that there was no official policy to ensure proper dress and appearance among students and employees. "Heretofore, it has been assumed that all hospital personnel would dress in accordance with good taste and custom. Such is no longer the case."[22]

Hahnemann students recognized quickly that dress and hair were both symbols and political rallying points that could inspire moderate students to unite with their radical peers. Most Hahnemann students felt that administrators were imposing old-fashioned values and treating medical students as high school or college students rather than as preprofessionals. The argument that students' lack of formal representation in college decision-making had led to such insensitivity was not difficult to sustain.

Hair and dress became such contentious issues that faculty and students formed ad hoc committees to formulate alternative policies. Hahnemann trustees had passed a bylaw whereby "Any student whose personal appearance is such as, in the opinion of the faculty, to disturb patients or professional personnel, will be excluded from Hahnemann and Hahnemann affiliated hospitals until such appearance is corrected to the satisfaction of the faculty and administration."[23] In 1969 the faculty's student affairs committee formed an ad hoc subcommittee on student-faculty relations to deal with the problem of "student dress and appearance," and in at least this case these discussions led the committee members on both sides to recognize the broader issues raised by the problem of long hair and casual dress. To "all the members" of the subcommittee, according to one student reporter, it became evident that this issue was "only one of the more obvious symptoms within the Hahnemann community and our society in general."[24]

Students identified the class and status issues implicit in protests against counterculture dress. They proudly defended their dress as effectively undermining middle-class medical professional culture and ideology. As one satirical piece in Hahnemann's student paper put it, "We must set an example for the unwashed masses; we must preserve our shining image that the poor can look up to. . . . And we must continue to dress in the traditional fashion because people have learned to identify sterility, grandiosity, and money with the role of doctor. Can we allow some long-haired anarchists to destroy our image?"[25] Another Hahnemann student questioned the notion that students threatened with disciplinary action must depend on the judgment of a clinician "even when it is clouded by his personal prejudice and political-social loyalties," adding that "it is imperative that patients lose the stereotype of doctors' being impersonal machines, all looking alike, sterile, and 'professional' (in traditional terms) in their appearance as well as their manner."[26] These radical students mocked the claim that conservative Hahnemann leaders were upholding the school's proud heritage: they showed a group of nineteenth-century Hahnemann faculty with their long beards and mustaches in *Grand Mal* with a caption that read, "Would you let these hirsute Hahnemann Homeopaths handle your health?"[27]

Student Participation

In 1967 a group of Hahnemann freshmen, including Mark Prager, Jerry Lindauer, Peter Eisenberg, Larry Kron, Forrest Lang, Thomas Liston, and Ron Feigin, became involved in the Philadelphia branch of SHO and began organizing at Hahnemann. They took over the student newspaper, set up a table at the college for antiwar petitions, and organized buses to go to the march on Washington to protest the war. When they heard that the Philadelphia County Medical Society was honoring an army officer, they protested outside the meeting and then walked in and demanded the microphone.[28] And they began to call for change at Hahnemann; they insisted on institutionalized structures that would provide students with a level of participatory democracy.

During 1968 and 1969 the freshman, sophomore, and junior classes complained of being alienated from the faculty and being evaluated unfairly.[29] The 1968–1969 sophomore class was especially vocal. In April 1969 a group of students including Mark Prager, an editor of *Grand Mal*, complained to the College Council that Hahnemann's Student Institute did not "currently reflect student opinion." The group brought with them to the council meeting a letter signed by 99 of the 111 sophomores, and proposed a series of changes for the incoming freshman class.[30] Students had long disliked the caution given at the beginning of their freshman year: "look to the right of you, look to the left of you . . . "[31] This letter argued that there should be a stated philosophy at Hahnemann that "every student admitted is qualified to complete the course of study."[32] The students also claimed that the "atmosphere between the faculty and students is characterized by mutual distrust" because faculty members' major responsibility was to test and grade students. Faculty evaluation, especially during the first two years, they explained, "concentrates on medical knowledge and ignores evidence of student character and habits essential to medical practice." In language similar to that used by American students nationwide, Hahnemann students regarded grades as "a crutch on which students learn to depend for motivation rather than develop personal responsibility for their own education," as forcing students "to place emphasis on material of little long run value." They noted that there were some courses with predetermined percentages of students who must fail. They called on the faculty and administrators to eliminate the "double paranoia syndrome, grade consciousness and meaningless cramming."[33]

The council members and the sophomore representatives discussed this letter. The council minutes later characterized this debate as showing the class's belief that "the faculty's emphasis is on weeding out failures rather than developing the physician in each man, and that the faculty does not recognize the students as adults and responsible men." After the sophomores left, the council agreed to form a new committee to make recommendations for change.[34]

In May, after a meeting between the dean and the new ad hoc sophomore class–faculty committee, which had been less than conciliatory, the dean reported to the faculty that he had "tried hard to listen to the demands of the students, many of which are justified, to be sympathetic to their interests although sometimes the students are unreasonable with respect to the timing of changes desired" and "will continue to maintain a sensible attitude and to attempt to make desirable changes in an orderly fashion but that he will not tolerate disruptive tactics."[35] In June the ad hoc committee recommended that "medical students be treated as graduate students in a professional field and their course work [be] designed with this role in mind." It suggested redesigning the student-faculty advisor system and instituting a pass-fail-honors comprehensive exam at the end of each instructional unit instead of the current exam and grading system.[36] Skeptical faculty were particularly swayed by the argument that other Philadelphia schools were already introducing such changes. The faculty's curriculum committee recommended to the executive council that one student from each of the four classes be elected by students as representatives on the curriculum committee, after noting the practice at Jefferson, Temple, and Woman's.[37] By the spring of 1969 there were student representatives on both the curriculum committee and the student affairs council, which was part of the faculty's College Council.[38]

In October 1969 Mark Prager and Jerome Lindauer, as editors of *Grand Mal*, asked permission to attend the faculty's College Council meetings. The council refused but agreed to make its minutes available and to have the dean ready to meet with the students to discuss the minutes.[39] The radical movement continued. In December 1969 one-half of Hahnemann's new sophomore class decided not to attend pathology lectures and to work in independent study groups instead, a gesture a student reporter called "Free University At Hahnemann."[40] The juniors, pointing to a lack of trust and communication among students, faculty, and administration, a lack of pride in Hahnemann, and steadily decreasing respect for human dignity at all levels of the institution, sent a questionnaire to the active clinical faculty, perhaps searching for allies. Their investigations discovered a high level of discontent, especially regarding faculty relations with the hospital and college administration. Faculty complained of growing competition, lack of communication, and the lack of a faculty dining room. One faculty member described the situation as "the half-dead feeling at Hahnemann."[41] During 1969, representatives from the Student Institute demanded no written exams of any kind during the junior and senior years and complained that the timing of the junior comprehensive exams interfered with students' performance of their final clinical clerkship because students had to take time away to cram for the exam.[42]

Not all faculty committees were responsive, however. The Clinical Science Promotions Committee, confronted by student complaints about clerkships, exams, and the National Boards, told the College Council that it was "unwise to have students participating in the detailed discussion at every meeting" but that some relationship would be helpful as students clearly had "extreme doubts and anxieties." The clinical science committee suggested organizing an open meeting or perhaps setting up an appeal mechanism.[43]

As a result of the growing stridency of student dissent the board of trustees issued a memorandum to the students and faculty in the spring of 1969, referring to the "present atmosphere of student unrest and militancy." Hahnemann, it argued, "is an academic institution with obligations to the public, to the government and to itself to maintain and preserve its academic environment and traditions." "Changes and improvements are desirable" but "must be brought about by an orderly process and along . . . democratic channels." The board pointed to the already established forums for student complaints at Hahnemann: faculty advisors, the student affairs committee, and class officers who "are responsible for reporting student desires and grievances to the instructors and Deans." These forums were spelled out in Hahnemann's student handbook: "orderly guide-lines which have been carefully constructed by past generations of students and faculty who had the welfare of the institution in mind as well as their own improvement." The board strongly disapproved of some of the tactics of the radical students, warning that "it is the firm resolve of the Administration to maintain law and order" and that it would not tolerate student "factions" that had begun to "demand immediate and unreasoned solutions to difficult problems, to agitate and irritate," and "to be patently militant and disruptive" by disrupting normal classes and administrative functions. The board threatened not only to call on the police but also to notify government and private agencies, an action that could lead to students' losing government loans and scholarships.[44]

The board also tried to undermine the motivation of Hahnemann's radical critics. The college "has a long tradition of friendly relations with students," but now "it is understood that the present generation are liberated and unfettered by past restraints and traditions." The board suggested that each radical examine his or her conscience and ask:

> Am I engaging in "doing Good" just to attract some attention to myself?
> Am I neglecting my studies to participate in the large issues of society which are undeniably important but which are actually out of context in my present capacity?
> Am I being used by other students who have selfish interests in disruptive activities?
> Am I permitting the inflammatory nature of campus disorders, the unpopular war and the general decline of societal morals to unduly influence my conduct?[45]

By 1970, however, Dean DiPalma reported to the trustees that "it is now a universally accepted principle to have students represented among the governing units of medical colleges and universities," and he gave as examples the University of Pennsylvania, Temple, and Jefferson. He pointed out that "our medical students are older, want to be involved, and are also capable of being involved," and Associate Dean Hugh Bennett noted that the contributions of the students on the curriculum committee "have been positive and significant."[46] In April 1970 the faculty's College Council agreed to allow two students elected by the student body on the council with full voting rights.[47]

Hahnemann and Civil Rights

Like many American teaching hospitals, Hahnemann Hospital had been in the comfortable position of being able to draw on its local inner-city population as teaching material. By the 1950s, poor African-Americans and Puerto Rican immigrants had replaced the children of Russian and Italian immigrants, who had begun to move out to the suburbs. These new neighbors were welcomed as public patients for teaching purposes and as janitorial and technical employees of the hospital. But until the civil rights movement of the 1960s, the professional staff at the college and hospital felt no need to have their institutions reflect or respond in any way to the needs of the local community. There were few Spanish translators in the hospital, and although many of the health problems faced by these patients stemmed from, for example, lead poisoning and poor nutrition, the hospital had no outreach programs and did not try to work with community leaders on these issues. The struggles between medical educators and community activists in the 1960s and 1970s—indeed the history of American medicine and the civil rights movement in general—has not been explored by historians.[48] Yet, as Hahnemann's experiences demonstrate, these struggles were crucial to understanding changes in health care services and public response.

"Community" was a central term defining the new approach to medicine in this period. In essence, it was a code word, used by radicals and liberals alike, to mean a concern for minority groups. Students and other medical advocates demanded that medical schools produce more black and ethnically diverse health professionals. In addition, activists who were promoting equity and combating discrimination believed that to improve the health care provided to inner-city communities, medical schools needed to produce more physicians who would return to care for their own "people." Few questioned the notion that only physicians of the same race and ethnicity would be attracted by such medical settings, but liberals did question the more radical idea, influenced by the Black Panther ideology of racial empowerment through separatism, that only a physician of the same race or ethnicity should practice there. Liberals had long called

Figure 33. Patients at Hahnemann Hospital's outpatient clinics, mostly poor, were by the 1940s and 1950s increasingly African American and Puerto Rican. *Medic* 1959.

for physicians to stop concentrating on wealthy white patients and go into the slums, but many became uncomfortable with what were in this period seen as radical demands for institutionalizing affirmative action policies based on a previous history of racial and ethnic discrimination.

The civil rights movement came slowly to Hahnemann, introduced by some of its black faculty and staff members. Psychiatrist Warren Smith (1922–1990), a 1957 graduate, for example, was a member of CORE and the NAACP and had been president in 1965 and 1966 of the Medical Society of Eastern Pennsylvania, the black medical society set up as an alternative to the Philadelphia

County Medical Society. Smith and Robert McMichael, an African-American pharmacology researcher, had helped organize summer programs initiated by Sam Evans, a powerful African-American city leader. These programs welcomed minority students into medical school laboratories, gave them experience, and boosted their résumés when they applied to the city's medical schools.[49] These efforts were at first quiet and unassuming. Few Hahnemann leaders could imagine that the 1964 North Philadelphia riots (which the hospital's emergency department residents had not been able to handle adequately)[50] would turn into demands some five years later to mend racist practices in Hahnemann's selection of students and hiring of professional staff. Beginning in the late 1940s Hahnemann, after almost forty years of segregation, began again to admit a handful of black men. In 1954 Hahnemann did receive an anonymous donation of two hundred dollars for a "negro students scholarship fund." In 1955 Hahnemann's dean counted 6 black students out of a total class of 393 undergraduates and noted that 15 of 1,122 applicants that year were black.[51] Until the 1970s, however, Hahnemann, according to George Gardiner, an African-American psychiatrist who was head of minority affairs, had a "bad reputation" in the local black community, and one North Philadelphia activist had a framed letter from Hahnemann hanging in his office, a letter that explained why "a colored student like you" would not be admitted to Hahnemann's medical school.[52] By the 1960s Hahnemann had begun to hire some black professional staff: the physiology department hired William Foster as an assistant and, by the end of the 1970s, the psychiatry department had six full-time black psychiatrists.[53]

By the late 1960s, Hahnemann faced stronger pressure to change. The civil rights movement in the South led by Martin Luther King Jr. began to come to the North. There was concern about the desperation of the urban poor as well as the discrimination faced by aspiring black professionals and the black middle class. Philadelphia was hardly welcoming to civil rights changes. Police chief Frank Rizzo, for example, responded violently to accusations of police racism and brutality and to the riots that followed. The quiet and gradual changes that had been occurring in higher education no longer seemed adequate to increasingly radical civil rights advocates. In 1969 the Black Panthers set up a free health clinic at Sixteenth and Susquehanna, at which some Hahnemann medical students volunteered.[54]

In 1968, the Philadelphia branch of SHO organized the Committee on Black Admissions (CBA) to pressure the city's medical schools to admit significant numbers of black candidates.[55] SHO had decided to make Philadelphia a special target because it was one of the few major American cities with a high proportion of both blacks and medical schools. Indeed, members of the CBA announced that they wanted Philadelphia to become a "model city," deliberately drawing on language from Johnson's Great Society.[56]

The CBA approached the deans of Philadelphia's six medical schools and demanded a policy of radical affirmative action: the immediate acceptance of 30 percent of the freshman class of September 1969 to be minority students, a figure similar to the percentage of African Americans in the city's population.[57] The University of California's medical school in San Francisco, Hahnemann's student paper announced, had already agreed to accept as 25 percent of its class what were termed "social and economic minorities" in September 1969, as the result of confrontations with the university's black student union (of the 136 new medical freshmen at San Francisco 32 were minorities, including 22 blacks and 8 Mexican Americans, and there were similar minority increases, although lower, in the university's nursing and dental schools).[58]

When their institutions were publicly accused of racism and insensitivity, the Philadelphia deans first asked for a ruling from the state's attorney general on affirmative action.[59] They then prepared a joint press release "on the Matter of Disadvantaged Students in Medicine," which defensively claimed that their admissions committees had always "exercised sympathetic interpretation of admissions criteria in applying them to those Negro applicants whom they could identify." The problem, they declared, was not racist medical administrators but too few qualified applicants. They agreed to begin working with medical student activists and the CBA, which had "a number of fresh ideas for recruiting more Negro applicants."[60]

Nonetheless, the deans worried that such students might alter the form of medical training. They warned of the "same old problems which have thwarted such efforts in the past, namely, how can a young person with a disadvantaged background overcome past education handicaps and meet the demanding standards of the medical school curriculum?" They were concerned that medical schools with "overburdened faculties" would have to take on the "new responsibility of additional tutoring." They were also not convinced of the basic premise of affirmative action, asking "when, if ever, is it fair to deny admission to one student with superior credentials in favor of another student with lesser ones because the latter has a disadvantaged background?" This question ignored the long-standing informal quota system practiced by Hahnemann and other Philadelphia schools against Jews, Italians, African Americans, women, and other nontraditional medical applicants. Still, conscious of the political power of the civil rights movements, the deans collectively agreed that this problem was "a matter of first priority for our medical schools," and they indicated that they were "confident that a profession which has soared so high in scientific advancement during the past few decades can surmount the problems which have been described above."[61] More practically, they proposed asking the help of SHO in recruiting and organizing two task forces: one where medical school admissions officers worked with student groups and the other where associate deans did long-range planning.[62] Showing awareness of local political sensibilities, the deans said they would seek "the advice of various community leaders who have been working with the problems of disadvantaged people for many years."[63]

The CBA gave a list of four hundred black and other disadvantaged students to the Philadelphia deans. In response, Hahnemann sent a catalog and letter to each person on the list and then sent an application form to those who expressed further interest. Of this group, approximately fifty applied, and Hahnemann offered places to three of them; two accepted.[64] In 1969, with the support of all of Philadelphia's medical schools, the CBA organized the Center for Medical Careers, which was a resource center for recruiting students who were termed (in what was clearly a language of compromise) "disadvantaged." This term could mean, a Hahnemann student pointed out, many different groups such as "Italian-American, Oriental, Black, etc."[65] The center also helped applicants find financial assistance. It was supported by the AAMC, the city of Philadelphia, and the United Health Services.[66] The medical schools, further, set up a few premedical programs in local high schools and colleges, such as the Cadbury Program at Haverford College to encourage "marginal applicants with an extra year of academic effort."[67] Such a program, however, as Hahnemann faculty recognized, made little difference to schools such as Hahnemann, for, of the Haverford black students interested in studying medicine in 1969, "the prestige medical schools have managed to recruit all of them."[68] Still, even in early 1969 Philadelphia activists at the Chicago meeting of SHO commented that "the Committee for Black Admission[s] program was swallowed up by the schools."[69]

SHO was also influential on the national level. The theme of the AAMC's 1969 annual meeting in Cincinnati was "The Health Care Dilemma—New Directions for Medical Education." Ron Feigin, a Hahnemann student, reported with some amazement that he had heard speakers using terms such as "dehumanization," "relevance," "accountability," and "community representation," terms, he commented, "which only a short time ago were considered by many as belonging to the rhetoric of the radical left."[70] For the first time representatives from various medical student organizations—SAMA (Students of the AMA), SNMA (Students of the black National Medical Association), and SHO—were invited to talk to the assembly. These students pointed out that although the convention focused on the role of medicine in the community, there were no representatives from the community and few medical students scheduled to participate.[71] By the early 1970s the AAMC had begun a campaign to increase the number of minorities in medical schools.[72]

Hahnemann faculty and trustees were unwilling to accede to all of SHO's demands but recognized that there was no easy middle path. Affirmative action was yet untested by the U.S. Supreme Court, and it was no coincidence that the Bakke decision in 1978 centered around the rejection of a white applicant to medical school. Even at the height of the liberal years, the idea had limited public support. After the Philadelphia newspapers reported the CBA meetings, John Scott, chair of physiology and head of Hahnemann's admissions committee, reported that he had received a number of letters from the general public "denouncing this quota" and urging the school to accept applicants "on the basis of ability only."[73] It was clear that the radical vision of civil rights activists was in conflict with the standard liberalism of some of Hahnemann's leaders. At a meeting in September 1968 discussing the CBA's demands, a trustee rejected affirmative action, saying "we are very anxious to receive qualified black students, but we think it important to give equal opportunity to all."[74]

Hahnemann, like the other medical schools, had always declared that it graduated few African Americans because so few applied and had "acceptable" qualifications. Admitting diverse ethnic groups, however, became a political issue with potentially serious ramifications for Hahnemann when in 1968 state senator Benjamin Donolow accused the school of racism and anti-Semitism, allegedly after a candidate he had proposed to Hahnemann had been rejected. Donolow claimed that Hahnemann discriminated against black and Jewish applicants, limited the numbers of students accepted from Pennsylvania, and gave unwarranted preference to applicants who were the sons of physicians. Donolow's accusations threatened Hahnemann's effort to increase its state appropriation.[75]

Hahnemann leaders pointed immediately to the conclusions of a recent state-commissioned survey of the state's medical schools, known as the Pechan Report, which showed that Hahnemann had a higher percentage of Catholic and Jewish students than most other medical schools.[76] The Pechan Report also showed that 72 percent of Hahnemann students were from Pennsylvania, a percentage exceeded only by Temple, and that 9 percent were children of physicians compared to 16 percent at Jefferson and 18 percent at the University of Pennsylvania. The number of black students, Hahnemann's president Charles Cameron explained, was low "because they do not qualify in competition with whites. Extensive efforts will have to be made to encourage and assist Negroes at earlier stages of their educational careers."[77]

In 1970, when President Cameron and Dean DiPalma went to Harrisburg to appear before the Senate Appropriations Committee to ask for an increase from thirty-six hundred dollars per medical student to five thousand dollars, pointing out that it cost ten thousand dollars per year to educate a medical student, the state senators asked difficult questions about the school's black admissions. Hahnemann's president and dean replied, as they reported to the trustees, that "Hahnemann offers admission to quite a few but they do not come here" and that "Hahnemann has a large number of disadvantaged students."[78]

In response to the accusations Hahnemann's trustees issued a statement claiming that it had always been the school's policy not to discriminate against a person "because of his race, color, religion or national origins." The board now felt "morally bound to take a more aggressive stand regarding the problems of discrimination in today's society," and Hahnemann would "do everything within its power to aid the fight against discrimination within the community." In an interesting addition, the board also resolved that there be no discrimination in its own membership.[79]

In the early 1970s Hahnemann set up recruitment programs to help attract and train minority students. It formed alliances with local black colleges, such as Cheyney State and Lincoln University, and accepted promising premedical students into a six-year B.S./M.D. program at Hahnemann and waived their tuition. A group of Hahnemann faculty got federal funding for what was termed the flexible curriculum, whereby minority students were accepted into a so-called decelerated program that allowed them to do the first basic science year in two years and that funded tutors from the basic science departments.[80]

The Patient and the Community: A New Kind of Physician and a New Kind of Medicine

Changing the way a doctor looked and changing the racial mix of the student body were part of the efforts by Hahnemann radicals to try to change the kind of physician they wanted to become and Hahnemann to produce. Medical schools and hospitals became the locus of a battle over what constituted legitimate medical authority and what empowering patients meant. Historians of the women's movement have pointed out that criticism of American medical care and practitioners by the feminist health advocates of the early 1970s largely concerned itself with the middle-class white woman and her doctor. But when Hahnemann students looked at the inner city in which their medical school and hospital were located and from which it drew the bulk of its teaching material, their sense of medicine's close relationship to urban racism and poverty meant that, for them, medical change had to deal with poor minority groups.

In trying to define what alternative kind of physician and medicine they wanted, Hahnemann students turned to other countries' medical systems, particularly—in a move that was provocative in this Cold War era—communist countries such as the Soviet Union and Cuba. *Grand Mal* had articles that praised Cuban health care,[81] and it reported on a 1970 conference held at the University of Pennsylvania's hospital by MCHR entitled "Health Care Systems in Other Countries: Why Not Here?" At that conference the health systems of Israel, Sweden, Yugoslavia, the Soviet Union, and Cuba, described as rationalized "comprehensive medical systems," were compared to the American profit-oriented, fee-for-service "non system." Patrick Storey, head of Hahnemann's new Department of Community Medicine, spoke on the Soviet Union and warned that the United States' present health care crisis was the result of "a grossly inadequate health structure."[82]

In this period medical schools like Hahnemann did try to introduce new programs or reorient old ones to show a responsiveness to the problems of the inner city. Pressures from Washington and growing welfare rights organizations had made medical administrators aware that they needed to institute projects that were "community oriented," both to placate a restless local population and to assure government and foundation funding. Thus, in 1966 Hahnemann founded the Department of Community Medicine; in 1970 renamed its psychiatric department the Department of Mental Health Sciences, which directed a series of successful community mental health clinics; and in 1971 established the state's first physician's assistants program.

One of the most searing critiques raised by radical students concerned the proper function of a teaching hospital. Students challenged the argument made by the AMA and AAMC that teaching hospitals provided the best care. The 1945 AMA/AAMC report that had placed Hahnemann on probation had argued that junior and senior students should be called "doctor" and that they should tell patients that the teaching-hospital system served "the best interest of the patient."[83] Students in the 1960s pointed to the racial and class inequities facing patients at Hahnemann clinics and tried to articulate the dissatisfaction among patients themselves.

Hahnemann students wrote devastating attacks on their educational system. In a powerful piece indicting American medical educators for racism, sexism, paternalism, and the exploitation of the poor, published in *Grand Mal* in 1969, one student wrote

> Being poor is watching all the residents practice passing a laryngoscope down your dead baby's throat.
>
> Being poor is being told in front of 115 people that you are a "veritable museum of pathology."
>
> Being poor is coming to the emergency room at 10:30 A.M., in severe pain, and not being seen until 1:30 P.M. in the clinic.
>
> Being poor is having four young men put their fingers in your vagina, and only one of them has his name end in M.D.
>
> Being poor is having a med student stick your arm seven times unsuccessfully while a staff physician stands by and watches.
>
> Being poor is being called "stupid" because you don't have the sense to feed your five kids more protein, when you get only $13,000 per year.
>
> Being poor is being afraid to go to the hospital, because you don't want to die.[84]

Blaming both the AMA as "one of the most powerful lobbies in Washington" and the federal government for its "inadequate health programs," Mark Prager berated "the hypocrisy of the medical profession, professing one goal (i.e. the best health care for all the people) yet following quite another (i.e. power, status, finances, ad nauseam)." "The time must come," he warned, "when health professionals themselves choose one side of the mirror and remain there—or the people may break the glass."[85]

Students countered the romanticized AMA picture of the small town doctor with the health care they encountered as urban medical students. Health care for many urban Americans, and especially the poor, they argued, took place not in a private office but in a hospital or outpatient setting. They used the language of SDS and SNCC to reconceptualize the problems with this kind of care. Comparing the treatment of patients in outpatient clinics to that of patients in private offices, students called for a new kind of medicine. They no longer accepted that idea that 1960s outpatient clinics should be run simply as a continuation of the nineteenth-century hospital dispensary, where free health care was provided to the poor so that doctors and donors could demonstrate their charitable spirit and so that a variety of patient ills could provide clinical experience for physicians and their students. Students, influenced by models developed by the radical health groups MCHR and SHO, called instead for community medicine, for facilities that would provide services beyond the traditional acute, emergency medical care. With the idea of participatory democracy and a view of the patient as an active participant, they also argued that the kind of care should no longer necessarily be defined by hospital administrators or medical practitioners.

By 1968 Hahnemann's medical training relied on two main outpatient clinics: the Hahnemann Hospital clinic on Race Street, an outgrowth of the school's original dispensary; and a clinic on Green Street, which was run by the school's Department of Community Medicine. The latter clinic was part of what was called the Spring Garden Community Services Center, a three-building complex that also provided a swimming pool, art classes, training for food handlers, an employment service, and a language laboratory.[86] Community medicine, radicals felt, was a liberal response to their more profound critique of American medicine and American society, and conservatives felt it was irrelevant to "real medicine." Mark Prager, while admitting that some of his peers thought the clinic was just "a way to hold the hands of the 'poor masses, who would most likely be better off if they just got a good job,'" praised it for giving the doctors and nurses there an opportunity "to treat people with the dignity they deserve, instead of as a disease with the drugs, the cardexes, and labs that it deserves." He also praised the day-care program, which served approximately fifty-five children. The clinic was sparsely fitted with hand-me-down medical equipment, like an examining table that had been repainted after being discarded at Hahnemann. The clinic was staffed by three doctors who received salaries from Hahnemann Hospital (an internist, an obstetrician, and Patrick Storey, head of the community medicine department) and by three nurses, two clerks, three community health workers who lived in the community, and a dentist and his assistant. The clinic treated around four hundred patients a month, two-thirds of them for general medicine and one-third for obstetrics and gynecology. Unlike most outpatients, patients at the Green Street clinic were allowed to make appointments rather than turn up and wait. The clinic's population ranged from Spring Garden Street to Fairmount Avenue, and from Broad Street to Twenty-fourth Street, an area of about thirteen thousand people, around 40 percent Puerto Rican, 40 percent black, and 20 percent white. Their average income was twenty-seven hundred dollars, the lowest in Philadelphia. Almost 90 percent of the clinic's patients were on Medicare or Pennsycare, a state system that paid four dollars a visit. While Prager recognized that some people would say "these are society's problems, not medicine's," he commented that "on Green Street the feeling seems to be that medicine can be used as a lever, a 'clout' in Dr. Storey's terms, to attack the basic problems of an area."[87]

Hahnemann students admitted that the Green Street clinic was the facility that Hahnemann teachers pointed out "to show how active Hahnemann is in the field of health care for the poor, especially when the Race Street clinic is mentioned in an accusatory tone by some 'student troublemakers.'"[88] More serious was the student criticism of the hospital's Race Street clinic, and during the late 1960s Hahnemann radicals were able to raise significant issues that unified students and helped to pressure administrators to rethink the nature and structure of Hahnemann health care.

During 1969 a number of Hahnemann students, Mark Prager prominently among them, began to protest about the conditions of the Race Street clinic. In November, Prager published the results of his study of the clinic, conducted during his junior year clerkship and based on his own interviews with seventeen patients. He found that the average waiting time for a doctor was about three hours. The patients he talked to said they wanted to wait in softer seats, but most thought their doctors were "good to excellent." Three had lost pay for the time spent in the clinic; four had a friend looking after their children; and twelve of the seventeen were on Medicare or Medicaid. Prager and other Hahnemann students used this study and their own experiences at Race Street to call for significant improvements in Hahnemann's treatment of its outpatients. They circulated a petition that noted the hard benches, especially uncomfortable for women, the lack of child care, and the treatment by students rather than physicians. They argued that the clinic should be made as comfortable and professional as Hahnemann physicians' private offices in the new Feinstein

Building.[89] A *Grand Mal* editorial blamed the values of the business world that was "all around us at Hahnemann":

> We see patients on Public Assistance, Medicare, and Medicaid on
> unyielding benches, waiting sometimes for as much as four to four and
> one-half hours to be treated by a junior medical student trying to
> impersonate a doctor. We see private patients waiting by appointment,
> in comfortable chairs, listening to Musak piped in air-conditioned
> splendor, for—yes, it's true—a real live M.D., perhaps even the head of
> the department.[90]

Most significantly, these students attacked the dissembling by medical students who did not explain to public patients that they were not doctors. "The patients are under the impression that all the young men in white coats are M.D.'s," Prager argued, for "the patient is the guinea pig for the student learning physical diagnosis."[91] These radical critiques of the teaching hospital threatened to undermine the mission of Hahnemann, as defined in response to the 1945 AMA/AAMC report, especially the efforts it had undertaken in the 1950s and 1960s to integrate the hospital into the college's teaching program.

Hahnemann radicals argued that, rather than providing the best care, the education of students was taking place through the exploitation of the urban poor, especially minorities. In 1969 *Grand Mal* featured a provocative letter written by Richard Thomas (Chip) Smith, a University of Pennsylvania student who had quit medical school because he was horrified by the experimentation on black men and women, whom he saw becoming guinea pigs in his clinical classes. Smith was about to enter his senior year and had been active in the Philadelphia branch of SHO. "To continue at Penn," Smith wrote, "is to continue exploiting poor people, primarily blacks, for narrow educational ends." It was not just Penn, but a more general problem, he explained, for everyone suffers in the traditional doctor-patient relationship practiced in teaching hospitals, a "brutal relationship," which "you expect me to honor and emulate." Smith blamed the organization of medical education in hospitals:

> medical students: kept off balance, made to feel guilty about their lack of
> knowledge, constantly caught up in meaningless busiwork [sic]; doctors:
> overworked, secure only in their professional image, harassed by patients
> and workers whose hostility they will never understand; and patients,
> rich and poor alike: ignorant about their own bodies gone haywire,
> fearful of death, desperately struggling to believe in their white-coated
> saviors, trapped in an environment that is death itself made visible.[92]

Poor black patients, he argued, suffered the most. "I've had my fill of putting it to blacks. I learned to draw bloods on old black ladies. I learned to do pelvics on young black women. I learned to do histories and physicals on black bodies and on a few wrinkled and run-down white ones. Now, in order to learn something about primary care, I am again faced with waiting black faces in the hospital clinics." Smith praised the indications of change such as the growing attacks on the AMA, the rise of malpractice suits, and the Black Panther's free health clinic. Smith concluded by linking the teaching hospital to American society: "It's a brutal system—a brutal, racist, materialistic, professionalized, technologized, dehumanized system. The American way—a white-washed health-care system in a brain-washed world. Vietnam, Bolivia, starvation, pollution: they all begin at home, baby. Those worldwide crimes are acted out each day inside our hospitals right before our eyes."[93]

Hahnemann did not change its hospital teaching program, although it did start to renovate the Race Street clinic. In 1970 Hahnemann also began to offer a new interdisciplinary course entitled "Medical Problems" for freshmen, which included fieldwork in the community, the study of a single family in detail, and thirty-six two-hour seminars on topics such as comparative health care systems, the cost of medical care, the role of the physician, concepts of prevention, and the relationship of physician to other health professionals. Students were pleased to see that not only the course's content but also its form reflected the radical health movement. "Active participation and direct experience," junior Thomas Liston wrote, would replace "the traditionally passive role of the first-year medical student."[94] Hahnemann also began introducing its new curriculum, known as the Core Curriculum, which taught all basic science courses in a grueling first year and then began some clinical work in the second year, encouraging students to select specialty areas. Throughout the late 1960s and early 1970s one of the most popular specialties for graduating seniors was psychiatry.[95] Of the group of radical students most became psychiatrists. Mark Prager, however, died suddenly in the spring of 1970 of an adrenal tumor, and Jerry Lindauer dropped out and never graduated.

Student radicals in this period were also uneasy about the priorities of medicine, particularly the stress on medical research and the topics considered important. In February 1970, in a *Grand Mal* editorial, Prager and Lindauer commented that: "The current medical student knows desperately little about the social problems of the people he treats. The reason, if you ask a basic scientist, is that knowledge of Marfan's syndrome is more important than Medicaid; Kuru is more important than lead poisoning; the deep sural nerve more important than how a community health center works."[96] Similarly, Peter Eisenberg, in his column "Maxwell's Silver Hammer," argued that "Medical schools are now trade schools, turning out highly skilled biological mechanics who tinker with the life processes of sick people." Yet, he explained, "the real world isn't in classroom A or B or in the Eccles Building (where 250 freshmen and sophomores spend 35 hours a week). . . . It's outside where children in North Philadelphia are eating lead paint and being bitten by rats."[97]

Jim Shames, a Hahnemann junior, recalled that one of his teachers had told him that "what I should try and strive for in medicine was blandness (his very words), so as not to offend anybody." But the woman waiting on the wooden bench all morning to be seen by the medical student was offended, he argued "not so much by my long-ish hair as by the degrading inadequate medical care this hospital and this country offer her." "We must radically alter the role of doctor," he concluded, "and to do so we must produce a new breed of physician." He proposed "new criteria for acceptance to medical school," such as recognition of the value of character rather than the ability to memorize skills, and proposed making medical education "relevant, and not with token Community Medicine courses, but by an entire redirection of goals." Shames wanted to see research and teaching on topics like pollution and malnutrition, which, he argued, "are killing more people in this country than Marfan's or Gaucher's disease, or Kuru, or Milkman's syndrome."[98]

The Vietnam War increasingly made faculty as well as students feel that an insular view of medicine was inappropriate. In 1969 the executive faculty decided that while the antiwar moratorium day would not be mentioned in the school's published calendar, "the response of each faculty member shall be at his discretion."[99] On that day a group of speakers gathered in Alumni Hall to talk about Vietnam, including Mattie Humphrey, a clinical instructor in community medicine, Walter Lear, deputy commissioner of the city's health department, and Jeffrey Bell, a Hahnemann graduate and intern at Philadelphia General Hospital. Later a group of one hundred medical students and nurses presented a resolution to the Philadelphia County Medical Society calling for an end to the war and redirection of energies for a better and more equitable health care system.[100]

HAHNEMANN MEDICAL COLLEGE and Hospital did not become a new institution as a result of these radical demands. Students were made members of a variety of faculty committees, and a few new courses were introduced to make medical training more "relevant." The most significant achievement of these students was that they managed to bring the concerns of a wider, angry world through the doors of the medical school and hospital—by means of their dress and hair, their petitions, their remade school newspaper, and their protests. Hahnemann never made 30 percent of its entering class minority students, but its outreach and decelerated programs attracted students who would otherwise have had no chance of being admitted, and during the early 1970s minority students made up as high as 18 percent of the freshmen class. In the mid-1960s the United States' involvement in Vietnam seemed distant and irrelevant to most

Hahnemann students, physicians, and staff. By the early 1970s the war had be-come recognized as an integral part of a wider problem with the distribution and provision of health care and the production of health professionals. In 1970, after the invasion of Cambodia, Hahnemann's dean issued a statement, and was one of fourteen medical school deans, including those at Temple, Pennsylva-nia, and Woman's, who sent a protesting telegram to President Nixon.[101]

In 1969 Mark Prager and Jerome Lindauer published a "Call to Action" to their peers and teachers:

> It is particularly easy for medical students and health professionals to avoid this reality, burying deeper into masses of particulate information, pleading the burdens of their studies, maintaining that these demanding routines are, after all, dedicated to life and the relief of suffering. But in our angular white isolation, our sensitivities can tragically atrophy, assaulted either by scientific trivia or the trauma of individual pathology and death. . . . The war in Viet Nam can be considered the moral crucible in which our generation is being tested."[102]

Chapter 8   Incorporating Change

The 1970s

IN THE LATE 1960s, radical students at Hahnemann had challenged their school to transform its mission and structure. Their voices had echoed in faculty and administrative meetings and had made those who ran the institution sensitive to the problems that confronted Hahnemann Hospital as an inner-city health care provider and Hahnemann Medical College as a producer of health care professionals and aware of the complex role of medicine in American society. During the 1970s these voices became muted, and, although student activism did not disappear, it dissipated somewhat with the end of formal American involvement in Vietnam. However, during this decade significant elements of the students' vision were adopted by Hahnemann, especially diversity in the student body and the faculty and curriculum changes emphasizing primary care.

In the 1970s, Hahnemann's administration adopted a liberal—but not radical—agenda. Hahnemann was remade not, as radical students like Mark Prager might have hoped, through rejection of the links between medical education and American capitalism but, ironically, through integration into the corporate world. Hahnemann's remaking was accompanied by more serious strain and conflict than the institution had experienced during its effort to adopt mainstream professional values in the 1940s. The radical Hahnemann students of the 1960s had wanted the power structure of American medicine to shift to its clients and consumers; and in the new corporate world of medicine, Hahnemann faculty, especially department heads, did lose power. But they lost it not to professional reformers, community representatives, federal bureaucrats, or patient advocates but to a new group of business-oriented executives who entered Hahnemann with the appointment in 1971 of Edward Wharton (Whartie) Shober as the first nonphysician president to lead the institution since the probation years of the 1940s.

Liberalism and the corporate world, at least in this era, were not necessarily incompatible. Shober, Hahnemann's most controversial president, adopted and continued aspects of the liberal agenda institutionalized during the Kennedy and Johnson administrations. Under Shober Hahnemann reached out to young men and women of diverse racial, geographic, and ethnic backgrounds, began to involve the local community in structuring Hahnemann's inner-city health services, and encouraged students to study not just the traditional specialties but also primary care, or what was termed family medicine. And he moved the institution firmly into the corporate world, inviting onto the board of trustees businessmen who knew how Philadelphia services worked and who had connections that could provide Hahnemann with services that it needed, such as data processing and food handling.

Nevertheless, this was an era not only of transformation but also of disaster. Groups based at Hahnemann experienced difficulty in coping with many of these changes, and Hahnemann's corporatization alienated so many of its constituencies that Shober's era has been written out of much of contemporary Hahnemann history. After the trustees and faculty asked Shober to resign in June 1977, they initially tried to turn back to a more traditional style of administration, choosing as the next president Hahnemann cardiologist William Likoff, a nationally recognized researcher. Likoff entered with the goodwill of a variety of Hahnemann groups who had been united by their dislike of Shober. But whatever may have been the hopes of those who chose him, Likoff did not and could not alter these major changes in the structure and mission of Hahnemann. It remained a corporatized institution and continued to experience the strains faced by many medical centers trying to maintain the necessary balance between the academic and the business worlds.

Unlike Hahnemann in the 1920s and 1930s, the remade Hahnemann found tradition a burden: the new was forward-looking, the old a sign of bad days when Hahnemann was unorthodox and rejected by the medical mainstream. A graphic example of this rejection of tradition is a story told by Ron Feigin, a student in the late 1960s. Feigin remembers walking through the old college building (originally the 1890 hospital), which was being demolished, and finding bookcases with glass cases, old anatomical drawings, hundreds of lantern slides, and a beautiful oak card catalog—all left to be thrown out. He rescued the card catalog, which he still has, and a metal stand that had held a skeleton.[1] Shober's predecessor, Charles Cameron, had begun this demolition of Hahnemann's physical past and, more quietly, had begun to transform Hahnemann administratively. But the Shober administration openly expressed its distrust for those who held onto Hahnemann's traditions; for them, a corporatized Hahnemann was the antithesis of tradition. It was not surprising, then, that in 1972, when Hahnemann's Alumni Association began to criticize the president, Shober swiftly broke with the association and refused it financial and administrative support. Shober was castigated as dismissive of the "old Hahnemann," but in fact this break was a dramatic symbol of a process that had begun in the 1950s. By the 1970s the institution no longer resembled the pre-war Hahnemann. It was increasingly staffed by men and women with no memory of Hahnemann training or traditions and administered not by promoted senior faculty but by professional managers trained in business. Although many Hahnemann alumni continued to see themselves as policymakers, they were reduced to upholding traditions through annual celebrations and keeping alive memories of famous Hahnemann graduates and some sense of Hahnemann's nineteenth-century past through a regular newsletter.

For Hahnemann, as for the White House, the 1970s were full of scandals and allegations of wrongdoing. The decade saw a decline in Hahnemann's local and national reputation, although not in its visibility. As one student commented in 1978, "When people used to ask us where we went to school, they'd say, 'Where?' Now people seem to know, even though, granted, it's for the wrong reasons. It hurts our pride a little bit, but we don't feel responsible and I'm not embarrassed to say I go to school here."[2] Under Shober Hahnemann faced increasing financial difficulties as local and federal agencies, as well as business and alumni groups, became more cautious of their support of Hahnemann-sponsored projects (both research and construction). Hahnemann maintained some respect as a teaching and health care center, although in 1977 it was ranked eighty-first of the United States' ninety-four medical schools, below every other medical school in Philadelphia.[3] Shober's major achievement was getting the funds to complete a new hospital wing, known as the North Tower, but this fundraising process also helped to lead to his downfall. Shober did help to make liberal policies a part of Hahnemann, but, like the constant construction in the 1960s and 1970s, which leveled almost all of Hahnemann's old buildings, Hahnemann's new organization destroyed the internal structure of the old Hahnemann that had lingered after the 1940s. It was not clear what the new Hahnemann would look like, but by the 1980s the sense of history as invigorating had largely disappeared under the noise of air-conditioning, audio-visual aids, and elevators that worked. Retelling Hahnemann's history—or even establishing and expanding an archive—became a political act. This chapter, more than any other in this book, seeks to show why even the bad and embarrassing times need to be not only remembered and recounted but also put into a larger context to highlight parts of Hahnemann's history that were critical to its remaking into a corporate academic institution.

A New President, a New Style

The position of president had been redefined by Hahnemann's trustees in 1961 to reflect the growing need for a full-time administrative leader. No longer just a formal title designating the head of the board of trustees, it became a professional executive position that more closely resembled a corporation's president, with power over the medical school's dean and the hospital administrator. The trustees had chosen Charles Cameron, who had been dean since 1956, as Hahnemann's first executive president. During his ten-year presidency Cameron continued his policies of improving and solidifying Hahnemann's academic reputation by attracting full-time faculty researchers and research funding. The trustees' selection in 1971 of Wharton Shober, a layman, suggested that the trustees, like those of many other medical centers, wanted to move Hahnemann in a new direction, away from the academic research emphasis of the postwar era and toward a vision of corporate medicine.

Wharton Shober seemed to offer a new style and a new kind of expertise. Shober had no senior academic qualifications, no M.D. or Ph.D., although he had attended Princeton, and he, like other men in their forties in this period, stressed his military experience.[4] He presented himself as a man of business, as having knowledge of and connections in industry and government. He and some of the trustees recognized, in ways that were initially less obvious to other Hahnemann groups, that institutions like academic health centers had to function on a new scale in the latter decades of the twentieth century, especially when it came to getting funding. Academic centers could no longer see themselves primarily as local or community institutions; they had to operate comfortably in the national and international medical marketplace. In the 1970s, financing Hahnemann no longer meant relying on individual contributions from alumni or on local fund-raising drives or on individual philanthropic trustees to donate money for pieces of medical equipment or for building renovation. In fact, in this new world a major medical institution could no longer depend on philanthropy at all: political patronage was the new leaven.

As in other periods in Hahnemann's history, the need for money in this period was the main factor that explained the attraction of Wharton Shober. From the start, it was money with a special twist: high society money, associated with the kinds of people that Hahnemann, unlike Philadelphia's more prestigious medical schools and hospitals, had rarely attracted, either as students, faculty, or trustees. In previous decades Hahnemann supporters had privately bemoaned the fact that many of their faculty and top administrators were not accepted in Philadelphia's high society, the Main Line suburban communities popularized in Hollywood's *High Society* (1956). Shober's combination of business flair and social background balanced out his lack of academic experience or qualifications. His background impressed the trustees, who were, as a reporter commented later, looking for someone "to streamline the operation, increase its fund-raising potential and improve its image."[5]

Shober made his image a crucial part of his appeal to the Hahnemann community, just as he later made Hahnemann's public image critical to Hahnemann's academic and financial standing. To an institution that was seeking to gain a greater regional and national presence, Shober was a breath of fresh air from the upper atmosphere of Philadelphia. His father was a Princeton graduate, and his mother was related to a former governor of Pennsylvania.[6] Described in the Philadelphia press as "the Philadelphia and Newport socialite," Shober flew his own plane and played polo at a Mainline horse club; he was a member of the Merion Cricket Club and the elite First City Troop.[7] Shober offered the promise of glitter and daring (he vacationed in the Swiss Alps, where he went on ballooning excursions),[8] and he proudly sought to integrate his high society connections with his role as a Hahnemann fund-raiser and executive leader. In 1975, for example, the Second Annual Radnor Hunt, run by the Radnor Hunt Club of Malvern, was held to benefit Hahnemann.[9]

Shober's military and business background, showing a mixture of confidence and successful entrepreneurship, also impressed the trustees. After a stint at Princeton, he had worked as a ditch digger, as a truck driver, and finally as an oil salesman for a New Jersey industrial oil company. In the 1950s, during the Korean War, he had been stationed in Germany as a lieutenant with the Twenty-eighth Pennsylvania Division, and after he returned to the United States, he founded his own business, an export firm for newspaper printing equipment called ATEC Corporation, which later merged with a larger company, the Joshua B. Powers Company.[10] Shober was described by his major supporter on Hahnemann's board, stockbroker Morton Jenks, as a millionaire with an altruistic interest in health care. To explain his willingness to consider leading Hahnemann, Shober claimed that after his wife had been saved from a life-threatening illness he had become interested in medical institutions and that because of this interest he was therefore willing to accept a salary from Hahnemann of forty-five thousand dollars, which was far below what he could have made elsewhere as a corporate executive.[11]

Shober took on the Hahnemann presidency in the shadow of its former occupant, Charles Cameron, who had become chairman of the board of trustees. Cameron had made the position of president a continuation of his dean's work as academic advocate. By the late 1960s, however, the trustees were facing increasing dissatisfaction at Hahnemann, mainly due to its chronic financial problems. Cameron had been an excellent dean, and he had improved Hahnemann's academic reputation by attracting respected clinicians to take up full-time positions and encouraging their research projects funded by pharmaceutical companies and the federal government. As dean and president, Cameron had helped

Figure 34. Edward Wharton Shober (1926–) brought corporate management to Hahnemann during his presidency (1971–1977) but at the cost of internal conflict. *Medic* 1974.

to change an institution freshly out of professional probation to one with a solid local and regional academic reputation. He had recognized the importance of dealing with Hahnemann's crumbling physical plant, its messy administrative structure, and its shaky financial base. What Cameron had not mastered was dealing with the major power brokers—in Philadelphia, Harrisburg, and Washington—to shore up Hahnemann's finances. A commentator later described Cameron as "a dedicated medical researcher but a lackluster fund-raiser."[12]

By the late 1960s Hahnemann's trustees were frustrated by the number of senior faculty members who had left for greener and richer pastures. Cameron told the trustees that many had been lured elsewhere by offers of academic advancement or larger salaries. But the trustees learned that this explanation was not complete. In 1969, for example, Daniel Downing, a pediatric cardiologist who had just left Hahnemann Hospital for Deborah Hospital, told one trustee privately about senior and junior faculty members who wished to stay but left because "the Administration [refused] to meet reasonable requests." Faculty members were motivated not by disloyalty to Hahnemann but "by complete disgust with the situation at Hahnemann," Downing claimed, and they were leaving because their "talents were not being utilized." One "felt that his future at Hahnemann was hopeless"; another that "his departure was forced by the shoddiest of expediencies." For himself, Downing explained, "Hahnemann had become, to me, so unhappy an institution that I could no longer enjoy my work."[13]

Charles Bailey's departure in 1958, the most disturbing loss, was seen as part of this trend. Bailey, Downing reminded the trustees, had "made Hahnemann famous and did so much to lift us from a third-rate status into the mainstream of world medicine." While Downing admitted that Bailey was "a difficult individual," he was not, Dowling argued, "completely unreasonable." Bailey had given Hahnemann an international reputation in innovative cardiology: "In any other institution in the country some accommodation would have been arranged for a genius. Not at Hahnemann." "Noone [sic] in the medical field in Philadelphia or in the nation can understand why Hahnemann is allowing its great claim to fame, its Cardiology-Cardiac Surgery groups, to slip away." Cameron had told the trustees, as Downing described it, that it was "harmful to the School to have this outstanding characteristic, as though it were a fungating growth on a shapely nose. Apparently, he wants no peaks in the academic scenery, preferring straight-line mediocrity." If the situation continued, Downing warned, Hahnemann would not close (for "every medical school is needed and tax dollars will keep it going"), but it would remain "a third-rate trade school, ever a morass in which talent will die or from which it will escape to firmer ground."[14] The trustees could see that there was money available for institutions like Hahnemann, especially through the federal government and business cooperation; they wanted a young and dynamic leader who knew how to tap into these networks. They suspected that to achieve this a new president would need to remake Hahnemann in ways that would cause various Hahnemann constituencies great pain; thus, when the complaining began, a number of trustees saw it as a sign that Wharton Shober was successfully doing his job.

By the time Shober entered Hahnemann's doors, fund-raising had become a different game than it had been in the immediate postwar decades that Cameron knew best. Cameron had seen the financial potential in attracting money from federal agencies with the government's new interest in medical research, especially NIH grants. But by the 1970s medical centers were operating in a world beyond peer review and individual faculty grants. Medical training and health care institutions, with their administrative and staff expenses, demanded a different kind of organization and a different kind of funding. Such institutions needed to run more as businesses; in fact, they were businesses. Shober recognized that connections in the corporate and political worlds would best enable Hahnemann to survive and expand.

Shober, like the new trustees he invited onto the board, took Hahnemann's growing academic reputation for granted. To some extent, the power that department heads and senior faculty held appeared old-fashioned, and promoting them to administrative positions was viewed as being akin to making shop boys executives. Shober's background and experience had well prepared him for the machinations of local and national business interests and the importance of political patronage. But he proved unable to integrate them into a culture built around faculty autonomy and academic freedom, without seeming to destroy Hahnemann's traditions.

A Liberal Philosophy as Good Politics

Shober and his administrative supporters recognized that Hahnemann would benefit from federal and state grants if it embraced and enhanced its role as an inner-city health care provider and if, instead of seeing its high quota of in-state students as a burden that lowered its national reputation and standards, Hahnemann remade itself as an innovative trainer and distributor of Pennsylvania's health professionals, especially from underserved communities. Adopting these ideas did not mean that Hahnemann officials needed to press for an American health care system based on Cuban or Soviet models; instead, embracing issues like geographic and racial diversity, high-quality urban health care, and interactions with community leaders became political assets not just radical dreams. Stripped of radical implications, elements of the liberal agenda made good politics. State and federal governments offered funding for education programs and health care facilities. Medical schools were able to attract federal money by designing programs to attract nontraditional students, to channel these students into primary care and family medicine, and to find ways of distributing them in underserved areas. Hahnemann also found that these programs provided an indirect way to appeal for an increase in class size to help deal with its financial problems. Embracing "diversity" in the 1970s (defined in acceptable bureaucratic terms) became a way of gaining community approval, government grants, and professional renown. Hahnemann might not be a leader in research but it could be an innovator in education and community health care. What these programs never resolved was the unacknowledged conflict between mainstreaming outsiders—helping poor minority students become wealthy specialists—and creating an alternative track that encouraged these students to become generalist health providers for the low prestige poor communities that most other physicians avoided.

A number of American medical schools, made aware of their politicized role as health care providers by the radical health groups in the 1960s, began to recognize that they could also benefit from the federal interest in the care of inner-city populations. They did not have to construct new facilities but could modernize old ones to make them seem more responsive to community needs. In the 1960s, Hahnemann, like many other medical centers, responded to federal initiatives like the 1963 Community Mental Health Centers Act by setting up a community mental health center with several satellite clinics. In the 1970s the pursuit of these options enabled Hahnemann to gain significant local political support. According to some reports, Shober began to assemble "an outpatient kingdom throughout the city."[15] He met with city bureaucrats, federal representatives from Philadelphia, and community groups. Reflecting the racial and ethnic makeup of the neighborhoods around Hahnemann, Shober hired black and Puerto Rican community leaders, or at least figures who claimed to represent these groups in local populations.[16] Many of these political alliances helped him. When he later came under attack, Hahnemann's trustees received a series of letters from local black leaders praising Shober as a "fine man" who had "outstanding capabilities as an Administrator" and had "demonstrated his compassion for humanity to our community."[17]

Although from the Republican Main Line, Shober reached out to local and state Democrats, such as Philadelphia's mayor Frank Rizzo and Congressmen Joshua Eilberg of Philadelphia and Daniel J. Flood of Wilkes-Barre. Flood was the ranking member of the House Health and Welfare Appropriations Subcommittee; in 1972 he was given an honorary degree and in 1974 was Hahnemann's commencement speaker.[18]

Before Shober arrived a group of Hahnemann faculty from the Department of Medicine and administrators in the dean's office initiated a few programs to bring racial and ethnic diversity to Hahnemann's student body. Charles Cameron developed an association with Cheyney State College, a predominantly black college in Chester County, Pennsylvania. Its president, Wade Wilson, was given an honorary degree in 1969, and in 1971 became the first African-American Hahnemann trustee. In 1970 a group of premedical students at Cheyney formed a club that became the basis for the Cheyney Hahnemann Medical Program (CHAMP), which built on a program already existing in medical technology. CHAMP encouraged black students to enter Hahnemann's medical school and its allied health programs. Cameron welcomed CHAMP as a way to "identify the talented and strongly motivated black students and prepare them to enter the field of medicine."[19] Initially it established lectures and visits by Hahnemann faculty and visits by Cheyney students to Hahnemann. Hahnemann hoped CHAMP would be a model for other medical schools and help to establish Hahnemann as a leader in innovative liberal medical education. CHAMP combined the recent federal legislation encouraging medical schools to push students into family medicine and other incentives to encourage medical schools to admit more diverse students.

Shober expanded Cameron's initiatives. He sought and obtained federal funding for both educational programs and health care facilities. That the focus of these new projects was eliminating racial and ethnic discrimination and trying to get greater community involvement was not surprising. During the 1960s and 1970s Congress had become actively involved in shaping health care policy and medical education, highly controversial areas. As educational institutions around the country became increasingly dependent on federal funds—whether as student loans or as funding for building construction or for research projects—the distinction between public and private schools, especially medical schools, became harder to maintain.

The Johnson administration in particular took advantage of this increasing dependence on federal dollars to try to link its social ideology to federal funding. With the 1963 Civil Rights Act, Congress tried to put into practice the 1954 antisegregation decision of the Supreme Court in *Brown v. The Board of Education.* Schools—and other institutions accepting federal funds—had to demonstrate a willingness not only to desegregate but to provide opportunities for minority candidates and employees. At Hahnemann, after a forty-year period of segregation, black students were readmitted in the late 1940s. Radical health groups had pointed out in the 1960s that graduating a handful of black physicians was hardly more than a gesture toward ameliorating Philadelphia's medical institutions' long-standing racial discrimination against prospective professionals and patients. In expanding programs of diversity already in place—welcoming community leaders into the administration of health clinics and seeking out nontraditional candidates for health training—Shober therefore reaped a benefit. Black community leaders wrote to the trustees praising Shober's effort to bring Hahnemann "out of the dark ages and [to] humanize and sensitize its administrative staff toward the needs of the total community [and its] involvement and participation." They pointed to the ways that the community had "worked with Hahnemann to reverse the poor image long held by the community-at-large in their negative feeling concerning your institution." Under Shober's leadership, the community no longer looked at Hahnemann "as a bulwark of racial and minority discrimination." Samuel L. Evans, the head of the American Foundation for Negro Affairs in Philadelphia, reminded Hahnemann's trustees pointedly of "the large amount of federal, state and other public funds allocated to the institution through grants and other means, largely tax payers['] money."[20] Indeed, in many ways by the 1970s, Hahnemann had become a public institution. When, for example, Vice President for Academic Affairs John Moyer sued Hahnemann for illegal dismissal in 1974 he did so in federal court, claiming the school should be considered a "public employer."[21]

CHAMP was expanded into a series of programs that Shober later called the Hahnemann Plan. Lincoln University was selected as another historically black institution that could direct promising premed minority students to Hahnemann. In 1971 a new program known as the Flexible Curriculum admitted a small number of minority students who took Hahnemann's four-year medical program in five years, a practice known, in the terminology of this era, as "deceleration."[22] Hahnemann also targeted underserved rural populations by linking up with regional colleges. In 1972 Hahnemann chose a selected group of premed students from Wilkes College in Wilkes-Barre. Wilkes-Barre was chosen partly because of its paucity of physicians: in the 1970s it had one doctor per thirty-five hundred people compared to the recommended ratio of one per one thousand. Further, Wilkes-Barre was the congressional district of Daniel Flood. Hahnemann established a six-year B.S./M.D. track for the selected Wilkes students, with a special family medicine curriculum. Students spent two years at Wilkes, two years at Hahnemann, and then two years doing their clinical training at hospitals in their local community. They were encouraged but not forced to stay and practice in the area. The undergraduates who entered Hahnemann, Shober later commented, had "two years of careful monitoring at their local college, making them perhaps the most closely observed group of trainees since the astronauts."[23] The Hahnemann-Wilkes program was approved by the NIH, the AAMC and the AMA, and the Commonwealth of Pennsylvania, and it improved Hahnemann's image as a regional health educator, as well as allowing Hahnemann medical school to increase its class size. It garnered Hahnemann much positive publicity; in March 1974, for example, an item that included student interviews aired on Philadelphia's local television news and was then proudly replayed at a Hahnemann Hospital Council meeting.[24]

A similar program was organized in 1974 with Lehigh University in Bethlehem, and in 1976 with Gannon College in Erie. Somewhat more ambitious was the combined program starting in 1976 linking Widener College and the Crozer-Chester Medical Center, a program that was expected to produce graduates willing to serve both the inner city and rural areas. Hahnemann was making special efforts to "prepare disadvantaged students early in their high school careers for eventual admission to Widener, and ultimately to Hahnemann Medical College," Shober explained. Hahnemann's full-time faculty rotated through each participating hospital for the purpose of transforming each into a true teaching hospital and attracting new physicians to these areas.[25]

The Hahnemann Plan was proposed as a solution for the scarcity of primary care physicians and for health care needs of the poor. The plan was, Shober claimed, "simple, low in cost, and since it is based on freedom of choice, ideal for a free society in which compulsion is considered repugnant." It placed an urban medical school in cooperation not only with rural colleges but also with rural hospitals, physicians' societies, and political, labor, and business leaders. Its most innovative feature was the creation of a "special student selection process" based on "both academic and non-academic criteria." Using language that would have sounded familiar in *Grand Mal*, Shober explained the philosophy behind the special admissions policy: "Hahnemann believes that non-academic attributes—personality traits—may be more significant than college grades in anticipating the performance of working physicians, and importantly, in selecting those students who are likely to become generalists rather than specialists."[26] Admission criteria were developed through interviews with family physicians and with residents in three family medicine programs (the University of Rochester's program at Highland Hospital, Harvard's program at Boston Children's Hospital, and the program at the Lancaster General Hospital) as well as from the results of a psychological test given to the residents of these programs. The program was a combination of innovative educational ideas and political sensitivity. Shober made this sensitivity clear: "Admission is completed by a committee with local community representation."[27] In essence, these programs offered certain students a different track, an alternative path from the medical mainstream. But the openness of the program meant that it could not ensure either that the students chose to practice family medicine or that they returned home to practice. Most significantly these programs enabled Hahnemann to select, admit, and monitor disadvantaged and minority students, thereby enabling it to continue its tradition of diversity.

1972: Annus Horribilis

After his inauguration Shober immediately began introducing profound internal changes including new bylaws and a new corporate structure. His administration was deliberately dismissive of Hahnemann's existing structures, partly because it apparently believed that this was the way a strong leader acted and partly because it wanted to demonstrate to the trustees that here was a new broom. Shober tried to bring business expertise to a sluggish academic complex. Most of the administrators that Shober appointed were people who had been at Hahnemann only a few years, people with executive experience, business training, and a national, corporate vision but no apparent previous ties to Hahnemann or Philadelphia or even medicine.[28] Shober set up a blue ribbon committee—so-called because it was outside Hahnemann's traditional committee structure—

to propose administrative changes, but he then ignored its recommendations.[29] Shober made the vice president for medical affairs more powerful, and appointed Robert Holmes, whom Hahnemann pediatrician Carl Fischer, then a reluctant acting director of medical affairs, had hired in 1968.[30] Holmes, a retired colonel in the Army Medical Corps with extensive service in Korea, became so unpopular that at one point he was called "the Nero behind the Zero."[31] Shober created a new position, vice president for academic affairs, for which he selected John Moyer, professor and head of the Department of Medicine, Hahnemann's most important department. Moyer had been at Hahnemann since 1957, was a skilled administrator and a respected researcher, and had played a crucial role in Cameron's effort to improve Hahnemann's academic reputation. It was a good choice, although Moyer was apparently not popular among the faculty, and he was placed over a capable and popular dean, Joseph DiPalma.[32] But the way his appointment was announced—one faculty member remembers Shober getting up in the middle of a faculty meeting and announcing Moyer's appointment—without any consultation of the faculty, was deeply distressing to the faculty and alumni observers.[33]

Some members of the faculty began to feel that they were being treated as employees who did not need to be consulted about executive decisions. The crucial year in Shober's administration was 1972, a year that saw a series of disasters and confrontations. During 1972, the Shober administration unsuccessfully attempted to fire Dean Joseph DiPalma, demoted John Moyer, chose a Latin American dictator as the recipient of an honorary degree, initiated a research project that ended after two controversial patient deaths, and broke with the school's Alumni Association.

SOMOZA, DOCTOR OF LAWS

In the spring of 1972 Shober announced that he had chosen General Anastasio Somoza, the former right-wing dictator of Nicaragua, to come to Hahnemann to receive an honorary degree at commencement. Somoza, who had recently relinquished his presidency but remained a powerful force in Nicaragua, was a graduate of West Point and, according to the *Evening Bulletin*, "had a wide circle of friends and business acquaintances in the Philadelphia area."[34] A Philadelphia paper reported that Shober had met the Somoza family while traveling in Latin America and had been an "honorary counsel" for Nicaragua in Philadelphia.[35]

Both faculty and student groups began to protest that this was an inappropriate choice. The faculty passed a series of motions indicating that they "could find no basis for an honorary degree to be awarded to General Somoza for meritorious service in areas of medicine and health education and any area deemed appropriate for an honorary degree."[36] In April a group also used the Somoza decision to bring together a number of grievances about the Shober presidency and present them to the board of trustees. In a thirteen-page position paper entitled "Faculty Position on Mr. Shober's Administration," this group outlined its vision of a proper leader of an academic institution, and the paper later reached the Philadelphia press.[37]

In this position paper Cameron became a somewhat romanticized version of the "perfect president." Without using Cameron's name, the paper compared Shober to "a distinguished president who is highly regarded in governmental and foundation circles" and works in "a quiet, behind-the-scenes capacity, [to] support strong departments in their efforts to secure financial backing."[38] This paper was not simply a personal attack but a cry against what these faculty members saw as the imposition of a different and antagonistic culture, the culture of business.

The faculty position paper complained of what it called Shober's "impulsive and unwise self-arrogated decisions" and claimed he had created a faculty "distrustful of administration's motives and tactics, torn and divided by deliberate polarization practiced by the administration, and seriously hampered by turmoil." The statement said, "we see administrative chaos, resulting from the creation of an unwieldy superstructure, and its implementation by fiat that bespeaks authoritarianism stemming from failure to understand how an academic institution should be administered."[39] Most revealing was a quotation from a recent report by the Josiah Macy Foundation entitled "Report of the Commission for the Study of the Governance of the Academic Medical Center":

> How does the academic medical center differ from a complex business organization? In a business the staff or employees work for pay under conditions arranged by and on tasks set by management. Money comes to a business as payment for goods and services, the quality and price of which being the chief consideration of the purchaser. In a medical center the three central activities—teaching, research, and care of patients—are carried out by people working according to their professional traditions. Much of the money comes not in payment for goods and services delivered to buyers but as support of activities within the medical center, or as payment for services rendered not to the payer but to a third party. . . . Much of the medical center's income is derived from grants to support specified activities. Grants are made not on the basis of completed results but on the abilities of individuals, the adequacy of supporting resources, and the quality of the program to be undertaken.[40]

The faculty group believed that Shober's action undermined the academic culture they knew and valued; the group castigated, for example, the "succession of essentially autocratic directives, memoranda, organizational charts, proposed Rules and Regulations, etc. which are essentially stripping the faculty of the academic prerogatives that are normal in a medical educational center." "It has clearly emerged," the group wrote, "that he regards a medical educational center and its faculty as mere employees who should serve at the pleasure of the President." Shober, they complained, did not recognize "that the fiscal stability of the institution rests largely on the ability of its scientists and teachers to attract research and teaching funds." Aware of what appeared to be a booming academic market, they remarked that "no capable professional needs to accept employment with, or remain with, an institution that is governed in an autocratic manner, whose faculty does not enjoy academic freedom and who may be subject to dismassal [sic] as a result of not being in agreement with the chief executive."[41]

However forceful and heated, these faculty protests were directed internally and could be (and apparently were) ignored by the Shober administration. More successful at altering Hahnemann policy in 1972—at least the policy concerning Somoza—were the protests from Hahnemann's seniors, who threatened to boycott the graduation ceremonies. It is not clear how radical students' dislike of Shober was reconciled with the positive community response over his antidiscriminatory policies. But in their petitions radical students found a way to link the local community to an opposition to both Shober and Somoza. In pamphlets with titles like "Somoza—A Study in Moral Prostitution," students argued that Hahnemann's board of trustees represented "the forces which regard health care and foreign policy as extensions of big business" and warned that the ancestors of the "Black and Puerto Rican citizens who make up the community that Hahnemann Hospital serves" were from Third World nations that were oppressed "under dictators such as General Somoza."[42] "Honoring this oppressor is an affront to our community and would threaten to strain any good faith now existing," argued the radicalized Student Institute; "We are honoring the forces which oppress Third World Peoples both inside and outside of the United States."[43]

Somoza's honorary degree of doctor of laws was awarded at a private party held at Pomona, the Chestnut Hill estate of Shober's main supporter on the board of trustees, Morton Jenks.[44] This party supposedly cost ten thousand dollars, which was billed to Hahnemann.[45] The Somoza incident drew the attention of the local press to Shober and his running of Hahnemann. There was quite a bit of coverage, some of it negative, but the incident was also a clear indication of Shober's ability to continue to do things his way. John Corr, a local columnist, for example, praised Shober's style in a story about Matt Naythons, a radical student who had decided to go to Pomona to protest. Shober supposedly suggested that Naythons join the guests for dinner. When Naythons replied, "I can't. . . . I don't have a tuxedo," Shober rented him one. The columnist concluded the story: "'I don't know,' Naythons said bewilderedly. 'But I think I've been co-opted.'" Corr commented, "Which demonstrates once again that a little finesse goes a long way."[46]

THE CDT RESEARCH DISASTER

During the 1970s, the most effective way that Hahnemann discontents found to have their voices heard inside the institution and to influence Shober and the trustees was to go to the popular press. The 1970s became the era of Hahnemann leaks, and Hahnemann's internal dissension became the subject of major local and, occasionally, national stories. A number of Hahnemann faculty and administrators were disturbed to see how quickly the Philadelphia press picked up and developed the story of the carbon dioxide therapy (CDT) research project, which many saw as the worst disaster of Shober's early administration. The alacrity with which the Philadelphia press moved onto this story can be explained in part because Shober had made Hahnemann's public image a crucial part of its academic and financial standing.

In the new world of corporate medicine, research played an uneasy part. Shober's concept of the CDT program suggests a sort of corporate research and discovery program rather than the free-floating scientific exploration that faculty researchers liked to believe they were undertaking. Part of the problems between Hahnemann executives and faculty appeared to be the effort to redefine not only administrative power but also power over research design. Seen this way, the funding structure of medical research was closer to a political process for getting money to build hospitals. Hahnemann faculty members were outraged at what they perceived as a lack of understanding of the national academic research culture. Thus, it is not surprising that when a research project that Shober supported ended in disaster, the press saw it as a sign of institutional mismanagement and medical malpractice.

Compared to Cameron, Shober was unfamiliar with the organization and culture of academic medicine, a field newly professionalized in the 1940s and 1950s. Shober's administration saw research as useful largely for its ability to contribute to improving Hahnemann's image. When Shober began to consider what research projects could best gain Hahnemann community and political attention he chose one that had immediate public appeal: the problem of drug addiction.

The problems of the inner city had become the focus of liberal federal reformers, especially after the publication of Michael Harrington's *The Other America* (1963). Kennedy and Johnson had established "model cities" programs to encourage mayors to deal creatively with the problems of poverty, disease, homelessness, and illegitimacy. Drug and alcohol addiction were seen as both a cause and a consequence of the crumbling of the inner city and, for medical researchers, seemed a perfect way to offer medicalized solutions to a social problem. Even better, from a purely business point of view, some addicts came from wealthy families. As Shober explained in 1972: "Drug addiction in the U.S. is now regarded as a disease of epidemic proportion. There is no known cure. Rehabilitation methods offer little hope. The public and the medical profession are urgently seeking an answer. . . . It is frequently stated that seventy percent of all crime is in some way associated with the drug problem. The tragic consequences to an entire family when a member becomes a drug addict are well known."[47]

On February 26, 1972, Ronald Brown, a twenty-four-year-old black drug addict, died at Hahnemann Hospital. At the autopsy Hahnemann physicians characterized his death as due to minor complications from treatment for his addiction. Marvin Aronson, the city's medical examiner, was not satisfied by this explanation when he heard that Brown had been a patient in Hahnemann's controversial carbon dioxide therapy program and that Brown, far from being a street transient, was the husband of Fawn Pitcairn, heir to the Pittsburgh Plate Glass fortune, and from a "socially prominent family" in Bryn Athyn.[48] Brown and Pitcairn had met at a halfway house for drug addicts, and their interracial, interclass marriage had made local headlines.[49]

Brown's death made an even better story when reporters learned of the death on March 2 of Morris N. Kallen Jr., who had just left the Hahnemann CDT program and was beginning outpatient therapy at the nearby Philadelphia Hotel, where Hahnemann had its psychiatric outpatient clinic. Kallen had died after his roommate gave him an overdose of methadone.[50] Both deaths, and Brown's in particular, became major local and then national stories: UPI called the story "Heiress Weeps for Husband," and AP, "The Heiress and the Junkie."[51]

The deaths of Brown and Kallen were linked to Hahnemann's CDT program, which had been developed in August 1971 and had been initiated not by a Hahnemann internist or psychiatrist but by Shober himself. He claimed to have begun to investigate medical solutions to the problem of urban drug addiction after being mugged by heroin addicts a few months before. "Right then," he told a reporter in January 1972, "I addressed myself to this problem of heroin."[52] Shober heard about the work of Albert A. LaVerne, a New York psychiatrist who claimed to have a cure for drug and alcohol addiction. Shober claimed to believe in LaVerne's program so much that he himself had inhaled the gas several times, and he told a reporter that "the inhalation of carbon dioxide has a beneficial effect on non addicts as well."[53] Within a month of his arrival at Hahnemann, Shober met with the head of Hahnemann's psychiatry and mental health sciences department to discuss the possibility of starting a CDT program, and he invited LaVerne to come and set up a research project to continue his work at Hahnemann.[54]

Even though the senior psychiatrists at Hahnemann had ridiculed the project, after Lewis Mills, an internist who had come to Hahnemann with Moyer in the 1950s, returned from New York somewhat impressed with the results after speaking to some of LaVerne's patients, Hahnemann began to set it up.[55] Shober was aware of CDT's stunning political and social implications. As he wrote privately to the publisher of Philadelphia's *Evening Bulletin*: "off the record, our preliminary information shows that we have found a relatively simple cure for alcoholism and heroin addiction. Naturally we don't want to raise the hopes of millions until we have complete scientific data."[56] In November 1971 Hahnemann advertised through local papers, radio, and television for addict volunteers.[57] By the time the CDT program ended in March 1972, after three months, forty-three patients had been treated.

The therapy was based on the idea that drug addicts needed a profound physical and mental break from their addictions and that an artificially induced coma could help them through the trauma of withdrawal. As Shober explained to the Hahnemann community in March, "following this experience, detoxification of the addict is usually managed with much less difficulty and subsequent psychologic behavior is most often improved. The disagreeable side effects of drug withdrawal are avoided. The addict expresses strong motivation to reform and seek a normal way of life."[58] A CDT patient breathed pure oxygen for ten minutes and then inhaled a mixture of 75 percent carbon dioxide and 25 percent pure oxygen for ten to twenty seconds, lapsed into a coma, and was revived with pure oxygen.[59] Ronald Brown had been in the program for three days and had received five treatments; before his death he had been in a coma for two days. Kallen had received a number of treatments before being released as an outpatient.[60] The introduction of the program had gained Hahnemann political and social accolades, and some CDT patients later acknowledged that they had sought it out, for the treatment had given them a feeling close to a high.[61]

CDT was never accepted as a mainstream psychiatric therapy, and during the furor after the March deaths, one outside psychiatrist described CDT as like "bloodletting . . . broiling or freezing."[62] During its brief three-month operation at Hahnemann the program had split the academic and hospital staff. Worse, as the story reached the press, internal conflicts among the faculty over the way it had been approved were made public, as was their dislike of publicity itself. At faculty meetings, Hahnemann physicians angrily protested what they called the "Madison Avenue" publicizing of the program.[63] One faculty member asked in a meeting why Shober, "a non-scientific person," had been publicly quoted "on such an extremely sensitive scientific experiment."[64] Hinted at in a number of press reports, and made explicit in the minutes of a private faculty meeting, was the faculty's concern that the program's protocols—especially its use of humans as experimental subjects—had not been approved by the institution's review boards and that at least in one case a CDT grant application had allegedly been

256 THE FINAL FIFTY YEARS

signed not by a department chairman or a dean but by Shober himself.[65] Not publicly expressed but undoubtedly present was the fear that there had been insufficient security and that the existence of the CDT program in Hahnemann Hospital had allowed patients access to illegal drugs.[66]

Hahnemann stopped the program in March at the time of the public reports of Brown's death, but spokesmen claimed the program was simply being postponed until the final report of the medical examiner. Shober issued an internal statement describing the program, explaining that "certain news stories may have given the impression that the carbon dioxide treatment was in some way involved in these deaths," but "there is no present evidence to substantiate such a conclusion."[67] In May the medical examiner's office issued the final death certificate for Ronald Brown, which indicated the cause of death as "complications of treatment of drug dependency" and called the manner of death "therapeutic misadventure."[68] By this time the district attorney's office, headed by Arlen Specter (who later became a United States senator), had begun its own investigation, and so had the Pennsylvania Medical Society. Specter called it a "poorly conceived alleged research program."[69]

In early May the press reported that Hahnemann researchers were redesigning a CDT grant application to modify the therapy, moving patients to intensive care units, and inducing comas less frequently.[70] With the continuing public controversy, however, Hahnemann had, by May 10, withdrawn its application to the NIMH for a two-million-dollar grant to expand the program.[71] Embarrassingly Hahnemann's public explanation for dropping the program—that there was insufficient money, time, and space allowed by the government to continue the program properly—was contradicted by its private explanations, which were leaked to the Philadelphia press on the same day. In a memo sent to hospital trustees, senior administrators, and department chairs, Shober and Moyer blamed the "the continuous release of prejudicial and inappropriate information through unauthorized channels in the institution leading to excessive publicity" that had resulted in probes "into the medical treatment of patients" that were "the invasion of privacy of the patient which is contrary to the welfare of the patients being treated, as well as to the institution and the physicians involved." "Our medical staff states that it is impossible to conduct a scientific evaluation of any medical therapeutic modality under the circumstances of repeated unauthorized news releases of medical information through the public press"; not only had two patients been named, but "the physicians are subjected to undue stresses which make the treatment of the patients most difficult since objectivity may be lost." Appealing to Hahnemann researchers' sense of scientific standards, institutional loyalty, and medical ethics, Shober and Moyer said "we hope that another institution which has not attracted the degree of unfavorable public attention that Hahnemann has with the program will undertake a scientific evaluation of the CDT treatment."[72]

The faculty called the program the "Carbon Dioxide Fiasco." They told the trustees that even before the publicity over the deaths the program had been "a citywide, statewide and national medical scandal." They attacked the "unprofessional manner in which the program was being conducted, with blatant publicizing in the press, over the radio, and by means of semipublic staged announcements to rather large groups on occasions which could not, by any stretch of imagination, be construed to be professional or scientific meetings." Further, they pointed out, the program had not been initiated by a scientific researcher, declaring that "the CDT project was Mr. Shober's own pet enthusiasm which he brought with him to Hahnemann and promoted vigorously, despite many cautionary statements made by members of the professional staff of the institution." LaVerne, they claimed, was a psychiatrist "whose standing among his peers in New York City was severely compromised by his past behavior." Worse, they claimed, he had treated heroin addicts at Hahnemann Hospital without having been appointed to the faculty or hospital staff and initially without having a Pennsylvania medical license. And most serious, the faculty believed the project had harmed Hahnemann's scientific reputation: "Responsible professional opinion at such critical places as the National Institutes of Health, and in general around the nation, has been that the CDT program has no scientific validity and, indeed, borders on the absurd. Members of Hahnemann's faculty, while attending professional meetings in places around the nation far removed from Hahnemann, have been the butt of jibes about it."[73]

Bad publicity led a number of uneasy trustees to resign rather than remain linked to Hahnemann. Shober was able to replace them with men who more strongly supported his policies.[74] In June 1972 he was reelected by the trustees and given a salary increase. As late as May 1977, a month before he was asked to resign, Shober defended the CDT program in a letter to the *Evening Bulletin*: "The program had some success, although not as much as we had hoped. I'm sorry it did not have more, but—and this is the point—I'm not sorry that we tried. In a new project we can never be sure of success or be immune to the hazards of sticking out our neck."[75]

A BREAK WITH TRADITION: SHOBER AND THE ALUMNI
Shober recognized that expanding Hahnemann Hospital was a critical part of his job. By the end of his first three years he was starting to gain better press; "Shober Proving He's the Man for Top Job at Hahnemann" was one headline in 1974.[76] In addition to building bridges with local community groups, Shober consolidated his business and political connections. He convinced Congressman Flood to find money in Washington to support a major hospital project; the number of outpatient visits from 1971 to 1974 doubled, and the length of in-patient stays decreased during his administration.

Within Hahnemann Medical College, however, conflict over some of the policies of the Shober administration became more fierce. In September 1972, for example, apparently dissatisfied with Moyer's inconsistent support, Shober fired him from his executive position as vice president for academic affairs, lowered his salary, and tried to remove him as chair of the Department of Medicine. However much some of the faculty had disliked Moyer and the power he had held, this action proved too much; Moyer began to be seen as one of Shober's victims. Moyer tried to negotiate for a few years and finally, in 1974, sued Hahnemann, Shober, and other top officials; the suit was settled out of court.[77]

Even less successful was Shober's effort to get rid of Dean Joseph DiPalma, who had been appointed by Cameron in 1967.[78] DiPalma remembers becoming more outspoken in his criticism of Shober, and after a particularly damaging article in the *Philadelphia Magazine* entitled "What's Festering at Hahnemann," Shober, seeking the source of the leaks, fired him. The faculty called an emergency meeting, asking Shober to attend, and instead of the usual sixty or seventy about three hundred members attended, including a number from the psychiatry department. The faculty chairman asked Shober to explain why the dean had been fired. Shober replied that "his views and attitudes are not in line with the forward progress which I and the Board have planned for the institution." As DiPalma tells the story in his memoirs:

> As he finished his statement the entire audience rose to their feet in unison as if it were a military movement. This gesture made an abrupt noise not quite the shot of a cannon but more as if a heavy crate had been dropped on the floor. This was followed by a moment of silence then again in perfect unison a single word was uttered by every person. That word was simply and effectively, "NO" exclaimed as if it were a clap of thunder. Shober was stunned. His jaw dropped. He looked around as if to seek a ready exit. . . . He knew that without the support of the faculty and the staff he could not succeed. While the Board might support him they were a weak lot and would collapse when the situation worsened. So with a smile he said, "Well! I didn't know that Dr. DiPalma was so popular. Perhaps I've misjudged the situation. I'm going to reinstate him with the understanding that he will support me in my efforts to make Hahnemann one of the best medical schools in the nation."[79]

During this period what were called poison pen letters began to appear. These letters—signed by "The Hahnemann Faculty Committee of Nine" or sometimes just "The Committee of Nine" (the members of the committee were never identified) and sent to faculty, staff, alumni and to the press—attacked Shober and his officials and brought to light difficulties, small and large, within the medical school, raising the level of antagonism on all sides.

Shober had come to Hahnemann as an outsider. His senior administration was made up almost entirely of men without long-standing connections to Hahnemann. This executive distance was typical of the direction of the corporate world of the United States, where business leaders sought to change institutions by drawing on values from outside the particular institution and community. The vision of Shober's appointees was the antithesis of tradition. Their distance from "old Hahnemann" became even sharper when Shober began to be attacked by officials from Hahnemann's Alumni Association. To the alumni Shober was not sufficiently sympathetic to Hahnemann traditions. To Shober the alumni's habit of writing to Hahnemann's trustees and offering their opinions of the policies of his administration was a problem.

By the 1970s the Alumni Association was largely supported by graduates from the 1930s and 1940s, physicians who remembered the dark days of probation and were proud to see the academic and physical changes introduced by Deans Brown and Cameron. More recent graduates, especially from the late 1960s, largely stayed away from Hahnemann boosterism, and many felt as alienated from Hahnemann's administrators and faculty, as they did from the politicians who were associated with Vietnam and now Watergate.[80]

The Alumni Association had gained its power in the interwar years and had become more conscious of itself as representing graduates rather than faculty as, pressured by the AMA/AAMC probation, the postwar deans began hiring department heads and junior faculty from outside Hahnemann. By the mid-1950s the association had gained two representatives on the board of trustees (a separate identity it had never needed before), and these representatives, such as Joseph Post and Charles Hollis, had been powerful figures in shaping Hahnemann policy. Until the Shober years the association maintained its influence in the medical school more because of its financial clout than because of its historical significance. Nonetheless, members of the association, especially its board of trustees, had come to see themselves as the holders of Hahnemann's conscience. Hahnemann alumni were already uneasy about Shober's forcing Cameron to retire as head of the board of trustees a year earlier than he had intended to. With Cameron and then Moyer leaving, they saw the true disappearance of the older, postwar Hahnemann.

Alumni, discontent with Hahnemann's constant financial problems, had initially embraced Shober's new ideal of the business world. They were quickly made aware that Shober was introducing not just new technical skills but a new style of administration and new values, many of them with little prior connection to Hahnemann traditions or the Philadelphia medical world.

Shober was particularly incensed when Harry K. Gabroy (class of 1943), the head of the Alumni Association's board of trustees, spoke against Shober's administration on the local television news in September 1972. Gabroy charged that the entire staff of Hahnemann Hospital was upset about the degree awarded to General Somoza and the demotion of Moyer and that the faculty had "no confidence at all" in Shober's administration. Gabroy also called the CDT program "a complete failure" and said that the "whole idea was Shober's."[81] Gabroy a few days earlier had written to the board of trustees expressing "vigorous protests" against the "precipitous actions of Mr. Shober" in dismissing Moyer, as the actions "not only violated the rights of Dr. Moyer but also reflected unfavorably upon the entire institution." Then on the first of December Gabroy wrote to all the alumni members asking for donations that would not be controlled by Hahnemann's board of trustees but would be spent for "specific projects" designated by the association.[82]

In response Shober simply abolished Hahnemann's formal ties to the association and set up an alternative alumni group, linked firmly to the administration. Hahnemann took away office space and its financial support of the alumni staff. Shober might have felt confident that doing this would not harm his new vision of the institution financially, for his major sources of funding came not from alumni contributions but from federal grants and industry contracts on a far larger scale. The legal firm engaged by Hahnemann's board of trustees wrote to Gabroy and told him that the association's actions were "wholly unacceptable." It advised him that the association was no longer authorized to solicit funds on behalf of Hahnemann and warned that it would tell alumni that "any contribution they may make to your Association is not a donation to Hahnemann so as to be included within Hahnemann's tax exemption." If the association protested, Hahnemann would complain to the state that the association was in violation of Pennsylvania's 1963 Solicitation of Charitable Funds Act.[83] Two trustees also wrote to the alumni, explaining that although "we are indeed sorry to have to take this action," "we hope that you will repudiate his action." If the association continued to ask for funds on behalf of Hahnemann, the letter said, "we will have no alternative but to hold all Trustees of the Association accountable therefor, reluctant as we would be to do so." The new alumni group, the Committee of Alumni Affairs, under the direction of the administration, would, the letter explained, far more effectively raise money for Hahnemann.[84]

The implication to donors that their contributions were no longer tax deductible was very serious. Gabroy immediately responded by assuring its members that "*your gifts to the Association continue to be fully tax deductible* as in the past" and that the association was "exempt under the Solicitation of Charitable Funds Act."[85] And in a sentence that was repeated many times, Gabroy claimed that Shober's administration had reduced "an academic institution to the level of a highly competitive business firm with autocratic management."[86] Shober had argued that the association was not "democratic," that it did not represent the voices of most alumni, and also that it was not effective in fund-raising.[87]

The association spent much energy trying to refute these charges.[88] But, even more important, the alumni were now no longer organized in an independent organization. Gabroy told the alumni that the association's representatives on the board were no longer "given posts of importance on major committees." And, noting the role its independence had played after the association was chartered as a separate corporation in 1931, he commented: "experience since that time has proven that on several occasions *this independence has made it possible for the Alumni Association to give vital assistance to the parent institution literally insuring its survival in times of great danger through both moral and financial support.*"[89] In January 1973 a committee of nine letter called on faculty and students to support the association, for "this is the only group that remains independent and is not subject to the devastations of the dictatorship of President Shober." "Keep your Alumni free of executive control so that there is at least one hope for freedom of speech at Hahnemann. At least this organization has professional leadership by professional people."[90]

Many of the alumni were horrified, not only by Shober's actions but also by the signs that the internal conflict was so serious that it was spilling out of the institution.[91] Numerous Hahnemann graduates wrote to Shober and Gabroy commenting on how much this conflict reminded them of the "bad old days" of the 1940s. But it was not clear what lessons they wished to draw from the comparison.[92]

The campaign against Shober heated up and became personal. Shober was accused of hiring crooks, of being the pawn of his vice president of medical affairs, and of having lied to the board of trustees about his credentials and experience.[93] Letters by the committee of nine claimed that through detective work they had discovered Shober's "true" past, and they presented a disturbingly tarnished image. A group of Hahnemann administrators and faculty began to circulate documents apparently showing that he had never graduated from Princeton and, worse, that he had been fired from the Joshua B. Powers firm, possibly for financial mismanagement.[94] Shober was not "a retired business executive who sold his company for a fortune," one letter claimed. Shober said that he "had sold his stock in the Joshua B. Powers Company for millions of dollars and that he was now in a position to make a contribution to society by becoming Hahnemann's president," but in fact "he bilked this Company into receivership [sic]!" "[T]he presentation of his credentials was completely deceitful and another indication of the personality of Mr. Shober. He is not the caliber [of] person we would want to follow in an academic institution."[95] This letter threatened that if the board did not take action, the writers would turn their information over to "a third-party carrier for the hospital since it is their money that is being wasted; and to the State Government as well since we are, in fact, a public utility and a charge of the State and Federal Government."[96] And, it continued,

We, the Faculty, are deeply shocked that the Board of Trustees would
defend a situation of this kind since undoubtedly, being business
executives, [the trustees] must have known that this whole deal had a
shady background and that it was most inappropriate to make such an
appointment in an academic institution. . . . Even more inappropriate is
the fact that an individual like this should have been allowed to make
academic decisions thereby smashing the professional futures of men like
Dean DiPalma, Dr. Lewis, Dr. Barbero, Dr. Moyer, Dr. Cameron and Mr.
Paxson, as well as many of our outstanding Clinical Chairmen who now
feel completely defeated and demoralized. These are the men who made
Hahnemann . . . NOT MR. SHOBER! They brought Hahnemann out
of the mire in the sixties and now Shober is taking Hahnemann right
back to the same condition again. Can these men be replaced who truly
were dedicated to Hahnemann's cause?[97]

Another letter explained that "we are pinpointing these issues so that when
Hahnemann is exposed to the next catastrophe—it will be absolutely and unmistakably clear as to where the responsibility lies for the pernicious errors in
policy and procedures. . . . NO FACULTY MEMBER WILL AGAIN BE USED
AS THE SACRIFICIAL LAMB."[98] Other letters attacked Hahnemann's new
alumni magazine, Hahnemann Today, as "a masterful deception and a phony reproduction of the Alumni News" containing photographs that made the faculty "appear to be a bunch of alcoholics on continuous partying escapades. This
may be appropriate for Mr. Shober and his society gatherings but certainly this
type of circular news is in poor taste as far as the serious minded Alumni are
concerned."[99]

These letters quickly found their way into the Philadelphia press. The story
of the break with the Alumni Association began to be included with other incidents, such as Somoza's private party at Pomona, the CDT program, and threats
of resignation by the faculty. One Alumni Association spokesman even claimed
there might be a tap on the association's telephone line.[100] Poison pen letters
quoted in the Evening Bulletin claimed that "the morale of the faculty is getting
lower and we are now progressing downward to a third-rate institution. Two years
ago, we may have been second rate but we were moving upwards."[101]

Within Hahnemann things worsened with the faltering American economy
and the cutbacks introduced by Nixon's administration. Dean DiPalma informed
the faculty in February 1973 that, with the reduction and elimination of so many
grants, Hahnemann "must announce that it cannot honor the previous policy
of absorbing income losses from grant sources which fund certain special projects
or programs," and that "this Institution cannot guarantee any individual salary
which is funded by a terminated grant source beyond the end of this fiscal
year."[102]

One effect of this turmoil was to unite the board of trustees behind Shober.

The End of the Administration in 1977

Shober's third, fourth, and fifth years as president were by comparison uneventful. Senior faculty members continued to leave: Jewell Osterholm, head of neurosurgery, went to Jefferson and took his staff; Joseph Linhart, head of cardiology, left, and so did Dominic DeLaurentis, professor of surgery.[103] In 1976 the new chair of obstetrics and gynecology was reported to have been denied research privileges by the FDA after submitting fraudulent results in his research on an IUD in the early 1970s. Even though this had occurred before his appointment to Hahnemann (and he had not mentioned it to Hahnemann), the story was entitled "Barred from Testing IUDs, Doctor Heads Hahnemann Unit."[104]

At the same time during this period Hahnemann confidently expanded its teaching, patient care, and research. In 1974 it opened the nineteen-story New College Building and the school's first student residence, the sixteen-story Stiles Hall. The Graduate School was formally organized under a dean, microbiologist Amedeo Bondi, and flourished with an array of masters programs including family therapy, creative arts therapy, and audiology and speech pathology. Hahnemann Hospital expanded into shock and trauma services, and established an innovative kidney dialysis outpatient unit. In 1976 the team of researchers and clinicians at Hahnemann's new Institute for Cancer and Blood Diseases performed the region's first allogeneic bone marrow transplant to treat a nineteen-year-old with leukemia. That year Sheila Moriber Katz, a Hahnemann pathologist, was one of the first to identify the etiological agent of Legionnaires' disease and subsequently became an expert on Legionella bacteria. That year as well Hahnemann received a strong accreditation report from the Middle States Association of Colleges and Schools, which led to its formal designation as Hahnemann University five years later.

Shober's changes at Hahnemann began to be more fully accepted, and earlier tensions were partly smoothed over. The poison pen letters stopped in 1974, and a year later the two alumni groups merged, organized in a single board of trustees with equal representation.[105] In September 1976 Shober was able to complete the hospital bond financing and Philadelphia's city council gave permission for Hahnemann to begin building the hospital wing.[106] When Hahnemann got the fourteen million dollars it needed, Shober later commented, "I was a hero for a short time. . . . No one thought I could get the money."[107] The student body began to look increasingly diverse, with around 10 percent minority students and around 20 percent women, and in 1973 Eunice F. Stanfield became Hahnemann's first African-American woman graduate.[108] The *Evening Bulletin* and the *Philadelphia Magazine* continued to run articles pointing to a Hahnemann scandal, but Shober seemed secure.

Then something happened: Shober was accused by the press of using Hahnemann employees and funds to renovate his apartment. It was a minor personal extravagance, but it occurred at a time when Hahnemann had frozen salaries and was having trouble paying city vendors. Suddenly the underlying tensions between the academic culture and the corporate world resurfaced, and with such force that the incident ultimately led to Shober's resignation. Shober's fall can be seen as the result of an effort to pull Hahnemann into the corporate world, where the image of a president was part of the institution's image and where, therefore, the president required facilities to impress those he wished to attract as donors and supporters.

Throughout the 1970s Hahnemann consistently had bad press, but by early 1977 negative articles were appearing daily. The Shober administration became convinced that inside Hahnemann there was a "Deep Throat" or perhaps several, and in Shober's final six months he fired his top executives, including five vice presidents.[109] Numerous disaffected administrators and faculty members used the newspapers to attack Shober and convince the trustees to fire him.[110] But Hahnemann's publicity was also the result of the changing culture of the professional mass media, especially the press, which had been profoundly altered by the Watergate experience and by the astonishing successes of the *Washington Post* reporters who had broken the story and helped to bring down a president. Many journalists not only sought out their own Deep Throat but also aspired to being the next Woodward or Bernstein. They shared the widespread skepticism about authority, especially the assumption that politicians were corrupt, and saw their role as bringing these people to the bright light of the public eye and thereby to justice.

Hahnemann became part of Philadelphia's testing grounds for these investigatory ideals. Newspapers, especially Philadelphia's *Evening Bulletin*, gleefully explored Hahnemann's scandals, and the paper's articles appeared to be personal attacks. But to a great extent, the paper's interest was not personal; it was part of many middle-class Philadelphians' dissatisfaction with Frank Rizzo and his administration, and part of a more general sense that there was a Richard Nixon in every hometown.

In 1974 Hahnemann bought a nearby apartment building on Benjamin Franklin Parkway known as the Windsor. It was initially intended to help Hahnemann's housing shortage, and for a while it housed medical and nursing students. But it was gradually renovated as a luxury apartment complex, typical of the buildings springing up around center city Philadelphia. In 1976 Shober began to live on the twenty-third floor.

Revelations about Shober's "Luxury Pad" came during a time of rising inflation and a growing awareness that Hahnemann was in serious financial danger.[111] Shober's firing of his top officials began to disturb the banking community, and in early June a Philadelphia brokerage firm that had earlier bought and promoted bonds for Hahnemann's Hospital extension now publicly warned its clients to sell these bonds because of the "substantially increased risk."[112]

Hearing this was made all the more difficult with the headlines that were appearing, such as "Hospital Boss in Luxury Pad." In these articles reporters claimed that Shober had allegedly spent "thousands of dollars" not authorized by the board to renovate his Windsor apartment, including a six-hundred-dollar ice machine, a stereo system installed by communications specialists from Hahnemann's television network, carpeting for four thousand dollars, and "a special wine closet . . . built and equipped with fans to keep air circulating over the president's stock," which cost "several hundred dollars." A group of vice presidents and trustees were quoted as describing this as "indulgent and extravagant." In his public reply Shober said that he had no wine closet and that the board had approved the apartment as a place for official functions and fund-raising activities "fully equipping such space in the manner which reflects upon the history and traditions of the Hahnemann Medical College and Hospital."[113] The press also reported that after the leak of a memo written by development director Wayne G. Rankin to his boss Douglas McArthur complaining that Hahnemann's consultant architect was designing this renovation rather than working on the new hospital wing, Rankin and then McArthur were fired.[114]

Shober's major defense was that the kinds of renovations he had undertaken and the kind of place the board had asked him to live in were appropriate for a senior executive. In a statement to the Hahnemann community, he explained that he did own the stereo ("an ordinary system") and "yes, there is an icemaker." But most significantly Shober tried to defend the idea behind the Windsor renovations: "the concept of using this facility and the occupation of it by the President is the same policy as approved by many universities and medical colleges in the United States."[115] To the press he added that more than three hundred people "associated with Hahnemann have used the premises in connection with plans and programs for the advancement of Hahnemann."[116]

Previously fired administrators began to speak out. In May, Richard Earl, who had worked as vice president for development for only a few months before being fired, told the *Evening Bulletin* that in November 1976 he had written a memo describing the report being written by Ketchum Inc. of Pittsburgh, a consulting firm hired to advise on fund-raising. According to Earl, and later confirmed by a Ketchum researcher, the report had concluded that the administration "has a terrible image; to wit, there is not one identifiable constituency that would support the institution in any major fund raising effort while Wharton Shober remains as president." The report had stated that "the make up of the board of trustees appears oriented more toward maintaining the job security of the president than toward the operation and betterment of the institution or the acquisition of financial support." Earl's memo commented that "the Ketchum representative was shocked to learn" that the alumni were "not being cultivated by the administration for participation in fundraising or, for that matter, any other effort," and that Earl had standing orders from Shober "not to speak to the alumni director."[117] Not long after writing the memo, Earl was fired.

Also in May, in a bizarre twist to the poison pen letters, Maurice Fox, one of Hahnemann's trustees, pursued a tip that a former partner of a public relations firm hired by Hahnemann in the early 1970s allegedly had an "original draft" of a committee of nine letter. The man, discovered in New Mexico, produced a draft apparently written in Shober's handwriting, which he claimed Shober had given him to type and mail.[118] Shober supposedly told the board that he had written this draft as an "intellectual exercise," explaining that "I had just finished reading Jonathan Swift . . . and I thought it would be amusing to write a letter criticizing myself for all the good things I had done."[119] He called on the trustees to dismiss Fox, which they refused to do, although they did censure Fox.[120]

The *Evening Bulletin* also gleefully reported that a group of trustees had tried to call an emergency meeting of the trustees to fire Shober and had gained the signatures of eleven (the required one-third), but that one trustee had withdrawn his name.[121] In May a group of trustees met with the editor and reporters of the *Evening Bulletin* to ask for "a policy of responsible journalism and offered to make available correct information so that neither the reputation of the Bulletin nor the reputation of Hahnemann would be injured by any further insinuations."[122]

Finally, in June, Shober went to the faculty and asked for personal assets to save Hahnemann from financial collapse. He blamed recent publicity about Hahnemann's financial problems for driving away potential lenders and said that the institution needed two million dollars worth of accounts from the private practices at the Hahnemann Professional Offices, a private medical complex administered by the hospital. These private accounts, he supposedly said, were the "only thing left" that Hahnemann could conceivably use as support for loans. If these accounts were not turned over, "there might not be a Hahnemann."[123] The faculty agreed but only if Shober resigned immediately. At its June meeting the trustees refused to appoint him to his suggested "chancellor" position but did allow him to resign quietly as president emeritus with an annual salary of eighty-two thousand dollars a year for the next eighteen months.[124]

At the faculty meeting following Shober's resignation the new chairman of the board, George McNeely, said, "We consider today Day One," and the faculty applauded at the announcement of Shober's resignation and greeted the announcement of William Likoff as acting president with a standing ovation.[125] When faculty members later asked Likoff why Shober had been treated so generously Likoff said, "our first priority was to see that Mr Shober resigned quietly with little trauma. . . . We had to dispense with this affair regardless of the cost. The matter could have continued on for months without end."[126] Still, as one reporter pointed out, "Hahnemann's money crisis did not happen in a vacuum. Most hospitals and medical colleges have been suffering cash-flow problems caused by inflation and slow payments from government agencies."[127]

The Lingering Effects

After Shober's resignation, publicized scandals continued to haunt Hahnemann. During 1977 and 1978 Philadelphians read about the federal investigation into possible funding improprieties by Congressmen Joshua Eilberg and Daniel Flood in the hospital's construction program. This became a national story in which Hahnemann's name always appeared.

Gradually the tangled web of political and corporate alliances whereby Shober had gained the financial support for the hospital became public. To raise money for the new hospital wing Hahnemann had needed the support of the state and federal governments, and to get that support it needed political clout. The Shober administration had therefore fired the hospital's law firm and hired Joshua Eilberg's firm at a cost of $500,000 in legal fees to convince the Philadelphia Hospital Authority that it should approve a proposed $39.5 million tax-exempt bond issue.[128] Shober had also apparently convinced Flood to find money for Hahnemann Hospital not through the regular government hospital construction channels but as a special line in a 1975 budget bill, in the form of a $14.5 million grant from the Community Services Administration budget (an agency that had been established in 1974 as a successor to Johnson's Office of Economic Opportunity). This money enabled Hahnemann to begin raising the money for the sixty-five-million-dollar wing, despite its shaky finances.[129] In addition, Flood allegedly influenced who should get some of the contract work around the building of the hospital, including the suggestion of a "project monitor" firm, CIDC which received an $835,000 contract.[130]

With the publicity over the investigations of Flood, Eilberg, and Shober, Hahnemann's trustees in January 1978 dropped Corson, Getson, and Tuteur, the law firm set up by Eilberg's partners to handle Hahnemann's accounts, and in April halted the payment of Shober's emeritus salary.[131] Dean DiPalma told the *Evening Bulletin* that

> Even in Paris they're aware of what's going on. We've had bad publicity
> in the past—in connection with Shober—and now this. With the young
> people and in the recruiting of faculty, that's where I think it's having its
> effect. We're trying desperately to create good publicity because we are
> on the verge of a fund-raising campaign. It's almost impossible when
> there is talk of collapse and blow-up. Our alumni contributions have

decreased and I think there is a definite connection with previous
publicity. It's not easy when I meet with deans from other medical
schools. I feel embarrassed talking to federal officials, almost as though I
had leprosy.[132]

In March 1978 the Community Services Administration (CSA) concluded,
after an internal investigation, that Hahnemann had financed its new wing with
money improperly obtained from the agency, the result of heavy political pressure from Flood. Hahnemann's grant of $14.5 million had avoided the Depart-
ment of Health, Education, and Welfare's strict standards for selection of
appropriate hospital grantees on aid to hospital construction and was thus a
"highly improper" use for CSA money.[133] Eilberg, Flood, and Shober were in-
dicted by a federal grand jury on charges associated with the hospital funding.
At the announcement of the indictments, William Likoff, Hahnemann's new
president, wrote to the *Evening Bulletin*, arguing that "it is now time to separate
the actions of certain individuals from the distinguished record of the institution itself and to permit Hahnemann to continue to concentrate all of its energies toward the advancement of the medical sciences in the best interest of
mankind."[134] And to the *Philadelphia Inquirer* he urged that the indictments of
Shober on "numerous counts of fraud" should "demonstrate to all that
Hahnemann has been suffering for entirely too long an unjust 'bum rap,' which
at times has threatened our very being and unfairly tarnished our long and distinguished record of service and leadership in patient care, medical education,
medical research and community service."[135]

Eilberg pleaded guilty to receiving a portion of fees from Hahnemann after
representing the hospital's interest before the federal government. Flood retired
from the federal government, not charged with anything to do with Hahnemann,
and he served a probation sentence for a separate influence-peddling case.
Shober, who had been charged with paying a ten-thousand-dollar bribe to Flood
for help in obtaining the hospital grant for Hahnemann, was found not guilty.
By 1980 he was working for General Arabian Medical and Allied Services, a
corporation that built and managed hospitals for the Saudi Arabian
government.[136]

Likoff was a man with impeccable academic credentials. A 1938 graduate
of Hahnemann, he was a professor of cardiology and the director of the (renamed) William Likoff Cardiovascular Institute. He announced that he intended
to name his own administrative staff to deal with hospital finances, development, and public affairs.[137] By September he was assuring the Philadelphia community that "it was the disastrous financial position of the institution—a serious
cash-flow situation that all but destroyed Hahnemann's line of credit with local
banks—that forced Shober's resignation" and that "the board of trustees was
duped as much as anyone else." He also presented himself as the opposite of his

predecessor, as a business executive so unskilled that "When I came aboard I couldn't read a cash-flow statement—let alone balance one. I couldn't even balance my own check book."[138]

THE YEARS of the Shober era made the Hahnemann community aware—in a way that radical students of the 1960s had been unable to—of the power of a major urban medical center as a purveyor of state and federal moneys to community groups and especially to industry. Who should direct this power, which legal firms should be chosen for advice, which firms should oversee contractors, which contractors and other firms should be negotiated with—these were questions that needed managers with special skills quite distinct from those required by the academic environment. Hahnemann had always had administrators—deans, registrars, secretaries—but they had played a minor role in directing the institution, especially the medical school. By the end of the 1970s and the end of the Shober administration, it was clear that although one corporate-oriented president had been forced to resign, that achievement had been, for the faculty, a pyrrhic victory. The 1980s and 1990s, with broader changes in medical economics, would be the era of a newly corporate Hahnemann. The purchase of Hahnemann in 1993 by a Pittsburgh health care company—however shocking it initially seemed to some academics—was a culmination of many of the changes Hahnemann had already faced and resolved in the previous decade.

Chapter 9   Coda

A New Alternative

I~N THE~ 1990s Hahnemann was transformed into a new institution. In 1993, Hahnemann's board of trustees announced Hahnemann's merger with the Medical College of Pennsylvania (MCP), which was part of a major consolidation by the Allegheny Health, Education, and Research Foundation (AHERF), a Pittsburgh-based health care company headed by Sherif S. Abdelhak. AHERF owned Allegheny General Hospital and several other health facilities and was seeking ways to expand into medical teaching and research. In 1995 the new MCP◊Hahnemann School of Medicine welcomed its first class, and in 1996 the institution was renamed Allegheny University of the Health Sciences. The newly amalgamated complex, described by the chair of Hahnemann's board of trustees as "a system of academic medicine," had assets of $1.5 billion and encompassed six hospitals, two psychiatric facilities, a research center, and a medical school second in size only to the University of Illinois.[1]

The choices and changes involved in this radically unorthodox strategy for survival seemed to many observers and participants to mark an obliteration of Hahnemann's century-and-a-half-long heritage. Hahnemann lost not only its name but, more fundamentally, its status as a freestanding, self-governing institution. Many were suspicious and resentful of this most profound of upheavals in Hahnemann's history. Some disliked the secrecy of the negotiations—"we read about it in the business pages first," one faculty member recalled.[2] Others worried that a new culture would engulf Hahnemann's academic traditions: a faculty group warned that "business will become the sole voice of the university."[3] During the heart of the disruption, students complained about the tuition increase and faculty members who seemed to spend more time writing grants than teaching; however, they also praised the "top notch personnel" and the "wide

Figure 35. Aware of the importance of rituals, first-year students of the class of 2000 entering a new institution, now called MCP◊Hahnemann School of Medicine of Allegheny University of the Health Sciences, take part in a new white-coat ceremony. *MCP◊Hahnemann School of Medicine Alumnae/i Magazine* 44 (fall 1996): 25.

array of hospitals available for clinical experience."[4] But viewed in the long light of history, the controversial decisions made in the 1990s, including the amalgamation, the new structure, and even the new name, appear somehow familiar. Hahnemann has always been engaged in the process of making and remaking itself, of enduring by following alternative paths.

This final chapter will not try to analyze or assess Hahnemann's most recent history. The merger with Allegheny is the subject of a study by the Acadia Institute of Bar Harbor, Maine, an independent research organization that studies issues in health care, medical ethics, and medical education. Instead, this chapter will look at Hahnemann's rediscovery of its past during the 1980s and 1990s and will then, in a reflective overview, examine a Hahnemann tradition that has been continued by Allegheny: the selection and dedications of memorial cornerstones as ways of preserving a moment in the institution's present and presenting a vision of its past. As Hahnemann categorized its achievements and milestones at intervals over the past 150 years it remade its own identity and rethought its place in the local community and in the national arena. For Hahnemann dedicating cornerstones offered an opportunity to express pride in past achievements but also awareness of its position as an institution slightly on the fringe of Philadelphia medicine, treading an alternative path that forced its supporters to define stridently yet carefully Hahnemann's special place.

The New Prestige of the Past

In 1979, for the first time, a Hahnemann archive was formally organized, headed by Barbara Williams, a librarian who had come to Hahnemann in 1958 under the library's director, Lucy Cooke, who had long tried to preserve the history of the institution. Williams tracked down, she later recalled, "the people and stuff I wanted from everywhere—administration, hospital, students, organizations, departments, individuals." She encouraged departments to deposit their materials in the archives and "talked history with everyone."[5] She was able to avoid the more controversial issue of Hahnemann's unorthodox past by initially concentrating on the postwar period and the important work of researchers brought to Hahnemann by Deans Charles Brown and Charles Cameron.

By the mid-1980s, however, Hahnemann administrators became more comfortable exploring the institution's homeopathic past, in part because so many Hahnemann executives, professors, and staff were now outsiders with no memories of the stigma of a homeopathic diploma or the 1940s probation period. President William Likoff, for example, was replaced in 1983 by Bertram Brown, a psychiatrist-administrator who had headed the National Institute for Mental Health for several years, and in 1987 by Iqbal Paroo, a professional hospital administrator and financial troubleshooter who had been brought to Hahnemann by Brown in 1984. There was also an increasing interest in homeopathy (along with other alternative medical systems) among both the lay public and academics. Book collectors, especially among physicians, began to seek out obscure homeopathic documents. Medical historians and sociologists in the 1970s had begun taking unorthodox medical groups seriously, and by 1980 William Rothstein, Martin Kaufman, and Harris Coulter had written major studies examining nineteenth-century American homeopathy. Philadelphia was no longer a center for active homeopathic teaching or practice: Boericke's pharmaceutical firm moved to California, and in 1986 the Homeopathic Medical Society of the County of Philadelphia, which had renamed itself the Philadelphia Hahnemann Alumni Society in 1948, disbanded and left its funds as an endowment to Hahnemann's archives.

The extensive collection of biographies, newspaper clippings, letters, and other documents relating to the history of Hahnemann and of American homeopathy left by Hahnemann's 1890s historian, Thomas Lindsley Bradford, began to appear intriguing and important rather than embarrassing. The almost two hundred volumes of the writings of sixteenth-century physician and alchemist Paracelsus that had been part of Constantine Hering's library were now recognized as the second largest such collection in North America. Retired homeopathic alumni and the widows of alumni found a sympathetic ear when they offered to donate to the institution letters and yearbooks. The development office chose the "Constantine Hering Society" as the name of the group of its most significant donors (those who contributed $10,000 or more), and the "Samuel Hahnemann Society" for those who contributed from $5,000 to $9,999.[6] The 1980 student yearbook included an article entitled "Homeopathic Medicine Revisited" by "Samuel Hahnemann, M.D."[7] In 1987 when Walter Hering's original building for his Globe Ticket Company, the 1900 Hering Building, was about to be demolished as part of the building of Philadelphia's Convention Center, Hahnemann rescued the large terra-cotta bust of Constantine Hering that had adorned the building. The rescue and restoration of the piece designed by German sculptor A.M.J. Mueller, who had designed other works of public art in Philadelphia's Fairmount Park, was announced proudly in the internal newsletter under the headline "Symbol of HU's Heritage Saved."[8] And in the mid-1980s Hahnemann's president Bertram Brown even briefly explored the possibility of setting up a homeopathic research program.[9]

One dramatic sign of the new value placed on Hahnemann's early history was a historical symposium organized by Barbara Williams, Ned Heindel of Lehigh University, and Henry Williams, a leading American homeopath. Commemorating the 150th anniversary of the Allentown Academy, the day-long symposium, held on September 21, 1985, was sponsored by Hahnemann, Lehigh University, the Homeopathic Medical Society of Pennsylvania, the National Center for Homeopathy, the historical societies of Lehigh and Northhampton Counties, and two local medical societies.[10] Speakers included Charles Cameron, who recalled the play he and fellow Hahnemann students had organized for the academy's centennial in 1935; Julian Winston, a well-known homeopathic advocate and editor of *Homeopathy Today*, the newsletter of the National Center for Homeopathy; and Harris Coulter, a homeopathic activist and historian whose books on homeopathy, developed from his doctoral dissertation at Columbia University, had helped give homeopathy prominence in American medical history. As a graduate student from the University of Pennsylvania, I attended the symposium on that cold and windy day, and although the room was filled mostly by the speakers and sponsors, the participants nonetheless felt that they were helping to bring homeopathy, or at least its nineteenth-century history, out of the closet.

Slices of History in Concrete

Collecting a set of symbolically freighted materials and inserting them into a cornerstone of an important building has been a Hahnemann tradition since 1835, when the founders of the Allentown Academy, Hahnemann's predecessor and the world's first homeopathic school, collected a number of items and put them into the cornerstone of their school building at a ceremony attended by faculty, students, and local supporters. Similar ceremonies occurred at

Hahnemann in 1884, 1927, 1938, 1974, 1979, and 1997. Like other commemorative events, and like a book commissioned to mark the vanishing of a name, these cornerstones were intended to cement connections between the past and present, physically and symbolically encapsulating tradition at junctures that transformed it, while at the same time easing the sometimes harsh transition between old and new. Opening these boxes of memory enables us to glimpse the past as contemporaries wished it to be remembered.

The Allentown founders saw themselves as medical pioneers, practitioners of a new kind of medicine that would revolutionize the treatment of all ills. Samuel Hahnemann, the man who had named and developed homeopathy and was then still practicing and teaching in Paris, was, they believed, a great man. He and his European followers had been unable to establish a formal teaching establishment, but Constantine Hering and the other founders of the academy hoped that their small medical school would be the beginning of an educational revolution in the United States and around the world.

They chose the items in the academy's 1835 cornerstone carefully and kept a list for posterity. The cornerstone included a portrait of Samuel Hahnemann and his major text, the *Organon*; samples of homeopathic medicines; a Philadelphia newspaper discussing the spread of homeopathy beyond Pennsylvania into Ohio; Hering's speech at the opening of the academy, entitled "The Necessity and Usefulness of Homeopathy"; a German-language homeopathic journal; the names of the academy's faculty and stockholders; and the school's constitution, both in German and in English.[11] These materials demonstrate the founders' awareness of the critical role of lay supporters, of the press as a vehicle for affirming identity and displaying pride, and of homeopathy as both a serious medical theory and a practical system based on learned texts and empirical evidence. The box and most of its contents are now part of the Hahnemann Collection of Allegheny's archives.

Half a century later, in the mid-1880s, Hahnemann Medical College built its first new building, a grand edifice on Broad Street, a place in the city that the institution never left. The cornerstone ceremony was held in 1884, and a list of the contents was published in the college's catalog. Once again Samuel Hahnemann's *Organon* was placed in this cornerstone—not his original work but the fifth American edition (1881). Also included were a sketch of Samuel Hahnemann and photographs of the college's ten professors and of Constantine Hering, who had died four years earlier. In a secularizing world where religious gestures were all the more dramatic, the cornerstone included a bible. There were fourteen newspapers, mostly local, but there were a few from New York. As a sign of the college organizers' awareness of the importance of the business world, there was a business card from the building contractors and one from the stone supplier, John Kolb. Most of the other items were self-consciously selected icons of medical professionalism and homeopathic culture. There were copies of homeopathic medical journals from the United States and Britain and also copies of the college's own *Hahnemannian Monthly*; catalogs of the college and a description of the Homeopathic Hospital; floor plans for the new college and the new hospital; a list of the college graduates from 1849 to 1884; and a copy of the transactions of the 1876 World's Homeopathic Convention, which included histories of American homeopathy in every state and country.[12] The contents of this cornerstone indicated that this was an institution confident of its place as an alternative and up-to-date medical school in the city, the region, and the nation.

Forty years later Hahnemann built a new hospital building that opened in 1928. The cornerstone ceremony was held in 1927, and the contents of the cornerstone were a strange combination of pride in Hahnemann's homeopathic heritage and paeans to a future consecrated to efficiency and expertise. What was honored from the nineteenth century was largely formulaic: a silver box holding the first brick removed from the 1886 college building, which was being razed to make room for the hospital; a vial of medicine from Constantine Hering's medicine case; a copy of speeches about Hering; and the program from the cornerstone-laying ceremony in 1884, as well as the 1884 box and all its contents. There was also a bible. Samuel Hahnemann was represented only as the subject of a pamphlet entitled "Samuel Hahnemann, Trail Blazer," which had been written during the 1927 fund-raising campaign for the hospital and was a request for donations in the form of a brief history of the man and the school. Of the texts, courses, professional activities, and teaching of almost eighty years, the organizers included only a signed photograph of the nervous system dissection by Rufus Weaver, who had recently retired as professor of applied anatomy after six decades of teaching at the college, and current catalogs of Hahnemann's medical, premedical, and nursing schools. That documents testifying to Hahnemann's financial health and organizational modernity to Philadelphia's business community took up most of the space is a revealing indicator of the main intended function of the ceremony. There were copies of six Philadelphia papers; a list of subscribers and other fund-raising material related to the greater Hahnemann fund-raising campaign for the hospital; photographs not of the faculty but of the trustees; a hospital annual report; and lists of the boards of trustees of the institution and the lay hospital association. There were also financial reports and two copies of "Diets," a pamphlet written by the dietary department of the hospital, indicating to Philadelphia's business leaders and prospective patients the institution's expertise in accounting as well as in nutrition and comfort.[13]

In the 1970s there were two ceremonies, part of the culmination of a building program initiated in the 1960s by Charles Cameron to consolidate Hahnemann's new identity as an orthodox academic medical center.[14] In 1974

Wharton Shober presided over a ceremony for Hahnemann's new college building, which was attended by local, state, and national politicians as well as faculty, students, and staff. The Shober administration was conscious of this tradition
as a means of gaining publicity and showing faculty, students, and alumni that
the administration—which a year earlier had severed relations with Hahnemann's ninety-year-old Alumni Association—did respect elements of Hahnemann's history. The items selected demonstrate an awareness of the tradition of
dedicating a cornerstone, but betray a sense of commemoration as ornamental
with little appreciation of its deeper meaning. The items in the cornerstone were
described in a press release and were also briefly on display in the building's lobby.
So distant did these organizers feel from Hahnemann's past that they included
a medicine box, supposedly owned by Samuel Hahnemann, as "a symbol of
Hahnemann's early homeopathic origins," although the press release did mention that "homeopathy has not been taught at Hahnemann for at least three
decades." There was also what the press release called "an antique college catalog" from 1892–1893. There were contemporary catalogs from Hahnemann's
schools of medicine and allied health, from the graduate school, and from the
schools of nursing and continuing education, as well as copies of local newspapers from the day of the ceremony, May 24, 1974. Students were represented by
a yearbook, and the faculty by a "gold plated stethoscope" that belonged to
Wilbur Oaks, chair of the Department of Medicine. The faculty was also represented by what the press release called a "small anatomically accurate gold heart"
designed by "an internationally renow[n]ed anatomist and executed by a
Hahnemann medical artist," Marjorie Stodgell, who had worked with Raymond
Truex, chair of anatomy in the 1950s. The heart trinket, which was not in fact
gold, was one of a number that had been handed out at the opening in 1961 of
an exhibit at the Franklin Institute, the walk-through heart designed by
Hahnemann's former cardiology professor George Geckeler. Items like this were
clearly intended to represent Hahnemann's research achievements since World
War II; as the press release put it, "the gold heart represented Hahnemann's pioneer role in cardiovascular research."[15] It was good spectacle and good press,
but showy rather than poignant.

In 1979, after a tumultuous half-dozen years of internal conflict that had
spilled out into the local and national press, Hahnemann laid a final cornerstone in a ceremony for the hospital's new North Tower, for which its previous
president, Wharton Shober, had helped raise the money. More than seventy
items were preserved in the cornerstone, in an effort to please numerous
Hahnemann constituencies. The choice of items consciously mimicked the 1884
and 1928 cornerstones, which had been recently opened and whose contents
were displayed on the day of the North Tower cornerstone ceremony.[16]

Twelve clinical departments had selected items representing their research.

Nephrology had chosen a Ramirez arteriovenous shunt for use in kidney dialysis, developed at Hahnemann in 1966 by Osvaldo Ramirez-Muxo, and a bottle of pills, the 1979 immunosuppressive dose for a kidney transplant patient, representing the department's role in the first kidney transplant operation in the region in 1963. The Cardiovascular Institute provided a pacemaker, a Satinsky clamp developed by Victor Satinsky in 1948, a prosthetic mitral valve representing Charles Bailey's pioneering operation, and a program of the 1978 fundraising ball given by CVI's women's division. The Department of Medical Oncology offered the filter used to process bone marrow for the region's first bone marrow transplant procedure, performed at Hahnemann in 1976. Reflecting recent publicity about acupuncture and the special interest in it by Teruo Matsumoto, professor and chair of the Department of Surgery and author of *Acupuncture and the Physician* (1974) and *Acupuncture and the Patient* (1975), there were acupuncture needles and an acupuncture mannequin. As part of the new president's efforts to mend connections between the alumni and the administration, the cornerstone included a list entitled "Alumni in Prominent Positions," as well as a copy of the March 1957 *Time* magazine issue featuring Charles Bailey on the cover, signed by Bailey. As a sign of Hahnemann's integration in the community there were programs not only of the Hahnemann Hospital Association's ball, but also of a fund-raising concert by the Philadelphia Orchestra and of the Philadelphia Flyers' Wives charity carnival.

William Likoff was represented in this cornerstone both as an administrative leader and as a cardiologist: there was his first presidential report to the board of trustees, a formal portrait, his inauguration program, a Bard-Parker stethoscope of "the kind used by Dr. Likoff," and a videotape of one of Likoff's grand rounds. Reflecting the high political profile Hahnemann had gained during and after the Shober administration, the cornerstone included a tribute from Pennsylvania's governor Milton Shapp and from Philadelphia's mayor Frank L. Rizzo. The copy of the North Tower's $39,500,000 bond prospectus, approved by the Hospital Authority of Philadelphia, was an uneasy reminder of the achievements of the previous administration and the investigations that were then taking place over the legality of the way this money had been raised. Like earlier cornerstones, this cornerstone included business cards from the hospital's architects and the building contractors. Echoing the 1928 hospital's cornerstone there was a hospital diet manual, but the designers also now included a copy of the hospital's room rates and its employee benefits for 1979, patient brochures, and a standard patient ID card, bracelet, and bill. Reflecting the prominent role of Hahnemann Hospital as an educational facility, there were audio and video teaching tapes, including some from Hahnemann's successful continuing education programs and from its television network. There was a tape of the fifty-first Hahnemann Symposium of 1978, the research series started by John Moyer in 1958. The institution's past was represented by the 1927 "Samuel Hahnemann, Trial Blazer" pamphlet, photographs of Hahnemann buildings old and new, the Bailey cover of *Time*, a list of Hahnemann "milestones," lists and photographs of the contents of the 1884 and 1928 cornerstones, and a brochure for the Hahnemann archives. Hahnemann's homeopathic past was emblemized mainly by photographs of nineteenth-century buildings and the names of its 1848 founders.

On May 23, 1997, Allegheny University of the Health Sciences dedicated a park designated for students, which was named after Alfred W. Martinelli, vice chairman of the Penn Central Corporation, who had headed Hahnemann's final board of trustees and was now a member of Allegheny's board of trustees. The ceremonies around the park—a place described in the dedication program as "an oasis for students amid the hustle and bustle of Center City life"[17]—were part of Allegheny's celebration of the forthcoming Hahnemann sesquicentennial. Martinelli Park's dedication included what was now termed a "time capsule." The items selected demonstrated an awareness of the increasingly precarious meaning of Hahnemann's past as well as an effort to create new traditions for a new institution. Reflecting the new historical interest in daily life, the cornerstone tried to capture a moment in the social history of Allegheny. It included student pocket medical guides, a medical school letter of acceptance, brochures and information packets from the medical school and the school of health professions, a class notebook with notes on a lecture on "ethics," a student's financial statement, and Allegheny's 1995–1997 financial aid handbook. There were photographs of the medical school classes of 1996, 1999, and 2000; student yearbooks; and various Allegheny memorabilia such as a pen, a key chain, and a bumper sticker. The momentous transformations of the previous four years were represented by trustee minutes and newspaper clippings dealing with the Hahnemann-AHERF merger. Hahnemann tradition was acknowledged by the creation of a cornerstone, and there were a few assorted references to Hahnemann's past: a 1947 medical school yearbook representing a major donor who had graduated from Hahnemann that year; a pair of dissecting scissors used in medical school by a 1938 graduate; a bronze plaque showing the Hahnemann University seal; and a program for the 1997 Hahnemann University School of Medicine's alumni weekend. New traditions, building on old ones, were shown by a description of Allegheny's 1997 continuing education course; a program of the "first annual" Medical Student Research, Education, and Community Service Day in 1995; a program of the "first annual" White Coat ceremony for first year medical students in 1996; and a prospectus for the new school of public health.

Hahnemann's history also spilled out into the park through freestanding three-sided pillars described as "a series of monuments highlighting the history and heritage of Hahnemann University."[18] Inscriptions on the 1848 pillar mentioned homeopathy, Samuel Hahnemann, Constantine Hering, Jacob Jeanes, and Walter Williamson and claimed (incorrectly) that the Homeopathic Medical College had been "the first medical school in the world to offer a homeopathic M.D. degree." The 1850 pillar referred to the 1869 name change, to the relocation to Broad Street, and to Rufus B. Weaver. The 1900 pillar mentioned the 1928 high-rise hospital, the school of X-ray technology, George Geckeler's heart sound recordings, and the founding of the Cardiovascular Institute. The 1950 pillar described the work of Charles Bailey and the postwar NIH funding that "began the transformation of Hahnemann into a major academic medical center." The 1997 pillar was dedicated to Martinelli, a Hahnemann trustee since 1987, who was "instrumental in effecting the merger between Hahnemann and Allegheny" and was "committed to the history and future of medical education." The 1998 pillar for the sesquicentennial described "a proud heritage shaping a bright new future." The pillars offered a positive and careful historical picture, concentrating on elements of Hahnemann's past that still had currency in the late 1990s, including a confident reference to its association with alternative medicine. Thus, a poster on a student bulletin board in the Klahr Building advertised a talk in February 1997 by a naturopath and a physician to "explain homeopathy and the experience of holistic medical practice," and asked, "Did you know Samuel Hahnemann was the father of Homeopathy? What is this system and how does it work? like cures like—dilutions—interview."

REFLECTING ON her experience of Hahnemann as a student in the 1960s and her subsequent career as a teacher and nephrologist, Patricia Lyons remarked that "Hahnemann has always had an inferiority complex, that it wasn't good enough—and that's been our strength and our weakness."[19] For its first fifty years Hahnemann graduates' pride in their unorthodox heritage gave them an identity as alternative healers but also as medical professionals. After the 1890s the institution became less comfortable with its homeopathic past. During the following fifty years Hahnemann developed yet another alternative identity—one neither proudly homeopathic nor integrated into professional orthodoxy. The medical school continued to teach homeopathic therapeutics and to train practicing physicians and began to accept students whose religious and ethnic backgrounds placed them outside the narrow bounds of American medical education. After the 1940s Hahnemann entered mainstream medicine, pursuing research and pedagogic programs that would enable its graduates to compete effectively. The distinctive Hahnemann traditions and culture that endured through this transformation were often unrecognized and unarticulated; now that being a Hahnemann alumnus no longer meant being recognized as a homeopath, it took some time for a new identity to be established. There remained a constant awareness of being ranked below other medical institutions; of searching for sources of pride without defensiveness; and of the financial and intellectual precariousness of being a multidisciplinary academic health center without the backing of a university or a major foundation. The tensions between contributing to the research enterprise and emphasizing teaching and clinical care were not resolved, nor was the contradiction implicit in Hahnemann Hospital's mission to both care for the city's poor and middle-class and also use them as research and pedagogic subjects. Hahnemann's clinical confidence and its long-standing emphasis on therapy remained strong, as did a commitment to accepting minority students.

For some faculty Hahnemann meant a lifelong home; for others it was a helpful way station on the path to a more prestigious career. For some students it was a place to make lifelong friends and colleagues; for others it was a means to a professional end. Hahnemann's traditions and culture, as Martinelli Park demonstrates, are tenuous but present nevertheless in the institution's new guise. The most recent remaking has forced all alumni, faculty, students, and staff to define what is and was Hahnemann.

Notes

Prologue   Medical Alternatives before 1848

1. Matthew Ramsey, "The Politics of Professional Monopoly in Nineteenth-Century Medicine: The French Model and Its Rivals," in Gerald L. Geison, ed., *Professions and the French State, 1700–1900* (Philadelphia: University of Pennsylvania Press, 1984), 225–305.
2. Charles E. Rosenberg, "The Therapeutic Revolution: Medicine, Meaning, and Social Change in Nineteenth-Century America," in Morris J. Vogel and Charles E. Rosenberg, eds., *The Therapeutic Revolution: Essays in the Social History of American Medicine* (Philadelphia: University of Pennsylvania Press, 1979), 3–25.
3. For a useful collection on the history of American alternative medicine, see Norman Gevitz, ed., *Other Healers: Unorthodox Medicine in America* (Baltimore: Johns Hopkins University Press, 1988).
4. See Alex Berman, "The Thomsonian Movement and Its Relation to American Medicine and Pharmacy," *Bulletin of the History of Medicine* 25 (1951): 405–428, 519–538; and Richard Harrison Shryock, *Medical Licensing in America, 1650–1965* (Baltimore: Johns Hopkins Press, 1967).
5. William G. Rothstein, *American Physicians in the Nineteenth Century: From Sects to Science* (Baltimore: Johns Hopkins University Press, 1972), 143–144.
6. See Jane B. Donegan, *"Hydropathic Highway to Health": Women and Water-Cure in Antebellum America* (Westport, Conn.: Greenwood Press, 1986); and Susan E. Cayleff, *Wash and Be Healed: The Water-Cure Movement and Women's Health* (Philadelphia: Temple University Press, 1987).
7. Alexander Wilder, *History of Medicine. A Brief Outline of Medical History and Sects of Physicians, From the Earliest Historic Period; With an Extended Account of the New Schools of the Healing Art in the Nineteenth Century, And Especially a History of the American Eclectic Practice of Medicine, Never Before Published* (New Sharon, Maine: New England Eclectic Publishing, 1901), 592–596. See also John S. Haller Jr., *Medical Protestants: The Eclectics in American Medicine, 1825–1939* (Carbondale: Southern Illinois University Press, 1994), 70–77; and Frederick C. Waite, "American Sectarian Medical Colleges before the Civil War," *Bulletin of the History of Medicine* 19 (1946): 148–166.
8. In 1851 Mary Grove Nichols (1810–1884) opened the first hydropathic school in

New York City, which lasted only a year and was not chartered to offer a degree; see Donegan, *"Hydropathic Highway,"* 169–174.

9. On the efforts of a group of French-speaking immigrants who brought homeopathy to New Orleans and published *L'Homoion*, one of the earliest homeopathic journals, see Thomas Lindsley Bradford, "Homeopathy in Louisiana," in William Harvey King, ed., *A History of Homeopathy and Its Institutions in America* (New York: Lewis Publishing, 1905), 1:189–190; and John Duffy, ed., *The Rudolph Matas History of Medicine in Louisiana* (Baton Rouge: Louisiana State University Press, 1962), 2:36–37.

10. Bibliographical information on Gram and all other homeopaths mentioned in the first four chapters is drawn from Thomas Lindsley Bradford, *History of The Homeopathic Medical College of Pennsylvania; The Hahnemann Medical College and Hospital of Philadelphia* (Philadelphia: Boericke and Tafel, 1898); Thomas Lindsley Bradford, *Biographical Index of the Graduates of the Homeopathic Medical College of Pennsylvania and the Hahnemann Medical College and Hospital of Philadelphia* (Lancaster: Achey and Gorrecht, 1918); William Harvey King, ed., *A History of Homeopathy and Its Institutions in America*, 4 vols. (New York: Lewis Publishing, 1905); Thomas Lindsley Bradford, "Biographies of Homeopathic Physicians: Collected and arranged in twenty years and now given in present form to the Librarian of Hahnemann Medical College of Philadelphia," 35 vols. (Philadelphia, 1916); and Joseph S. Hepburn, "Medical Annals of the Central High School: With a historical sketch of medical education in Philadelphia," *The Barnwell Bulletin* 18 (1940): 1–94. Note that I have modernized the spelling "homoeopathy" to "homeopathy" throughout.

11. For a history of Allentown, see Joseph C. Guernsey, "Homeopathy in Pennsylvania," in *Transactions of the World's Homeopathic Convention, held at Philadelphia, under the auspices of the American Institute of Homeopathy, at its twenty-ninth Session, June 26th, 27th, 28th, 29th, 30th, July 1st, 1876* (Philadelphia: Sherman and Co., 1880), 773–786; and Thomas Lindsley Bradford, "Homeopathy in Pennsylvania," in King, ed., *History of Homeopathy*, 1:114–118.

12. On homeopathic domestic health guides, see Lamar Riley Murphy, *Enter the Physician: The Transformation of Domestic Medicine, 1760–1860* (Tuscaloosa: University of Alabama Press, 1991), 220–224.

13. Naomi Rogers, "Ärtze, Patienten, und Homöopathie in den USA [Doctors, patients, and homeopathy in the USA]," in Martin Dinges, ed., *Weltgeschichte der Homöopathie: Länder, Schulen, Heilkundige* (Munich: Verlag C. H. Beck, 1996), 269–300; and see King, ed., *History of Homeopathy*, vol. 1 (and Barbara Williams has counted in this source around twenty-five hundred physicians in forty-four states). For the major studies of American homeopathy see Rothstein, *American Physicians*; Martin Kaufman, *Homeopathy in America: The Rise and Fall of a Medical Heresy* (Baltimore: Johns Hopkins Press, 1971); and Harris L. Coulter, *Divided Legacy: A History of the Schism in Medical Thought*, 4 vols. (Washington, D.C.: Wehawken Book Co., 1973–1994).

14. For a brief but useful overview see Lester S. King, *The Medical World of the Eighteenth Century* (Chicago: University of Chicago Press, 1958), 591–592. Born Christian Friedrich Samuel Hahnemann and known by that name during his lifetime, Hahnemann was later referred to as Samuel Christian Friedrich Hahnemann.

15. Joseph Kett, *The Formation of the American Medical Profession: The Role of Institutions, 1780–1860* (New Haven: Yale University Press, 1968), 134.

16. See John Harley Warner, *Against the Spirit of System: The French Impulse in Nineteenth-Century American Medicine* (Princeton: Princeton University Press, 1998).

17. Kett, *Formation of American Medical Profession*, 162.

18. For a useful analysis of historians' views on this question, see John B. Blake, "Homeopathy in American History: A Commentary," *Transactions and Studies of the College of Physicians of Philadelphia* 3 (1981): 83–92.

19. For this argument, see John Harley Warner, "Medical Sectarianism, Therapeutic Conflict, and the Shaping of Orthodox Professional Identity in Antebellum American Medicine," in W. F. Bynum and Roy Porter, eds., *Medical Fringe and Medical Orthodoxy, 1750–1850* (London: Croom Helm, 1987), 234–260.

20. See Robert Jütte, "The Professionalisation of Homeopathy in the Nineteenth Century," in John Woodward and Robert Jütte, eds., *Coping with Sickness: Historical Aspects of Health Care in a European Perspective* (Sheffield: European Association for the History of Medicine and Health Publications, 1995), 47.

21. On orthodox protests at the term, see Kett, *Formation of American Medical Profession*, 161–162.

22. Pitman Dinsmore, "Homeopathy and Its Founder" (M.D. thesis, Homeopathic Medical College of Pennsylvania, 1852), n.p., Hahnemann Collection, Archives and Special Collections, Allegheny University of the Health Sciences, Philadelphia (hereafter cited as Hahnemann Collection).

23. On homeopathic domestic kits, see Ronald L. Numbers, "Do-It-Yourself the Sectarian Way," in Guenter Risse, Ronald L. Numbers, and Judith Walzer Leavitt, eds., *Medicine without Doctors: Home Health Care in American History* (New York: Science History, 1977), 67.

24. Harris L. Coulter, *Science and Ethics in American Medicine, 1800–1914*, vol. 3 of *Divided Legacy* (Washington, D.C.: McGrath Publishing Co., 1973), 3:290–297. In 1872 a homeopath estimated that nineteen out of twenty homeopaths were Republicans; see Coulter, *Science and Ethics*, 3:293.

25. Kaufman, *Homeopathy in America*, 65. See also Walker Rumble, "Homeopathy in the Lehigh Valley, 1881–1920," *Pennsylvania Magazine of History and Biography* 54 (October 1980): 483; Kett, *Formation of American Medical Profession*, 149, 153–154.

26. Kett, *Formation of American Medical Profession*, 141–142.

27. Quoted in Bradford, *History*, 62.

28. See Kett, *Formation of American Medical Profession*, 149–155; and Robert C. Fuller, *Alternative Medicine and American Religious Life* (New York: Oxford University Press, 1989), 24–35, 49–56. For examples of some Swedenborgians who disdained homeopathy, see Wilder, *History of Medicine*, 339.

29. Rothstein, *American Physicians*, 166, 177–179; Kaufman, *Homeopathy in America*, 35–46.

30. See Naomi Rogers, "American Homeopathy Confronts Scientific Medicine," in Guenter B. Risse, Robert Jütte, and John Woodward, eds., *Culture, Knowledge, and Healing: Historical Perspectives of Homeopathic Medicine in Europe and North America* (Sheffield: European Association for the History of Medicine and Health Publications, forthcoming); and Murphy, *Enter the Physician*, 219–220.

31. See Rogers, "Ärtze, Patienten, und Homöopathie," 271.

Chapter 1   *Proudly Homeopathic, 1848–1869*

1. Quoted in Thomas Lindsley Bradford, *History of The Homeopathic Medical College of Pennsylvania; The Hahnemann Medical College and Hospital of Philadelphia* (Philadelphia: Boericke and Tafel, 1898), 4, 5–6. The first three chapters of my book rely heavily on Bradford's *History*, not so much on his interpretation as on his compilation of documents about the institution, many of which are no longer in existence. For other useful histories of Hahnemann, see Pemberton Dudley, "Hahnemann Medical College and Hospital of Philadelphia," in William Harvey King, ed., *A History of Homeopathy and Its Institutions in America* (New York: Lewis Publishing, 1905), 2:37–141; Joseph C. Guernsey, "Homeopathy in Pennsylvania," in *Transactions of the World's Homeopathic Convention, held at Philadelphia, under the auspices of the American Institute of Homeopathy, at its twenty-ninth Session, June 26th, 27th, 28th,*

29th, 30th, July 1st, 1876 (Philadelphia: Sherman and Co., 1880), 2:654–764; and Thomas Lindsley Bradford, "Hahnemann Medical College and Hospital of Philadelphia," in Frederick P. Henry, ed., *Founders' Week Memorial Volume* (Philadelphia: City of Philadelphia, 1909), 291–304.

2. Thomas Lindsley Bradford, "Homeopathy in New York," in King, ed., *History of Homeopathy,* 1:45.

3. Quoted in Bradford, *History,* 18.

4. William G. Rothstein, *American Physicians in the Nineteenth Century: From Sects to Science* (Baltimore: Johns Hopkins University Press, 1972), 162.

5. On patients who frequented both homeopaths and hydropaths in the 1840s, see Lamar Riley Murphy, *Enter the Physician: The Transformation of Domestic Medicine, 1760–1860* (Tuscaloosa: University of Alabama Press, 1991), 188.

6. *Fourteenth Annual Announcement of the Homeopathic Medical College of Pennsylvania: Session of 1861–1862* (Philadelphia: Bryson's Caloric Power Printing Rooms, 1861), 6.

7. Martin Kaufman, *Homeopathy in America: The Rise and Fall of a Medical Heresy* (Baltimore: Johns Hopkins Press, 1971), 35–46.

8. Thomas Lindsley Bradford, "Homeopathy in Pennsylvania," in King, ed., *History of Homeopathy,* 1:40. A copy of Hering's thesis is in the Hahnemann Collection.

9. Harris L. Coulter, *Science and Ethics in American Medicine, 1800–1914,* vol. 3 of *Divided Legacy* (Washington, D.C,: McGrath Publishing Co., 1973), 3:42.

10. C[onstantine] Hering, *The Homeopathist, or Domestic Physician,* 2d American ed., 4th German ed. (Philadelphia: Beilert and Bauersachs, 1844), iii.

11. A. R. Thomas, "Medical Education and Homeopathic Medical Colleges in the United States," in *Transactions of the World's Homeopathic Convention, held at Philadelphia, under the auspices of the American Institute of Homeopathy, at its twenty-ninth Session, June 26th, 27th, 28th, 29th, 30th, July 1st, 1876* (Philadelphia: Sherman and Co., 1880), 2:776. Thomas does not give a reference for this quotation.

12. *Constitution and By-Laws of the Philadelphia Branch of The American Institute of Homeopathy. Together with the Constitution and By-Laws of The American Institute, and an Abstract of The Proceedings of Its Third Annual Session* (Philadelphia: C. L. Rademacher, 1846), 12.

13. Alexander Wilder, *History of Medicine. A Brief Outline of Medical History and Sects of Physicians, From the Earliest Historic Period; With an Extended Account of the New Schools of the Healing Art in the Nineteenth Century, And Especially a History of the American Eclectic Practice of Medicine, Never Before Published* (New Sharon, Maine: New England Eclectic Publishing, 1901), 317.

14. Bradford, *History,* 62.

15. Ibid., 50–52.

16. See advertisement in *The Homeopathic News* [published by Constantine Hering and Adolph Lippe] 1 (1855): 47.

17. Kaufman, *Homeopathy in America,* 53–55.

18. Bradford, *History,* 8–9.

19. *Third Annual Announcement of the Homeopathic Medical College of Pennsylvania: Session of 1850–1851* (Philadelphia: Union Office, 1850), 4–5; Bradford, *History,* 48, 49.

20. *Third Annual Announcement: 1850–1851,* 5.

21. Ibid., 6.

22. *Fourth Annual Announcement of the Homeopathic Medical College of Pennsylvania: Session of 1851–1852* (Philadelphia: C. Sherman, 1851), 6–7.

23. Ibid., 15–16.

24. *Twentieth Annual Announcement of the Homeopathic Medical College of Pennsylvania: Session of 1867–1868* (Philadelphia: Jas. B. Rodgers, 1867), 6.

25. See William G. Rothstein, *American Medical Schools and the Practice of Medicine: A History* (New York: Oxford University Press, 1987), 48–55.

26. Bradford, *History*, 10.
27. Ibid., 257.
28. Arthur M. Eastman, *Life and Reminiscences of Dr. Constantine Hering* (Philadelphia: By the Family, 1917), 12.
29. Naomi Rogers, "Women and Sectarian Medicine," in Rima D. Apple, ed., *Women, Health, and Medicine in America: A Historical Handbook* (New Brunswick, N.J.: Rutgers University Press, 1992), 291; and Regina Morantz Sanchez, *Sympathy and Science: Women Physicians in American Medicine* (New York: Oxford University Press, 1985), 46.
30. [Samuel A. Jones, E. Hahnemann Ehrman, and Jacob Reed Jr.], *Who, Which, What, and Wherefore, or, A Few Facts for the Homeopathic Profession* (Philadelphia: n.p., 1860), 8.
31. Naomi Rogers, "The Proper Place of Homeopathy: Hahnemann Medical College and Hospital in an Age of Scientific Medicine," *Pennsylvania Magazine of History and Biography* 108 (1984): 179–201.
32. Bradford, *History*, 54. Bradford could not find the history drafted by this committee.
33. A. W. Morse, "Medicine as a Science" (M.D. thesis, Homeopathic Medical College of Pennsylvania, 1853), n.p., Hahnemann Collection.
34. David R. Hindman, "Pre-Hahnemannic Homeopathy" (M.D. thesis, Homeopathic Medical College of Pennsylvania, 1857), Hahnemann Collection.
35. *Sixteenth Annual Announcement of the Homeopathic Medical College of Pennsylvania: Session of 1863–1864* (Philadelphia: Brysons Stationery and Printing Rooms, 1863), 5.
36. William Nephew King, "Homeopathy" (M.D. thesis, Homeopathic Medical College of Pennsylvania, 1857), Hahnemann Collection.
37. George W. Dennett, "The Physician and His Duties" (M.D. thesis, Homeopathic Medical College of Pennsylvania, 1857), Hahnemann Collection.
38. Bradford, *History*, 84.
39. Ibid., 139.
40. Samuel Gibbs Tucker, "Homeopathic Surgery" (M.D. thesis, Homeopathic Medical College of Pennsylvania, 1865), n.p., Hahnemann Collection. On homeopaths and surgery see Martin S. Pernick, *A Calculus of Suffering: Pain, Professionalism, and Anesthesia in Nineteenth-Century America* (New York: Columbia University Press, 1985), 30. Pernick argues that homeopaths were closer to the orthodox view than were most other alternative groups; see also Ira M. Rutkow, "William Tod Helmuth and Andrew Jackson Howe: Surgical Sectarianism in Nineteenth-Century America," *Archives of Surgery* 129 (June 1994): 662–668.
41. Tucker, "Homeopathic Surgery."
42. On the public appreciation of surgery and surgeons, see Gert H. Brieger, "Surgery," in Ronald L. Numbers, ed., *The Education of American Physicians: Historical Essays* (Berkeley: University of California Press, 1980), 186–187.
43. *Second Annual Announcement of the Homeopathic Medical College of Pennsylvania: Session of 1849–1850* (Philadelphia: Merrihew and Thompson, 1849), 9; see Bradford, *History*, 41.
44. *Third Annual Announcement: 1850–1851*, 7; see also Bradford, *History*, 51; *Fourth Annual Announcement: 1851–1852*, 9.
45. *Sixteenth Annual Announcement: 1863–1864*, 5–6.
46. *Third Annual Announcement: 1850–1851*, 7.
47. After 1861 no student from the deep South attended the college until 1869, and between 1862 and 1865 there were no students from the Confederate states.
48. Cited in Bradford, *History*, 137.
49. Harold J. Abrahams, *Extinct Medical Schools of Nineteenth-Century Philadelphia* (Philadelphia: University of Pennsylvania Press, 1966), 179–181.

50. *Twentieth Annual Announcement: 1867–1868*, 6.
51. Brieger, "Surgery," 189.
52. Before 1860, medical jurisprudence had been combined with other chairs, including botany.
53. In 1894, the chair was held by Charles Platt (1869–1928), who had a Ph.D. in chemistry; had taken courses at Johns Hopkins University, at the University of Edinburgh, and at the Sorbonne and the École de Médecine in Paris; and had worked at Thomas Edison's laboratory.
54. Bradford, *History*, 26–29.
55. *Third Annual Announcement: 1850–1851*, 8.
56. This neighborhood had a number of small private medical schools. The Medical Department of Pennsylvania College, founded in 1840 and taken over in 1859 by the Philadelphia College of Medicine, was on Filbert and Seventh. At Eleventh and Locust was the Franklin Medical College (1847–1852), formerly the Philadelphia School of Anatomy.
57. Bradford, *History*, 31, 34.
58. Ibid., 34–38.
59. His collection of homeopathic materials, especially the thirty-five volumes of scrapbooks of biographical information about American homeopaths, remains one of the richest archives of American homeopathic history anywhere. These materials are held in the Hahnemann Collection, Allegheny University of the Health Sciences.
60. Rothstein, *American Medical Schools*, 50–51.
61. In 1845 Charles Julius Hempel (1811–1879), a German immigrant who later briefly taught materia medica at the college and became a translator of German homeopathic works, was studying orthodox medicine at New York University and practicing as a homeopath; see Murphy, *Enter the Physician*, 188.
62. Bradford, *History*, 37; and see *Third Annual Announcement: 1850–1851*, 8.
63. *Fourth Annual Announcement: 1851–1852*, 9; see also *Fifth Annual Announcement of the Homeopathic Medical College of Pennsylvania: Session of 1852–1853* (Philadelphia: C. Sherman, 1852), 9.
64. Harrison O. Apthorp, "Scientific Lecturing" (M.D. thesis, Homeopathic Medical College of Pennsylvania, 1856), Hahnemann Collection.
65. Kaufman, *Homeopathy in America*, 65–67.
66. *Twenty-first Annual Announcement of the Homeopathic Medical College of Pennsylvania: Session of 1868–1869* (Philadelphia: Jas. B. Rodgers, 1868), 12.
67. *Second Annual Announcement: 1849–1850*, 11, 10.
68. Ibid., 9–10; *Fourth Annual Announcement: 1851–1852*, 11.
69. *Second Annual Announcement: 1849–1850*, 12.
70. Ibid., 10.
71. I. T. Talbot, "The Alumni—Present," *Medical Institute* 1 (October 1886): 88.
72. *Fifth Annual Announcement: 1852–1853*, 10; *Fourteenth Annual Announcement: 1861–1862*, 7.
73. In an unusually reflective moment, Bradford remembered "that dingy room in the basement of the old College, where students were allowed to prescribe for the sick. The table, the stove, the benches" (Bradford, *History*, 578).
74. Ibid., 34. After the school opened a separate hospital in 1852, the dispensary was moved to the top floor next to the dissecting rooms.
75. Charles E. Rosenberg, "Social Class and Medical Care in Nineteenth Century America: The Rise and Fall of the Dispensary," *Journal of the History of Medicine* 29 (1974): 32–54; and see Rosenberg, *The Care of Strangers: The Rise of America's Hospital System* (New York: Basic Books, 1987). The first in the country to build a teaching hospital was the University of Michigan in 1869.
76. Bradford, *History*, 577, 575.

77. *Fourth Annual Announcement: 1851–1852*, 11.
78. Students, the catalog claimed, "will be admitted on certain terms, to witness Clinical practice in this Institution"; see *Fifth Annual Announcement: 1852–1853*, 10; and Bradford, *History*, 405.
79. *Fifth Annual Announcement: 1852–1853*, 17, 10; Bradford, *History*, 405–406.
80. See brief histories by A. R. Thomas and Charles Mohr in the 1880s, cited in Bradford, *History*, 406–407.
81. Ibid., 407–411. Their failure to gain government support came despite efforts to circumvent the power of the regular Army Medical Corps and an 1862 act that allowed the president to make appointments without approval; see Kaufman, *Homeopathy in America*, 68–72.
82. Bradford, *History*, 408–413; and see Thomas Lindsley Bradford, *Biographical Index of the Graduates of the Homeopathic Medical College of Pennsylvania and the Hahnemann Medical College and Hospital of Philadelphia* (Lancaster: Achey and Gorrecht, 1918), xv.
83. *Third Annual Announcement: 1850–1851*, 8, 11; *[Twenty-first] Annual Announcement and Catalog of The Hahnemann Medical College of Philadelphia: Session of 1868–1869* (Philadelphia: King and Baird, 1868), 8. Surgical operations "will be performed in the presence of the class, either upon the living or recent subject" (*Fourteenth Annual Announcement: 1861–1862*, 7).
84. Bradford, *History*, 137–138. In 1860 it cost the same amount, fifteen dollars, to repair a skeleton as it did to buy a dissecting body (Bradford, *History*, 84). "An Act for the Promotion of Medical Science, and to Prevent the Traffic in Human Bodies," passed on March 18, 1867, applied only to Philadelphia and Allegheny counties; see Francis R. Packard, *History of Medicine in the United States* (New York: Paul B. Hoeber, 1931), 2:784–785.
85. Bradford, *History*, 35.
86. *Fifth Annual Announcement: 1852–1853*, 9.
87. Ibid.
88. Indeed one of the college's first research treasures was Alvan Small's presentation of a double fetus. The college trustees paid to have a wax model of the fetus made, and the fetus was reported in a local homeopathic journal (Bradford, *History*, 597–598).
89. Bradford, *History*, 599, see also 142, 148.
90. Ibid., 189.
91. Ibid., 599. This mannequin was purchased by the college from faculty member Arrowsmith in 1868 for $342.
92. Ibid., 38.
93. Ibid., 156–157.
94. Ibid., 11–12, 19–22, 26.
95. *Third Annual Announcement: 1850–1851*, 12.
96. *Fourteenth Annual Announcement: 1861–1862*, 5.
97. Minutes, Faculty of the Homeopathic Medical College of Pennsylvania, November 24, 1854, Hahnemann Collection. See also Bradford, *History*, 67, quoting from a faculty report that no longer exists.
98. Bradford, *History*, 67–68.
99. Ibid.
100. Amy R. Stiles to T. L. Bradford, May 23, 1895, Humphreys File, Bradford Scrapbook, Hahnemann Collection.
101. See, for example, John B. Blake, "From Buchan to Fishbein: The Literature of Domestic Medicine," and Ronald L. Numbers, "Do-It-Yourself the Sectarian Way," in Guenter B. Risse, Ronald L. Numbers, and Judith Walzer Leavitt, eds., *Medicine without Doctors: Home Health Care in American History* (New York: Science History, 1977), 11–30, and 49–72.

102. "On the Social Position of Medicine," *North American Journal of Homeopathy* 3 (1853), quoted in Kristin M. Mitchell, "'Her Preference Was to Heal': Women's Choice of Homeopathic Medicine in the Nineteenth-Century United States" (B.A. thesis, History Department, Yale University, 1989), 16.

103. Bradford, *History*, 69.

104. In 1866, for example, the faculty secretary was told by one group of faculty members to sell all of the allopathic medical journals in the library, but Thomas Lindsley Bradford assured the readers of his history in the 1890s that this did not happen; see Bradford, *History*, 107.

105. *Seventeenth Annual Announcement of the Homeopathic Medical College of Pennsylvania: Session of 1864–1865* (C. Sherman, Son and Co., 1864), 5.

106. Bradford, *History*, 108 ff.

107. See Rogers, "The Proper Place of Homeopathy," 182–183.

108. *Third Annual Announcement: 1850–1851*, 10, 7.

109. Tucker, "Homeopathic Surgery," n.p.

110. Bradford, *History*, 118.

111. Ibid., 95.

112. Ibid., 142.

113. *[Twenty-first] Annual Announcement (Hahnemann): 1868–1869*, 6.

114. Bradford, *History*, 138.

115. *[Twenty-first] Annual Announcement (Hahnemann): 1868–1869*, 5.

116. Bradford, *History*, 137.

117. *[Twenty-first] Annual Announcement (Hahnemann): 1868–1869*, 9, 16.

118. Bradford, *History*, 137.

119. *Fourteenth Annual Announcement: 1861–1862*, 6.

120. Bradford, *History*, 116, 118.

121. *Twentieth Annual Announcement: 1867–1868*, 7.

122. *Twenty-first Annual Announcement (Homeopathic): 1868–1869*, 5–6.

123. *Third Annual Announcement: 1850–1851*, 6.

124. Morse, "Medicine as a Science."

125. Dennett, "The Physician and His Duties."

126. Bradford, *History*, 94.

Chapter 2   *Becoming a Homeopathic Leader, 1869–1898*

1. Quoted in Thomas Lindsley Bradford, *History of The Homeopathic Medical College of Pennsylvania; The Hahnemann Medical College and Hospital of Philadelphia* (Philadelphia: Boericke and Tafel, 1989), 154.

2. Quoted in Bradford, *History*, 155, 156.

3. *The [22nd] Annual Announcement and Catalog of The Hahnemann Medical College of Philadelphia: Session of 1869–1870* (Philadelphia: William P. Kildare, 1859), 5–6.

4. Ibid., 6–7.

5. By 1880, 26.8 percent of medical schools in the United States required three years; see Martin Kaufman, *Homeopathy in America: The Rise and Fall of a Medical Heresy* (Baltimore: Johns Hopkins Press, 1971), 19. The first medical school to experiment with course grading was Lind University in 1859; see Edward C. Atwater, "Internal Medicine," in Ronald L. Numbers, ed., *The Education of American Physicians: Historical Essays* (Berkeley: University of California Press, 1980), 160. See also Frederick C. Waite, "Advent of the Graded Curriculum in American Medical Colleges," *Journal of the Association of American Medical Colleges* 25 (1950): 315–322.

6. Bradford, *History*, 162.

7. Ibid., 298–299.

8. Advertisement in *Homeopathic Recorder* [ca. 1897], in Thomas Lindsley Bradford, "Scrapbook of Newspaper Cuttings, 1896–1906," Hahnemann Collection.

9. See Richard Harrison Shryock, *Medical Licensing in America, 1650–1965* (Baltimore: Johns Hopkins Press, 1967), 48; James H. Cassedy, *Medicine and American Growth, 1800–1860* (Madison: University of Wisconsin Press, 1986), 232 nn. 18, 19; see also Naomi Rogers, "Ärtze, Patienten, und Homöopathie in den USA [Doctors, patients, and homeopathy in the USA]," in Martin Dinges, ed., *Weltgeschichte der Homöopathie: Länder, Schulen, Heilkundige* (Munich: Verlag C. H. Beck, 1996), 281–282.

10. See John H. Ellis, *Yellow Fever and Public Health in the New South* (Lexington: University of Kentucky Press, 1992), 73, 193 n. 53.

11. Bradford, *History*, 414–415.

12. Ibid., 419.

13. Ibid.

14. Ibid., 420.

15. Ibid., 422.

16. Ibid., 420.

17. Ibid., 422.

18. Ibid., 423–424, 417–418.

19. Ibid., 431.

20. Ibid., 423

21. See Naomi Rogers, "Women and Sectarian Medicine," in Rima D. Apple, ed., *Women, Health, and Medicine in America: A Historical Handbook* (New Brunswick, N.J.: Rutgers University Press, 1992), 284–286; and Regina Morantz-Sanchez, *Sympathy and Science: Women Physicians in American Medicine* (New York: Oxford University Press, 1985), 65–70; and see Leonard Paul Wershub, *One Hundred Years of Medical Progress: A History of the New York Medical College, Flower and Fifth Avenue Hospitals* (Springfield, Ill.: Charles C. Thomas, 1967), 148–154.

22. J. Thomas Scharf and Thompson Wescott, *History of Philadelphia, 1609–1884* (Philadelphia: L. H. Everts and Co., 1884), 1:1637.

23. Mercy B. Jackson, "A Plea: For the Admission of Women to the Medical College and Institute of America," *Hahnemannian Monthly* 3 (1867): 21–25.

24. Samuel Hahnemann to Dear Friend [1841], reprinted in Thomas Lindsley Bradford, *The Life and Letters of Samuel Hahnemann* (Philadelphia: Boericke and Tafel, 1895), 412 and 468–472.

25. Bradford, *History*, 183.

26. Ibid., 183–184. On a homeopathic school that changed its mind about admitting women, see William Barlow and David O. Powell, "Homeopathy and Sexual Equality: The Controversy at Cincinnati's Pulte Medical College, 1873–1879," in Judith Walzer Leavitt, ed., *Women and Health in America: Historical Readings* (Madison: University of Wisconsin Press, 1984), 422–428.

27. See A. R. Thomas to Drs Sartain, Branson & others of the Women's Medical Club of Philadelphia, September 1, 1886, Harriet Judd Sartain Papers, Historical Society of Pennsylvania, Philadelphia; and see also Bradford, *History*, 272.

28. [Anon.], *Philadelphia and Popular Philadelphians* (Philadelphia: The North American, 1891), 276–277; Scharf and Wescott, *History of Philadelphia*, 1:1637. See also Kirsten Swinth, "Emily Sartain and Harriet Judd Sartain, M.D.: Female Influence and a Community of Women Professionals," unpublished paper, 1997, American Studies Department, George Washington University, Washington, D.C.

29. A. R. Thomas to Drs Sartain, Branson & others of the Women's Medical Club of Philadelphia, September 1, 1886; Bradford, *History*, 184.

30. See A. R. Thomas, "A New Preparation of the Nervous System," *Hahnemannian*

Monthly 24 (1889): 65–68; William Weed Van Baun, "The Golden Jubilee of Rufus Benjamin Weaver, A.M., M.D., Sc.D., Master Anatomist," *Hahnemannian Monthly* 50 (1915): 401–413.

31. Charles E. Rosenberg, *The Care of Strangers: The Rise of America's Hospital System* (New York: Basic Books, 1987), 201–209.

32. John Harley Warner, *Against the Spirit of System: The French Impulse in Nineteenth-Century American Medicine* (Princeton: Princeton University Press, 1998).

33. Kaufman, *Homeopathy in America*, 41–43.

34. *Twenty-first Annual Announcement of the Homeopathic Medical College of Pennsylvania: Session of 1868–1869* (Philadelphia: Jas. B. Rodgers, 1868), 9.

35. Bushrod Washington James, *Echoes of Battle* (Philadelphia: Henry T. Coates and Co., 1895), 101–102, 103.

36. Ibid., 78.

37. See, for example, the efforts by James Otis Moore to conceal his homeopathic training in order to work as a surgeon in the Civil War; John Harley Warner, *The Therapeutic Perspective: Medical Practice, Knowledge, and Identity in America* (Cambridge: Harvard University Press, 1986), 181.

38. My thinking about the role of travel in medical education has been shaped by the work of John Harley Warner, especially his *Against the Spirit of System*.

39. Charles H. Haeseler, *Across the Atlantic: Letters from France, Switzerland, Germany, Italy, and England* (Philadelphia: T. B. Peterson and Brothers, 1869), 260, 340.

40. *Twenty-first Annual Announcement (Homeopathic): 1868–1869*, 7.

41. Bradford, *History*, 306; see also *Twenty-sixth Annual Announcement and Catalogue of The Hahnemann Medical College of Philadelphia: Session of 1873–1874* (Philadelphia: William P. Kildare, 1873), 7.

42. W. E. Leonard, "Homeopathic Medical Education," *Hahnemannian Monthly* 26 (1891): 293.

43. See Naomi Rogers, "The Proper Place of Homeopathy: Hahnemann Medical College and Hospital in an Age of Scientific Medicine," *Pennsylvania Magazine of History and Biography* 108 (1984): 198–200.

44. Bradford, *History*, 257.

45. Rosenberg, *Care of Strangers*, 203–209.

46. Bradford, *History*, 427, 432. My discussion in the rest of this section draws heavily on Bradford's account; see Bradford, *History*, 227, 433–438, 451–453, 212–220.

47. Joseph C. Guernsey, "Reminiscences of Dr Charles G. Raue," *Homeopathic Recorder* 9 (1896): 530.

48. William R. King (unpublished transcription of speech at the Banquet of the Hahnemann Alumni Association, Hotel Walton, Philadelphia, May 10, 1899), 3–4, Hahnemann Collection.

49. *Medical Institute* 1 (1886): 79.

50. Thomas Creigh Imes, "The Physiognomy of Disease" (M.D. thesis, Hahnemann Medical College of Philadelphia, 1884), Hahnemann Collection.

51. For a history of Philadelphia black hospitals see Vanessa Northington Gamble, *Making a Place for Ourselves: The Black Hospital Movement, 1920–1945* (New York: Oxford University Press, 1995). Gamble makes no explicit mention of homeopathic physicians.

52. See [Obituary], William Edwin Morgan, *Philadelphia Tribune*, July 28, 1938.

53. See Rogers, "A Proper Place," 159; and Bradford, *History*, 279–280.

Part II   The Second Fifty Years

1. The other was the New York Homeopathic Medical College, renamed the New York Medical College in the 1930s. The number of homeopathic schools peaked

in 1900, when there were twenty-two schools (15 percent of all medical schools in the United States); by 1912 there were only twelve, and by 1920, only five. The number of homeopathic graduates also peaked around this time (420 graduates in 1903, 7 percent of the nation's medical graduates) and then dropped to 97 in 1920; see Naomi Rogers, "American Homeopathy Confronts Scientific Medicine," in Guenter B. Risse, Robert Jütte, and John Woodward, eds., *Culture, Knowledge, and Healing: Historical Perspectives of Homeopathic Medicine in Europe and North America* (Sheffield: European Association for the History of Medicine and Health Publications, forthcoming).

Chapter 3   The Turbulent Years: 1898–1928

1. William A. Pearson, "The Hahnemann Medical College of Philadelphia, 1898–1948," *Hahnemannian Monthly* 82 (1947): 445.
2. See for example D[ouglas] S. Kistler, "A Summary of My Twenty-five Years' Experience in the Practice of Medicine," *Hahnemannian Monthly* 53 (1918): 30–31.
3. B. F. Betts, "Valedictory: Address to the Graduating Class of Hahnemann Medical College at the Thirty-ninth Annual Commencement, April 7, 1887," *The Medical Institute* 2 (March 1887): 54–55. For a fuller exposition of these ideas see Naomi Rogers, "American Homeopathy Confronts Scientific Medicine," in Guenter B. Risse, Robert Jütte, and John Woodward, eds., *Culture, Knowledge, and Healing: Historical Perspectives of Homeopathic Medicine in Europe and North America* (Sheffield: European Association for the History of Medicine and Health Publications, forthcoming).
4. On homeopaths in Massachusetts working for a state licensing law, see Samuel L. Baker, "A Strange Case: The Physician Licensure Campaign in Massachusetts in 1880," *Journal of the History of Medicine and Allied Sciences* 40 (1985): 301.
5. J. Stuart Moore, *Chiropractic in America: The History of a Medical Alternative* (Baltimore: Johns Hopkins University Press, 1993), 83. On medical licensing see Richard Harrison Shryock, *Medical Licensing in America, 1650–1965* (Baltimore: Johns Hopkins Press, 1967); and Joseph F. Kett, *The Formation of the American Medical Profession: The Role of Institutions, 1780–1860* (New Haven: Yale University Press, 1968); William G. Rothstein, *American Physicians in the Nineteenth Century: From Sects to Science* (Baltimore: Johns Hopkins University Press, 1972); and Martin Kaufman, *Homeopathy in America: The Rise and Fall of a Medical Heresy* (Baltimore: Johns Hopkins Press, 1971).
6. Harold F. Alderfer, "Legislative History of Medical Licensure—Pennsylvania," *Pennsylvania Medical Journal* 64 (December 1961): 1605–1609.
7. Editorial, "You Cannot Bridge the Gulf," *Homeopathic Recorder* 26 (1911): 338.
8. Moore, *Chiropractic in America*, 86.
9. Editorial, "Concerning Medical Licensing Boards, and Their Members," *Homeopathic Recorder* 27 (1912): 71, 70; and see Kaufman, *Homeopathy in America*, 162.
10. Kenneth M. Ludmerer, *Learning to Heal: The Development of American Medical Education* (New York: Basic Books, 1985), 235.
11. On the medical profession in Philadelphia, see Leo James O'Hara, *An Emerging Profession: Philadelphia Doctors, 1860–1900* (New York: Garland, 1989).
12. Joseph G. Guernsey, "State Board Report," *Hahnemannian Monthly* 41 (1904): 695–699. Between 1894 and 1904, of 435 candidates 10.34 percent failed.
13. Carl C. Fischer, "The Hahnemann Story" (talk delivered at the Hahnemann Club Annual Dinner, Union League, Philadelphia, April 1, 1970), 7.
14. There is an enormous literature on the Flexner report; for a useful overview see Ludmerer, *Learning to Heal*, 166–190.
15. Abraham Flexner, *Report on Medical Education in the United States and Canada: A*

Report to the Carnegie Foundation for the Advancement of Teaching (New York: Carnegie Foundation, 1910), 156, 161.

16. Ibid., 159.
17. Ibid., 160–161.
18. Ibid., 157.
19. Ibid.
20. The homeopathic schools were Hahnemann of San Francisco, Hahnemann and Hering both of Chicago, homeopathic departments at the University of Iowa and the University of Michigan, Southwestern Homeopathic (Louisville), Boston University, Detroit Homeopathic, Kansas City Hahnemann, New York Medical College and Hospital for Women, New York Homeopathic, Pulte (Cincinnati), Cleveland Homeopathic, Atlantic Medical (Baltimore), and Philadelphia's Hahnemann. Two, both in the Midwest, were state universities, and one, Boston, was a municipal university; all three of these were established in the 1870s (Boston 1873, Michigan 1875, and Iowa 1877). Twelve were private medical colleges. Of the fifteen schools, four were in the East, two were in the South (Baltimore and Louisville), eight were in the Midwest, and one was in the West (San Francisco). Of the fifteen, four were founded before the Civil War (the two schools in New York, the Philadelphia school, and the Hahnemann Medical College of Chicago), five were established in the 1870s, and the remaining six, during the mid-1880s.
21. Flexner, *Report*, 158, 161.
22. Ibid., 161–162.
23. See Norman Gevitz, *The D.O.'s: Osteopathic Medicine in America* (Baltimore: Johns Hopkins University Press, 1982); see also Norman Gevitz, ed., *Other Healers: Unorthodox Medicine in America* (Baltimore: Johns Hopkins University Press, 1988).
24. See, for example, Martin Kaufman, "Homeopathy in America: The Rise and Fall and Persistence of a Medical Heresy," in Norman Gevitz, ed., *Other Healers: Unorthodox Medicine in America* (Baltimore: Johns Hopkins University Press, 1988), 99–123; Norman Gevitz, "The Fate of Sectarian Medical Education," in Barbara Barzansky and Norman Gevitz, eds., *Beyond Flexner: Medical Education in the Twentieth Century* (New York: Greenwood Press, 1992), 83–97; W. H. Roberts, "Orthodoxy vs. Homeopathy: Ironic Developments following the Flexner Report at the Ohio State University," *Bulletin of the History of Medicine* 60 (1986): 73–87; and Stow Persons, "The Decline of Homeopathy: The University of Iowa, 1876–1919," *Bulletin of the History of Medicine* 65 (1991): 74–87. And on the continuation of Temple University's medical school, an orthodox school distinct in other ways from the Flexner model, see Janet A. Tighe, *"A Key of Gold": Science, Money, and the Public Good in an American Medical School* (forthcoming).
25. William Van Lennep, "Report of the Dean of the Hahnemann Medical College and Hospital of Philadelphia [1911–1912]," *Hahnemannian Monthly* 47 (1912): 533. "We have changed our entire curriculum to conform with that of the most advanced medical schools in the country" (540).
26. William A. Pearson, "Report of the Dean of the Hahnemann Medical College of Philadelphia for the Year 1917 and 1918," *Hahnemannian Monthly* 53 (1918): 402–403.
27. *Sixty-fourth Annual Announcement Hahnemann Medical College and Hospital of Philadelphia: College Department: Session of 1911–1912*, 22; Flexner, *Report*, 160.
28. *Annual Announcement: 1911–1912*, 20, 15; see also William Van Lennep, "Dean's Report [1910–1911]," *Hahnemannian Monthly* 46 (1911): 465–466.
29. Van Lennep, "Report of the Dean [1911–1912]," 533. William A. Pearson, "History of the Hahnemann Medical College, 1848–1948," *Hahnemannian Monthly* 83 (1948): 51; and see also William A. Pearson, "History of the Hahnemann Medical College, 1898 to 1948," *Hahnemannian Monthly* 83 (1948): 123.

30. *Annual Announcement: 1911–1912*, 15, 20–23. On the use of "laboratory" as a weapon in the competitive medical marketplace of 1910, see Flexner's scathing comments on Eclectic schools: "They talk of laboratories, not because they appreciate their place of significance, but because it pays them to defer thus far to the spirit of the times" (*Report*, 163).

31. Van Lennep, "Dean's Report [1910–1911]," 465, 466. In spite of the funding of the Hering Laboratory, by 1931 senior students working at the dispensary were taught to make only "some of the simple diagnostic tests, such as the von Pirquet, Mantoux and the allergic skin tests" and for the rest were "permitted to order the indicated laboratory work" (Carl V. Vischer, "Student Instruction in the Medical Out-Patient Department of Hahnemann Hospital, Philadelphia," *Hahnemannian Monthly* 66 [1931]: 662).

32. Van Lennep, "Report of the Dean [1911–1912]," 535.

33. [William Pearson], "The Annual Report of the Dean of Hahnemann Medical College, Philadelphia, for the Year 1914–1915," *Hahnemannian Monthly* 50 (1915): 532.

34. This paragraph is based on readings of the catalogs for 1910–1911 and 1911–1912 from these four other schools.

35. *Annual Announcement: 1911–1912*, 16–18, 43. William Van Lennep, "Report of the Dean of Hahnemann Medical College and Hospital of Pennsylvania [1913–1914]," *Hahnemannian Monthly* 49 (1914): 445. The requirement for two confinements was typical for Philadelphia schools, except for the Woman's Medical College, which demanded ten.

36. *Annual Announcement: 1911–1912*, 19. All the schools' catalogs mention moral behavior.

37. Ibid., 54.

38. [William Pearson], "Annual Report of the Dean, 1914–1915," 532.

39. Flexner himself recognized the financial problem by pointing out that of the homeopathic schools, apart from the two state universities and the New York schools, "all the others are dependent on tuition. Their outlook for high entrance standards or improved teaching is, therefore, distinctly unpromising. Only a few command tuition fees enough to do anything at all: the Chicago Hahnemann, Boston University, and the Philadelphia Hahnemann, with annual fees ranging between $12,000 and $18,000" (*Report*, 161). Of the Eclectic schools, he commented: "The utter hopelessness of the future of these schools is apparent on a glance at their financial condition. All are dependent on fees" (*Report*, 163).

40. By 1911, Hahnemann had seven faculty members on salary; see Van Lennep, "Report of the Dean [1911–1912]," 533. The faculty are "poorly paid and all made personal sacrifices to conform with requirements" (Pearson, "History of the Hahnemann Medical College, 1898 to 1948," *Hahnemannian Monthly* 83 [1948]: 123).

41. Minutes, Faculty Meeting, January 19, 1920, Hahnemann Collection. The minutes for all of the Hahnemann bodies cited hereafter are contained in the Hahnemann Collection, unless otherwise noted.

42. In 1911 Frederick Gates, chair of the board of trustees of Rockefeller's General Education Board, had sent Rockefeller "five essays in which he derided homeopathic doctrines and praised the merits of scientific medicine" ("Notes on Homeopathy," Gates Papers, cited in Ludmerer, *Learning to Heal*, 202, 320 n. 55). On Gates's effort to deflect Rockefeller's desire to place homeopathy on equal footing with regular medicine, see E. Richard Brown, *Rockefeller Medicine Men: Medicine and Capitalism in America* (Berkeley: University of California Press, 1979), 105, 109–111.

43. Pearson, "History of the Hahnemann Medical College, 1898 to 1948," *Hahnemannian Monthly* 83 (1948): 123; see also Dean F. Smiley, "History of the Association of American Medical Colleges, 1876–1956," *Journal of Medical Education* 32 (July 1957): 512–525.

44. Thomas Lindsley Bradford, "List of the Homeopathic Magazines published in the United States and in Foreign Countries, from 1825 to the present time," unpublished manuscript, 1918, Hahnemann Collection. I would like to thank Barbara Williams for her research on this point.

45. Van Lennep, "Dean's Report [1910–1911]," 469.

46. On antivivisectionists in the 1910s and 1920s see Susan E. Lederer, *Subjected to Science: Human Experimentation in America before the Second World War* (Baltimore: Johns Hopkins University Press, 1995), 101–125.

47. Minutes, Faculty Meeting, November 6, 1914.

48. Minutes, Special Faculty Meeting, September 22, 1913; Minutes, Faculty Meeting, July 14, 1914.

49. Minutes, Faculty Meeting, June 11, 1915.

50. [Editorial], "Drugless Healers in the Army Medical Department," *Hahnemannian Monthly* 53 (1918): 285–286.

51. G. H. W[ells], "Medical Education and the War," *Hahnemannian Monthly* 53 (1918): 298–299.

52. "The demand for homeopathic physicians is so great that it is imperative that we increase the number of our students. Never were there better opportunities for homeopathic physicians than now"; see William Pearson, "The Annual Report of the Dean of the Hahnemann Medical College, Philadelphia, for [the] Year 1915–1916," *Hahnemannian Monthly* 51 (1916): 402.

53. Kaufman, *Homeopathy in America*, 153; and see Frederick M. Dearborn, ed., *American Homeopathy in the World War* (n.p.: American Institute of Homeopathy, 1923).

54. Pearson, "History of the Hahnemann Medical College, 1898 to 1948," *Hahnemannian Monthly* 83 (1948): 266; William A. Pearson, "Report of the Dean of the Hahnemann Medical College for the Year 1916–1917," *Hahnemannian Monthly* 52 (1917): 432. The other member was Charles E. Kalke, president of the Illinois Homeopathic Medical Association and dean of Chicago's Hahnemann Medical College.

55. Pearson, "Report of the Dean, 1917 and 1918," 402; and see Dearborn, ed., *American Homeopathy in the World War*.

56. William A. Pearson, "Epidemic Influenza Treated by Homeopathic Physicians," *Journal of the American Institute of Homeopathy* 12 (1919): 11–13.

57. Pearson, "History of the Hahnemann Medical College, 1898 to 1948," *Hahnemannian Monthly* 83 (1948): 128; and see M. W. Van Denburg, "Gelsemium Sempervirens, Ait.," *Hahnemannian Monthly* 35 (1900): 145–151. There is unfortunately no historical study of the impact of homeopathic therapy and the influenza pandemic or of the reason that homeopathy's successes made so little difference in its declining national reputation; but for a brief discussion of osteopaths and the pandemic, see Gevitz, *The D.O.'s*, 72. A Hahnemann student later recalled that when she went to the Student Health Service in the 1940s with the flu she was given gelsemium (Beatrice Troyan, telephone interview by Naomi Rogers, August 26, 1997).

58. See Charles O. Jackson, *Food and Drug Legislation in the New Deal* (Princeton: Princeton University Press, 1970), 15–16. My thanks to Suzanne White Junod for pointing this out.

59. Pearson, "History of the Hahnemann Medical College, 1898 to 1948," *Hahnemannian Monthly* 83 (1948): 123.

60. Boone was "reputed to have won more decorations, while serving with the Marines, than any other medical officer"; see Carl C. Fischer, "The Hahnemann Story" (talk delivered at the Hahnemann Club Annual Dinner, Union League, Philadelphia, April 1, 1970), 4.

61. Pearson, "History of the Hahnemann Medical College, 1898 to 1948," *Hahne-*

mannian Monthly 83 (1948): 266; and Warren G. Harding, "Address to the Graduating Class of Hahnemann Medical College of Philadelphia," *Hahnemannian Monthly* 54 (1919): 496–502.

62. *Sixty-second Annual Announcement Hahnemann Medical College and Hospital of Philadelphia: Session of 1909–1910*, 12.
63. *Annual Announcement: 1911–1912*, 15.
64. Hahnemann was Philadelphia's largest, with 350 beds. Children's Homeopathic had 175, and Women's Homeopathic had 135. The only homeopathic hospital larger in the state was the Homeopathic State Hospital in Allentown, with 1,150 beds; see "Business Transactions of the Fifty-Fourth Annual Session of the Homeopathic Medical Society of the State of Pennsylvania Continued, September 18th, 19th, 20th, 1917: Homeopathic Hospitals," *Hahnemannian Monthly* 53 (1918): 149–152.
65. *Medic* 1933, 92.
66. Minutes, Faculty Meeting, December 23, 1918.
67. Minutes, Faculty Meeting, May 23, 1921.
68. Minutes, Faculty Meeting, April 19, 1938.
69. *Medic* 1936, n.p.
70. Higinio Mendoza, "A Misconception," *Medic* 1928, 23. Mendoza, born in 1902, was the son of Agustin Mendoza and while a student was president of the Federation of Filipino Associations in America and of the Filipino Association of Philadelphia. He described himself as a Liberal Christian. According to Fischer, Mendoza's family campaigned for him during his time at Hahnemann and got him elected governor of the Island of Palawan. When the Japanese invaded, he led the resistance on his island and was captured and hung. See Fischer, "Hahnemann Story," 6.
71. *Medic* 1929, 120, 131.
72. B. J. Baute, "The Past, Present and Future of Homeopathy," *Medic* 1929, 49.
73. Ibid.
74. *Medic* 1934, 188.
75. Wyrth Post Baker, telephone interview by Naomi Rogers, August 13, 1997.
76. Ibid., 257.
77. "Homeopathy: Historical Glimpses," *Medic* 1930, 12.
78. Kistler, "A Summary," 30.
79. Vischer, "Student Instruction," 663.
80. *Medic* 1936, n.p.
81. Charles S. Cameron, "1935: Remembering the Centennial" (transcript of a speech given at a historical symposium entitled "The Allentown Academy [1835–1843]: 150 Years of Homeopathy in America, September 21, 1985," Allentown Public School Administration Building, Allentown, Pennsylvania), Hahnemann Collection.
82. William G. Rothstein, *American Physicians in the Nineteenth Century: From Sects to Science* (Baltimore: Johns Hopkins University Press, 1972), 300–301 n. 5.
83. Pearson, "History of the Hahnemann Medical College, 1898 to 1948," *Hahnemannian Monthly* 83 (1948): 125; G. H. W[ells], "Co-education at Hahnemann Medical College," *Hahnemannian Monthly* 53 (1918): 178.
84. Note that a Miss Butler gave four lectures to seniors on social science; Minutes, Faculty Meeting, December 17, 1917.
85. W[ells], "Co-education," 177.
86. Minutes, Faculty Meeting, October 27, 1919; ibid., April 26, 1920. See also Pearson, "Report of the Dean, 1917 and 1918," 404–405.
87. Minutes, Special Faculty Meeting, June 5, 1928.
88. Minutes, Medical Council, May 5, 1938.
89. Quoted in [Barbara Williams], "Thomas Creigh Imes" [April 1988], in "Archiva: Contributions to the Hahnemann University Library Newsletter, 1985–1989," 20.

90. David McBride, *Integrating the City of Medicine: Blacks in Philadelphia Health Care, 1910–1965* (Philadelphia: Temple University Press, 1989), 94.

Chapter 4 Survival through Diversity: The 1920s and 1930s

1. The New York Homeopathic Medical College deserves a comprehensive history, but one has not been written; however, see L. C. Aldrich, "The New York Homeopathic Medical College and Hospital," in William Harvey King, ed., *A History of Homeopathy and Its Institutions* (New York: Lewis Publishing, 1905), 2:259–302; and Leonard Paul Wershub, *One Hundred Years of Medical Progress: A History of the New York Medical College, Flower and Fifth Avenue Hospitals* (Springfield, Ill.: Charles C. Thomas, 1967). Charles Rosenberg once commented that as a graduate student at Columbia University in the early 1960s he was given the opportunity to write this history as a commissioned piece, with the proviso that there be nothing about homeopathy in it (conversation with Naomi Rogers, around 1983).
2. Louis S. Reed, *The Healing Cults* (1932), cited in Ronald L. Numbers, "The Fall and Rise of the American Medical Profession," in Judith Walzer Leavitt and Ronald L. Numbers, eds., *Sickness and Health in America: Readings in the History of Medicine and Public Health* (Madison: University of Wisconsin Press, 1985), 193; Norman Gevitz, *The D.O.'s: Osteopathic Medicine in America* (Baltimore: Johns Hopkins University Press, 1982), 50; J. Stuart Moore, *Chiropractic in America: The History of a Medical Alternative* (Baltimore: Johns Hopkins University Press, 1993), 89–90.
3. For the important point that alternative medical groups did not just vanish in the twentieth century, see Numbers, "Fall and Rise," 191–194.
4. Morris Fishbein, *The Medical Follies: An Analysis of the Foibles of Some Healing Cults, Including Osteopathy, Homeopathy, Chiropractic, and the Electronic Reactions of Abrams, with Essays on The Antivivisectionists, Health Legislation, Physical Culture, Birth Control, and Rejuvenation* (New York: Boni and Liveright, 1925), 36.
5. Fishbein, *Medical Follies*, 37–38, 41.
6. See, for example, D[ouglas] S. Kistler, "A Summary of My Twenty-five Years Experience in the Practice of Medicine," *Hahnemannian Monthly* 53 (1918): 32; and see G. H. W[ells], "Medical Education and the War," *Hahnemannian Monthly* 53 (1918): 299.
7. Annie Riley Hale, *"These Cults:" An Analysis of the Foibles of Dr. Morris Fishbein's "Medical Follies" and an Indictment of Medical Practice in General, with a Non-Partisan Presentation of the Case for the Drugless Schools of Healing, Comprising Essays on Homeopathy, Osteopathy, Chiropractic, The Abrams Method, Vivisection, Physical Culture, Christian Science, Medical Publicity, The Cost of Hospitalization and State Medicine* (New York: National Health Foundation, 1926), 32.
8. Martin Kaufman, "Homeopathy in America: The Rise and Fall and Persistence of a Medical Heresy," in Norman Gevitz, ed., *Other Healers: Unorthodox Medicine in America* (Baltimore: Johns Hopkins University Press, 1988), 113.
9. See *Medic* 1921, 17. Pearson was a "32nd degree Mason," and in 1920 he was president of the American Chemical Society.
10. *Medic* 1933, 92.
11. *Medic* 1921, 17.
12. See, for example, *Medic* 1928, 95; and Carl C. Fischer, "The Hahnemann Story" (talk delivered at the Hahnemann Club Annual Dinner, Union League, Philadelphia, April 1, 1970), 5.
13. Dorothy Ann Harrison, "Picking 'Doctors-to-Be' for Twenty Years Has Made Dean Rare Judge of Men," *Evening Bulletin*, August 7, 1932.
14. *Medic* 1933, 114, 92.
15. "Ernest L. Tustin, City Welfare Head, Victim of Cancer," *Philadelphia Inquirer*, December 19, 1921.

16. Minutes, Board of Trustees College Committee, May 10, 1920.
17. Frederic J. von Rapp, "Address Made by the Chairman of the College Commit[t]ee: At a Meeting of the Faculty of the Hahnemann Medical College on the Evening of October 21, 1935," *Hahnemannian Monthly* 70 (1935): 875.
18. W. A. Pearson, "Dreams Come True," *Hahnemannian Monthly* 73 (1938): 773.
19. Hahnemann listed these seven salaried faculty on a 1913 Application for Membership in the Association of American Medical Colleges, question 17, "List of Salaried Teachers (Full Time)," Hahnemann Collection. For a similar list from an uncited source see Fischer, "Hahnemann Story."
20. Minutes, Board of Trustees College Committee, June 10, 1925, April 19, 1926, May 31, 1928. By 1928 Pearson was paid $4000; Phillips $5000; Sappington $3600; Widman $4000; and Boericke $5000.
21. John Storer, telephone interview by Naomi Rogers, April 18, 1997. See also *Medic* 1944, n.p.: "like some wizened elf, dwelt in that first floor labyrinth marked STUDENTS KEEP OUT (as if they'd wander in of their own accord.) With a wit like a Bard-Parker blade, he cunningly dissected delinquents without benefit of anesthesia, and walking into his lecture late was like tweaking a leopard's nose."
22. *Medic* 1941, 73.
23. Horst Agerty and Charles Cameron, joint interview by Naomi Rogers and Barbara Williams, Philadelphia, November 13, 1996.
24. Eichi Karl Koiwai, telephone interview by Naomi Rogers, August 20, 1997.
25. *Medic* 1928, 105.
26. See, for example, Fischer, "Hahnemann Story," 5.
27. Agerty and Cameron, joint interview; *Medic* 1935, 132; *Medic* 1938, 45; *Medic* 1949, n.p.
28. *Medic* 1929, 130.
29. *Medic* 1928, 112.
30. Storer, interview.
31. Wyrth Post Baker, telephone interview by Naomi Rogers, August 13, 1997.
32. Ibid.
33. Minutes, Board of Trustees Executive Committee, August 11, 1938.
34. *Medic* 1935, n.p.; *Medic* 1936, n.p.
35. Baker, interview.
36. Storer, interview; see also *Medic* 1940, 208, on the mock "Handbook of Dispensary Medicine." Under "G-I Dispensary": "this dispensary is dedicated to the proposition that any patient who doesn't have a rubber tube shoved down his gullet at least once a week is the unhappiest of mortals and probably a nasty Communist to boot."
37. Sidney Zubrow, telephone interview by Naomi Rogers, May 21, 1997.
38. *Medic* 1945, 145: Ashcraft had an extensive private practice and was described as an "able surgeon, and popular, inspiring teacher," and students praised "his pleasing personality, his gentlemanly demeanor and his scholarly attainments."
39. Minutes, Special Faculty Meeting, April 22, 1930. I have not been able to discover what the content of the letters was.
40. See von Rapp, "Address," 870.
41. Minutes, Board of Trustees Executive Committee, July 3, 1940.
42. W. B. Trites, *Paterfamilias* (New York: Cosmopolitan Book Company, 1929), 113–114. All other quotes from this novel will be documented with parenthetical page numbers in the text. On the autobiographical element of the novel, see [review of *Paterfamilias*], *Evening Bulletin*, September 28, 1929.
43. "[W]e homeopaths have to profess a rule that we know is false" (329); compare this statement to comments by Clarence Bartlett, professor of medicine, in 1918: the law of similars "had its limitations. This fact is now recognized by all of us. Individually we have decided differences as to the extent or number of the excep-

tions. Such variations in opinion [call] . . . for tolerance respecting conflicting views while years and experience bring us nearer to unanimity" (Clarence Bartlett, "A Review of Forty-three Years of Medical Education," *Hahnemannian Monthly* 53 [1918]: 498).

44. Minutes, Hahnemann Club, October 10, 1944.
45. *Medic* 1928, 119–120; *Medic* 1929, 142.
46. *Medic* 1928, 119; *Medic* 1929, 142.
47. Bartlett, "A Review," 498.
48. *Medic* 1929, 130.
49. "Fourth Year," *Medic* 1936, n.p.
50. *Medic* 1928, 97.
51. Fischer, "Hahnemann Story," 5.
52. *Medic* 1928, 100; see also Fischer, "Hahnemann Story," 5.
53. *Medic* 1928, 101.
54. Ibid., 96.
55. Ibid., 101.
56. Ibid., 98.
57. The professor, William G. Schmidt, was attacking the charge that his "scholastic controls are puerile and as unbecoming professional students" (William G. Schmidt to Stauffer Oliver, September 10, 1945, Accred. Survey Reports, Box 5, AAMC Archives, Washington, D.C.).
58. Warren Landau, telephone interview by Naomi Rogers, July 31, 1997.
59. Agerty and Cameron, joint interview.
60. Ibid.
61. See, for example, [Charles S. Cameron], "The Class History," *Medic* 1935, 132.
62. Abraham Flexner, *Report on Medical Education in the United States and Canada: A Report to the Carnegie Foundation for the Advancement of Teaching* (New York: Carnegie Foundation, 1910), 295, 158–159. The schools were The Universities of Iowa and Michigan, Detroit Homeopathic, and the two New York schools.
63. Pemberton Dudley, "The Faculty Address to the Alumni Association of Hahnemann College, May 17, 1900," *Hahnemannian Monthly* 35 (1900): 435.
64. Ibid., 434.
65. *Sixty-sixth Annual Announcement Hahnemann Medical College and Hospital of Philadelphia: College Department: Session of 1913–1914*, 27.
66. Minutes, Faculty Executive, July 26, 1912.
67. William A. Pearson, "Report of the Dean of the Hahnemann Medical College of Philadelphia for the Year 1917 and 1918," *Hahnemannian Monthly* 53 (1918): 402. For a description of the curriculum, with its emphasis on chemistry, physics, and biology, see pp. 403–404. See also Frederick B. Wagner Jr., *Thomas Jefferson University: Tradition and Heritage* (Philadelphia: Lea and Febiger, 1989), 793–794.
68. William Pearson, "The Annual Report of the Dean of the Hahnemann Medical College, Philadelphia, for [the] Year 1915–1916," *Hahnemannian Monthly* 51 (1916): 402.
69. See Minutes, Board of Trustees College Committee, June 10, 1925, April 19, 1926, May 31, 1928, May 19, 1929. The amount of surviving information on the budgets in the 1920s is limited.
70. Minutes, Faculty Meeting, May 2, 1913.
71. [William Pearson], "The Annual Report of the Dean of the Hahnemann Medical College, Philadelphia, for the Year 1914–1915," *Hahnemannian Monthly* 50 (1915): 533. The premedical class numbered thirty-nine.
72. Pearson, "Annual Report of the Dean, 1915–1916," 402–403.
73. Agerty and Cameron, joint interview.
74. William Van Lennep, "Dean's Report [1910–1911]," *Hahnemannian Monthly* 46 (1911): 468.

75. Dudley, "Faculty Address," 433.
76. *Medic* 1928, 118; see also Carl Castle Fischer, "As I Remember It: Autobiography," unpublished manuscript, 1981, Hahnemann Collection.
77. Agerty and Cameron, joint interview.
78. *Medic* 1944, 244.
79. *Medic* 1944, 5.
80. Fischer, "As I Remember It," chap. 5, p. 1.
81. Landau, interview.
82. "As Chairman of the College Committee, I have advocated the belief—that the future of Hahnemann Hospital lies—in taking by our institution as large a freshman class as you can possibly accommodate" (von Rapp, "Address," 873).
83. Minutes, Faculty Executive, September 12, 1933.
84. Minutes, Board of Trustees College Committee, December 22, 1936.
85. Zubrow, interview.
86. Zubrow's fiancée, Molly Cohen, who had come for the application interview to assure administrators that she was working and could help repay the loan, asked the committee, "were those your only bad experiences?" Zubrow's application was then supported by his physiology professor, Frank Widman, and he received the loan (Zubrow, interview).
87. Minutes, Medical Council, April 7, 1938.
88. Saul Jarcho, "Medical Education in the United States, 1910–1956," *Journal of Mount Sinai Hospital* 26 (1959): 357; for a brief discussion of discrimination against Jews and Catholics at the University of Michigan, see Horace W. Davenport, *Fifty Years of Medicine at the University of Michigan, 1891–1941* (Ann Arbor: University of Michigan Medical School, 1986), 17–19. And for a footnote on this issue as "one of the truly shameful episodes in the history of American medical education," see Kenneth M. Ludmerer, *Learning to Heal: The Development of American Medical Education* (New York: Basic Books, 1985), 328 n. 54.
89. *Medic* 1921, 28.
90. *Medic* 1928, 120, 45.
91. *Medic* 1921, 61.
92. *Medic* 1933, 127.
93. Zubrow remembers that one Italian (the "first body builder I ever knew") used to lift weights, but the others "put him down as a freak" (Zubrow, interview).
94. Application for Membership in the AAMC.
95. *Medic* 1929, 185.
96. *Medic* 1933, 118.
97. *Medic* 1945, n.p.
98. *Medic* 1928, 58, 67, 84. There are few indications of class background, but Stephen Steinbey (class of 1928), who was born in 1895 in Poland and was nicknamed the Baron, described himself as the son of a "country gentleman." He attended premedical classes at Crane College and then completed three years of medical work at the University of Michigan; see *Medic* 1928, 58.
99. *Medic* 1933, 196. Sohn directed a hospital in Seoul until he retired in 1959, and in Korea he was elected head of the Korean Medical Association; see *Hahnemann Alumni News* (fall 1970): 6.
100. Zubrow, interview.
101. Storer, interview.
102. "Regulations," *Medic* 1936, n.p.
103. "The Curriculum," *Medic* 1935, 78.
104. "Suggestions for Improving the Curriculum," *Medic* 1934, 54.
105. Minutes, Faculty Executive, March 8, 1932.
106. "Suggestions," 54.

107. Fischer, "Hahnemann Story," 7.
108. Herman G. Weiskotten, Alphonse M. Schwitalla, William D. Cutter, and Hamilton H. Anderson, *Medical Education in the United States, 1934–1939* (Chicago: American Medical Association, 1940).
109. Martin Kaufman, *Homeopathy in America: The Rise and Fall of a Medical Heresy* (Baltimore: Johns Hopkins Press, 1971), 177; H. G. Weiskotten and M. W. Ireland, "The Hahnemann Medical College of Philadelphia, Philadelphia, Pennsylvania, January 17, 18, 19, 1935," cited in Victor Johnson and Fred C. Zapffe, "The Hahnemann Medical College and Hospital of Philadelphia, Pennsylvania, April 3–6, 1945," Accred. Survey Reports, Box 5, IM Box 238, AAMC Archives, Washington, D.C., 3.
110. Cited in Johnson and Zapffe, "1945 Report," 3.
111. Cited in ibid., 4.
112. *The Hahnemann Medical College and Hospital of Philadelphia: Announcement for the Eighty-Ninth Annual Session: 1936–1937,* 26.
113. *The Hahnemann Medical College and Hospital of Philadelphia: Announcement for the Eighty-Eighth Annual Session: 1935–1936,* 35; *Announcement: 1936–1937,* 37.
114. *Announcement: 1935–1936,* 26.
115. Ibid., 62–63.
116. *Announcement: 1936–1937,* 65–66.
117. Frederick von Rapp, "A New Department of Pharmacology at Hahnemann," *Hahnemannian Monthly* 71 (1936): 577; von Rapp, "Address," 872.
118. Minutes, Board of Trustees College Committee, December 22, 1936.
119. *Medic* 1937, 58.
120. Minutes, Medical Council, December 14, 1944.
121. Von Rapp, "A New Department of Pharmacology," 577.
122. Minutes, Faculty Executive, October 22, 1934.

Chapter 5   *Turning Points: Hahnemann in the 1940s*

1. Warren Landau, telephone interview by Naomi Rogers, July 31, 1997.
2. Margaret Giannini, telephone interview by Naomi Rogers, August 24, 1997.
3. These examples were gained from the following interviews: Beatrice Troyan, telephone interview by Naomi Rogers, August 26, 1997; Giannini, interview; Seth Fisher, telephone interview by Naomi Rogers, May 5, 1997.
4. Fisher, interview.
5. Giannini, interview; Troyan, interview.
6. *Medic* 1951, n.p.
7. "Hahnemann Going Co-Ed in Fall," *Evening Bulletin,* May 22, 1941.
8. Mary Walsh, *Doctors Wanted: No Women Need Apply: Sexual Barriers in the Medical Profession, 1835–1975* (New Haven: Yale University Press, 1977), 245.
9. Irena Koprowksa, "American Women Health Scientists Today: A Global Perspective" (transcript of a speech given at the First Annual Hahnemann University Lectureship and Recognition Award for Women in Science and Medicine, April 22, 1986, Hahnemann University, Philadelphia, Pennsylvania), Hahnemann Collection.
10. See Adrian, "Female View," and Julie, "a little inconvenience," *Impulse* 1 (October 1971).
11. Fred C. Zapffe to Joseph S. Conwell, June 12, 1945, 1945 Accred. Survey Reports, Box 5, Association of American Medical Colleges Archives, Washington, D.C.; and see J. Conwell to Fred C. Zapffe, June 22, 1945, Accred. Survey Reports, Box 5, AAMC Archives, Washington, D.C. Additional cites of the letters contained in

these survey files will be cited with the name of the sender, the name of the recipient, the date, and AAMC Archives.

12. Stauffer Oliver to Victor Johnson, June 26, 1945, AAMC Archives. See also Victor Johnson to Stauffer Oliver, July 2, 1934, AAMC Archives.
13. In 1943, medical schools at the University of Arkansas and the University of Texas were on public probation; but my reading of the AMA's Council on Medical Education and Hospital's "Educational Data" published in the *Journal of the American Medical Association* from 1944 to 1949 shows no other school listed. However, it is probable that a number of schools were on probation that was not made public. For one example of a medical school placed on "private" probation but listed by the AMA as "acceptable," see Martin Kaufman, *University of Vermont College of Medicine* (Hanover, N. H.: University of Vermont College of Medicine, 1979), 157–168.
14. "Forty-first Annual Presentation of Educational Data by the Council on Medical Education and Hospitals, 1941," *JAMA* 117 (1941): 686–687.
15. "Council on Medical Education and Hospitals," *JAMA* 128 (1945): 603.
16. William Schmidt to Medical Council, August 24, 1945, in minutes, Medical Council, August 24, 1945.
17. Victor Johnson and Fred C. Zapffe, "The Hahnemann Medical College and Hospital of Philadelphia, Pennsylvania, April 3–6, 1945," Accred. Survey Reports, Box 5, IM Box 238, AAMC Archives, Washington, D.C., 8, 9, hereafter referred to as "1945 Report."
18. Oliver to Johnson, June 26, 1945, AAMC Archives.
19. See also "Budget and Finances," in Johnson and Zapffe, "1945 Report," 8; and minutes, Board of Trustees College Committee, January 31, 1947.
20. Johnson to Oliver, July 2, 1945, AAMC Archives.
21. Johnson and Zapffe, "1945 Report," 5–7.
22. Johnson and Zapffe called it an "alarmingly high figure" ("1945 Report," 47).
23. Minutes, Medical Council, June 22, 1943.
24. Ibid.
25. See a reference to this petition in Johnson and Zapffe, "1945 Report," 48–49.
26. Minutes, Faculty Meeting, May 2, 1940; and see Minutes, Faculty Meeting, April 21, 1941.
27. See Johnson and Zapffe, "1945 Report," 48–49.
28. Minutes, Faculty Meeting, October 18, 1943; minutes, Medical Council, June 22, 1943; and see Johnson and Zapffe, "1945 Report," 49–50; and Victor Johnson to Carl C. Fischer, July 6, 1945, AAMC Archives.
29. Minutes, Medical Council, June 22, 1943.
30. Johnson and Zapffe, "1945 Report," 10, 52.
31. Minutes, Faculty Meeting, October 18, 1943; For additional discussion of faculty demands see minutes, Medical Council, March 6, 1945.
32. Schmidt to Medical Council, August 9, 1945, in minutes, Medical Council, August 9, 1945.
33. He had also taught chemistry, physics, engineering, pharmacy, and mathematics at local high schools, at Temple University, and at the Drexel Institute; see Johnson and Zapffe, "1945 Report," 7.
34. Schmidt to Oliver, September 10, 1945, AAMC Archives.
35. Schmidt to Medical Council, August 24, 1945, in minutes, Medical Council, August 24, 1945. He also urged faculty "to refrain from expressing an overly confidential and palsy-walsy attitude toward our students."
36. Schmidt to Oliver, September 10, 1945, AAMC Archives.
37. Editorial, "The Prognosis of a Move," *Hahnemannian Monthly* 80 (1945): 474; and

see Schmidt to Johnson and Zapffe, November 2, 1945, AAMC Archives; Schmidt to Zapffe, October 28, 1945, AAMC Archives.

38. Editorial, "Prognosis of a Move," 474; and see "Homeopaths Fire Dr. W. G. Schmidt," *Evening Bulletin,* January 11, 1946; "Schmidt Fired as Director of Medical Paper," *Philadelphia Record,* January 11, 1946.
39. Minutes, Medical Council, December 21, 1945.
40. Minutes, Medical Council, October 6, 1944.
41. Carl C. Fischer, "The Hahnemann Story" (talk delivered at the Hahnemann Club Annual Dinner, Union League, Philadelphia, April 1, 1970), 8.
42. Minutes, Medical Council, March 6, 1945.
43. Johnson and Zapffe, "1945 Report," 15.
44. Ibid., 15, 16.
45. Schmidt to Oliver, September 10, 1945, AAMC Archives.
46. Minutes, Board of Trustees College Committee, May 16, 1938.
47. Minutes, Medical Council, November 30, 1945.
48. Minutes, Medical Council, August 9, 1945.
49. Minutes, Faculty Meeting, April 30, 1945; and Conwell to Eberhard, April 13, 1944, AAMC Archives.
50. E. Burke Wilford to Medical Council, November 30, 1945, in minutes, Medical Council, November 30, 1945.
51. Carl C. Fischer to Fred Zapffe, August 15, 1945, AAMC Archives; Stauffer Oliver to Fred C. Zapffe, August 23, 1945, AAMC Archives.
52. Fischer, "Hahnemann Story," 8; and see minutes, Medical Council, June 22, 1943.
53. Johnson and Zapffe, "1945 Report," 21. Additional cites to this report will be documented with parenthetical page numbers in the text.
54. Minutes, Special Faculty Meeting, January 4, 1946.
55. See Charles E. Rosenberg, *The Care of Strangers: The Rise of America's Hospital System* (New York: Basic Books, 1987), 190–211; Kenneth M. Ludmerer, *Learning to Heal: The Development of American Medical Education* (New York: Basic Books, 1985), 219–233.
56. *Medic* 1940, 212; *Medic* 1945, 83; Giannini, interview; "Requirements for Promotion," *Medic* 1936, n.p.
57. In 1941 Hahnemann had eighteen departments: anatomy, chemistry, physiology, pathology and bacteriology, medicine, pediatrics, gastroenterology, neurology, homeopathic materia medica and therapeutics, surgery, urology, obstetrics, otolaryngology, ophthalmology, gynecology, pharmacology, oncology, preventive medicine and public health.
58. Schmidt and Scott to Board of Trustees, July 23, 1945, in minutes, Medical Council, July 24, 1945.
59. Fischer, "Hahnemann Story," 9.
60. *The Hahnemann Medical College and Hospital of Philadelphia Announcement for the One-Hundredth Academic Year: 1946–1947* ([Philadelphia]: n.p.), 48.
61. Charles Brown, "Facts about the Present and Spirit of the Future," in minutes, Board of Trustees College Committee, January 31, 1947; and see minutes, Medical Council, August 20, 1946.
62. William G. Schmidt to Fred C. Zapffe, June 12, 1945, AAMC Archives.
63. Ibid.
64. Oliver to Zapffe, July 19, 1945, AAMC Archives.
65. Minutes, Medical Council, November 30, 1945; Newlin F. Paxson, John C. Scott, Edmund C. Hessert, Stanley P. Reimann, Wm. L. Martin, G. Harlan Wells [letter to Board of Trustees], December 7, 1945, in minutes, Medical Council, December 11, 1945.
66. Paxson et al., in minutes, Medical Council, December 11, 1945.

67. Minutes, Medical Council, June 18, 1946.
68. Schmidt to Oliver, September 10, 1945, AAMC Archives. For another example of the lack of power of the Medical Council, see minutes, Medical Council, March 7, 1946.
69. Oliver to Fischer, September 7, 1945, Schmidt to Oliver, September 10, 1945, and Oliver to William G. Schmidt, September 7, 1945, AAMC Archives.
70. Schmidt to Oliver, September 10, 1945, AAMC Archives.
71. Schmidt to Johnson and Zapffe, November 2, 1945, AAMC Archives.
72. Although he was not Jewish, one candidate was rejected because his major interest seemed to be in business rather than in medicine; see minutes, Board of Trustees College Committee, March 16, 1945.
73. Minutes, Medical Council, August 20, 1946.
74. *Annual Announcement: 1946–1947*, 11.
75. Minutes, Medical Council, May 14, 1946; ibid., June 18, 1945; minutes, Board of Trustees, College Committee, October 22, 1947.
76. Minutes, Special Faculty Meeting, March 8, 1949.
77. Minutes, College Council, March 11, 1947; and see minutes, Faculty Meeting, October 19, 1949.
78. Minutes, Board of Trustees Executive Finance Committee, October 15, 1947; minutes, Board of Trustees Executive Committee, November 1, 1946.
79. Minutes, Board of Trustees Executive Finance Committee, October 15, 1947.
80. Johnson to Brown, September 8, 1947, in ibid.
81. Minutes, Board of Trustees Executive Finance Committee, October 15, 1947.
82. Donald G. Anderson to Charles L. Brown, November, 15, 1948, in minutes, Board of Trustees Executive Committee, November 22, 1948.
83. Minutes, Board of Trustees Executive Committee, March 25, 1949.
84. *Annual Announcement: 1946–1947*, 31; and Barbara Williams, interview by Naomi Rogers, Philadelphia, September 12, 1997.
85. Minutes, Board of Trustees, June 10, 1947; minutes, College Council, June 17, 1947.
86. *Annual Announcement: 1946–1947*, 70–71. On the number of freshmen who chose the homeopathy elective, see minutes, College Council, December 9, 1947; and minutes, Board of Trustees College Committee, December 3, 1947.
87. Minutes, Board of Trustees College Committee, April 21, 1948; minutes, College Council, June 17, 1948; minutes, Board of Trustees, June 10, 1947; minutes, College Council, September 9, 1947; minutes, College Council, December 9, 1947.
88. William A. Pearson, "History of the Hahnemann Medical College, 1898 to 1948," *Hahnemannian Monthly* 83 (1948): 268, 269.
89. Minutes, Faculty Meeting, October 19, 1949.
90. "Inscription," *Medic* 1949, n.p. See also William G. Schmidt: "As a group, you have been mauled by the ax of drastic change as it has carved your destiny on the chopping block of experimental education" (*Medic* 1949, n.p.).

Chapter 6   *Embracing Orthodoxy: The 1950s and 1960s*

1. "A university is really a state of mind on the part of the faculty of a college . . . [and their attitudes] towards basic research, teaching and community service" (Dean Joseph DiPalma, minutes, Board of Trustees College Committee, April 9, 1968).
2. Walter S. Wiggins, James M. Faulkner, John Hinman, Stockton Kimball, and Arthur Ebbert Jr., "Survey Report of Hahnemann Medical College, Philadelphia, Pennsylvania; October 1–4, 1956," in Accred. Survey Reports, Box 5, IM Box 238, AAMC Archives, 19 (hereafter "1956 Report").
3. Victoria A. Harden, *Inventing the NIH: Federal Biomedical Research Policy, 1887–1937* (Baltimore: Johns Hopkins University Press, 1986), 180.
4. *Medic* 1950, n.p.

5. Saul Jarcho, "Medical Education in the United States: 1910–1956," *Journal of Mount Sinai Hospital* 26 (1959): 379.
6. Jarcho, "Medical Education," 365, 378.
7. Ibid., 373; and see minutes, Board of Trustees, May 22, 1957, on an additional donation of $100,000 from the Ford Foundation.
8. Harden, *Inventing the NIH*, 182.
9. Ibid., 183.
10. "1956 Report," 14.
11. See, for example, Charles Cameron's report on the "current efforts of the six medical schools of Pennsylvania to secure an increased allotment" of $750 per student (minutes, Board of Trustees, October 29, 1958).
12. "1956 Report," 18. The Longwood Foundation gave $300,000 to each school.
13. Warren Landau, telephone interview by Naomi Rogers, July 31, 1997.
14. William Kellow, "The Forces of Society," *Hahnemann Alumni News* 28 (spring 1963): 15, 14.
15. Joseph R. DiPalma, "Memoirs of a Medical School Dean," unpublished manuscript, 96, Hahnemann Collection.
16. Minutes, Board of Trustees Executive Finance Committee, October 15, 1947. Brown also felt that some of the older members deserved pay increases but was not sure whether it should be "straight across the board" or by merit: "I may say that in dealing with professional academic faculty, it is difficult or almost impossible to have any one measuring rod to determine the merit, ability and usefulness of different individuals to the institution" (ibid.).
17. See James T. Patterson, *The Dread Disease: Cancer and Modern American Culture* (Cambridge: Harvard University Press, 1987), 136–151, and especially 141–142; and Stephen P. Strickland, *Politics, Science, and Dread Disease: A Short History of United States Medical Research Policy* (Cambridge: Harvard University Press, 1972), 32–54.
18. In 1957 the American Heart Association had raised half a million dollars for distribution for research; Minutes, Cardiovascular Research Institute, April 26, 1957. For one medical school's expansion through heart research and surgery, see Leonard S. Wilson, *Medical Revolution in Minnesota: A History of the University of Minnesota Medical School* (St. Paul: Midewiwin Press, 1989), 481–528.
19. On the Institute for Cancer Research at Lankenau Hospital founded by Hahnemann oncologist Stanley Reimann, see Jean Barth Toll and Mildred S. Gillam, eds., *Invisible Philadelphia: Community through Voluntary Organizations* (Philadelphia: Atwater Kent Museum, 1995), 768–769, 1263. The Institute for Biomedical Studies of Cancer was founded at Hahnemann in 1958 with the help of the American Cancer Society and the National Cancer Institute.
20. George Geckeler, interview by Barbara Williams, [notes], February 16, 1981, Philadelphia, Hahnemann Collection; Annual Report: Division of Anatomy, Department of Cardiology, 1954–1955, Hahnemann Collection. See also John Moyer, "Memoirs," unpublished manuscript, 1997, chap. 15, p. 10: "George had a particular kind of sing-song voice which I remembered quite well on the records. . . . As soon as he began to speak, I recognized his voice from the records that I had used 15 years previously [as a student]."
21. Likoff interned and did his pathology and medical residencies at Mount Sinai Hospital. He had a cardiac fellowship under Samuel Levine at the Bent Brigham Hospital, one of the few academic cardiology centers in the United States.
22. Minutes, Board of Trustees, December 15, 1948; "this group will require considerable space and accommodations preferably in the Hospital unit, and it is for this purpose that the doctors supporting this proposal plan to solicit outside financial

aid, to which the Federal Government will probably contribute." See also minutes, Board of Trustees, August 12, 1953.

23. William Likoff to Barbara Williams, July 15, 1974, Hahnemann Collection. Likoff claimed that CVI had "disintegrated when institution[al] administrative policy dictated growth and support of departments rather than cross-disciplinary units."

24. Minutes, Cardiovascular Research Institute, [1949]. On Bailey's continuing involvement with the Deborah Hospital in Brown Mills, New Jersey, see Dryden P. Morse, *Congenital Heart Disease: Pathogenic Factors, Natural History, Diagnosis, and Surgical Treatment: An International Symposium under the Direction of Charles P. Bailey, M.D.* (Philadelphia: F. D. Davis, 1962).

25. DiPalma argued that Bailey had a "retinue of grateful patients" who were "largely a Jewish group and they were intensely loyal and supportive" ("Memoirs," 109).

26. Likoff to Williams.

27. "Hahnemann Heart Work Continues to Grow," *Hahnemann Hospital Tidings* (midwinter 1951): 95; minutes, Board of Trustees, March 28, 1958; Charles Zeitz was a truck driver for Likoff's father's food business. Zeitz gave the son $75,000 in return for an $1,800 loan he had received from the father some years earlier that had helped make him a wealthy businessman; see William Likoff in Likoff, Victor Satinsky, and Joseph DiPalma, "History of the Hahnemann Cardiovascular Institute, April 10, 1981," transcript of audiotape, Hahnemann Collection.

28. Minutes, Cardiovascular Research Institute, April 30, 1962.

29. Ibid.

30. L. Stauffer Oliver to Board of Trustees, Hahnemann Medical College and Hospital, "Important and Confidential," August 24, 1953, Hahnemann Collection.

31. Ibid.

32. Minutes, Board of Trustees, February 16, 1949; October 19, 1949.

33. DiPalma, "Memoirs," 112. DiPalma vividly remembers having lunch with Charles Laughten and Harry Bellefonte.

34. Minutes, Cardiovascular Research Institute, January 18, 1954.

35. Annual Report: Division of Anatomy, 1954–1955, n.p., Hahnemann Collection.

36. Minutes, Joint Meeting of the Liaison Committee of the Council on Medical Education and Hospitals and the Association of American Medical Colleges and the Committee for the Survey of Medical Education, November 5, 1949, LCME Agenda and Minutes, 1949, AAMC Archives, 7.

37. "Forty-sixth Annual Report on Medical Education," *JAMA* 131 (August 1946): 19.

38. "Dr. Starr Appointed U. of P. Medical Dean," *Philadelphia Inquirer,* November 6, 1945.

39. Annual Report: Division of Anatomy, 1954–1955, n.p., Hahnemann Collection.

40. Minutes, Board of Trustees College Committee, November 16, 1945.

41. Cyrus C. Sturgis, "Dr. Brown Resigns," *University [of Michigan] Hospital Bulletin* 1 (August 1935): 35; Thomas M. Durant, "Memoir of Charles Leonard Brown (1899–1959), *Transactions and Studies of the College of Physicians of Philadelphia* 28 (1960–1961): 104–105.

42. Victor Johnson and Fred C. Zapffe, "The Hahnemann Medical College and Hospital, Philadelphia, Pennsylvania, April 3–6, 1945," in Accred. Survey Reports, Box 5, IM Box 238, AAMC Archives, Washington, D.C., 8 (hereafter "1945 Report").

43. Victor Wierman Jr. to Dear Sir, February 14, 1947, addendum to minutes, Board of Trustees College Committee, January 31, 1947. See also DiPalma, "Memoirs," 117: Brown did "a magnificent job of regaining for Hahnemann a respectable place in the medical community."

44. Donald G. Anderson and John E. Deitrick, "Survey of Hahnemann Medical School and Hospital of Philadelphia, Pennsylvania: May 9–13, 1949," Accred. Survey Re-

ports, Box J, IM Box 238, AAMC Archives, Washington, D.C., 64 (hereafter "1949 Report"), mentions a grant of $37,000 from the U.S.P.H.S. [sic], perhaps the new NIMH.

45. "1949 Report," 63, 66.
46. Margaret Giannini, telephone interview by Naomi Rogers, August 24, 1997.
47. "1949 Report," 39.
48. John C. Scott and Emerson A. Reed, "History of the Department of Physiology: Hahnemann Medical College and Hospital, Philadelphia, Pennsylvania," unpublished manuscript, 1978, 6, 9–10, 14. Frank Widman (Hahnemann M.D. 1893) had been professor of physiology since 1918.
49. DiPalma, "Memoirs," 106.
50. "The Hahnemann Faculty," *Hahnemann Hospital Tidings* (January 1948): 6. DiPalma also describes Gregory as a man who "kept to himself" and seemed apart from the other chairmen ("Memoirs," 97).
51. Gregory left in 1953, as the result, DiPalma claims, of a fight over a cancer biopsy that Gregory F. Froio, an associate professor of pathology, sent to New York (without telling Gregory) after Gregory had said it was not cancerous. The New York pathologist said it was cancerous. Gregory fired Froio for insubordination, and, supported by Brown, the College Council reluctantly supported him. But "this was an empty triumph for now he [Gregory] was completely discredited. All the clinicians avoided him and he soon found it expedient to leave for another position" ("Memoirs," 117).
52. "The Hahnemann Faculty," 6.
53. Raymond C. Truex (1911–1980) had been teaching anatomy at the College of Physicians and Surgeons in New York City (assistant professor 1942–1945, associate professor 1945–1948). He left in 1961 and was professor of anatomy at Temple until 1978.
54. "1956 Report," 38.
55. DiPalma, "Memoirs," 98; "1956 Report," 44. George Paff, hired in 1949 as an anatomist from Long Island College of Medicine, urged DiPalma to apply, saying that he had doubled his salary and found living conditions in Philadelphia "much superior" (DiPalma, "Memoirs," 96).
56. DiPalma, "Memoirs," 100, 97. He became involved in cardiology research and studied the effect of drugs on cardiovascular disease, especially arrhythmias, and later used ECG analysis of Venus-flytrap plants.
57. Johnson and Zapffe had argued that full-time basic science faculty "should have a majority in determining the policies of the institution" ("1945 Report," 10–11).
58. "1956 Report," 77.
59. Annual Report: Division of Anatomy, 1954–1955, Hahnemann Collection; Annual Report: Division of Microbiology, 1954–55, Hahnemann Collection.
60. Indeed, Hahnemann's bylaws in the 1950s stated that a majority of the College Council should always be preclinical faculty; see "1956 Report," 9, 32.
61. DiPalma, "Memoirs," 108.
62. The 1950 *Medic* was dedicated to Brown:
    We entered Hahnemann together.
    We experienced many changes together.
    Our associations have been pleasant and fruitful through a trying period.
    The class of 1950 is proud to honor a great clinician and respected teacher.
    After Brown resigned in 1955, Charles M. Thompson was acting head until July 1957, when John Moyer was appointed.
63. Charles S. Cameron, "A Fresh Dean's View of Hahnemann," *Hahnemann Alumni News* 23 (April-May 1957): 4.
64. Horst Agerty and Charles Cameron, joint interview by Naomi Rogers and Barbara

Williams, Philadelphia, November 13, 1996. Cameron recalled that there were some questions from the Philadelphia General Hospital staff at the beginning that subsequently disappeared.

65. "I was greatly affected by it" (Agerty and Cameron, joint interview). In a later interview he again recalled his two months caring for the patients in the cancer wards; he said he became "emotionally involved with cancer, a pitiful thing, needed to be solved; I wanted to take care of these people, sort of sounds stupidly altruistic" (Cameron, interview by Naomi Rogers and Barbara Williams, December 4, 1996).

66. Cameron, interview.

67. DiPalma, "Memoirs," 119.

68. Charles S. Cameron, *The Truth about Cancer* (Englewood Cliffs, N.J.: Prentice-Hall, 1956).

69. Cameron, interview.

70. There were two distinct exceptions: the Department of Radiology was headed by Stauffer Lehman (Hahnemann M.D. 1931), who was full-time, and had six other full-time staff; and the Department of Therapeutics was headed by homeopath Garth Boericke, who was also full-time; see "1956 Report," 48.

71. Moyer, "Memoirs," chap. 15, pp. 24–25.

72. "1956 Report," 48.

73. Ibid., 69.

74. Ibid., 70, 74.

75. Ibid., 62, 64.

76. Ibid., 62.

77. Ibid., 70.

78. Ibid., 46.

79. Ibid., 63.

80. See Jarcho, "Medical Education," 379: "clinical departments [in the 1950s] remained an area of conflict."

81. Moyer, "Memoirs," chap. 15, p. 8.

82. Ibid., 1–3.

83. Ibid., 8, 10.

84. Ibid., 11.

85. Ibid., 13.

86. "1956 Report," 49.

87. Minutes, Board of Trustees, June 25, 1958.

88. Moyer, "Memoirs," chap. 15, pp. 23–24.

89. Ibid., 22, 24.

90. Wilbur Oaks, interview by Naomi Rogers, Philadelphia, November 13, 1996; George Harlan Wells, "A History of the Department of Medicine at the Hahnemann Medical College and Hospital of Philadelphia," unpublished manuscript, June 1965, 14–18.

91. Minutes, Board of Trustees, December 17, 1958.

92. Wells, "History," 19.

93. John Storer, telephone interview by Naomi Rogers, April 25, 1997: see also Cameron, interview, on Hahnemann surgeons "who value speed."

94. Minutes, Board of Trustees, January 29, 1958.

95. Statement by Lee G. L. Thomas, in minutes, Board of Trustees, January 29, 1958.

96. Watson Malone III, [Remarks], *Medical Staff News*, August 8, 1958.

97. Charles S. Cameron, "A Statement by the Dean," *Medical Staff News*, August 8, 1958: "where called for on academic grounds, full time appointments will be considered, and again, merit and only merit will determine the appointments."

98. Ibid.

99. Charles Philamore Bailey, "The Surgical Treatment of Mitral Stenosis (Mitral Com-

missurotomy)," *Diseases of the Chest* 15 (April 1949): 377–397. His patient was twenty-four-year-old Claire Ward. "Because of her evident good condition she was transported without incident by train to a 1,000 mile distant medical convention [probably the American College of Chest Physicians, annual meeting, Chicago June 20, 1948] for presentation in person" (390). He also designed a special "guillotine" knife for the operation.

100. William Likoff to Barbara Williams, July 15, 1974.
101. Bailey also benefited from the widespread interest in heart surgery. A 1945 graduate who later became a surgeon remembers that surgery was so popular that he first applied to do a pathology rather than a surgical residency, as it was easier to get into at Hahnemann Hospital (Storer, interview).
102. Geckeler, interview.
103. Moyer, "Memoirs," chap. 15, p. 29.
104. Storer, interview.
105. Moyer, "Memoirs," chap. 15, pp. 29, 31.
106. Ibid., 9.
107. Storer, interview; and see Moyer, "Memoirs," chap. 15, p. 32: "if he thought it was a good idea, he would try anything."
108. DiPalma, "Memoirs," 127.
109. Ibid., 129: "at that time there was no such mechanism as informed consent much less a human research committee."
110. *Time,* March 25, 1957; and see Charles P. Bailey, Brian A. Cookson, Daniel F. Downing, Wilford B. Neptune, "Cardiac Surgery under Hypothermia," *Journal of Thoracic Surgery* 27 (January 1954): 73–91; and "Girl Recovering after 'Deep-Freeze' Heart Operation," *Evening Bulletin,* September 30, 1952.
111. DiPalma, "Memoirs," 107.
112. *Medic* 1951, n.p.
113. Charles P. Bailey to Watson Malone III, July 3, 1958, Hahnemann Collection; and see Moyer, "Memoirs," chap. 15, p. 33: "Dean Cameron was quite reluctant to make this appointment because he was quite sensitive to the erratic and mercurial behavior of Bailey."
114. Bailey to Malone, July 3, 1958. Years later Bailey saw the reasons for his departure differently: see Charles P. Bailey to Burton J. Landau, May 15, 1990, Hahnemann Collection: "Why should I have been so irrational as to resign just because the student teaching was taken away from my new department. Looking back, that would seem to have been one of the great mistakes of my life. . . . if I had stayed, at the age of 65 I would have been retired—or made Emeritus, or something. And here I am at 79 1/2, pioneering in the field of medical malpractice. And that is very exciting."
115. Bailey to Malone, July 3, 1958.
116. "Agreement Between Charles P. Bailey, M.D., and the HAHNEMANN MEDICAL COLLEGE & HOSPITAL Represented [sic] by Watson Malone, III, Charles S. Cameron, M.D., and Charles S. Paxson, Jr, September 1, 1958," Hahnemann Collection.
117. "Notes from Meeting with Dr. Bailey, Dr. Cameron, Messrs. Malone, Vogel, Davis, Paxson, July 31, 1958," Hahnemann Collection. See also Chas. S. Paxson Jr., "Confidential," July 21, 1958, in "Notes for File of Charles P. Bailey," Hahnemann Collection.
118. Minutes, Board of Trustees College Committee, November 6, 1966.
119. Eichi Karl Koiwai, telephone interview by Naomi Rogers, August 20, 1997.
120. "1945 Report," 18.
121. *Hahnemann Alumni News* (1961–62), 22.
122. Joseph DiPalma, Burton Landau, Suzanne Zarro, and Vincent Zarro, joint interview by Naomi Rogers, November 12, 1996.

123. Cameron, "A Fresh Dean's View," 6.

124. "1956 Report," 77.

125. Abstract of Charles Cameron, "Hahnemann; The Next Twenty-five Years," *Hahnemann Alumni News* 29 (May 1964): 5.

126. Minutes, Board of Trustees, March 26, 1958, and December 17, 1958.

127. *Hahnemann Alumni News* (1961–62), 16; minutes, Board of Trustees, February 25, 1959.

128. DiPalma, Landau, Zarro, and Zarro, joint interview.

129. Sidney Zubrow, telephone interview by Naomi Rogers, May 21, 1997; he also felt "Everything was old."

130. DiPalma, Landau, Zarro, and Zarro, joint interview.

131. William Francis Kellow graduated from the University of Notre Dame and Georgetown School of Medicine. He was previously associate dean of the University of Illinois College of Medicine and was certified by the American Board of Internal Medicine and the American Board of Pulmonary Diseases.

132. "Squibb Presents Original Painting to Hahnemann," *Medical Staff News* (May-June 1967): 2.

133. Charles Cameron, telephone interview by Barbara Williams, November 26, 1997; "Elmer Bobst, Executive Dies at 93," *Evening Bulletin*, August 3, 1978.

134. "Dedication of the Elmer Holmes Bobst Institute of Clinical Research," *Medical Staff News* (May-June 1967): 4–5.

135. William Likoff to Charles Cameron, January 25, 1972, Hahnemann Collection.

136. Minutes, Ad Hoc Joint Committee of the Council for Affairs on GFT-Volunteer Physicians' Interrelationships, January 20, 1976; the committee discussed a meeting on December 2, 1975, commenting on "the feeling that there is a deliberate exclusion of volunteer staff."

137. William Pearson, "The Hahnemann Medical College of Philadelphia, 1898–1948," *Hahnemannian Monthly* 82 (1947): 413.

138. Ibid.

139. Minutes, Medical Council, March 26, 1939.

140. Minutes, College Council, December 10, 1946. Margaret Giannini (Hahnemann M.D. 1945) does not remember graduating with an H.M.D. (Giannini, interview); and Seth Fisher (Hahnemann M.D. 1948) remembers graduating with both an M.D. and an H.M.D. (Fisher, telephone interview by Naomi Rogers, May 5, 1997).

141. Minutes, Medical Council, November 19, 1940.

142. Oaks, interview.

143. Storer, interview by Naomi Rogers, April 18, 1997. For histories of the Huron Road Hospital, see Nan Murphy, *A History of Huron Road Hospital* ([Cleveland]: Today Magazine [The Bulletin of Huron Road Hospital], 1974); and Frederick Clayton Waite, *Western Reserve University Centennial History of the School of Medicine* (Cleveland: Western Reserve University Press, 1946).

144. Oaks, interview.

145. Herbert Harkins, telephone interview by Naomi Rogers, June 11, 1997.

146. Fisher, interview.

147. Garth Boericke, "Homeopathic Trends," *Medic* 1942, 174. Hahnemann graduates, he claimed "are recognized and accredited everywhere . . . [and] our school has kept pace with American medicine, which is a tribute to our leaders, particularly those at Hahnemann. We must admit, however, that this broad minded policy has curtailed homeopathy, the art, to an appreciable degree"; and he urged students to "trim our sails to catch the steady trade wind of medical progress"; and see also G. Harlan Wells, "Recent Progress in Medicine," *Hahnemann Hospital Tidings* 52 (January 1947): 5–9.

148. "1949 Report," 40.
149. DiPalma, "Memoirs," 102–103.
150. John Moyer, telephone interview by Naomi Rogers, August 4, 1997.
151. [Garth Boericke], Annual Report: Department of Therapeutics, 1954–55, Hahnemann Collection.
152. Giannini, interview.
153. *The Hahnemann Medical College and Hospital Bulletin: 1950–1951*, 20.
154. *Medic* 1945, 101.
155. See *The Hahnemann Medical College Bulletin: 1958–1959*, 43; *The Hahnemann Medical College Bulletin: 1959–1960*, 44.
156. *Medic* 1943 II, 8; see also *Medic* 1946, n.p.: "years of experience in all schools of therapeutics" and "a masterful prescriber in homeopathy and allopathy."
157. *Medic* 1946, n.p. *Medic* 1943 was dedicated to Boericke: "in him our class sees a paragon—the perfect example insofar as humans are perfect—of what a doctor should be. Good, sympathetic, understanding of Man's frailties and generous with his faults, full of the milk of human kindness and tender quality of mercy"; "an authority on therapeutics, whatever the school"; "his great wealth of knowledge"; "conducting the most enlightening bed-side clinics of the four years"; "a sharp wit and eloquent tongue" (*Medic* 1943 II, 8).
158. *Medic* 1941, 226–227: Boericke is "Hahnemann's homeopathic star."
159. Charles S. Cameron, "Hahnemann and Rush: A Re-evaluation," *Hahnemann Alumni News* 34 (spring 1969): 16, 20; and see Charles S. Cameron, "Homeopathy in Retrospect," *Transactions and Studies of the College of Physicians of Philadelphia* 27 (1959–1960): 28–33.
160. Charles S. Cameron to Editor, *Evening Bulletin*, October 30, 1962.
161. Charles Cameron, "Change of Name," in minutes, Board of Trustees, September 30, 1970.
162. "1949 Report," 24.
163. *Sixty-third Annual Announcement of Hahnemann Medical College and Hospital of Philadelphia: Session of 1910–1911*, 37.
164. *Medic* 1932, 254, 255.
165. *Medic* 1934, 134.
166. *Medic* 1929, 127; see also James Krauss, "Report of the Chairman of the Committee on the Formation of a National Association for Clinical Research," *Journal of the American Institute of Homeopathy* 1 (January 1909): 364–365.
167. Charles W. Shaffer, "Hahnemann Research Foundation," *Hahnemannian Monthly* 74 (1939): 1052–1053.
168. H. M. Eberhard, "Hahnemann Medical College and Hospital of Today," *Hahnemannian Monthly* 77 (1942): 112–115; H. M. Eberhard, "Research Work at Hahnemann," *Hospital Tidings* 48 (November 1939): 8–9.
169. See H. M. Eberhard, "Some Facts Regarding the Hahnemann Medical College and Hospital of Philadelphia," *Hospital Tidings* 46 (October 1941): 6–7.
170. "1949 Report," 33.
171. See, for example, *Medic* 1943 II, 83: Stephen Edgar Dunlap, of Lancaster, was "very naive," "always altruistic and upright," and "a firm believer in homeopathy. One can see his ears perk up when some rare drug is mentioned and before the day passes he will study its virtues. After the war he hopes to practice homeopathy in Lancaster county."
172. Fisher, interview.
173. Koiwai, interview; Storer, interview.
174. Ana Nuñez, interview by Naomi Rogers, August 15, 1997.
175. Minutes, Hospital Council, November 9, 1948, and December 7, 1948.

176. *Medic* 1950, n.p.; see also minutes, Hospital Council, March 14, 1950, and April 3, 1963.

177. Report of the President, in minutes, Board of Trustees College Committee, May 13, 1969.

178. Minutes, Hospital Council, March 2, 1971.

179. Ibid., May 1, 1963.

180. Ibid., January 5, 1971.

181. Minutes, College Council, August 1, 1972. See also minutes, College Council, January 6, 1970; and minutes, Board of Trustees College Committee, January 13, 1970.

182. "1949 Report," 3, 20–21.

183. "1956 Report," 7.

184. Lonnie Fuller, telephone interview by Naomi Rogers, July 28, 1997; on racial segregation at inner-city hospitals see Rosemary Stevens, *In Sickness and in Wealth: American Hospitals in the Twentieth Century* (New York: Basic Books, 1989), 252–254.

185. Minutes, Board of Trustees, September 30, 1959. Fifteen hospitals in the region, including Hahnemann, were "talking to the Unions," and Hahnemann's board and solicitors were "keeping their eyes on the situation."

186. Minutes, Assembly of the General Faculty, May 13, 1965.

187. Minutes, Hospital Council, October 5, 1971.

188. On closings see minutes, Hospital Council, June 8, 1948, and May 2, 1967.

189. Minutes, Hospital Council, June 8, 1948.

190. Abraham Flexner, *Report on Medical Education in the United States and Canada: A Report to the Carnegie Foundation for the Advancement of Teaching* (New York: Carnegie Foundation, 1910), 57.

191. Minutes, Board of Trustees College Committee, February 6, 1966.

192. "1949 Report," 26.

193. See Susan E. Lederer, *Subjected to Science: Human Experimentation in America before the Second World War* (Baltimore: Johns Hopkins University Press, 1995); and David J. Rothman, *Stranger at the Bedside: A History of How Law and Bioethics Transformed Medical Decision Making* (New York: Basic Books, 1991).

194. Minutes, Board of Trustees College Committee, February 6, 1966.

195. See, for example, [E. Merton Hill], "Changing Concepts," *Hahnemann Alumni News* 23 (spring 1957): 2: in the minds of alumni the hospital and the college "are separate and autonomous units," but alumni need to change this thinking, for "modern education from a medical point of view requires and includes hospital facilities as an integral portion of the program and teaching of a medical school." "[W]e have long standing mental barriers to break down."

196. Minutes, Hospital Council, June 5, 1957; minutes, Hospital Council, December 7, 1971.

197. Ibid., January 5, 1971.

198. Ibid., July 6, 1971.

199. See ibid., January 8, 1964; see also Stevens, *In Sickness*, 245–248.

200. Minutes, Hospital Council, February 6, 1968.

201. [John Moyer], Annual Report: Department of Medicine, 1957–1958, Hahnemann Collection.

202. Minutes, Hospital Council, February 10, 1948.

203. See the discussion of the 1967 Pechan Report in chapter seven.

204. DiPalma, "Memoirs," 115; and DiPalma, Landau, Zarro, and Zarro, joint interview.

205. DiPalma, Landau, Zarro, and Zarro, joint interview.

206. "Self Portrait by George," *Medic* 1947, 187.

207. Robert McMichael, telephone interview by Naomi Rogers, September 12, 1997.
208. Art Peters, "Dr. King's Doctor Also Had a Dream: A Health Center," *Evening Bulletin,* January 29, 1973; David Cleary, "U.S. Assigns Doctors to Critical Health Areas," *Evening Bulletin,* May 26, 1972.
209. Margo Downing, "Doctor Bucks Unhealthy Trend," *Evening Bulletin*, June 4, 1980.

Chapter 7   Radical Alternatives: 1968–1972

1. See Flora Davis, *Moving the Mountain: The Women's Movement in America since 1960* (New York: Simon and Schuster, 1991), 157–183; Sheryl Burt Ruzek, *The Women's Health Movement: Feminist Alternatives to Medical Control* (New York: Praeger, 1978); James Jones, *Bad Blood: The Tuskegee Syphilis Experiment* (New York: Free Press, 1993); Paul Lowinger, "The Doctor as a Political Activist. Progress Report," *American Journal of Psychotherapy* 22 (October 1968): 616–625.
2. Lowinger, "Doctor as Political Activist," 617–619.
3. Ibid., 619.
4. Robert J. Bazell, "Health Radicals: Crusade to Shift Medical Power to the People," *Science* 73 (August 1971): 509.
5. Ibid., 508.
6. Lowinger, "Doctor as Political Activist," 622–623; Bazell, "Health Radicals," 508; Michael R. McGarey, Fitzhugh Mullan, and Steven Sharfstein, "A Study in Medical Action: The Student Health Organization," *New England Journal of Medicine* 279 (1968): 74–80; and Fitzhugh Mullan, *White Coat, Clenched Fist: The Political Education of an American Physician* (New York: Macmillan Publishing Co., 1976), 51–67.
7. Peter Eisenberg, telephone interview by Naomi Rogers, August 4, 1997.
8. Minutes, College Council, October 8, 1946.
9. Ibid., November 11, 1947, including letter from Charles Fineberg [president of the sophomore class] to Dean Charles Brown, October 24, 1947.
10. "Dedication: Grant Orante Favorite," *Medic* 1944, 5.
11. Irving Lichtenstein, "Foreword," *Medic* 1944.
12. "The Next Hundred," *Medic* 1948.
13. Philip Scranton, "Yes, Maxwell, There Is a Way Out," *Grand Mal* (February 1970).
14. Minutes, Board of Trustees College Committee, March 10, 1970.
15. Minutes, Hospital Council, December 7, 1965.
16. John C. Burnham, "American Medicine's Golden Age: What Happened to It?" in Judith Walzer Leavitt and Ronald L. Numbers, eds., *Sickness and Health in America: Readings on the History of Medicine and Public Health* (Madison: University of Wisconsin Press, 1985), 248–258.
17. Charles S. Paxson Jr., "An Administration Perspective," *Grand Mal* (December 1969).
18. Ibid.
19. Eisenberg, interview.
20. Stephen Baer and Phyllis Baer, joint telephone interview by Naomi Rogers, May 11, 1997.
21. Minutes, Hospital Council, January 4, 1972.
22. Ibid., January 6, 1970.
23. As reported in M. Prager, "The Student Faculty Subcommittee: Will It Work?" *Grand Mal* (February 1970).
24. "Student Faculty Relations Conference Planned," *Grand Mal* (February 1970).
25. "F. T. Babbitt, M.D., F.D.I.C.," "Filth and Dirt," *Grand Mal* (February 1970).
26. Prager, "The Student Faculty Subcommittee."
27. *Grand Mal* (February 1970).

28. Examples drawn from Eisenberg, interview; and Ron Feigin, telephone interview by Naomi Rogers, August 7, 1997.
29. "Chairmen Reports—June Faculty Conference [1969]," minutes, College Council, June 24, 1969.
30. Minutes, College Council, April 29, 1969.
31. Eisenberg, interview.
32. Review of College Council minutes, April 29, 1969, in minutes, Board of Trustees College Committee, May 13, 1969.
33. Minutes, College Council, April 29, 1969.
34. Ibid.
35. Minutes, Assembly of the General Faculty, May 22, 1969.
36. Minutes, College Council, June 24, 1969.
37. Ibid., September 24, 1968.
38. "Memorandum to the Students and Faculty," in minutes, Board of Trustees College Committee, May 13, 1969.
39. Minutes, College Council, October 28, 1969.
    Note that the council continues to refer to the paper as the *Impulse*.
40. [Karl] Emory Robinson, "Free University at Hahnemann," *Grand Mal* (December 1969).
41. Ibid.
42. Minutes, College Council, January 6, 1970.
43. Ibid., June 24, 1969.
44. "Memorandum to the Students and Faculty."
45. Ibid.
46. Minutes, Board of Trustees College Committee, March 10, 1970.
47. Review of minutes of the College Council, April 28, 1970, report in minutes, Board of Trustees College Committee, May 12, 1970. Students had originally requested five representatives.
48. For an analysis of the impact of civil rights and liberal activists on a black medical school, see James Summerville, *Educating Black Doctors: A History of Meharry Medical College* (Tuscaloosa: University of Alabama Press, 1983), 156–181.
49. Robert McMichael, telephone interview by Naomi Rogers, September 12, 1997; Kendall Wilson, "Warren E. Smith, Noted Doctor and Civic Leader Succumbs," *Philadelphia Tribune*, September 18, 1990.
50. Minutes, Hospital Council, September 1, 1964.
51. Harold A. Taggart, "Report of the Dean of the Faculty of the Hahnemann Medical College and Hospital for the Academic Year ending August 31, 1955," Hahnemann Collection.
52. George Gardiner, interview by Naomi Rogers, November 14, 1996.
53. Minutes, Board of Trustees College Committee, May 1, 1947; ibid., March 17, 1954; Gardiner, interview.
54. "Panther Clinic Opens," *Grand Mal* (February 1970). [Mark Prager and Jerome Lindauer], "Black Panther Clinic," *Grand Mal 2* (February 1970).
55. "Still Hold," *Grand Mal* (November 1969).
56. Minutes, College Council, September 24, 1968.
57. Minutes, Board of Trustees College Committee, September 10, 1968; ibid., October 8, 1968. The percentage of African-Americans in Philadelphia was 26 percent.
58. "CBA Demands Met but Not Here," *Grand Mal* (November 1969).
59. Minutes, College Committee, October 8, 1968.
60. "Public Statement of the Six Philadelphia Medical School Deans on the Matter of Disadvantaged Students in Medicine," in minutes, Board of Trustees College Committee, October 8, 1968. See also John Rhodes, "Committee Demands Phila. Medical Schools Admit More Negro Students," *Philadelphia Tribune*, September 14,

1969; "Medical Deans Study Bid on Negroes," *Philadelphia Inquirer*, September 19, 1968.

61. "Public Statement of the Six Philadelphia Medical School Deans."

62. Minutes, Board of Trustees College Committee, October 1968; minutes, College Council, September 24, 1968.

63. "Public Statement of the Six Philadelphia Medical School Deans."

64. Minutes, College Council, January 28, 1969; minutes, Board of Trustees College Committee, February 11, 1969; minutes, College Council, October 28, 1969. See also David M. Cleary, "Thirty-four Negroes Admitted to Medical Schools Here," *Evening Bulletin*, September 21, 1969: eleven went to Pennsylvania, eleven to Jefferson, eight to Temple, two to Hahnemann, one to Woman's, and one to the osteopathic college.

65. Bruce Tapper, "Medical Career Center," *Grand Mal* (December 1969).

66. Ibid.; minutes, College Council, January 28, 1969.

67. Minutes, Board of Trustees College Committee, September 10, 1968.

68. Minutes, College Council, October 28, 1969.

69. Minutes, SHO, February 27, 1969, box 1, folder 9, Fitzhugh Mullan Papers, State Historical Society of Wisconsin, Madison, Wisconsin.

70. Ron Feigin, "Med. Schools Put Heads Together," *Grand Mal* (December 1969).

71. Ibid.

72. Timothy Ready and Herbert W. Nickens ("Black Men in the Medical Education Pipeline: Past, Present, and Future," *Academic Medicine* 66 [April 1991]: 181–187) note that 23 percent fewer black men enrolled in medical school in 1990 than in 1971.

73. Minutes, College Council, September 24, 1968.

74. Minutes, Board of Trustees College Committee, September 10, 1968.

75. Donald McDonough, "Rep. Bersonto to Push $1.5 Million Bill for Hahnemann," *Philadelphia Inquirer*, August 6, 1968; Leonard H. Gashel and George Ingram, "Many Donolow Constituents Back Hahnemann Dispute," *Philadelphia Inquirer*, August 5, 1968; Duke Kaminski, "State Approves $1.5 Million for Hahnemann," *Evening Bulletin*, November 13, 1968.

76. Minutes, Admissions Committee, Board of Trustees College Committee, October 10, 1967. The percentage of Jewish students at Hahnemann was 38 percent higher than that of any other school in the state. The next highest percentage was 33 percent for Osteopathic and the University of Pennsylvania. For a report on the Task Force on Admission Policy of Schools of Medicine, Dentistry, and Nursing, chaired by Senator Albert Pechan, see Albert R. Pechan, "Medical Training Facilities and Medical Practice in Pennsylvania," *Pennsylvania Medicine* 70 (1967): 67 ff., 117–120 ff., 97 ff.

77. Minutes, Board of Trustees College Committee, July 9, 1968.

78. Ibid., May 12, 1970.

79. Report of Board of Trustees meeting, in minutes, College Council, April 29, 1969.

80. Chip Jackson, telephone interview by Naomi Rogers, August 19, 1997.

81. [Mark Prager and Jerome Lindauer], "Why Cuba?" *Grand Mal* (February 1970).

82. Jerome M. Lindauer, "Health Care in Cuba and USSR," *Grand Mal* (February 1970).

83. Victor Johnson and Fred C. Zapffe, "The Hahnemann Medical College and Hospital of Philadelphia, Pennsylvania, April 3–6, 1945," Accred. Survey Reports, Box 5, IM Box 238, AAMC Archives, Washington, D.C.

84. Larry Kron, "On Being Poor," *Grand Mal* (November 1969); for a similar critique see David E. Reiser, "Struggling to Stay Human in Medicine: One Student's Reflections on Becoming a Doctor," *New Physician* 22 (May 1973): 295–299.

85. Mark Prager, "Mirror, Mirror, on the Wall," *Grand Mal* (December 1969).

86. "Philly Battles Poverty with Center Opening," *New Pittsburgh Courier*, December 14, 1968; Mark Prager, "Green St. Clinic," *Grand Mal* (December 1969).
87. Prager, "Green St. Clinic."
88. Ibid.
89. Mark Prager, "Is the Medium the Message?" *Grand Mal* (November 1969).
90. [Mark Prager and Jerry Lindauer], "Are We in the Business of Healing; Or Are We in the Business?" *Grand Mal* (November 1969).
91. Prager, "Is the Medium the Message?"
92. "Medical Brutality Blamed for Penn Med. Student Leaving School," *Grand Mal* (November 1969); see also Maury Levy, "My Son, the Radical Doctor," *Philadelphia Magazine* 62 (September 1971): 81, 184, 186.
93. Ibid. Smith began to work with Walter Lear on the Philadelphia Board of Health.
94. T. Liston, "Interdisciplinary Course Planned," *Grand Mal* (February 1970).
95. In 1966, 6.8 percent of graduating seniors said they would like to practice psychiatry (compared to 19 percent for general practice, 25 percent for internal medicine, and 26 percent for surgery). By 1972, this had increased to 13.5 percent (compared to 18 percent for general practice, 18 percent for surgery, and 33.7 percent for internal medicine).
96. [Mark Prager and Jerome Lindauer], "New Freshman Course," *Grand Mal* (February 1970).
97. Peter Eisenberg, "Maxwell's Silver Hammer," *Grand Mal* (November 1969).
98. Jim Shames, "Cream Cheese," *Grand Mal* (November 1969).
99. Minutes, Board of Trustees College Committee, October 14, 1969.
100. Peter Eisenberg, "October 15 a Success," *Grand Mal* (November 1969); and see [Mark Prager and Jerry Lindauer], "A Call to Action," *Grand Mal* (November 1969).
101. Minutes, Board of Trustees College Committee, May 12, 1970.
102. [Prager and Lindauer], "A Call to Action."

Chapter 8 *Incorporating Change: The 1970s*

1. Ron Feigin, telephone interview by Naomi Rogers, August 7, 1997.
2. Tom Dugdale, quoted in Doris B. Wiley, "Hahnemann's Stiff Upper Lip: Hospital Stoics Taking Lots of Bad Publicity in Stride," *Evening Bulletin*, April 3, 1978.
3. Jonathan R. Cole and James A. Lipton, "The Reputations of American Medical Schools," *Social Forces* 55 (March 1977): 662–684. This ranking was based on a questionnaire sent to full-time faculty members at eighty-seven American medical schools. The University of Pennsylvania was ranked eleventh, Temple fifty-fifth, Jefferson seventy-second, and the Medical College of Pennsylvania eightieth (Cole and Lipton, "The Reputations," table 2, 669–671). In the "visibility" ranking Hahnemann scored higher than Jefferson and the Medical College of Pennsylvania.
4. See "Curriculum Vitae: Edward Wharton Shober, Jr.," [dated] 12/15/73, Hahnemann Collection.
5. Ellen Karasik, "How Shober Lost out at Hahnemann," *Philadelphia Inquirer*, June 27, 1977.
6. "Subject: Edward Wharton Shober," in the Faculty Committee (of Nine) to Members of the Board of Trustees of the Hahnemann Medical College and Hospital, Attention: Isadore H. Krekstein, May 7, 1973, Hahnemann Collection. This document is a dossier on Shober described in the main letter as "a brief rundown on Mr. Shober" containing information "all available as public information" from a "consultant working on information."
7. "Newporter Appointed President of Hospital," *Newport Daily News*, August 24, 1971. This article also described him as the director of the Newport Casino, a gov-

ernor of the New School, and trustee of the Newport branch of the English Speaking Union.

8. During his Hahnemann presidency he returned from a summer vacation with an injured back, the result of a faulty balloon landing in the Swiss Alps. As one Philadelphia gossip columnist commented, "anybody can get a bad back shooting the rapids in Colorado" (Suzy Says, "Pretty and Perky," *Daily News*, July 22, 1975).

9. "Second Annual Radnor Hunt Is Scheduled This Fall: Will Benefit Hahnemann," *The World of Hahnemann* (July 1975): 1.

10. "Subject: Edward Wharton Shober." Shober left the company in 1970.

11. See Wharton Shober, "First Person: Absence of Redress," *Princeton Alumni Weekly* (February 1982): 54.

12. Len Lear, "Is 'Shoberism' Killing Hahnemann?" *The Drummer*, February 18, 1975. DiPalma argued that the clinicians wanted a new and modern hospital and were pressuring the board for a new president: "Cameron was nearing retiring age. Let us push him upstairs and get us a younger and vigorous president who will stir up the institution and raise more money was the pervasive thought" (Joseph R. DiPalma, "Memoirs of a Medical School Dean," unpublished manuscript, 181).

13. Daniel F. Downing to Harry L. Buck, September 17, 1969, Hahnemann Collection.

14. Ibid.; see also "Faculty Turnover: Is It Cause for Alarm?" *Hahnemann Alumni News* 36 (spring 1970): 8.

15. Lear, "Is 'Shoberism.'"

16. Ibid.

17. The quotes in the text are from Charles W. Bowser to Isadore Krekstein, January 24, 1973; Edward S. Lee to Isadore Krekstein, January 25, 1973; and Melvin L. Hardy to Isadore Krekstein, January 23, 1973, in minutes, Board of Trustees, January 31, 1973, letters sent by Shober to Krekstein for circulation. These letters had obviously been coordinated after a community meeting, for they used much the same language and made the same points. See also Samuel L. Evans to Isadore Krekstein, January 22, 1973, commenting on efforts by "a small number of faculty and alumni . . . to control the policy making operation of [Hahnemann] . . . against the will of its president" and offering "our unqualified support of President Schober [sic]" (in ibid.).

18. On Shober organizing fund-raising for Flood, see Shober, "First Person," 54.

19. "Cheyney, Hahnemann Join to Recruit Black Pre-Meds," *Coatsville (Pennsylvania) Record*, December 28, 1970; and see "Cheyney, Hahnemann Begin Co-op Program," *Ardmore (Pennsylvania) Main Line Times*, January 7, 1971.

20. Edward S. Lee to Isadore Krekstein, January 25, 1973; Hardy to Krekstein, January 23, 1973: "speaking for the more than 500,000 poor people in Philadelphia"; Evans to Krekstein, January 22, 1973.

21. "Dr. John H. Moyer vs. The Hahnemann Medical College and Hospital et al., United States District Court for the Eastern District of Pennsylvania, July 22, 1974," 12, Hahnemann Collection; and see David M. Cleary, "Doctor Sues Hospital, Officials in Long Dispute at Hahnemann," *Evening Bulletin*, July 24, 1974.

22. Hahnemann offered full tuition waivers to all these minority students until the mid-1970s, when the children of middle-class minority groups began applying. A federal grant provided money to encourage basic science departments to provide tutoring and participate in summer programs; Chip Jackson remembers that some departments were more helpful than others; see Chip Jackson, telephone interview by Naomi Rogers, August 19, 1997.

23. *Congressional Record*, 94th Congress, 1st sess., 1975, 21: E 1561.

24. Minutes, Council on Medical and Ambulatory Health Affairs, March 4, 1974.

25. *Congressional Record*, 94th Congress, 1st sess., 1561.

26. Ibid.
27. Ibid.
28. Hahnemann Public Relations Department, [editor, Mildred C. Plenty], "Hahnemann News," January 1972. Four new vice presidential posts were created: Charles S. Paxson Jr. was executive vice president; Robert H. Holmes was vice president for medical affairs (and later senior vice president for corporate and fiscal affairs); John H. Moyer was vice president for academic affairs; Joseph R. DiPalma was vice president and dean. Other appointments included Douglas G. McArthur as treasurer (and later senior vice president for corporate affairs); Robert E. Snyder, executive assistant to the president (and later vice president for Ambulatory Health Services, that is, the director of Hahnemann Professional Offices); Douglas C. Geary, vice president for development; and Robert Hunt, hospital director. McArthur had been at Hahnemann since 1967 as assistant treasurer and was a graduate of the Wharton School; Snyder was formerly associate administrator and was a graduate of Villanova; Hunt had been assistant administrator for the previous three years and had an MBA in health care from George Washington University.
29. See, for example, minutes, Executive Faculty meeting, December 8, 1971, February 2, 1972, March 8, 1972, and July 5, 1972.
30. Carl Castle Fischer, "As I Remember It: Autobiography," unpublished manuscript, 1981, 12: Holmes impressed Fischer "most favorably."
31. The Committee to the Faculty of Hahnemann, memorandum, April 25, 1974, Hahnemann Collection. And see also the Hahnemann Faculty Committee of Nine to Morton Jenks, May 18, 1973, Hahnemann Collection; the Hahnemann Committee of Nine to John A. D. Cooper, memorandum, December 4, 1974, Hahnemann Collection; and Lear, "Is 'Shoberism,'" quoting "one knowledgeable observer": "Holmes is a very autocratic Heinrich Himmler–type. He's always talking about the fact that Gen. Patton is his idol."
32. See, for example, Dowling to Buck, September 17, 1969: Moyer was "inspiring resignations in droves. He made the Department of Medicine the largest full-time service in the Hospital and Medical School but he also made it the one with the biggest turnover."
33. DiPalma, "Memoirs," 186; minutes, special meeting of General Faculty, September 22, 1971.
34. Karl Abraham, "Hahnemann to Honor Gen. Somoza Despite Student, Faculty Protests," *Evening Bulletin,* June 7, 1972.
35. Quoted in Abraham, "Hahnemann to Honor Gen. Somoza"; see also "Subject: Edward Wharton Shober," stating that in 1964 Shober had been appointed honorary consul to Nicaragua. Shober said he had known Somoza since 1952; in 1965 Shober took a six-week tour of Latin America to "confer with their chiefs of State," and "it is not known for whom, and for what purpose this trip was made." Hahnemann had a previous connection with Somoza: Desiderio Roman (1870–1950), clinical professor of surgery from 1913–1948, was Anastasio Somoza's uncle; "Dr. Roman Dies, Famed Surgeon," *Philadelphia Inquirer,* September 8, 1950.
36. Quoted in Abraham, "Hahnemann to Honor Gen. Somoza"; see also minutes, General Faculty meeting, May 18, 1972.
37. See a reference in Jeff Nesmith and Warren Froelich, "Trustee Alters Stand, Hahnemann Parley Off," *Evening Bulletin,* April 29, 1977; "Faculty Position," 1, 5.
38. "Faculty Position," 9.
39. Ibid., 2.
40. "Report of the Commission for the Study of the Governance of the Academic Medical Center," quoted in "Faculty Position," 2.
41. "Faculty Position," 3, 4.

42. "Somoza—A Study in Moral Prostitution" [1972], and "A Statement," April 1972, Hahnemann Collection.
43. "Somoza—A Study in Moral Prostitution"; and "Statement of Student Institute, Hahnemann Medical College and Hospital," June 7, 1972.
44. Abraham, "Hahnemann to Honor Gen. Somoza."
45. See Lear, "Is 'Shoberism'"; and Henry R. Darling, "Alumni Group Is Ousted by Trustees in Smoldering Dispute at Hahnemann," *Evening Bulletin*, December 21, 1972.
46. John Corr, "Serving Up a Hearty Meal for the Condemning Man," *Philadelphia Inquirer*, June 9, 1972.
47. "Statement by Wharton Shober, President, Hahnemann Medical College and Hospital, March 10, 1972," in "What's New? A Weekly Newsletter of the Hahnemann Medical College and Hospital," Special Edition, March 13, 1972, Hahnemann Collection.
48. "Heroin Treatment Blamed in Death," *Pittsburgh Press*, May 18, 1972.
49. Both spent eleven months at Gaudenzia House in West Chester; see "Subject: Edward Wharton Shober."
50. "Addict Found Dead: Patient in Test Program," *Evening Bulletin*, March 3, 1972.
51. "CDT File 7/23/72," Hahnemann Collection.
52. See "Subject: Edward Wharton Shober" on the January 14, 1972, mugging: "It is alleged that this violent act caused subject to become interested in addicts and their rehabilitation (how similar to the near death of his wife that caused him to become interested in the medical field)." Shober told reporters that he knew his assailants were drug addicts because he had recognized the telltale sign of dripping noses. "When I was mugged, down on the ground, I got a good look at the kids who kicked me. . . . their noses were running, a symptom of heroin addiction" (Lou Antosh, "Mugging of Hospital Prexy Led to Heroin Program Here," *Daily News*, January 14, 1972).
53. Antosh, "Mugging of Hospital Prexy."
54. Minutes, Special Executive Faculty, May 17, 1972.
55. See DiPalma, "Memoirs," 188: "Mills who had no genuine interest in this haphazard research was certainly no match for the domineering Vice President Holmes much less the reckless President Shober. Besides the poor fall guy, Mills had lost any respect the faculty and staff might have had for him and most were after his scalp."
56. Wharton Shober to Robert L. Taylor, November 29, 1971, Hahnemann Collection, asking for free publication of notice as a "public service"; after the *Daily News* and the *Philadelphia Inquirer* ran the notices as "minor news" on the first day, the program got "more than 104 telephone calls" and on the second day "approximately 150 calls."
57. Minutes, Special Executive Faculty, May 17, 1972: advertisements were run in the *Evening Bulletin*, the *Inquirer*, and the *Daily News*, and there were over twelve hundred applicants. In January 1972, Shober, LaVerne, and five addicts were seen on numerous television stations. See "Radio Spot Announcement," [November 1971], Hahnemann Collection: "Heroin addicts and alcoholics are invited to join Hahnemann's new, free, out-patient treatment program. Volunteers will be seen three times a week. Treatments are brief, safe, non-addictive, and non-toxic, and do not involve psychotherapy. Volunteers should be able to return to daily activities immediately following treatment. Volunteers will be treated in strict confidence." The advertisement was paid for by the Committee for CDT Treatment of Heroin Addiction and Alcoholism, which consisted of Senator Claiborne Pell (Rhode Island), Congressman William Anderson (Tennessee), Congressman Daniel J. Flood (Pennsylvania), James Stevenson, Mrs. Edward Labvisdon, and Mrs. Allen

Evans. Supposedly families complained about a twelve-hundred-dollar fee required prior to treatment; see "Subject: Edward Wharton Shober."

58. DiPalma believed that during the treatment a therapist spoke to the patient to convince him or her to stop; DiPalma, "Memoirs," 187.

59. "Death Stops Carbon Dioxide Use for Addicts," *Psychiatric News*, May 3, 1972; and minutes, Executive Faculty Special Meeting, May 17, 1972.

60. Patricia McBroom, "Therapy Is Linked to Addict's Death," *Philadelphia Inquirer*, May 18, 1972; Karl Abraham, "Addict's Death Blamed on Drug Treatment," *Evening Bulletin*, May 17, 1972.

61. Lear, "Is 'Shoberism.'"

62. Ibid.

63. "Faculty Position," 4, 12.

64. Angelakos, in minutes, Special Executive Faculty Meeting, May 17, 1972.

65. Ibid.; "Faculty Position," 12.

66. Joseph DiPalma, Burton Landau, Suzanne Zarro, and Vincent Zarro, joint interview by Naomi Rogers, November 14, 1996.

67. "Statement by Wharton Shober."

68. McBroom, "Therapy Is Linked to Addict's Death"; Abraham, "Addict's Death Blamed on Drug Treatment."

69. McBroom, "Therapy Is Linked to Addict's Death"; Abraham, "Addict's Death Blamed on Drug Treatment."

70. "Hahnemann Asks Aid to Resume Dope Addict Cure," *Connellsville (Pennsylvania) Daily Courier*, May 5, 1972; "Addict Treatment Plan," *New York Times*, May 5, 1972.

71. The Governor's Justice Commission withdrew its support of a $286,000 grant; according to other reports Hahnemann withdrew grant applications from the National Institute of Mental Health (NIMH) and the federal Law Enforcement Assistance Administration; see "Aid Denied for Drug Therapy," *Daily News*, May 10, 1972.

72. Karl Abraham, "Hahnemann's Versions Differ on Dropping Drug Program," *Evening Bulletin*, May 10, 1972.

73. "Faculty Position," 11–13.

74. See DiPalma, "Memoirs," 184.

75. Wharton Shober, letter, "Hahnemann: Sticking Neck Out," *Evening Bulletin*, May 6, 1977; and Wharton Shober to John H. Moyer, memorandum, April 3, 1972, Hahnemann Collection.

76. David M. Cleary, "Shober Proving He's the Man for Top Job at Hahnemann," *Sunday Bulletin*, November 3, 1974.

77. "Dr. John H. Moyer vs. The Hahnemann Medical College and Hospital et al."

78. DiPalma, "Memoirs," 164.

79. Ibid.; see also minutes, Special Meeting of the General Faculty, May 30, 1972; minutes, College Council, May 30, 1972.

80. Feigin, interview.

81. "Subject: Edward Wharton Shober."

82. Harry K. Gabroy to YOU as a Trustee of Hahnemann, September 12, 1972, Hahnemann Collection; Harry K. Gabroy to Dear Fellow Alumnus, December 1, 1972, Hahnemann Collection.

83. Herbert A. Fogel to Harry K. Gabroy, December 15, 1972, Hahnemann Collection; and see the Hahnemann Committee of Nine to John A. D. Cooper, memorandum, December 4, 1974, Hahnemann Collection.

84. I. H. Krekstein and Charles B. Hollis to Dear Doctor [Board of Trustees and Officers, Hahnemann Alumni Association], December 15, 1972, Hahnemann Collection.

85. Harry K. Gabroy to Dear Fellow Alumnus, January 1973, Hahnemann Collection;

see also YOUR Committee of Nine to Dear Friends, January 30, 1973, Hahnemann Collection.

86. See Darling, "Alumni Group Is Ousted by Trustees"; and John O'Connor, "Alumni, Faculty Assail Hahnemann President," *Daily News,* January 22, 1973.

87. An administration statement signed by DiPalma claimed that the present alumni association was "not representative" and that "to make our organization more responsive to needs of our alumni" it had instituted a complete reorganization of Hahnemann's alumni programs. It referred to the lack of democratic elections of alumni officers and to inefficient solicitation of funds; see Darling, "Alumni Group Is Ousted by Trustees."

88. The poison pen letters also challenged Shober's claims; see YOUR Committee of Nine to Dear Friends, January 30, 1973, Hahnemann Collection.

89. Harry K. Gabroy to Dear Fellow Alumnus, December 1, 1972, Hahnemann Collection.

90. A Faculty "Committee of Nine" to Dear Colleagues, January 9, 1973, Hahnemann Collection.

91. [name erased], Philadelphia, Class of 1964 to I. H. Krekstein and Charles B. Hollis, January 3, 1973, Hahnemann Collection; and see N. Eugene Shoemaker to Board of Trustees, December 21, 1972, Hahnemann Collection: "I TORE UP THE CHECK TO MY ALMA MATER today, when I recieved [sic] your correspondence."

92. See Ernest Leiss, telephone interview by Naomi Rogers, August 14, 1997. See, for example: "He needs removal at once before the whole place comes tumbling down. These times are reminiscent of those awful years 1943 to 1947 when Hahnemann's future was shaky. How well I remember those days. I was there"; Robert M. Mattson to Ernie Leiss, December 8, 1972, Hahnemann Collection.

93. See, for example, the Hahnemann Committee of Nine to John A. D. Cooper, memorandum, December 4, 1974, Hahnemann Collection.

94. Karasik, "How Shober Lost."

95. "The Clinical Faculty of Hahnemann" to "Members of the Board of Trustees," May 10, 1973, Hahnemann Collection; and see also "The Committee to Investigate the Actions and Recommendations of the Hahnemann Search Committee for President" to "Members of the Board of Trustees," May 12, 1973, Hahnemann Collection.

96. "The Clinical Faculty of Hahnemann" to "Members of the Board of Trustees," May 10, 1973, Hahnemann Collection.

97. Ibid.

98. The Hahnemann Faculty Committee of Nine to Morton Jenks, May 18, 1973, Hahnemann Collection.

99. The Faculty Committee of Nine to Dear Colleagues, February 11, 1973, Hahnemann Collection.

100. Darling, "Alumni Group Is Ousted by Trustees."

101. Jeff Nesmith, "Letters Stir Storm at Hahnemann," *Sunday Bulletin,* May 22, 1977.

102. Joseph R. DiPalma to Dear Faculty Member, February 20, 1973, Hahnemann Collection.

103. The Hahnemann Committee of Nine to John A. D. Cooper, memorandum, December 4, 1974, Hahnemann Collection.

104. John Benditt, "Barred from Testing IUDs, Doctor Heads Hahnemann Unit," *Evening Bulletin,* January 18, 1976.

105. "Two Hahnemann Alumni Groups Bury the Scalpel, Agree to Merge," *Evening Bulletin,* April 23, 1975; and see Lear, "Is 'Shoberism.'"

106. John T. Gillespie, "Unit OKs Hospital Addition," *Evening Bulletin,* February 5, 1976.

107. Karasik, "How Shober Lost."

108. See Joseph R. DiPalma, "The Hahnemann Medical College of Philadelphia: An-

nual Report, Wednesday, October 26, 1977," 10, Hahnemann Collection. From 1972 to 1977, first-year classes increased from fifteen to nineteen "minorities" (9.8 percent to 10.6 percent) and from twenty-five to forty-six "females" (16.3 percent to 25.6 percent).

109. "Fifth VP at Hahnemann Resigning," *Gettysburg Times*, May 28, 1977; and Jeff Nesmith, "Fourth Vice President Leaves Hahnemann," *Evening Bulletin*, May 18, 1977.

110. Nesmith, "Letters Stir Storm."

111. Editorial, "Can Hahnemann Afford an 'Official Residence'?" *Evening Bulletin*, May 14, 1977; Jeff Nesmith and Warren Froelich, "Hospital Renovated Apartment, but Needed Toilet Paper," *Evening Bulletin*, May 8, 1977.

112. Warren Froelich and Jeff Nesmith, "Hahnemann President Appeals to Aides to Bail Out Hospital," *Sunday Bulletin*, June 19, 1977.

113. Warren Froelich and Jeff Nesmith, "Hospital Boss in Luxury Pad: Hahnemann Buzzes over Decor," *Evening Bulletin*, May 4, 1977.

114. Froelich and Nesmith, "Hospital Boss in Luxury Pad"; Warren Froelich, "FBI Probes Hahnemann Contract," *Sunday Bulletin*, December 18, 1977.

115. "Statement Given to Inquirer and Daily News by Shirley Laird Responding to Article Appearing in Evening Bulletin Today," May 4, 1977, Hahnemann Collection.

116. Ibid.

117. Jeff Nesmith and Warren Froelich, "Shober Fired Consultants Whose Data Criticized Him," *Sunday Bulletin*, May 29, 1977.

118. Nesmith, "Letters Stir Storm."

119. Karasik, "How Shober Lost."

120. Nesmith, "Letters Stir Storm."

121. Jeff Nesmith and Warren Froelich, "Trustee Alters Stand, Hahnemann Parley Off," *Evening Bulletin*, April 29, 1977.

122. Wharton Shober to Members, Board of Trustees, memorandum, May 6, 1977, Hahnemann Collection.

123. Ellen Karasik, "Hahnemann Vote Backs Bank Loan," *Philadelphia Inquirer*, June 23, 1977; and Froelich and Nesmith, "Hahnemann President Appeals."

124. "Fifth VP at Hahnemann Resigning."

125. Warren Froelich and Jeff Nesmith, "Hahnemann and Banks Meet on Loan," *Evening Bulletin*, June 22, 1977.

126. Karasik, "Hahnemann Vote Backs Bank Loan."

127. Karasik, "How Shober Lost."

128. Wendell Rawls Jr., "Hospital Says Fund-Raising Lags Because of Eilberg-Flood Matter," *New York Times*, February 28, 1978.

129. Rawls, "Hospital Says Fund-Raising Lags"; Aaron Epstein, "Hahnemann Aid Called 'Improper,'" *Philadelphia Inquirer*, March 16, 1978.

130. Epstein, "Hahnemann Aid Called 'Improper.'"

131. "Hahnemann Drops Law Firm, Cites Eilberg," *Philadelphia Inquirer*, January 24, 1978; "Hahnemann Halts Paying Ex-President," *Philadelphia Inquirer*, April 28, 1978; "Hahnemann Halts Salary to Shober," *Evening Bulletin*, April 27, 1978; Rawls, "Hospital Says Fund-Raising Lags."

132. Doris B. Wiley, "Hahnemann's Stiff Upper Lip: Hospital Stoics Taking Lots of Bad Publicity in Stride," *Evening Bulletin*, April 3, 1978.

133. Epstein, "Hahnemann Aid Called 'Improper.'"

134. William Likoff, letter to editor, *Evening Bulletin*, October 30, 1978.

135. William Likoff, letter to editor, *Philadelphia Inquirer*, October 27, 1978. On Likoff to the Hahnemann community, see William Likoff to Dear Colleague, October 27, 1978, Hahnemann Collection: "The events of the past week have moved swiftly and very favorably for Hahnemann." Likoff noted that there were federal indict-

ments over construction of Hahnemann Hospital Tower Project against Congressman Joshua Eilberg, Shober, George L. Guerra, and John P. Dixon. "Let us now put this unpleasant part of history in its proper place. Let it be an era that most of us lived through, and some of us only heard about. We must not permit the actions of one president to diminish and tarnish the reputation this institution has developed over the past 130 years."

136. L. Stuart Ditzen, "Gerald Ford: A Probe Target?" *Evening Bulletin*, June 25, 1980; D. I. Strunk, "Insider: Good Show, Whartie," *Evening Bulletin*, July 10, 1980. For Shober's own description of his experience ("as I introduced modern business methods to it [Hahnemann] I was surrounded by controversy"), see Wharton Shober to Editor, *London Daily Telegraph*, September 12, 1997; and see Shober, "First Person."

137. "Top Cardiologist Is Elected President of Hahnemann," *Evening Bulletin*, November 22, 1977.

138. Jack Severson, "Can He Heal His 'Family'?" *Philadelphia Inquirer*, September 26, 1978.

Chapter 9   Coda: A New Alternative

1. Alfred W. Martinelli to All Hahnemann Faculty, Employees and Students, memorandum, November 18, 1993, Hahnemann Collection; Gilbert M. Gaul, "The New Principle for Health Care," *Philadelphia Inquirer*, November 21, 1993.

2. Patricia Lyons, telephone interview by Naomi Rogers, August 25, 1997; see also similar protests by some trustees in minutes, Special Meeting of Board of Trustees, November 17, 1993.

3. Quotation from a faculty grievance to Hahnemann's Committee of Faculty Affairs, cited in Marian Uhlman, "Hahnemann Faculty Hold Line on Tenure," *Philadelphia Inquirer*, December 11, 1994.

4. See Thomas J. Doyle, "The Hahnemann University-Medical College of Pennsylvania Merger: A Historical and Personal Perspective," *JAMA* 276 (1996): 1773.

5. Barbara Williams, note to author, October 1997.

6. *Degrees and Stitches* 12 (June 1988): 2.

7. *Medic* 1980, n.p.

8. "Symbol of HU's Heritage Saved," *Degrees and Stitches* 12 (May 1988): 5.

9. Information from Barbara Williams, telephone interview by Naomi Rogers, October 2, 1997.

10. Program of "150 Years of Homeopathy in America," September 21, 1985, Hahnemann Collection.

11. J. C. Guernsey, "A Brief Sketch of the Allentown Academy," section in A. R. Thomas, "Medical Education and the Homeopathic Medical Colleges in the United States," in *Transactions of the World's Homeopathic Convention, held at Philadelphia, under the auspices of the American Institute of Homeopathy, at its twenty-ninth session, June 26th, 27th, 28th, 29th, 30th, July 1st, 1876* (Philadelphia: Sherman and Co., 1880) 2:777–778.

12. See "Actual Contents of Cornerstone 1884," in [program], "Cornerstone Laying of the Hahnemann Medical College and Hospital of Philadelphia: Monday Afternoon, April Twenty-third Nineteen Hundred and Twenty-Eight at Four O'Clock," n.p., Hahnemann Collection.

13. Inventory list, 1979, prepared by Barbara Williams, Hahnemann Collection.

14. There was a cornerstone prepared for the opening of the Klahr Building (which is still extant) in 1938, but the list of its contents has not survived; see "The Laying of the Cornerstone," *Hospital Tidings* 46 (1938): 18.

15. Hahnemann Medical College and Hospital, "Cornerstone Setting Ceremonies for

Hahnemann's Twenty-one Story, 445,000 Square Foot New College Building, Friday, May 24, 1974," Hahnemann Collection.

16. *Alumni News* (October 1979), n.p.
17. Program of "Alfred W. Martinelli Sesquicentennial Park Dedication, May 23, 1997," Hahnemann Collection.
18. Ibid.
19. Lyons, interview.

Sesquicentennial Circle

**Allegheny University of the Health Sciences
gratefully acknowledges the following members
of the Sesquicentennial Circle.**

The Sesquicentennial Circle is comprised of leadership donors to the annual fund. Sesquicentennial Circle members chose to generously support future endeavors while honoring the unique history and rich heritage of Hahnemann University founded in 1848 and Medical College of Pennsylvania founded in 1850.

President's Circle

Sherif S. Abdelhak and Marlynn
Singleton, M.D. MCP 1995

David E. Barensfeld

Phillip S. Brackin, M.D. HU 1970

Stanley K. Brockman, M.D.

Stuart Caine and Ruth H. Caine, M.D.
HU 1987

Nancy T. Caputo, M.D. WMC 1948

D. Walter Cohen, D.D.S.

Drs. Gail and Albert Cook, HU 1954,
and Family

Verdi J. DiSesa, M.D.

Thomas A. Gennarelli, M.D.

Dr. and Mrs. W. Clark Hargrove III

Sue Haines

Dr. and Mrs. Richard Hayden

Margaret E. Hurley, M.D. MCP 1974

Drs. Janet and Donald Kaye

Patricia and Philip Kind

June F. Klinghoffer, M.D. WMC 1945,
and Sidney Wenger, M.D. HU 1939

Dr. and Mrs. Robert Maddalon, MCP
1980

Marie Hren Manno, M.D. WMC 1958

Alfred and Aline Martinelli

Dr. and Mrs. Theodore Matulewicz

Leona V. Crook Miller, M.D.

Leslie A. Miller, Esq., and Richard B. Worley

The Dr. M. Lee Pearce Foundation, Inc.

Pittsburgh Cardiology Associates

    Michael A. Fallert, M.D.

    Jerome E. Granato, M.D.

    Howard P. Grill, M.D.

Rhoda S. Pomerantz, M.D. WMC 1963, and Irwin Feinberg, M.D.

Marcella+ and Leonard L. Ross, Ph.D.

Theodore R. Sadock, M.D. HU 1938

Dr. Bernard L. and Idajane Segal

James D. Sink, M.D.

Lorraine I. Stengl, M.D. WMC 1947

Mr. and Mrs. Leon C. Sunstein Jr.

Theodore W. Uroskie, M.D. HU 1970, Theodore W. Uroskie Jr., M.D. 1995, and Jonathan A. Uroskie, M.D. HU 1996

Gary Veith, M.D. HU 1972

David K. Wagner, M.D.

Dr. and Mrs. Glenn J. R. Whitman

Margaret Gray Wood, M.D. WMC 1948

Thomas J. Zaydon, Sr., M.D. HU 1944 In honor of my sons, successful Hahnemann graduates Thomas J. Zaydon, Jr., M.D., and Samuel J. Zaydon, M.D.

Dean's Circle

Sucha Order Asbell, M.D. WMC 1966, and Michael J. Asbell

Barbara F. Atkinson, M.D., and G. W. Atkinson, M.D.

Gerald E. Beck, M.D.

Janice C. Benson, M.D. MCP 1974

Jeffrey Bettinger, M.D. HU 1974

Dr. and Mrs. Jules Blake

Calvin Bland

John Brennan

Dr. and Mrs. Fredric Brownstein, MCP 1975

Lawrence H. Byrd, M.D. MCP 1973

W. Morgan Churchman III

Betsy Z. Cohen

Cooke & Bieler, Inc.

Glenda D. Donoghue, M.D.

Bert Green, M.D. MCP 1974

Dr. and Mrs. Willard P. Green

Michael I. Greenberg, M.D. HU 1987

Barbara A. Hajjar, M.D. WMC 1965

Frances M. Hunter, M.D. MCP 1981

Dorothea R. Johnson, M.D. WMC 1956

Theodore R. Kantner, M.D.

Dwight and Pam Kasperbauer

Uwe Koepke, M.D., Ph.D. MCP 1977, and Anne E. Mauks, M.D. MCP 1972

Lila Stein Kroser, M.D. WMC 1957, and Albert S. Kroser, D.O.

Flora B. Leigh, M.D. WMC 1961

Irving L. Lichtenstein, M.D. HU 1944

David M. Long Jr., M.D., Ph.D. HU 1956

Robert M. McNair Jr., Esq.

Dr. and Mrs. George J. Magovern Sr.

Francis E. Marchlinski, M.D.

Mildred Milgrom, M.D. WMC 1960

Mary S. Oda, M.D. WMC 1946

P. M. Procacci, M.D. HU 1969

Dr. Richard and Rosalie Regnante HU 1964

Henrietta Rosenberg, M.D. MCP 1970, and Henry Rosenberg, M.D.

Priscilla and Joel J. Roslyn, M.D.

R. Douglas Ross, M.D. HU 1974

Anthony C. Santopolo, M.D. HU 1976

John E. Schiller, M.D. HU 1968

Barbara A. Schindler, M.D. WMC 1970, and Alan M. Schindler, M.D., Ph.D. MCP 1977

Jan Schneider, M.D.

David W. Sculley

Carol S. Shapiro, M.D. WMC 1965

James A. Shaver, M.D. HU 1959

Fong Y. Tsai, M.D., and Jean C. Tsai

William E. and Nanette J. Welton

Myron Yanoff, M.D.

Faculty Circle

Dr. and Mrs. George J. Amrom, HU 1972

Margaret I. Anderson, M.D. WMC 1954

William M. Anderson, M.D. HU 1967

James S. Atkinson, D.D.S., and Kay M. Atkinson

Virginia M. Badger, M.D. WMC 1961

Phyllis Baer, M.D. HU 1972, and Stephen Baer, M.D. HU 1972

Lee A. Barber, M.D. MCP 1977, and Joseph Nowoslawski, M.D.

Dr. and Mrs. Willis Barnes, HU 1957

Frances R. Batzer, M.D. MCP 1972

Ericha Benshoff, M.D. MCP 1987, and Richard Moyer

Doris M. Benzenhoefer-Tobin, M.D. WMC 1956

Barbara and Richard Berkowitz, M.D. HU 1960

Arnold T. Berman, M.D. HU 1965

Drs. Dominick, Michael, Patrick, and Joseph Bianchi, HU 1938, 1983, 1984, and 1985

John J. BianRosa, M.D., J.D.

Dorothy McKnight Blasco, M.D. WMC 1954

Helen W. Boigon, M.D. WMC 1946

Michael J. Booth, R.N., M.S.N. HU 1997

Conrad M. Brahin, M.D. HU 1948

Eddy and Gloria Bresnitz and sons

Karen Brinton, M.D. MCP 1976

Linda S. Brodsky, M.D. MCP 1979

Laurette M. Bryan, M.D. WMC 1955

Victoria Sandoe Burkhart

Stanley H. Bushkoff, M.D. HU 1957

Janice and Donald R. Buxton Jr., M.D. HU 1967

Marylou Buyse, M.S., M.D. WMC 1970, and Carl N. Edwards, J.D., Ph.D.

Pamela S. Callahan

Frederick W. Campbell III, M.D.

Elizabeth T. Cancroft, M.D. WMC 1962

Kathleen J. Catalano, M.D. WMC 1964

Mary M. Cavasina, M.D. WMC 1952

Joan A. Celebre, M.D. WMC 1960

Mrs. William A. Chapman+

Jerome H. Check, M.D. HU 1971

Cathe Chiaramonte, M.D., and Richard
    Baum, M.D. MCP 1987

Barbara E. Chick, M.D. WMC 1959

Kathryn E. Chizik

Dr. and Mrs. James E. Clark

Maurice C. Clifford, M.D.

Milton Coll, M.D. MCP 1981, and
    Andrea Becker, M.D.

Marjorie Conrad-Peatee, M.D. HU 1946

James F. Conroy, D.O.

Jeanne A. Cooper, M.D. HU 1947

Oscar Corn, M.D. HU 1943+, Selma
    Corn, Robert C. Corn, M.D. HU
    1975, and Holly C. Corn, M.D. HU
    1979

Elizabeth Cornfield, M.D. WMC 1943

Ellen Cosgrove, M.D. HU 1978, and
    Jeffrey Fahl, M.D. HU 1978

Thomas S. Cretella, M.D. HU 1945

Susan Croushore

Simindokht Dadparvar, M.D., and
    Bizhan Micaily, M.D.

Jeffrey I. Damsker, M.D. HU 1967

Douglas D. Danforth

Dr. and Mrs. J. Thomas Danzi

Harriet J. Davis, M.D. WMC 1935

Nancy K. Davis

Dr. and Mrs. Nicholas G. DePiero, HU
    1942

The Lawrence Dinenberg, M.D. HU
    1970, Family

Paul DiPlacido

Gloria Donnelly, Ph.D., R.N., F.A.A.N.

Joanne Barone Dragun, M.D. HU 1988

M. Gay Wasas Ducharme, M.D. WMC
    1958

Amy Papalia Early, M.D. HU 1976

Mr. and Mrs. Leonard T. Ebert

Gail Eisenberg, M.D. MCP 1976, and
    Mitchell Eisenberg, M.D. MCP
    1976

Dr. and Mrs. Kenneth D. Emkey, HU
    1972

Gerald H. Escovitz, M.D.

Cherie S. Evans, M.D. MCP 1972

Donald S. Faber, Ph.D.

Michael B. Faucher

Mary S. Fay

Stanley Fiel, M.D. MCP 1973, and Carol
    Fiel

Judith Haschak Figura, M.D. WMC 1969

William S. Frankl, M.D., and Razelle
    Frankl, Ph.D.

June M. Fry, M.D., Ph.D. MCP 1977

Lonnie E. Fuller Sr., M.D. HU 1960

George C. Gardiner, M.D., and Margarita
    Gardiner, M.D. MCP 1985

Shelley R. Gebar

James C. Gehris, M.D. HU 1954

Mr. and Mrs. Joseph E. Gembala Jr., Esq.

Dr. Patricia Gerrity

Andrea F. Gilbert

Kim A. Gilchrist, M.D. HU 1985

Fruma W. Ginsburgh, M.D. WMC 1951

Dan I. N. Giurgiu, M.D. MCP 1990

Carol and Jeff Glassroth, M.D.

Jacqueline T. Gomberg, M.D. MCP 1982, and Jonathan Gomberg, M.D. MCP 1982

Betty Gottlieb, Ph.D. MCP 1985, and Harry Gottlieb, M.D.+

Polly Graham, M.D. WMC 1969, and Roger Graham, Ph.D.

Mark Granick, M.D., and Carol Singer Granick, M.D.

Lucille C. Gunning-Blackwood, M.D. WMC 1949

Lorraine F. Gutowicz, M.D. MCP 1978, and Charles B. Weinberger

F. Todd Harad, M.D. HU 1987, and Family

Judy and William Harrington

Virginia B. Hartridge, M.D. WMC 1950

S. Jane Hayashi, M.D. WMC 1953

Kathleen Heidelberger, M.D. WMC 1965, and Charles Davenport, M.D.

Enrique Hernandez, M.D.

Wilbert E. Hernandez, M.D. HU 1941

William J. Hickey, Ph.D., and Barbara R. Hickey

Linda B. Hiner, M.D.

Dr. and Mrs. John C. Hoak, HU 1955

Bruce Hoffman, M.D., and Karen Hoffman

Betty J. Hohmann, M.D. WMC 1959

Jan C. Horrow, M.D., and Mindy M. Horrow, M.D. MCP 1980

Dr. and Mrs. Ramachandra U. Hosmane and Vinay and Sunil

Christie Huddleston, M.D. MCP 1978, and Rafael Porrata-Doria, Esq.

Mary H. Hudson, M.D. WMC 1961

Ami E. Iskandrian, M.D., and Greta P. Iskandrian, M.D.

Dr. and Mrs. Leonard S. Jacob, MCP 1978, HU 1972

Mariell Jessup, M.D. HU 1976

Rosaline R. Joseph, M.D. MCP 1953, and Robert Joseph, M.D.

Stephen Kalstein, M.D. HU 1967

Parviz Kambin, M.D.

Honey and H. Lawrence Karasic, M.D. HU 1960

Andrea C. Kay, M.D. MCP 1984

Herbert Kean, M.D. HU 1956

Mary Ann Keenan, M.D. MCP 1976

Gerald J. Kelliher, Ph.D.

Margaret and Peter I. Kenmore, M.D. HU 1947

Denis R. King, M.D. HU 1969, and Joan King

Lorraine C. King, M.D. MCP 1971

Dorothea Kleppinger, M.D. HU 1948,

and Richard Kleppinger, M.D. HU 1948+

Linda J. Kline

Lucille M. Koehler, M.D. WMC 1949

Janet P. Kramer, M.D. WMC 1968

Marion R. Kramer, M.D. WMC 1967

Audrey Krauss-Angelides, M.D. HU 1958

Dr. and Mrs. Herbert L. Kunkle Jr., HU 1979

Dr. and Mrs. Carl Lam, HU 1963

David Laskow, M.D.

Leslie Y. Lee, M.D. HU 1944

Roger B. Lee, M.D. HU 1968, and Sylvia Lee

George A. Levine, M.D.

Yale S. Lewine, M.D. HU 1934, and Ella Lewine

Donald H. Lieberman, M.D. MCP 1973

Gilbert R. Lipshutz, M.D. HU 1973+, and Jacqueline Lipshutz

Helen Nobel Lipsitz, M.D. WMC 1939, and Herman Lipsitz

Brian W. and Pamela A. Little

Mary C. Lizzul

Beverly and Walter P. Lomax Jr., M.D. HU 1957

Madeleine Long, M.D. MCP 1980

Diana E. Kostyra Lopez, M.D. WMC 1964, and George Lopez, M.D.

Emily Jean S. Lucid, M.D.

Dr. Sissell Lund-Katz and Dr. Alan Katz

Terry Lyman, R.N.

Dr. and Mrs. James D. Lynch, HU 1975

Alice L. McElhinney and Thomas McElhinney, Ph.D.

Meg McGoldrick

Mrs. Robert J. McKain Jr.

Mary L. McKenzie, M.D. WMC 1959

Dr. and Mrs. Robert M. McNamara

Mary Ellen McNish and David R. Miller, Ph.D.

JoAnn Magnatta

Phyllis C. Marciano, M.D. WMC 1960

Joseph C. Maroon, M.D.

Anna Mascolo, M.D. WMC 1960

Matsumoto-Sanego Surgical Associates Ltd.

Dorothy A. Wludyka Matthews, M.D. WMC 1958

Catherine A. Michon, M.D. WMC 1965

Kathleen Mirante, M.D. MCP 1971

Eleanor D. Montague, M.D. WMC 1950

Carol Hansen Montgomery, Ph.D.

The Moreschi Family, MCP Classes of 1954, 1987, and 1990

Jean M. Moroney, M.D. WMC 1965

Dr. and Mrs. Rohinton J. Morris, HU 1984

Charles P. and Denise L. Morrison

Drs. Venu and Prashant Mukerjee

Donna M. Murasko, Ph.D., and Kenneth J. Blank, Ph.D.

Gordon D. Myers, M.D. HU 1947

Joel B. Nadler, M.D. HU 1967

David Naide, M.D. HU 1960, and Joan Naide

Elaine Needell, M.D. HU 1950, and Mervin H. Needell, M.D. HU 1950

Herbert F. Neuwalder, M.D. HU 1959

Teruko S. Neuwalder, M.D. WMC 1961

Wilbur W. Oaks Jr., M.D. HU 1955

Mr. and Mrs. Michael W. O'Mahoney

Anna C. O'Riordan, M.D. HU 1957

Barbara O'Sullivan, M.D., M.P.H. MCP 1983

Nan and Bob Palmer

Deon Patten, M.D., M.P.H. WMC 1952

Frances K. Patterson, M.D. WMC 1962, and Paul Wigler

Constantinos A. Pavlides, M.D.

Michael C. Phillips, Ph.D., D.Sc.

Harry A. Pinsky, M.D. HU 1936, and Helen Pinsky

Sonja Stahl Pinsky, M.D. WMC 1958, and S. Theodore Pinsky, M.D.

Donna M. Pisera, M.D. HU 1982

Gene-Ann Polk, M.D. WMC 1952

Joel Posner, M.D., and Mary Scanlon, M.D. MCP 1980

Trevor R. P. Price, M.D., and Margaret Ann B. Price, M.D.

Sandra M. and John S. Pulizzi, M.D. HU 1961

Reed Edwin Pyeritz, M.D., Ph.D.

Kathleen Engles Quigley

Joseph H. Reichman, M.D. HU 1973

Anthony J. Ricketti, M.D. HU 1978

Richard Ricklefs, M.D. HU 1951

L. Rigberg, M.D. HU 1968, and Family

Stephen E. Risen, M.D. HU 1967, and Andrea Risen

Deloris E. Rissling, M.D. WMC 1964

Dr. and Mrs. Jay Roberts, Ph.D.

Lois May Roberts, M.D. WMC 1950

Charles L. Rojer, M.D. HU 1960

Louis F. Rose, M.D., D.D.S. MCP 1972

Hubert L. Rosomoff, M.D. HU 1952

Dr. and Mrs. Walter Rubin

Shirley and Morton F. Rubinstein, M.D. HU 1961

Gail S. Rudnitsky, M.D. MCP 1982

Dr. and Mrs. John M. Russell

Dr.+ and Mrs. Nathan L. Samuels

M. Elizabeth Sandel, M.D. MCP 1981

Kathleen Sazama, M.D., J.D., and Franklin Jed Sazama, Ph.D.

John C. Schantz, M.D. HU 1971

Jeffrey I. Scharf, M.D. HU 1975, in memory of Marcia T. Scharf

Ronald Schaupp, M.D. HU 1960

Phyllis Salit Scher, M.D. WMC 1962, and Robert A. Scher, M.D.

Martin Schimmel, M.D. MCP 1972

Louise Schnaufer, M.D. WMC 1951

Raymond S. Schreyer, M.D. HU 1978, and Nancy Schreyer, Ph.D. HU 1979

Dr. and Mrs. Alan Jay Schwartz

Jean Retta Schwartz, M.D. WMC 1959

Joseph A. Sciuto, M.D. HU 1940

Security Elevator Company

Gretchen Sennott

Millard S. Seto, M.D. HU 1957

Lenore Sherman

Jamie E. Siegel, M.D. MCP 1982

G. Harton Singer III

Mary Ann Skidmore, M.D. MCP 1972

Marguerite Singer Smith

Suzanne J. Smith, M.D. MCP 1971

Renee Solow, M.D. MCP 1973

Louise A. Sonnenberg, M.D. WMC 1967

David A. Sorber, M.D. HU 1979, and
    Rosalind P. Sorber

Susan Sordoni, M.D. MCP 1997

Hardy L. Sorkin, M.D. MCP 1972

Barbara and Richard Spielvogel, M.D.

Melody Ann Stancil, M.D. MCP 1971

Barbara Starrett, M.D. WMC 1970

Robert Steeb, M.D. HU 1965, and Mrs.
    Steeb

Alice M. Stein

Angela Stupi, M.D. MCP 1976, and
    Joseph M. Romano, M.D. MCP 1975

Elinor H. Suitor, M.D. WMC 1945

Vanlila Swami, M.D., and Kumar
    Swami, M.D.

Albert S. Terzian, M.D. HU 1945

Anne Neering Tessaro, M.D. WMC 1961

Mary A. Thomas, M.D. HU 1947

Jill Tillman

Benjamin C. K. Tom, M.D. HU 1955

Lloyd C. Tom, M.D. HU 1959

Bram J. Trauner, M.D. HU 1976

Harvey Tritel, M.D. HU 1969

Mary Ann Tsao, M.D. MCP 1979

Ross M. Ufberg, M.D. MCP 1982

Marjorie Uhalde, Ph.D., M.D. MCP 1979

Alice Ai-Lie Uong, M.D. MCP 1971

Malin Van Antwerp

William Van Decker, M.D.

Mark F. Victor, M.D. HU 1976

Lawrence M. Wells, M.D. HU 1969

Warren Werbitt, M.D. MCP 1973

J. J. White Incorporated

Michael P. White

Shirley T. Whiteman, M.D. WMC 1953

Libby F. Wilson, M.D. WMC 1963

Dr. and Mrs. Nelson M. Wolf

Robert J. Wolfson, M.D. HU 1957, and
    Mrs. Wolfson

Christine Wan-Ming Wu, M.D. WMC
    1955

Meriel Lee Wu, M.D. MCP 1972

C. Thomas Yarington Jr., M.D. HU 1960,
    and Barbara Yarington

Jeffrey and Margaret Yarmel

James P. Yeager Jr., M.D. HU 1957

Jerold J. Yecies, M.D. HU 1966

Dr. and Mrs. Daryl N. Zeigler, HU 1979

Audrey Ann Zelkovic, M.D. WMC 1965

William J. Zukel, M.D. HU 1947

The symbol + indicates the donor is
deceased.

Index

Page numbers in italics refer to illustrations.

About the Author

Naomi Rogers, who was born in Melbourne, Australia, is a historian of medicine. She teaches at Yale University in the School of Medicine and in the Women's Studies Program. At the University of Pennsylvania she received her Ph.D. in American history and also her knowledge and love of Philadelphia. She has published works on the history of alternative medicine, on gender and medicine, and on disease and public health, including a study of polio in America (*Dirt and Disease: Polio before FDR* [New Brunswick, N.J.: Rutgers University Press, 1992]). She is currently working on a study of an Australian nurse, Sister Elizabeth Kenny, whose alternative methods transformed polio therapy in the 1940s.